# FDR, THE VATICAN, AND THE ROMAN CATHOLIC CHURCH IN AMERICA, 1933–1945

# The World of the Roosevelts

General Editors: Arthur M. Schlesinger, Jr., William vanden Heuvel, and Douglas Brinkley

# FDR, the Vatican, and the Roman Catholic Church in America, 1933–1945

Edited by

David B. Woolner and
Richard G. Kurial

FDR, the Vatican, and the Roman Catholic
Church in America, 1933–1945
© David B. Woolner and Richard G. Kurial, 2003

First published 2003 by
PALGRAVE MACMILLAN™
175 Fifth Avenue, New York, N.Y. 10010 and
Houndmills, Basingstoke, Hampshire, England RG21 6XS
Companies and representatives throughout the world

PALGRAVE MACMILLAN is the global academic imprint of the Palgrave
Macmillan division of St. Martin's Press, LLC and of Palgrave Macmillan Ltd.
Macmillan® is a registered trademark in the United States,
United Kingdom and other countries. Palgrave is a registered trademark in
the European Union and the other countries.

ISBN 1–4039–6168–9 hardback

Library of Congress Cataloging-in-Publication Data
FDR, the Vatican, and the Roman Catholic Church in America,
1933–1945/edited by David B. Woolner and Richard G. Kurial.
    p. cm.
    Proceedings of a conference held in Oct. 1998 in Hyde Park, N.Y.
    Includes bibliographical references and index.
    ISBN 1–4039–6168–9
    1. Roosevelt, Franklin D. (Franklin Delano), 1882–1945—Relations with
Catholics—Congresses. 2. Catholic Church—United States—History—
20th century—Congresses. 3. Catholic Church—Foreign relations—
United States—Congresses. 4. United States—Foreign relations—Catholic
Church—Congresses. 5. United States—Foreign relations—1933–1945—
Congresses. 6. World War, 1939–1945—Diplomatic history—Congresses.
7. United States—Politics and government—1933–1945—Congresses.
I. Woolner, David B., 1955– II. Kurial, Richard G.

E807.F345 2003
282'.73'090430—dc21                                    2003040568

A catalogue record for this book is available from the British Library.

Design by Newgen Imaging Systems (P) Ltd., Chennai, India.

First edition: September, 2003
10 9 8 7 6 5 4 3 2 1

Printed in the United States of America.

*In memoriam*
*Thomas Casey*
*Friend, Mentor, Teacher*

FDR attends Notre Dame Convocation and receives honorary LLD Degree from Notre Dame, South Bend, Indiana, December 9, 1935. Left to right: George Cardinal Mundelein, FDR, and Col. Edwin Watson, Military Aid. Courtesy of Franklin D. Roosevelt Presidential Library.

# CONTENTS

## Acknowledgments

A CONFERENCE ON THE SCALE OF *FDR, the Vatican, and the Roman Catholic Church in America, 1933–1945,* could not have happened without the assistance of many individuals and the support of a number of key institutions. The inspiration for the conference came from William J. vanden Heuvel, cochair of the Franklin and Eleanor Roosevelt Institute (FERI), whose vision and dedication to the legacy of Franklin D. Roosevelt helped make this event possible. The president of Marist College, Dr. Dennis Murray, also deserves special recognition for embracing the conference idea and becoming the driving force behind it. We are also grateful to Verne Newton, the former director of the Franklin D. Roosevelt Presidential Library, and to John F. Sears, the former executive director of FERI, for their help, as well as to Lynn Basanese, Elaine Murphy, and the staffs of the FDRL and FERI for their cheerful and unceasing assistance. Special thanks must also go to Marist's Director of College Relations, Tim Massie, and to Marist's Director Special Events, Valerie Hall, for their strong support. We are also grateful to Lawrence Fuchs of Brandeis University and David O'Brien of the College of the Holy Cross for their wise counsel.

Our appreciation also goes out to our friends and colleagues at the Department of History at the University of Prince Edward Island, including a special thank you to Anna Fisher for logistical support; as well as to our friends and colleagues at Marist College in the History, Political Science, and Religious Studies Departments. Here we wish to express special thanks to the former dean, Reginetta Haboucha, as well as to the current dean, Thomas Wermuth; and also to Professors Mar Peter-Raoul, Robyn Rosen, Louis Zuccarello, and the late Thomas Casey, to whom this book is dedicated.

For providing us with a contemporary perspective on the issues raised by the conference we wish to acknowledge with our thanks the participation of Corrine C. Boggs, American ambassador to the Holy See; former ambassadors to the Holy See, Ray Flynn and Thomas Melady; Rev. Dr. Remi Hoeckman, O.P., secretary to the Holy See's Commission for Religious Relations with the Jews and Professor at the Department of Ecumenical Studies, Pontifical University of St. Thomas, Rome; Rabbi Joseph Ehrekranz, Sacred Heart

University Center for Jewish Christian Understanding; Peggy Obrecht, director of Church Relations, United States Holocaust Museum; Eugene Fisher, National Conference of Catholic Bishops; the Reverend John Pawlikowski, O.S.M., Professor of Social Ethics at the Catholic Theological Union; John J. Gilligan, former congressman and governor of Ohio; Brigadier General Casey Brower, dean of faculty, Virginia Military Institute; Arthur Schlesinger, Jr., chair emeritus of FERI; Charles R. Morris, author of *American Catholic*, and Amanda Smith of Harvard University. For providing us with the Eleanor Roosevelt dimension of this story we wish to thank Dr. Allida Black, Director of the Eleanor Roosevelt Papers Project, and Professor Anne Constantinople of Vassar College.

The editors would like to extend a special thank you to Marist Trustee Jack Gartland, whose sage advice, unflinching support, and constant encouragement both in New York and in Rome made this project possible. We also wish to thank the the McCann Foundation; the Charlotte Cunneen Hackett Charitable Trust; and the Gannett Foundation for their financial support, and to acknowledge the financial assistance of Marist College, the Franklin and Eleanor Roosevelt Institute, and the Department of History of the University of Prince Edward Island.

Finally, we would like to express our thanks to participants of the conference who so graciously accepted our invitation to share their knowledge of this fascinating aspect of the Roosevelt era; to Kevin Lundy and the many Marist students who helped make the conference a success; and to those involved in the final preparation of this book—Douglas Brinkley, the Director of the Eisenhower Center for American Studies at the University of New Orleans, Michael Flamini, Deborah Gershenowitz, Brendan O'Malley, and Ian Steinberg of Palgrave, Mary McFarland of FERI, and Lisa MacGregor and Jane McKay of the University of Prince Edward Island.

*Richard Kurial and David B. Woolner*

# FOREWORD

IN OCTOBER 1998, THE FRANKLIN AND ELEANOR ROOSEVELT INSTITUTE, the Franklin D. Roosevelt Presidential Library, and Marist College organized a major international conference on FDR, the Vatican, and the Roman Catholic Church in America. Initially planned as a prestigious, but small, academic conference, it grew considerably in scale after the March 1998 publication of the Vatican document *We Remember: A Reflection on the Shoah*. Given the importance of this document to both the history of the Roosevelt era and to the contemporary debate over the Vatican's response to the Holocaust, the conference organizers decided to expand the mandate of the conference to include a discussion of this important issue. To facilitate this effort, the organizers invited a number of key individuals involved in this debate to take part in the conference, including the Rev. Dr. Remi Hoeckman, O.P., secretary to the Vatican Commission for Religious Relations with the Jews, Rabbi Joseph Erenkranz, the director of the Sacred Heart University Center for Jewish Christian Understanding, Peggy Obrecht, the director of Church Relations at the United States Holocaust Museum, and Dr. Michael Marrus, a leading Holocaust Historian and the dean of the University of Toronto's School of Graduate Studies. Much to the satisfaction of those involved, the goodwill generated by the frank and open debate of this important issue at the conference moved the participants to call for further dialogue between the two communities and contributed to the subsequent decision by the Vatican and the International Committee for Interreligious Consultation to convene a small group of Jewish and Catholic scholars to review the Vatican records from World War II—something that might not have happened but for the wonderful experience at the Hyde Park conference.

A second wonderful consequence of that conference is this book. It consists of 16 selections, which, for the editors, proved eminently difficult to choose, given the quality of papers written and presentations delivered. Divided into four parts, the book opens with two overviews outlining the relationship between the Protestant president and both the Catholic people in America and the Catholic Church in America. In "Franklin D. Roosevelt: A

Protestant Patrician in a Catholic Party," Michael Barone discusses the remarkable positive tension between FDR and his Democratic party and the urban Catholic American voters who were so instrumental in sustaining him in power. Barone's essay is followed by the eminent Catholic scholar Gerald Fogarty's examination of "Roosevelt and the American Catholic Hierarchy." Fogarty assesses the Catholic heavyweights in FDR's America: Mundelein, Spellman, O'Connell, Mooney, Dougherty, and Hayes. With broad strokes, he outlines the Catholic leadership in transition from World War I through the development of the Catholic alliance with the New Deal and, beyond, to Roosevelt's relations with the Catholic hierarchy during World War II.

With this grounding intact, Part 2 of *FDR, the Vatican, and the Roman Catholic Church in America* focuses on the intricate and diverse relationship between the New Deal and American Catholicism. Anthony B. Smith begins with an analysis of one of the New Deal's strongest Catholic supporters, the liberal theologian John A. Ryan. While seeking to "offer a Catholic sanction...to a consumer culture in America," Ryan's vision of abundance had definite constraining limits. Smith effectively evokes the underlying Catholic dichotomy that Ryan embodied even as he consistently supported both FDR and the New Deal.

In "Al and Frank: The Great Smith–Roosevelt Feud," Robert Slayton addresses the personal political conflict that existed between the Big City immigrant's son, Al Smith, and the upstate privileged patrician, Franklin Roosevelt. In this masterful tale, Slayton reveals how Smith, a denizen of a Lower East Side neighborhood, lost his vision and his innocence on the national political stage. He also captures the anger that grew inside this Catholic Democratic stalwart when, much to his utter dismay, the Protestant lightweight from Hyde Park succeeded in capturing the hearts and votes of the urban Catholic masses. Political triumph and failure added a stark contrast to the careers of these two Democratic giants of the interwar years and contributed, no doubt, to the deepseated hostility that existed between them, a hostility so effectively evoked in Slayton's essay.

Steven Avella's examination of "California Catholics and the Gubernatorial Election of 1934" offers a microcosmic view of the politics of American Catholicism and indicates the distance American Catholics were prepared to go in supporting radical reform during the Depression years. Avella reveals that, notwithstanding Upton Sinclair's sincere efforts to court the Catholic vote in California during his EPIC gubernatorial campaign, his earlier anti-Catholic diatribes came back to haunt him and contribute to his electoral defeat. As obvious as this historical conclusion might appear, Avella's careful quantitative analysis effectively captures the complexity of the Catholic response to Sinclair's candidacy. While California Catholics may not have supported Sinclair, the evidence suggests they gave his candidacy the most careful consideration. As for Sinclair, he went off to lick his political wounds, no doubt rueing all the excess anti-Catholic baggage he had acquired prior to his campaign.

Francis Sicius offers a remarkable comparison of FDR's New Deal with the radical reform measures contained in the pages of the *Catholic Worker* as outlined by its founder, mentor, and resident guru, Peter Maurin. Contrasts abound, as evident in Maurin's invocation of a "back to the land" movement, his emphasis on communtarianism, and his essentially anti-capitalist message. But Sicius focuses, as well, on the close comparisons of the two contemporaries, noting that both Maurin and FDR were prepared to do just about anything to put equity and prosperity back into the American system. What that "anything" might be, of course, varied from man to man, but Sicius captures the mutual spirit of reform that the age demanded and that both Maurin and FDR embodied in their own unique ways.

In "Francis E. Lucey and President Franklin D. Roosevelt," Ajay K. Mehrotra examines the ambivalent response of a leading Catholic lawyer to the New Deal. In so doing, he seeks to establish a connection between New Deal economic and social policies and classical Catholic scholastic teaching. For Mehrotra, scholars like Lucey envisioned the New Deal as an opportunity to engage in the political dialogue that would shape America's future evolution. Still, even as he praised the role of the state in engineering reform, he was highly critical of the negative impact this increasingly regulatory state had on individual independence and freedom. As with all New Deal policies, there was always something to criticize, but for Mehrotra, Lucey's social theories provided an opportunity for Catholic intellectuals to connect with the Protestant roots of America, thereby placing at least all the Christian community on board the American train.

Philip Chen adds further fuel to the freedom fire in his chapter, "Religious Liberty in American Foreign Policy, 1933–41." Chen focuses exclusively on the second of Roosevelt's Four Freedoms—Freedom of Worship—and in so doing, he seeks not only to define religious liberty, but to determine whether and when issues of religious liberty should be factors in foreign policy decision-making. Chen concentrates on four of the most important foreign policy issues that directly impacted the American Catholic community in order to assess the contrasting responses of both FDR and his Catholic constituency. In each case (the diplomatic recognition of the Soviet Union; Mexican anticlericalism; the Spanish Civil War; and Soviet Lend-Lease), Chen outlines the parameters of the administration's position and contrasts it with a variety of Catholic responses drawn primarily from leading Catholic journals such as *Commonweal* and *America*. Besides capturing the complexity of the foreign policy debate, Chen also reveals that Catholic opinion was hardly monolithic, as the dialogue within Catholic circles often matched or exceeded the Catholic critique of FDR's pragmatic foreign policies.

As World War II engulfed Europe, President Roosevelt began to transform himself, as Michael Barone writes, from "Dr. New Deal" to "Dr. Win-the-War." In so doing, his relationship with the Catholic Church and American Catholics increasingly moved from the national and domestic arena on to the international stage. As such, the intricate and intimate relationship between Washington and the Vatican, between FDR and Pope Pius XII, took on added significance. Out of the conflagration of war came, of course, new controversy. The goals of the Vatican, American objectives, the diplomatic interplay between the United States and the Vatican, the Holocaust itself—all of these factors and more contributed to the progressive evolution in the relationship between the United States and the Catholic Church. In the third part of this book, then, the contributors endeavor to assess and analyze the scope and impact of these dramatic changes.

This section opens with John Conway's balanced assessment of the policies of Pope Pius XII. In "Pope Pius XII and the Myron Taylor Mission," Conway carefully examines the policy options available to the Vatican as the war unfolded. Conway rejects arguments regarding ulterior motives and hidden designs. Instead, he suggests that papal diplomacy during the war constituted an exercise in survival, an exercise in determining the possible in an increasingly impossible situation. The Vatican discovered all too quickly that moral authority in wartime carried little weight and to exercise it too freely might well have been profoundly counterproductive. Stalin's oft-quoted reference to how many divisions the pope possessed captures succinctly the diplomatic dilemma confronted by the Vatican during World War II.

Michael Phayer, in "Catholics, Jews, and the Bombardment of Rome," examines in greater depth the priorities of Pius XII during the war. In so doing, Phayer also rejects the historical stereotype of Pius as a cold, heartless, and uncaring pope. However, personal character aside, his assessment of the pontiff's wartime conduct is highly critical. In a world of stunning, dramatic, and violent change, Phayer marvels at the singleminded determination of Pius XII. For Phayer, Pius' refusal to reassess or reexamine his diplomatic assumptions seriously undermined his ability to play a positive diplomatic or moral role during World War II. He argues that Vatican diplomacy focused exclusively on one issue: protecting Catholics and Catholic infrastructure in Rome and Rome alone. All else paled in comparison and, as a consequence, Pius XII, who was prepared at any cost to save the Holy City, often appeared "callous" to those witnessing and, indeed, experiencing the horror of war.

In many ways, Peter C. Kent's article mirrors the Phayer critique. In "Toward the Reconstitution of Christian Europe: The War Aims of the Papacy," he contends that Pius XII was remarkably detached from the stunning changes that war wrought. He argues, as well, that Vatican diplomacy was similarly rigid and inflexible over the course of the war. For Kent, the primary focus of Vatican diplomacy during the war rested on the postwar reconciliation of Christian Europe. In this regard, Pius XII recognized the importance of defeating Fascism, but he remained consumed with the fear that atheistic communism might rush in to fill the vacuum occasioned by the vagaries of victory. Unprepared to make changes in a world utterly changed, Kent concludes that Pius XII and the Vatican could do little to heal the "wounds of the war." As a sad consequence, the Vatican, although relatively unscathed physically during the war, would emerge all the same as a significant diplomatic, political, and moral loser of this conflict—and these wounds, many self-inflicted, would take years to heal.

In "Diplomacy's Detractors: American Protestant Reaction to FDR's 'Personal Representative' at the Vatican," Michael Carter turns his attention to the domestic Protestant response to Roosevelt's decision to send a personal emissary to the Vatican. In assessing Protestant anger and opposition to Roosevelt's appointment of Myron Taylor and, later, at Truman's effort to appoint General Mark Clark as the American ambassador to the Vatican, Carter assesses the two standard historical interpretations. While accepting the arguments regarding outbursts of anti-Catholic bigotry and a defense of Church–State separation, Clark contends that the negative response to an American diplomatic appointment to the Vatican had far more to do with efforts to attain Protestant ecumenical unity in America than with constitutional or anti-Catholic initiatives. Clark's analysis suggests that, not for the first time, domestic issues and concerns (interdenominational unity, to be precise) constituted the primary source of opposition to the foreign policy initiative of both Roosevelt and Truman.

Still, when all was said and done, Roosevelt overcame any Protestant opposition to his diplomatic engagement with the Vatican. In his contribution, Robert Trisco describes in detail the nature and complexity of the wartime diplomatic relationship between the United States and the Holy See. He does so, however, not through the eyes of the Taylor mission, but from the perspective of the archbishop of Laodicea, better known as the apostolic delegate to Washington, Amleto Cicognani. Through Cicognani, Trisco introduces all of the key diplomatic players in the U.S.–Vatican relationship: Taylor, Maglioni, Spellman, Welles, and, of course, Pacelli— Pius XII himself. In terms of Trisco's analysis, the key word that drives Vatican diplomacy is "persistence." Whether on the issue of recognition, POWs, Vatican relations with Japan, the bombing of Rome and, indeed, the feeding of Rome following the Allied victory, Trisco captures the relentless essence of Vatican diplomacy. In the latter stages of his analysis, Trisco addresses the issue of intervention, or the lack thereof, on behalf of the

Jewish population of Rome, of Italy, and indeed, of Europe. He suggests that, relative to the possible destruction of the Catholic Church in Rome, this occupied a lesser priority diplomatically, but, in his estimation, the Church did all that could be done to address this unfolding catastrophe.

Off on the fringes of the diplomatic world dwell the spies and operatives so essential to the acquisition of information for states in a complex and often violent world. In "A Few Bits of Information: American Intelligence and the Vatican," David Alvarez reveals that FDR was clearly conscious of the intelligence gathering potential inherent in the decision to send a personal representative to the Vatican. However, as Alvarez reveals, in terms of acquiring vital diplomatic and military information over the course of the war, the American record was decidedly lacking in accomplishment. Alvarez attributes this failure primarily to weaknesses within the American intelligence stucture. He points out that American military and civilian intelligence operatives were slow to exploit the available sources in and around the Vatican. With the fall of Rome, however, the intelligence situation offered the promise of improvement in terms of sources and information. However, relative to potential, Alvarez spares few prisoners as he pillories the laughable human intelligence gathered over time and marvels at the contradictory conclusions drawn from signals intelligence. Indeed, in judging the American intelligence results with regard to the Vatican as "lackluster," Alvarez might well be guilty of considerable understatement.

In the concluding chapter to this section, Charles Gallagher, citing new documentary evidence, offers a new perspective on the Coughlin case. In assessing why the Catholic Church failed to halt the anti-Semitic diatribes broadcast from Royal Oak, Michigan, Gallagher points the finger directly at Monsignor Patrick Hurley, a rabid anti-Semite originally from an Irish neighborhood near Cleveland. For Gallagher, the evidence suggests that Hurley, in his capacity as the first American attached to the Secretariat of State in the Vatican, proved to be a master of obfuscation and, notwithstanding entreaties emanating from Roosevelt himself, succeeded in burying the anti-Semitic component of Charles Coughlin deep in the bowels of the Holy See.

Clearly, anti-Semitism penetrates beyond the boundaries of any one faith, nation, or people. In that context, it would be illogical to attribute to all Catholics the prejudiced perceptions of a single Catholic, even if that Catholic was located in high places. In the concluding chapter of this book, the Reverend Dr. Remi Hoeckman's address on the purpose of the document *We Remember: A Reflection on the Shoah* is presented. A Catholic document for the world's Catholics, *We Remember* seeks to provide an explanation for Catholics on "this terrible tragedy of our century." However, Dr. Hoeckman was not unmindful of the potential for this document to open sources, to open dialogue, and to open communication in order that the past could be both remembered and overcome. In seeking to enhance and enrich the lines of communication to the past, Hoeckman held out the hope that the Catholic and Jewish faiths might transcend the difficult memories of horrors past and move on into the future, if not in concert, at least in understanding.

At this conference, it was a considerable joy to witness, for a moment in time, the establishment of a positive and enriching dialogue between men and women of different denominations, different faiths, and different perspectives on the world. Of course, the conference did not resolve all issues or repair all damage. Not surprisingly, even in the few intervening years, more bumps on the road to dialogue, to understanding, to faith and trust have appeared. Well might the road to travel be long, but the journey remains in the interests of us all. We hope this book helps to smooth the way in order that we might all know the past and embrace the future together.

PART 1

# FRANKLIN D. ROOSEVELT AND AMERICAN CATHOLICS

# CHAPTER 1

# FRANKLIN D. ROOSEVELT

## A PROTESTANT PATRICIAN IN A CATHOLIC PARTY

### MICHAEL BARONE

ONCE, WHEN ASKED HIS PHILOSOPHY, FRANKLIN ROOSEVELT ANSWERED simply, "I am a Christian and a Democrat." As always with Roosevelt, there was more to it than that. He was not just a Christian, but also a Protestant, an Episcopalian, a descendant on his mother's side of Huguenot and Yankee New Englanders. And he was not just a Democrat, but a New York Democrat, a member of a state party whose leaders and whose most faithful voters were overwhelmingly Catholic, especially Irish Catholic. There was a tension, always, between this Protestant patrician and his Catholic political party, a tension that this congenial country squire and shrewd politician sought to resolve, with much success, but never with finality. For there remained a tension between the Democratic Party he created in his own image and the Catholics who were such a large part of its constituency, until the tie between them snapped some time in the late 1960s.

But that is far ahead of our story. Franklin Roosevelt grew up in the late nineteenth century and the first decade of the twentieth in an American patriciate that was almost entirely Protestant. There were a few rich Catholics who reached a tenuous foothold in New York society, and probably more Jews of the type portrayed in Edith Wharton's *The House of Mirth* and Anthony Trollope's *The Way We Live Now*. But I gather none were likely to gain an invitation to Springwood or Campobello or Mrs. James Roosevelt's houses in New York City. Catholics, which mostly meant Irish Catholics, were present as servants, or perhaps French governesses. Years later James A. Farley complained, "the president never took me into the bosom of his family" and "never was I invited to spend the night in the historic mansion"—although he adds with almost pathetic gratitude that Eleanor Roosevelt, presumably out of her innate courtesy, made him feel welcome at lunch in Hyde Park.

The history that the young Franklin Roosevelt absorbed was in many ways a Protestant history. I do not know whether he read Macaulay's *History of England*, though I think it likely; but in any case this story of how Protestant England was rescued from a Catholic tyrant was the basis of what Herbert Butterfield called the "whig interpretation of history," which influenced so much of the history of the times. I do read in Kenneth S. Davis's biography that in his early teens Roosevelt read Francis Parkman's *Montcalm and Wolfe* and Alfred T. Mahan's *The Influence of Sea Power on History*, both of which can be called Protestant history. Mahan showed how sea power—a central focus always of the "former naval person" Roosevelt—determined the outcome of the great struggles between Protestant Britain and Catholic France (it ends in 1783, before France became revolutionary). And Parkman presents a history of North America in which the central struggle is between Jesuit Quebec and Puritan Boston, and in which the Revolution and Civil Wars are just incidental sortings-out of the Protestant victors.

The Democratic Party of New York was quite another thing. As a five-year-old child, Roosevelt visited the White House with his father and met his friend, President Grover Cleveland (who, in a sour mood, said, "My little man, I am making a strange wish for you. It is that you may never be President of the United States." This, from the only man who won three popular-vote pluralities for president to the only man who won four popular-vote majorities). James Roosevelt was a gold Democrat, a profoundly conservative man who was attracted to a party whose major principle was laissez faire—low taxes and low tariffs, no interference with local custom, whether segregation in the South or the saloon in the North. But New York Democrats, in James Roosevelt's old age, were increasingly Irish Catholics. Daniel Patrick Moynihan, in his wonderful chapter on the Irish in his and Nathan Glazer's 1963 classic *Beyond the Melting Pot*, tells the story of New York Congressman Timothy J. Campbell, a native of Cavan, calling on President Cleveland for a favor. The president refused on the grounds it was unconstitutional. "Ah, Mr. President," replied Tim, "what is the Constitution between friends?"

Between friends—but Roosevelt opposed the Irish Catholic leaders of New York's Democratic Party at almost every turn in his career. During the whole of his lifetime, the leader of Tammany Hall—the Manhattan Democratic party—was an Irish Catholic. The most notable was Charles F. Murphy, leader from 1902 until his death in 1924, a grim, taciturn teetotaler with a great eye for political talent. In his first election as an adult, Roosevelt voted against the 1904 Democratic presidential nominee, Judge Alton B. Parker, and for his cousin Theodore Roosevelt. In 1910 he won election to the state Senate in heavily Republican Dutchess County by campaigning against bossism. In his first month in the Assembly, he bolted the Democratic caucus and refused to vote for Murphy's candidate for the U.S. Senate (then still elected by the legislature), "Blue-eyed Billy Sheehan." When Murphy sought him out and asked his support, he coolly replied, "No, Mr. Murphy." Then he refused to vote for a compromise candidate, James A. O'Gorman, formerly president of the Friendly Sons of St. Patrick. And he opposed Murphy's choice for president and supported Woodrow Wilson at the 1912 Democratic National Convention.

Murphy was surely relieved when Roosevelt went to Washington in 1913 to become assistant secretary of the Navy. But in those days a Roosevelt was not easily put down. Assemblyman "Big Tim" Sullivan spied him when he first came to Albany: "You know these Roosevelts. This fellow is still young. Wouldn't it be safer to drown him before he grows up?" Murphy must have thought so. In 1913 he brought about the impeachment of Democratic Governor William Sulzer when he would not allow Tammany members to control appointments. In 1914 Roosevelt threw his hat into the ring for U.S. senator—now elected by popular vote. Murphy championed James W. Gerard, ambassador to Germany. In absentia, Gerard beat Roosevelt, 68 to 25 percent. Roosevelt telegraphed Gerard that he would support him if he would declare his unalterable opposition to Murphy's leadership.

How can we account for what seems, at this distance, such animus, and arguably such irrational animus? For the acquiescence of Murphy and his friends, it seems plain, was, if not absolutely essential then at least exceedingly helpful for a young New York Democrat interested in winning higher office. And there were things to be said in Murphy's behalf. He elevated to the leadership of the legislature in 1911, the same year Roosevelt bolted the caucus, young men of great talent and integrity, Al Smith in the Assembly, Robert Wagner in the Senate. He acquiesced in their efforts to enact welfare state measures in New York that led the nation. Tammany-backed mayors of New York built in record time bridges and subways that even today, though somewhat frayed, are an essential part of the awesome infrastructure of New York City.

Against this, Roosevelt had the example of his cousin Theodore, who built a great political career over the opposition of the bosses of his own party. And he shared the view of the upper-class elite, nurtured by James Bryce in *The American Commonwealth* and Lincoln Steffens in *The Shame of the Cities*, that city governments and party machines were thoroughly corrupt, and must be opposed at all turns. Underneath that, not much articulated, was a sense that the mostly Catholic masses of New York—for the Irish were being joined by hundreds of thousands of Germans, Italians, Jews, and other immigrants—were not really capable of democracy. Only Anglo-Saxons—Protestants—were in this view deeply imbued with the principles of liberty and democracy that were central to the American republic. Other races—a term often used by elite spokesmen at the time—were unreliable. A contrast was often drawn between the authoritarian character of the Catholic Church, whose members were expected to defer to the authority of the clerical elite, and the Protestant tradition that seemed to emphasize the freedom of the individual conscience. By analogy, Catholic voters were seen as slavish followers of political bosses, rather than as autonomous citizens making individual decisions. It is not clear to me how much Roosevelt shared these attitudes, but they were the conventional wisdom in his social class; and if we can draw inferences from his actions—so often the only way to guess what Roosevelt really thought—he shared them to some considerable extent.

Yet for the practical politician, confronted with the political map of New York, it was still plain that somehow the votes of the Catholic masses must be won. The facts were simple: by 1910, New York City had 52 percent of the population of New York state; that figure rose to 54 percent in 1920 and peaked at 55 percent in 1930 and 1940; indeed, in 1944 New York City cast 7 percent of the votes in the whole country; and most residents of New York City were Catholic. After his early fights with the Democratic bosses, Roosevelt seemed more disposed to cooperate with them. In 1920, when James M. Cox offered the vice presidential nomination to Franklin Roosevelt, his campaign manager ran it by Murphy, who agreed, with the revealing comment, "this is the first time a Democratic nominee for the presidency has shown me courtesy." In 1924, Roosevelt stood up on crutches at Madison Square Garden, and delivered his "happy warrior" nomination speech for Governor Alfred E. Smith, Murphy's great ally, a Catholic of Irish and Italian descent. Admiring his great skills, and also appreciating his great power over his future career, the recuperating Roosevelt supported Smith as governor and again for the presidential nomination in 1928. His reward, of course, was the nomination for governor, and an election that he would not have come close to winning without Catholic votes.

Yet the tension with Tammany and with Catholics continued. To investigate Tammany, Governor Roosevelt appointed Samuel Seabury, the personification of the white Anglo-Saxon elite. Al Smith, despite earlier disavowals, decided to run for president, with Tammany support. Then, just after Roosevelt won the nomination, the Seabury commission forced him to hold hearings on New York City Mayor Jimmy Walker, who abruptly resigned. He had "walked the political tightrope expertly," wrote James MacGregor

Burns. "He stripped the Republicans of a national issue without losing Tammany, which was divided on the matter and in any case did not dare to turn against Roosevelt openly."

Neither Catholic voters or Catholic bosses turned against Roosevelt openly in the 1930s, when he became the greatest Democratic vote-winner since Andrew Jackson. The First New Deal of 1933–34 ended the downward spiral of depression and got the economy growing again, and produced the only gains in off-year elections for the party in power in the twentieth century. Democratic gains were especially great in the big cities of the East Coast and Great Lakes and in the industrial communities of Pennsylvania and Ohio, offsetting losses in rural and small town districts. Though there were no exit polls in 1934—Gallup conducted his first random-sample poll in October 1935—it is apparent that Roosevelt's Democrats were gaining votes from Catholics even as they were losing some from Protestants. The Second New Deal of 1935–36 did not upset this pattern: the Democratic vote in congressional elections, closely tracking Roosevelt's landslide reelection margin, also closely tracked the 1934 results. The old Democratic minority coalition of the South and the big cities had been replaced by a Democratic majority coalition of the South, the big cities, the industrial belt, and the Progressive belt of the Upper Midwest and the West. Catholic voters were more heavily Democratic than in the 1920s or in Woodrow Wilson's 1910s.

But this was a different kind of Democratic Party in one important way. The traditional Democratic Party, the party of the first Democratic President Franklin Roosevelt had ever met, Grover Cleveland, was a laissez faire party, a party that believed in a minimalist federal government that pretty much left all kinds of Americans alone. The domestic programs of Woodrow Wilson and, even more, the wartime policies of the Wilson administration, were more interventionist, but they did not all prove to be popular: his decision to go to war and the government's suppression of German culture hurt Democrats in the Progressive Upper Midwest, while Prohibition hurt in the heavily Catholic cities of the Northeast. The Democratic Party of the 1920s, while deeply riven, was also something of a laissez faire party: pro-saloon and pro-immigrant in the big states of the North, anti-liquor and pro-segregation in the South.

Then Roosevelt's New Deal suddenly inserted the federal government into every local community. NRA set all prices and wages. AAA controlled agricultural production. The Wagner Act established huge industrial unions, which became major institutions in the industrial belt from Pennsylvania to Illinois. WPA employed workers in almost every city and county. Roosevelt critic Frank Kent, an admirer of laissez faire Democrats, was not far wrong when he wrote, "What Mr. Roosevelt has done—if plain words are to be used—is adopt neither Democratic nor Republican politics, but rather he has taken over the policies of that small group of so-called Progressive Republicans, typified by Senator Norris of Nebraska and Senator LaFollette of Wisconsin."

Holding a majority coalition together is not easy in American politics, and it is more difficult for an interventionist than for a laissez faire party. What is noteworthy is not that Roosevelt had difficulty holding Catholics in the Democratic coalition but that he had such a high degree of success. Some of his New Deal programs—Repeal—had special appeal to Catholics. So did his evident openness to people of immigrant origin—as when he addressed the Daughters of the American Revolution as "My fellow immigrants." In Joseph Alsop's splendid phrase, "on a very wide front and in the truest possible sense, Franklin Delano Roosevelt included the excluded"—and of course many Catholics felt that they were somehow excluded from being regarded as fully Americans.

Including the excluded also meant appointing Catholics to more high positions than any previous president. The two most visible appointments were those of James A. Farley and Joseph P. Kennedy. Both had been instrumental in Roosevelt's election in 1932: Farley was his top political organizer and Kennedy was one of two men who contributed $50,000—an enormous sum in the depression year of 1932. Neither was a product of the New York City Democratic organization. Farley was from Stony Point on the Hudson in Rockland County—suburban territory now, upstate then. Kennedy's father had been a ward politician in East Boston, but he made his money in banking and in 1927, refused entry to Massachusetts's posh clubs, moved his base to New York, and raised his large family in Bronxville. Farley was made postmaster general, the traditional post for dispensing patronage, and also one of great interest to the philatelist-in-chief. Kennedy became the first chairman of the Securities Exchange Commission; then, when he sought to become treasury secretary, was fobbed off with the one office Roosevelt knew an Irish American with political ambitions could not refuse, ambassador to the Court of St. James.

In the meantime, Roosevelt, with Farley's help but also through WPA Administrator Harry Hopkins, stayed in close political alliance with the heavily Catholic Democratic machines in Chicago, Philadelphia, and other big cities. But in New York he opposed Tammany and backed Mayor Fiorello LaGuardia, who was elected on the Republican and American Labor Party lines, whose strongest ethnic support was among Jewish voters.

Foreign policy produced tensions in this new Democratic coalition. Roosevelt stretched the patience of liberal advisers like Harold Ickes and his ambassador to Spain, Claude Bowers, with his support of the embargo against both sides in the Spanish Civil War, which worked to the detriment of the leftist Republican government. The reason, he told Ickes, was the support of the Catholic hierarchy for the Franco regime; to raise the embargo would, he said, exaggeratedly, lose the support of every Catholic voter in the 1938 election. That was exaggeration. But Roosevelt's increasing support of Britain in 1939 and 1940 angered many anti-British Irish Catholic voters. And when Italy attacked France in June 1940 he declared, "the hand that held the dagger has struck it into the backs of its neighbor"—a comment that antagonized some Italian Americans for years to come. His support of Britain also brought a clash with one Kennedy, who resigned and attacked Roosevelt's policies. It was only by playing on Kennedy's political ambitions for his sons that Roosevelt secured his endorsement in November 1940. Roosevelt's decision to run for a third term also brought bitter opposition from Farley, who was running for president himself. Two years later Farley secured the nomination of a conservative Catholic for governor of New York; he lost by a wide margin to Republican Thomas E. Dewey.

As Roosevelt transformed himself from "Dr. New Deal" to "Dr. Win-the-War," he avoided domestic issues, which would have split Catholics and Protestants in his enlarged Democratic coalition. Such issues did arise after Roosevelt's death. When Democrats pushed for federal aid to education, Catholics insisted that parochial schools be included, a position strongly opposed by southerners and many northern Protestants. One of the most vocal was Eleanor Roosevelt, who engaged in a bitter correspondence with Cardinal Spellman on the issue. The coming of the Cold War also divided some Democrats from others, with strongly anti-Communist Catholics and their liberal anti-Communist allies coming out ahead of those liberals personified by Henry Wallace who favored a softer line. Later, in the 1960s and 1970s, the issue of abortion would also split the Democratic coalition along religious lines. We can only speculate on how Franklin Roosevelt would have handled these divisive issues, though with his characteristic tendency to "weave the two together" he might have made them less divisive. On education, for example, the approach of the G.I. Bill of Rights he signed was to extend aid to the student, who could then choose public or religious schools, and leave the state out of the choice altogether.

So far I have mostly stressed the tensions between this patrician Protestant and his heavily Catholic political party. So perhaps it should end on a more positive note. One of the strengths of our majority-forcing politics is that it gives politicians a strong incentive to hold together large numbers of what has always been a diverse people. From the beginning, Americans have been divided along lines of region, religion, race, ethnicity, and, in recent years, cultural values. Such coalitions have been especially hard to hold together as the federal government has become larger and more intrusive in the lives of its citizens. And they were especially difficult to create and hold together in the long century from the beginning of massive Irish Catholic immigration in the 1840s until the reforms of the Vatican II Council of the 1960s—and the election of John Kennedy in 1960—made American Catholics less religiously and culturally distinctive.

It was the achievement of Franklin Roosevelt to build a political coalition that included significant majorities of Protestants, Catholics, and Jews—arguably the only such political coalition in American history. And if he had trouble holding it together, and if his successors were ultimately unable to do so, it should also be said that the existence of that coalition, the highly visible effort to include the excluded, contributed greatly to the common American effort in the great hour of the nation's—and the world's—need in the 1940s and to the strength and cohesiveness of the nation in the half-century since. Roosevelt may have started off a particular kind of Christian and a particular kind of Democrat, but in time he transcended these limitations and expanded the happily elastic definition of what it means to be an American. That is no mean achievement, nor one that should be forgotten.

CHAPTER 2

# ROOSEVELT AND THE AMERICAN CATHOLIC HIERARCHY

## GERALD P. FOGARTY, S.J.

AMERICAN CATHOLICS HAD TRADITIONALLY BEEN DEMOCRATS, but they had been through two traumatic events before the election of Franklin D. Roosevelt. First, their relationship with the previous Democratic administration of Woodrow Wilson had been frequently strained on both the domestic and foreign fronts. Second, the defeat of Al Smith, the first Catholic candidate for president, in 1928 made them feel like second-class citizens. When Roosevelt took office, he confronted a body of American bishops who were in transition. Some, like Cardinal George Mundelein, had been partially shaped by some of the anti-German sentiment of World War I. Others were newcomers on the American episcopal scene, like Francis Spellman who had been named auxiliary bishop to the cantankerous Cardinal William O'Connell, in September 1932, or Archbishop Edward Mooney who became bishop of Rochester in 1933, after serving as apostolic delegate first to India and then to Japan. Behind the rise of each of these members of the American hierarchy was Cardinal Eugenio Pacelli, the secretary of state, who was elected pope in 1939. His early experience of the United States was shaped by Wilson's coolness toward Vatican peace initiatives in World War I.

To place Roosevelt's dealings with the American hierarchy in perspective, this chapter will treat: (1) the background of World War I in shaping the Vatican's attitude toward the United States; (2) the development of the Catholic alliance with the New Deal; and (3) Roosevelt's relations with the Catholic hierarchy during World War II.

## WORLD WAR I, THE AMERICAN HIERARCHY
## AND THE VATICAN

American Catholicism was the product of immigration. Its ethnic pluralism was both its strength and its weakness. As World War I approached, those of German ancestry were sometimes held suspect, a suspicion that may have led some to seek to demonstrate their American patriotism at every opportunity. One such German American later became one of Roosevelt's most ardent supporters. In 1915, the Sees of both Chicago and Buffalo were vacant. Rumors made the rounds that Dennis J. Dougherty, bishop of Jaro in the Philippines would be the new archbishop of Chicago. In the meantime, the Holy See intended to appoint George Mundelein, then auxiliary bishop of Brooklyn, to Buffalo, when the British Foreign Office requested that the Holy See not appoint a bishop of German ancestry to a See on the border between the United States and Canada during World War I. The Holy See, therefore, appointed Mundelein to Chicago and Dougherty to Buffalo. Within three years, Dougherty was transferred to the Archdiocese of Philadelphia and became its first cardinal in 1921. Mundelein, however, seemed sensitive to his German ancestry and soon became identified as fully American.[1]

But World War I brought strained relations both between the bishops and President Woodrow Wilson and between the United States and the Vatican. Wilson had shown himself singularly ill-disposed toward non–Anglo-Saxons in general and the pope in particular. As a historian, he had written in 1902 about the predominantly Catholic immigrants from eastern and southern Europe, "multitudes of men of the lowest class from the south of Italy, and the men of the meaner sort out of Hungary and Poland . . . as if the countries of the south of Europe were disburdening themselves of the most sordid and hapless elements of their population."[2]

American Catholics were divided on the war. Irish Americans were suspicious of British designs. When they later tried to introduce Irish independence on the agenda at the Versailles Peace Conference, they learned Wilson's attitude toward hyphenated Americans. He remarked about the incident: "My first impulse was to tell the Irish to go to hell, but, feeling that this would not be the act of a statesman, I denied myself this personal satisfaction."[3]

In dealing with the Church, Wilson's sole contact was Cardinal James Gibbons of Baltimore. Although by 1911, there were two other cardinals in the American Church, John Farley of New York and William O'Connell of Boston, the aging Gibbons had the task of carrying messages from Benedict XV to the president. But here his personal vanity may have made him indiscreet and to bask in the newspaper attention he drew on his infrequent visits to the White House. As early as December 1916, Archbishop Giovanni Bonzano, the apostolic delegate, thought the cardinal guilty of indiscretion.[4] Regardless of what influence Gibbons had on Wilson, he nevertheless ardently led the hierarchy to support American entry into the war.[5]

Once the United States was in the war, however, Gibbons was more hesitant to act as an emissary between the Vatican and Wilson. In August 1917, Benedict XV proposed a series of points for negotiating peace. When Bonzano asked Gibbons to intervene with the president to examine the papal proposals, he hesitated. Wilson and Robert Lansing, the secretary of state, rejected the papal note on the grounds that it would return Germany to the *status quo ante bellum*. Wilson, however, alienated the Allies by ignoring them in his rejection of the papal initiative and thus appearing to be their spokesman.[6] Gibbons himself had made no effort personally to intervene with the president.[7]

On January 8, 1918, soon after rejecting the papal peace plan, Wilson issued his own "Fourteen Points." While Gibbons and other bishops sought to show the similarities between Wilson's points and the pope's, American newspaper propaganda increasingly portrayed the pope and his plan as pro-German.[8]

The increase in anti-Catholic propaganda provided the context within which Gibbons next attempted to persuade Wilson to conclude a separate peace with Austria–Hungary. As early as May 1917, the Holy See had learned from Archbishop Eugenio Pacelli, then the nuncio to Bavaria, that the Austro-Hungarian emperor was interested in pursuing a separate peace and ending the alliance with Germany.[9] Even after the United States declared war on Austria–Hungary on December 7, 1917, the emperor made overtures for peace through the pope.[10] Gibbons urged Wilson to cooperate with the pope in seeking to detach the Empire from Germany, but his efforts were thwarted by two factors. First, the secret Treaty of London between the Allies in 1915 contained an article excluding the Holy See from any peace negotiations, due to Italian desires to keep the Roman Question from coming before an international body. Second, Italy convinced the Allies that Benedict was concerned for Austria–Hungary only because of its large Catholic population. Gibbons had to steer a delicate course in his efforts at mediation. On the one hand, he denied that the pope wished to introduce the Roman Question at a peace conference and urged the president to counter the British exclusion of the Vatican. On the other hand, he would neither call for public demonstrations in favor of the Holy See's participation nor join the bishops of the British Empire in protesting the exclusion.[11] Faced with increased anti-Catholic propaganda, he was ineffective in the final plea to Wilson for a separate Austro-Hungarian armistice.[12]

During the last days of the war, Austria–Hungary made one more plea to Wilson for a separate armistice and asked for papal mediation. On October 11, Bonzano received a cable from Cardinal Pietro Gasparri, the

secretary of state, enclosing a separate telegram to Wilson. He was to have
Gibbons intervene with the president. In order not to avoid any publicity,
however, the delegate sent his secretary with the telegram and a letter of his
own to Wilson, who was then out of town.[13] On October 17, Wilson
responded to the pope that the people of the United States desired peace, "if
peace can be founded with some prospect of permanence upon genuine and
impartial justice." While he would endeavor "to pursue such a course as will
bring the world the blessings of such peace," he continued: "I warmly appreciate the generous confidence you express in my personal influence in this
time of tragedy and travail."[14] It was an innocuous letter with no mention
of the conditions that Wilson envisioned for such a permanent peace that
included his concept of allowing self-determination for the populations of
the Austro-Hungarian Empire.

On October 28, Bonzano forwarded Wilson's letter to the pope. But he
also informed Gasparri that only a few days earlier Gibbons had informed
him that a visit to the White House would be inopportune because of the
indiscretion of the press, but agreed it would be effective to write Wilson.
However, the delegate now openly stated that the cardinal was not "very jeal-
ous of the secrecy in this regard."[15] Although Benedict XV's overtures to
Wilson had been thwarted either through Gibbons' hesitation or the president's polite but firm rejection, the pope, nevertheless, recognized the role of
the United States in world affairs. On November 8, he thanked Wilson for
his letter and called on him "to become the champion of peace and of a just
and durable peace." He also praised Wilson for recognizing the independence of Poland, a concern of the Holy See for some time, and called on him
now to work for the independence of Armenia, on whose behalf he had
already written to the sultan of Turkey. Now, he declared, "that is why all
humanity has fixed its eyes on the great president of the greatest democracy
in the world." Together with Wilson, he wanted a just and lasting peace, but
believed the president would agree that "peace cannot be lasting," if conditions were imposed that left "seeds of rancor" and "plans for revenge." "The
history of the past," he concluded, "is the mistress of the future."[16] It was a
gracious letter, especially considering that Wilson was following the lead of
his Italian allies in rejecting any role for the Holy See in the forthcoming
peace conference.

But not every Vatican diplomat was happy at the new role given to the
United States, at least when it meant a diminished role for the Holy See. In
October, the new German government had also made overtures to Wilson
for an armistice. This prompted Pacelli to write to Gasparri that this was
effective recognition of Wilson as the head of the nations allied against
Germany. For his own part, he added, "on this occasion I cannot hide from
Your Eminence my sadness in seeing Germany turning directly to the

President of the United States, rather than having had recourse to the good offices of the Holy Father." Although many German leaders, including some Protestants, wanted papal mediation, this was precluded by article 15 of the Treaty of London.[17] The president's rejection of the papal initiatives shaped Pacelli's approach when he was later cardinal secretary of state and pope and was dealing with the United States during World War II. One final episode illustrated the difference in approach between European Church leaders and the United States. On March 25, 1919, Cardinal Desire Mercier, archbishop of Mechlin, Belgium, had written to both Wilson and Georges Clemenceau, the president of France, asking that they conclude the peace treaty at Versailles with an invitation for a "public act of religion in the church of Notre Dame in Paris." He further proposed that the cardinals from the allied nations be invited. On May 19, he informed Gasparri of his plan and enclosed a response from Clemenceau offering half-hearted support for the project. In regard to Wilson, however, he reported a Belgian emissary had been unable to see the president, but was informed by Colonel House, the president's assistant, that there was little hope of interesting Wilson in "a project of a religious, Catholic character."[18] Mercier, the symbol of Belgian resistance, had received his first lesson on the president's attitude toward the Church, just as he was about to embark on a triumphal tour of the United States where he received the accolades of both Protestants and Catholics and was awarded doctorates from some of the nation's leading non-Catholic universities, including Harvard, Yale, Princeton, Brown and Columbia.

On both the diplomatic and home fronts, therefore, Catholics were estranged from Wilson. In 1924, Archbishop Patrick Hayes of New York bluntly commented that the president "certainly was not sympathetic to us."[19] In 1928, American Catholics became even more alienated from society with the defeat of Al Smith, the first Catholic candidate for president. Alienated they may have been, but their leaders, under John A. Ryan, professor at the Catholic University of America and director of the Social Action Department of the National Catholic Welfare Conference (NCWC), had developed a progressive social policy in the wake of the war that would gradually build a bridge to the New Deal.

CATHOLICS AND THE NEW DEAL

When Roosevelt ran for his first term, Catholic spokesmen were divided. Ryan was lukewarm with severe reservations about the candidate's program to get the nation out of the Depression. Father Charles Coughlin was enthusiastic with his war cry on his weekly radio program of "Roosevelt or Ruin." Both would change. When Roosevelt took office, he encountered several prominent members of the hierarchy who had taken office in the era of

World War I. O'Connell in Boston, Hayes in New York and Dougherty in Philadelphia were indifferent to him, to judge from lack of surviving correspondence. But Roosevelt's champion in these early days was Mundelein in Chicago. Roosevelt's personal advisers were well aware of the conservatism of the eastern bishops, but became increasingly enamored of Mundelein's social programs under the direction of his auxiliary, Bernard J. Sheil.[20] What the president needed was an entree, which he found when he learned that Mundelein collected presidential autographs.[21] On April 22, 1933, one month after his inauguration, Roosevelt wrote Mundelein on the feast of St. George. The cardinal was delighted that "the busiest man in the land, one who now carries the weight of the world on his shoulders" took the time "to write me on my feast-day." He decided to push his luck further by asking for an appointment when he was in the east in a week "to pay my respects and congratulate you on the remarkable record for achievement you have made in the past few weeks you have been our national leader and chief executive."[22] This was the first recorded exchange between the two who soon developed a strong friendship, based on their mutual concern for social reform. On May 5, Roosevelt granted the cardinal's request for the first of several meetings at the White House.[23]

Most, but not all, Catholics rallied to the New Deal. Ryan saw Roosevelt's first-term programs as compatible with Catholic social teaching as most recently articulated by Pius XI in *Ouadragessimo Anno*. Coughlin, however, turned increasingly against his former idol. Late in 1934, he founded the National Union of Social Justice to lobby for legislation in Washington. The only ecclesiastical restriction placed on his actions was the prohibition from Archbishop Amleto Cicognani, the apostolic delegate, of broadcasting from his church in Royal Oak, Michigan, a Detroit suburb. In May 1935, Cardinal Dougherty explained the difficulty to Filippo Bernardini, former professor of canon law at the Catholic University and then apostolic delegate to Australia. Coughlin, he said, was "aided and abetted by his Most Reverend ordinary, Bishop [Michael J.] Gallagher" and was "now quite beyond control." He had become "a hero in the minds of the proletariat and especially those members of that rabble, who are of Jewish extraction or belong to the Socialists or Communists."[24]

Detroit was at that time a suffragan diocese of the Province of Cincinnati. Archbishop John T. McNicholas, O.P., became the reluctant emissary first for Archbishop Pietro Fumasoni-Biondi, who completed his term as apostolic delegate in 1933, and then for his successor, Archbishop Amleto Cicognani, to intervene with Gallagher to have Coughlin cease his attacks on Roosevelt. Early in 1935, McNicholas informed Gallagher that the delegate wished Coughlin not to mention names in his broadcasts, but to no avail. As McNicholas told his friend, Archbishop Edward Mooney, bishop of

Rochester, "Bishop Gallagher says, 'Well, St. John the Baptist denounced Herod and his wife because of their adulterous union!' "[25]

Despite Coughlin's rabid attacks, however, Roosevelt continued to gain Catholic favor. On December 9, 1935, he received an honorary doctorate from the University of Notre Dame. Mundelein presided over the ceremonies and praised the president's "indomitable persevering courage." In response, Roosevelt spoke of the national life depending on the rights of man, supreme among which were "the rights of freedom of education and freedom of religious worship."[26]

While Roosevelt and Mundelein were becoming closer, Coughlin continued to be a problem. Early in 1936, Cicognani asked McNicholas if the administrative committee of the NCWC could make a statement. The archbishop proposed to Mooney a generic statement acknowledging that Coughlin was exercising his rights as a citizen to express his opinions on social issues, but was not speaking "for the Catholic Church of the United States, nor the American Hierarchy." McNicholas wanted to spare the Holy See from bearing the brunt of censuring Coughlin, but also desired to find a formula that would not bring the acrimony of the people upon the bishops who issued it.[27] For his part, Mooney thought the only ecclesiastical authorities who could "step into this affair" were "his own Bishop and the Holy See. His own Bishop has spoken—and how! Evidently the Holy See does not care to speak. . . ."[28] In short, regardless of their sympathies for or against Roosevelt, the two bishops were powerless to do anything about Coughlin, as long as he had his bishop's approval.

But Coughlin escalated his assault. In the summer of 1936, he launched his own third party with Congressman William Lemke of North Dakota as its presidential candidate. In September, however, after Bishop Gallagher had visited Rome, the *Osservatore Romano* condemned Coughlin's attacks on Roosevelt. The paper further stated that Gallagher had new directives from Rome and was incorrect in saying Coughlin had Vatican approval.[29] At this juncture, Roosevelt added to his episcopal followers a newcomer and, in the eyes of some, a relatively obscure bishop, Francis Spellman, auxiliary bishop of Boston.

A favorite of Cardinal Eugenio Pacelli, now the secretary of state, Spellman was in fact Pacelli's man in the hierarchy and, while enduring the repressive regime of Cardinal O'Connell, cultivated a friendship with Joseph P. Kennedy and, through him, made contact with Roosevelt. Soon after the *Osservatore Romano* rebuked Coughlin, Spellman first wrote and then visited Cicognani to convey Roosevelt's annoyance with Coughlin. As long as Coughlin had Gallagher's support, however, the delegate said he could do nothing, but Spellman thought "he could at least rebuke Gallagher or demand that he keep Coughlin in Detroit." Spellman further recorded in his diary that Cicognani was "weak and frightened and I am sure that he is suspicious and too cautious." He added the provocative note, "I did not tell him of Cardinal Pacelli's visit."[30] Spellman had in fact known of the forthcoming visit since early August.

As events unfolded, Spellman seems to have advised Pacelli on the Coughlin case. The day after he saw Cicognani, he visited Roosevelt at Hyde Park to discuss both Coughlin and Pacelli's coming visit, which did not become public for several more days.[31] As will be seen, however, Coughlin was not the only reason why Pacelli was making his American visit.

But Coughlin continued to be an irritation as the election of 1936 approached. Late in October, James A. Farley, chairman of the Democratic National Campaign Committee, urged Roosevelt to obtain from Mundelein, not a direct endorsement, but a statement "that he sees no communistic tendencies in the present administration." He thought this strategy necessary to neutralize Coughlin's charges that were becoming ammunition for the Republicans.[32]

Mundelein had, in fact, already issued a statement that narrowly missed being a specific endorsement. After registering to vote in September, he gave a newspaper interview in which he called Roosevelt "his friend" and spoke of the gratitude the American people should feel "for the prosperity, the happiness, and the freedom now abroad in our land." He was, however, careful to note that he had "called the priests together and told them to get out the vote, but not to tell people how to vote."[33] The Chicago *Times* interpreted the cardinal's remarks as a "slap" at Coughlin, but by this time the priest had lost his following, except for the lower, less-educated classes.[34] Democratic leaders, nevertheless, prevailed on John A. Ryan to make a radio broadcast defending Roosevelt's legislative initiatives. Coughlin then branded him "Right Reverend New Dealer," and Archbishop Michael J. Curley of Baltimore, who had jurisdiction over the Catholic University, authorized his newspaper to publish an attack on both Ryan and Coughlin.[35]

Roosevelt's election to a second term was virtually a foregone conclusion, but it did elicit responses from bishops who had hitherto been silent—or whose correspondence with the president was not retained. Two days after the election, Cardinal Patrick Hayes of New York congratulated him "on your triumphal victory—an outstanding event in American history."[36] The cardinal may well have been influenced by Monsignor Robert F. Keagan, director of Catholic Charities for New York, who had already effusively congratulated the president. Keagan thought the victory "effectively" answered "the carping criticism, the abuse, and the vilification to which you were unwarrantably subjected during the last six months." In particular, he cited "the misrepresentation of the provisions of the Social Security Act" and "the grossly intemperate remarks of the radio gentleman from Royal Oak," but was "proud and happy that my vote and the vote of every friend whom I could influence, went to swell the magnificent total which must have heartened and strengthened you yesterday."[37]

Two days after Roosevelt's triumph, he established a historical precedent by meeting with Cardinal Pacelli. On October 8, Pacelli had arrived in the United States ostensibly as the house guest of Genevieve Garvin Brady, a papal countess, but Spellman, probably acting under the cardinal's instructions, took charge of the visit and in the process alienated Hayes, Cicognani and Mrs. Brady. After visiting the cities of the east coast, Pacelli and Spellman left by a chartered plane to visit most of the principal cities in the Midwest and California. On October 30, they were in Cincinnati, where Coughlin later claimed Pacelli discussed his case with McNicholas, but refused to see Gallagher or Bishop Joseph Schrembs of Cleveland. Pacelli then supposedly ordered Gallagher to forbid Coughlin from engaging in any further political activities after the election.[38] Spellman, however, reported nothing of any discussion about Coughlin in his otherwise detailed accounts in his diary. Once back in New York and with the election over, Pacelli could now realize one of the purposes of his visit—to meet the president. His experience during World War I made it imperative to establish some direct contact with the United States government as Europe was again moving toward war. From his arrival in the United States, NCWC officials had been trying to arrange such a meeting, but Cicognani received word from Pacelli that Spellman had orchestrated it through Joseph Kennedy. Spellman's solitary action now alienated him from Cicognani and from the NCWC, the organization of the American bishops.[39]

On November 5, Roosevelt hosted both Pacelli and Spellman at Hyde Park. Newspapers speculated that the president and cardinal discussed establishing diplomatic relations between the United States and the Holy See, an issue on which Spellman had been working since at least November 1935, through Kennedy and Farley, but without any consultation of Cicognani. But Roosevelt seems to have wanted to keep Mundelein informed of the proceedings. Even as he was agreeing to the Hyde Park meeting, he asked his Chicago friend to meet him at the White House on November 9.[40] What transpired between the two is unknown, but, a few weeks after the meeting, Spellman heard rumors that Roosevelt would like him to be the papal representative in Washington, a position he recognized was impossible. In February 1937, he was a guest at the White House, but recorded nothing about the issue of diplomatic relations. Late in the summer, Roosevelt again broached the question in the context of building Catholic support for a revision of the neutrality laws. Thomas Corcoran, a presidential aide, and James Roosevelt, the president's son, discussed the issue with Spellman.[41] Roosevelt, however, preferred to take direct initiative through Mundelein.

American Catholic attitudes toward neutrality or intervention in part reflected their ethnic origin. Some of Irish ancestry, and particularly Coughlin, interpreted anti-German propaganda in terms of their own anti-British prejudice. If Roosevelt sought a Catholic spokesman against Nazi aggression, Mundelein fit the bill perfectly. Here was a prelate of German ancestry who was decidedly anti-Nazi. On March 14, 1937, Pius XI had issued *mit brennender Sorge*, a condemnation of National Socialism. Because the German government had placed restrictions on Church presses, the encyclical had to be read from the pulpits in German parishes. On May 22, 1937, Mundelein delivered an address to his clergy in which he expressed his dismay that the German people had accepted Adolf Hitler, "an inept paper hanger," as their leader.[42] There is some evidence that his statement was made at the request of Pacelli and several German bishops who had helped draft *mit brennender Sorge*.[43] The forum he chose was neither a pastoral letter nor a public statement, but a supposedly private statement to his clergy that happened to be picked up by the international press. Whatever may have been the background to the cardinal's statement, it drew the praise of other American bishops. But the German government made a formal protest to the Vatican and demanded that the cardinal retract his remark. When the Vatican defended Mundelein's right to freedom of speech within his own diocese, Germany then withdrew its ambassador to the Holy See.[44] Not only did the speech alienate the German government, it also served to enlist the support of German American Catholics for the Allied cause. As well, it provided the occasion for reintroducing the topic of diplomatic relations when Roosevelt and Mundelein next met.

On October 5, 1937, Roosevelt delivered an address in Chicago proposing a pact of nations committed to isolating and severing all contacts with aggressor nations. He then had lunch at Mundelein's residence—the first time a president had visited a Catholic prelate. As Mundelein reported their conversation to Cicognani, Roosevelt wished to have the Holy See participate in a movement to establish "permanent peace in a war-torn old world." With the Holy See's approval, the president intended "to send a special envoy to the Vatican . . . of ambassadorial rank."[45] What Roosevelt meant by "special envoy" was not specified, but the overture was a far cry from Wilson's aloofness during World War I. Enclosing a copy of his letter to Cicognani, Mundelein assured Roosevelt that he would receive "the most cordial cooperation in your efforts to arrest the spread of this gangster spirit in nations which is menacing present and future generations."[46]

Less than a week after meeting Roosevelt, Mundelein had a visit from Spellman, who, unfortunately, did not record whether they discussed diplomatic relations. From the available evidence, however, Roosevelt may have made his overtures to Mundelein as a result of Spellman's earlier initiatives.

On September 21, Spellman had written Pacelli apparently about his conversation that summer with James Roosevelt. On November 26, Pacelli responded asking the bishop's advice on drafting a pro-memoria for Pius XI about diplomatic relations. Alluding to Spellman's earlier letter, he said "the Holy See always required that its representative be recognized as the Dean of the diplomats of the same grade" and that the American ambassador to Italy not also be accredited to the Holy See. The cardinal could see no other obstacles to establishing diplomatic relations and concluded "The practical procedure to arrive at the establishment of relations is simple, it would be enough that the Government express a desire that everything can be easily prepared."[47]

For several weeks, Spellman discussed Pacelli's proposals with various people close to the president. On Kennedy's advice, he broached the questions raised in Pacelli's letter with James Roosevelt. Both Roosevelt and Cordell Hull, the secretary of state, did not see how the United States government could recognize the nuncio as the dean of the diplomatic corps. The government, moreover, preferred to have the ambassador to Italy also accredited to the Holy See—a position that the government had long favored because it bypassed the necessity of gaining Senate approval for the appointment of an official ambassador, which the Vatican could not accept. On January 7, 1938, Spellman therefore reported to Pacelli that he was not "too optimistic about the eventual success" of his negotiations, but he still planned to submit a memorandum on the topic to the president.[48] A few days later, he visited James Roosevelt at the White House and gave him his memorandum. This time, moreover, he had informed Cicognani of his actions. He then explained his activities to Pacelli, who responded on February 26 that while "it would be more dignified for the United States to have a true and proper Ambassador, nevertheless the Holy See could not raise a difficulty if it preferred to give to the Representative only the designation of Minister."[49] Precisely what Spellman had reported of his White House meeting and what Pacelli would have been willing to accept at this time is unknown. For several more months the question of diplomatic relations was in abeyance.

In the meantime, the Coughlin problem continued. After his Union Party was defeated in 1936, he announced that he would cease his radio broadcasts unless his supporters increased his subscriptions to his journal, *Social Justice*. Next, on January 20, 1937, Bishop Gallagher died. Almost immediately, Coughlin resumed his broadcasts, because, he claimed, the dying bishop had requested it. On May 26, the Holy See announced that Detroit was to be an archdiocese with Edward Mooney, chairman of the administrative board, as the first archbishop. Mooney, who had sought to advise McNicholas on what the NCWC could do about Coughlin, now found himself having to deal with the fractious priest. He had to live out what he had earlier predicted to his Cincinnati colleague—any bishop who sought to restrain Coughlin would himself become the object of rebuke.[50] On the advice of Frank Hall, director of the National Catholic News Service, Roosevelt wrote to congratulate Mooney on his new post.[51] For several more years, however, Mooney and the NCWC were negligible quantities in Roosevelt's equation for dealing with the American hierarchy. The same was not true of his relations with Mundelein and Spellman.

The development of Roosevelt's relationship with the American hierarchy now centered on three events that occurred in rapid succession—Mundelein's attending as legate the Eucharistic Congress in New Orleans; the death of Cardinal Patrick Hayes of New York; and the death of Pius XI. In September, 1938, Hayes died, and Mundelein presided at the funeral. Roosevelt asked friends in attendance at the funeral to discuss with both Mundelein and Spellman the issue of diplomatic relations—the first evidence for the cooperation of both prelates on the issue.[52] For the next month, Spellman conferred with government officials on the issue and then attended the Eucharistic Congress, where he spoke about the matter with Mundelein.[53] For the moment, however, Mundelein would be the principal negotiator. Just prior to his departure for Rome to report on the congress, he was Roosevelt's guest at the White House where he discussed his trip to the Holy See. The president then instructed the American ambassador to Italy, William Phillips, to make every effort to impress upon both Vatican and Italian officials that Mundelein enjoyed his government's complete respect. Phillips met Mundelein's ship in Naples, feted him on board the flagship of the United States Navy, escorted him on the special train provided by the Italian government to Rome, and there turned him over to Vatican officials. He also hosted Mundelein at a dinner at the embassy. The Irish embassy likewise honored the American cardinal, for Mrs. Brady, an old friend of Mundelein's, had then married the Irish ambassador to the Holy See.[54] The respect shown Mundelein had the effect Roosevelt had intended. German newspapers now reported that the cardinal was in Rome to announce the establishment of diplomatic relations—a report that Mundelein did nothing to dispel.[55]

What Mundelein discussed with Vatican officials is, unfortunately, unknown. Whatever may have been his role in influencing Roosevelt, it was now coming to an end. On February 10, 1939, Pius XI died. In the conclave to elect his successor, the cardinals chose Pacelli, who took the name Pius XII. This had a direct effect on the American Church and on negotiations with the government. In an unprecedented move, Roosevelt sent Kennedy, then ambassador to the United Kingdom, to represent him at Pius XII's coronation. In the United States, the major issue awaiting the pope's decision was the New York succession. Other churchmen owed their rise to a Roman patron, and Spellman now had the most powerful of them all. Yet, it was not a foregone conclusion. The Consistorial Congregation, charged with episcopal appointments, had actually recommended McNicholas of Cincinnati to be the new archbishop of New York, but Pius XI died before confirming him. Pius XII must have known of his reservations about Roosevelt, for, on June 29, 1938, the archbishop had written to Domenico Tardini, secretary of the Congregation of the Extraordinary Affairs of the Church:

> Our political situation here grows more perplexing. President has been given unprecedented powers by Congress. I cannot think that he is a serious-minded man or that he studies any questions profoundly. He has no prejudice whatever against the Catholic Church. On the contrary, he is very kindly disposed to things Catholic. He is an opportunist. Consistency means nothing to him. What seems to me the most serious objection to be made to the Federal Administration of our Government during six years is radical and subversive teachings have everywhere been tolerated and even encouraged.[56]

Even if the new pope did not have his own candidate, such negative views on Roosevelt would have been enough to convince him that McNicholas was not suited for New York. On April 12, Spellman was named archbishop of New York. Within six months Mundelein had died, and Spellman initially became the principal negotiator with Roosevelt. Yet, from the available evidence, Spellman never inherited Mundelein's mantle of personal friendship with the president. But he lost no time in trying to ingratiate himself with the president.

Though Secretary of State Hull and Assistant Secretary Sumner Welles desired official diplomatic relations with the Holy See on the pragmatic grounds of having a listening post within Rome, Roosevelt's actual attitude was ambiguous.[57] Anti-Catholicism was a fact in American political life, and the president would have to proceed cautiously. On October 24, he summoned Spellman to the White House. The next day, the archbishop submitted a report of his conversations to Cardinal Luigi Maglione, the secretary of state, through Cicognani. He had urged that the president disregard all opposition and establish diplomatic relations. Though well disposed, Roosevelt hesitated because he could not get the necessary majority in Congress to appropriate funds, but he had already shown his favorable attitude toward the Holy See and the Holy Father by sending Kennedy to represent him at the coronation. The president suggested that after Congress had revised the Neutrality Act in November, it would recess until January 3. During that time, he would "name a special mission to the Holy See, explaining as the motivation for his action his belief that such an association would be a help for the peace of the world." For the time being, Spellman continued, diplomatic relations "would consist in a mission of the government in Rome accredited to the Holy See, without the necessity that the mission of the Holy See in Washington be recognized as an Apostolic Nunciature." Roosevelt also suggested two names to Spellman, either Myron C. Taylor, chairman of the board of the United States Steel Corporation, or Breckenridge Long, former ambassador to Italy. By naming a "special mission," Roosevelt could bypass the necessity of having the Senate confirm an ambassador. Spellman was confident, however, that if the mission went well, congress would appropriate the necessary funds to make it permanent. He was careful to note for Maglione that he had discussed all the details of his conversation with Cicognani and was forwarding his report to Rome through the delegate.[58] Up to this point Spellman had been speaking of the establishment of official diplomatic relations, but Roosevelt's proposal of a "special mission" echoed "the special envoy" of which he and Mundelein had spoken two years earlier.

On November 28, 1939, Cicognani notified Spellman that Maglione had cabled him that "The Holy Father has learned of the report with pleasure and hopes that Your Excellency as well as I will make opportune overtures to the President, that he may carry out his proposal." The delegate further suggested that Spellman might want to arrange another confidential meeting with Roosevelt.[59] Spellman immediately made another appointment with Roosevelt and notified Cicognani, who made the further recommendation, "perhaps you can open the discussion by mentioning that the previous conversation was referred to the Holy See, and that His Eminence the Cardinal Secretary is deeply interested in the matter."[60]

Spellman may well have been piqued at receiving Cicognani's further advice, for he now devised a better way of opening the discussion with the president. He took Cicognani's letter of November 28 and totally rewrote it. He incorporated into it much of his report to Maglione. Instead of Maglione's terse message telling Cicognani and Spellman jointly to make overtures to the president, the new letter stated that the Holy Father was pleased to learn that the president intended to send a mission sometime while Congress was in recess, that Spellman alone was to take the initiative, and that the pope believed "the proximate fulfillment of his gracious intention will be most conducive to the welfare of a world sadly torn by misunderstanding, malice and strife." Spellman was to communicate through the apostolic delegate "the approximate time that the President intends to make the announcement."[61] This was the version that was finally published in the official documents of the Holy See and World War II.

On December 7, Spellman scheduled a confidential meeting with Roosevelt. In the morning, he flew from New York, had his new version of the letter retyped on the apostolic delegate's stationary, and took it to the

White House. Roosevelt agreed to make the announcement on Christmas Day that he was sending an emissary to the pope. As Spellman recorded, "my letter from the Delegate which I left with President was sufficient to give official assent of the Holy See."[62] It is difficult now to determine whether Spellman had rewritten the letter simply to force Roosevelt to take action on an issue that he had been discussing for four years or to let the president know that the Holy See would accept a "special mission."

Whatever may have been Roosevelt's motivation, on December 23, he again summoned Spellman to the White House to give him a handwritten letter to Pius XII saying that he was sending Myron Taylor as his "personal representative." The text was immediately sent by cable to the Vatican, and the original letter was dispatched by Cicognani. The delegate acknowledged that the mission was not "in itself, of a permanent character; to reach this point an Act of the Federal Congress is required. But everybody understands that, after such a decision, *alea iacta est* and the only thing is to hope that the problem will be settled as it deserves."[63] Cicognani, as it turned out, was a bit too optimistic. On December 24, Roosevelt's letter to the pope was made public. In an effort to offset public opposition, he also sent letters to Cyrus Adler, president of the Jewish Theological Seminary in New York and to Dr. George A. Buttrick, president of the Federal Council of Churches.

In the meantime, Roosevelt was not finding the Vatican as malleable as he may have wished, at least in regard to choosing bishops. After Mundelein's death, he made no secret that he would like to have seen Bernard Sheil, Mundelein's auxiliary and administrator of the archdiocese, succeed his friend. Spellman, too, may have attempted to promote Shiel. But, on December 27, 1939, Pius XII transferred Archbishop Samuel Stritch from Milwaukee to Chicago. From the outset, Roosevelt expressed reservations. In his instructions to Taylor who was about to embark on his first visit to the pope in February 1940, he referred to Stritch as "somewhat of a Fascist." Since Washington had just been made an archdiocese, moreover, he stressed "it is important" that the first ordinary "be a reputable and liberal-minded Bishop. Bishop Bernard J. Sheil, who was understudy to Cardinal Mundelein would be an agreeable choice."[64] Roosevelt may have compromised in regard to establishing diplomatic relations, but the Holy See was not going to allow the compromiser to intrude into the internal affairs of the Church. His urging the appointment of Sheil may have been one reason why Washington was left under the jurisdiction of Archbishop Michael J. Curley of Baltimore until his death in 1947—and why Sheil spent the rest of his days as auxiliary of Chicago.

In addition to having Taylor discuss Stritch in Rome, however, Roosevelt turned to Spellman who was all too eager to please his president. Spellman first phoned Stritch, who had not yet left Milwaukee, and then wrote him about articles that appeared in the Milwaukee *Catholic Citizen* that seemed favorable to Coughlin. Writing in reply, Stritch emphatically denied the accusations that he was a Coughlin supporter, noted that he had issued rebuttals of some of the reports mentioned, and declared his support for Roosevelt's general policies. Spellman sent a copy of the letter to Enrico Galleazzi, a friend in the Vatican and, in what was a breach of confidence, forwarded the original to Roosevelt.[65]

Spellman was clearly the Vatican's man in the American hierarchy, but he never came to enjoy the same prominence among the bishops. From 1936 to 1939 and from 1941 to 1945, Mooney was chairman to the administrative board of the NCWC; Stritch held the office in 1941 and 1946. Until World War II, however, the available evidence indicates that Roosevelt largely ignored the official organization of the American hierarchy in favor of dealing with those whom he perceived to be powerful individuals like Mundelein and Spellman. McNicholas, moreover, though largely under Mooney's influence in the prewar years, belonged to a group, including Cardinal O'Connell in Boston and Archbishop Curley in Baltimore, that failed to see Hitler as a threat to the Church. Roosevelt was concerned and wished to determine whether these bishops and other Catholics were isolationists or pro-German. In June 1941, Taylor, whose mission was now permanent, was in Washington and discussed the issue with Cicognani. He pointed out that many bishops of Irish descent tended to see only a German attack on Britain but not the danger of Nazism. On May 23, moreover, the isolationist American First Committee in New York held a rally at which it distributed a pamphlet quoting phrases from the statement of the administrative board of the NCWC issued the previous April. In the statement, the bishops said they could not give directives on the political situation, but referred to the pope's five points for peace in his Christmas address in 1940. Taken out of context, however, these sentences were construed to mean that the bishops favored isolationism. With Mooney's authorization, Michael Ready, the general secretary of the NCWC, protested the misuse of the statement. Explaining these actions to Taylor, Cicognani noted that, while some prelates, notably O'Connell and Curley, opposed armed intervention, neither had ever spoken in favor of Nazism. In a church of 116 bishops and about 30,000 priests, Cicognani told Maglione, divergence of opinion was to be expected. With this evaluation, he was careful to mention, Spellman was in agreement.[66] What was needed to overcome that divergence of opinion was some major event.

Many American Catholics embraced isolationism, a posture that was reinforced by and must be interpreted in the context of the dispute in the United States over the Spanish Civil War from 1936 to 1939. In 1937, in response to reports of the murder of Spanish bishops, priests, nuns, and lay people, the American bishops issued a letter of sympathy with the Spanish hierarchy.[67]

At the same time, they issued a further statement of solidarity with the German Church, then undergoing persecution from the increasingly repressive Nazi regime.[68] The two statements illustrated the divided sentiment of the American bishops and people. On the one hand, Communism, represented by the Spanish Loyalists, who had some vocal American support, was a threat to the Church. On the other, Nazism was an equal threat. Caught between these two forces, American Catholic opinion, nevertheless, seemed to favor Franco, whose Fascism appeared preferable to Communism.[69] Some leaders, like Hayes and McNicholas, were publicly pro-Franco, but others, like Mundelein and Mooney, maintained silence on the issue.

By 1941, however, the tendency some Catholics may have had toward involvement in European affairs was challenged by the possibility of cooperating with Communism. On June 21, 1941, Hitler broke his pact with Stalin and invaded the Soviet Union. Roosevelt responded by announcing the extension of Lend-Lease to the Soviet Union. The bishops were publicly divided as to whether this policy violated Pius XI's prohibition in *Divini Redemptoris* of cooperation with Communism. On July 6, 1941, Bishop Joseph Hurley of St. Augustine broadcast from Washington in favor of Roosevelt's policy. Hurley was a close friend of Mooney and an ardent supporter of Roosevelt. Within his Florida diocese, Taylor maintained a residence, and the two were in close contact. Roosevelt seems to have cultivated him, principally through Sumner Welles, then undersecretary of state. With the State Department paying his fare to Washington and with material provided by Welles, he distinguished between lending arms to the beleaguered Russian people and cooperation with Communism.[70] That Hurley had also served until recently in the Vatican Secretariat of State seemed in the public mind to give his words more weight, but not with all the bishops. Curley privately complained that he had spoken from Washington without his permission. Archbishop Francis Beckman of Dubuque went on the radio to protest against Hurley. Cardinal O'Connell likewise protested. Coughlin, of course, broadcast against him. Cicognani reported to Cardinal Maglione that the dispute, widely reported in the secular press, created an unfavorable impression. Spellman, usually so favorable to Roosevelt's policies, wrote Pius XII directly to repudiate Hurley's action. On September 15, Tardini replied to Cicognani's report to Maglione. He deprecated the public disagreement among the bishops and urged that such differences be expressed in private.[71]

But even before Tardini had written to disapprove the public division of the bishops, Maglione had sent Cicognani new instructions. On August 11, he stated that bishops were to enjoy full freedom and were not being asked to speak against the war, but, at the same time, without compromising the

Holy See, they were to inform the American Catholics of the religious situation in Germany. Cicognani replied in a lengthy letter that, although the United States was moving toward greater involvement, most Americans preferred only a defensive war. Catholics realized what Nazism had done to the Church, but the bishops, except Hurley and John Mark Gannon of Erie, opposed intervention. The most outspoken critics of intervention remained O'Connell, Curley, Gerald Shaughnessy of Seattle, and McNicholas. The nub of the problem, Cicognani explained, was whether adherence to Pius XI's prohibition of cooperation with Communism now meant American Catholics would have to oppose the American policy of extending Lend-Lease to the Soviet Union. After Mooney and Ready, the NCWC officials, had consulted Welles, Mooney urged that the Vatican publicly declare that cooperation with the Russian people was not tantamount to cooperation with Communism and that it publish this declaration in the *Osservatore Romano* before the annual bishops' meeting in November in order to avoid further cleavage in the hierarchy that would surely result from varied interpretations of the encyclical.[72]

In the meantime, Taylor was commissioned to make Mooney's interpretation of the issue of Lend-Lease to the Soviets part of what he would discuss in his second visit to the pope. After meeting Taylor, Tardini privately informed Cicognani that Pius XII had no trouble with Mooney's position, but, rather than publishing that interpretation in the *Osservatore Romano*, the delegate could make it known to Mooney and any other bishops who inquired. Cicognani now notified Mooney of the Vatican position, but Mooney and Ready, with Cicognani's acquiescence, decided on a more effective way of disseminating it to American Catholics. They recommended that McNicholas, not known for his support of Roosevelt and publicly opposed to intervention, embody the interpretation in a pastoral letter. Cicognani, accordingly, summoned McNicholas to Washington and informed him of the Vatican's desires. After consulting Mooney, Stritch, and Bishop John Peterson of Manchester, the archbishop issued his pastoral that was then distributed by the National Catholic News Service. Urging his people to have charity in matters of political opinion, he drew attention to Pius XI's encyclical *mit brennender Sorge* that distinguished between Nazism and the German people. He then made the same distinction between Communism and the Russian people. The passages of *Divini Redemptoris* that prohibited cooperation with Communism, he argued, did not apply "to the present moment of armed conflict." Reporting these events to the Vatican, Cicognani noted that some American bishops remained in opposition. Beckman, who may have been alerted to McNicholas' forthcoming pastoral, announced on the radio that he refused to accept the validity of any distinction between the Soviet state and the Russian people. Cicognani had tried, unsuccessfully, to prevent

Beckman's broadcast, but had succeeded in preventing Shaughnessy from joining him. In late October, Cicognani admitted to Maglione that he had revealed to Taylor that he had received instructions on interpreting the encyclical, but now he was afraid some government official would leak the information that the interpretation had come directly from the Vatican.[73]

By the fall of 1941, the American bishops were still divided. Spellman had been noticeably absent from the negotiations over Lend-Lease. While Roosevelt recognized that he was Pius XII's point man in the American hierarchy, he also now realized that Mooney had greater authority among the American bishops and influence over critics like McNicholas. On October 23, he met secretly with Taylor and Mooney to inform the latter that the Justice Department might take action against Coughlin's National Union for Social Justice. But Mooney still had to preside over the annual meeting of the hierarchy in November, when McNicholas' pastoral would surely be a topic of discussion. McNicholas, for his part, while respecting his colleague in Detroit, still had reservations about intervention. He reported that Senator Robert Taft of Ohio had already queried him about certain aspects of his pastoral and held fast to the position that Germany's invasion of Russia illustrated a European problem of no immediate concern to the United States. Mooney thought otherwise and perhaps spoke for the majority of American bishops in identifying the cause of the Church with American intervention. "Of course it is easier for a non-Catholic than for a Catholic to be an isolationist," he wrote:

> They have not the world view of the worldwide spiritual interest that is our heritage of faith. Of course, too "the conflict in Europe is based largely on national interest." The real question is—on that side—whether or not we have a deep national interest in Hitler's defeat. But the opposition of a sincere and moderate man like Taft may be providential drag on precipitate action. But— like yourself—"I do not want to get into the arena of politics"—and I hope we can keep the boys out of the arena in Washington the week after next—and still within the orbit of good Catholic American citizenship. You have helped very much to lay one ghost at any rate.[74]

The annual meeting of the American bishops from November 12 to 13 displayed Mooney's ability to keep "the boys out of the arena of politics."

The bishops deputed the administrative board of the NCWC to issue a statement on "the crisis of Christianity." Drawing on McNicholas' pastoral, it acknowledged that Nazism and Communism were enemies of the Church, but then drew the now familiar distinction between Nazism and the German people and between Communism and the Russian people. It recalled Pius XII's Christmas message of 1939 outlining five points "for a just and honorable peace." Drawing on Leo XIII's teaching on Church and State, it called for respect for both authorities. In more specific terms, perhaps aimed at Becknan and Coughlin, it stated, "we deplore the presumption of those who, lacking authority, strive to determine the course of action that the Church should take within her clearly defined field. Recognizing the liberty of discussion, and even of criticism, which our democratic form of government guarantees, we urge and commend respect and reverence for the authority of our civil officials which has its source in God." The bishops ended their statement with a prayer for the guidance of civil officials.[75] The statement received favorable comment in the secular press, including the *New York Times*, which published it in its entirety.

Only a few days after issuing their statement, however, the bishops were called upon practically to show their support for the administration. On December 7, the Japanese bombed Pearl Harbor. The next day, the United States declared war on Japan. Three days later, Germany and Italy declared war on the United States, which immediately took the same action. On December 22, Mooney, after consulting the administrative board of the NCWC, wrote Roosevelt to offer the support of the hierarchy. Two days later, Roosevelt responded with gratitude to this example of "national unity" and with the pledge that the American purpose was not to seek "vengeance but the establishment of an international order in which the spirit of Christ shall rule the hearts of men and of nations."[76]

Roosevelt's mention of a new "international order" may have been intended to assuage those bishops who still opposed U.S. entry into the war. But not all were satisfied. Cicognani won Beckman's silence only by referring to Tardini's dispatch of the previous September, opposing public dissent among the bishops, and by reminding him of the consequences of acting contrary to the unanimous opinion of the episcopate, the way he now interpreted Mooney's letter to Roosevelt. Curley, the blunt spoken archbishop of Baltimore, also won a demand for an explanation from Cicognani, but his problem seems to have been more the result of an off-the-cuff remark rather than open opposition to the government. All that remained of the opposition to Roosevelt was Coughlin, whose Social Justice continued to challenge the war. He ceased publication only through the intervention of the United States Post Office, which threatened to withdraw the journal's mailing privileges, and of Mooney, who ordered him to cease all non-religious activities or face suspension from the priesthood. By this time, however, Coughlin's followers had diminished to a small group of insignificant fanatics.[77]

With the nation now at war and the bulk of the hierarchy strongly behind it, Roosevelt and his administration now dealt with both Mooney and Spellman. Each had different claims on the president's attention: Mooney, because of his leadership in the NCWC, and Spellman, because of his friendship with the pope and his position as military ordinary with jurisdiction over members of the armed forces. Though the two archbishops were not personal friends, each recognized their different entrées to the president. Roosevelt, for his part, was generally deft in his approach to the two.

On September 17, Taylor returned for a third visit to the pope, this time for nine days.[78] In his official memorandum, presented to the pope in the first of three audiences, he explained that the purpose of his visit was to explain that the United States was waging war against the Nazis and the Japanese, but had no enmity for the Italian people. He then presented a second memorial in his own name, but actually drafted by Mooney, Hurley, and Ready, in collaboration with Welles. It pointed to the similarities between papal pronouncements and American objectives and pledged that the United States would be satisfied with nothing "less than complete victory" and would prosecute "this war until the Axis collapses."[79] Despite the memorandum's origin with members of the American hierarchy, there is no evidence that Vatican officials learned of its actual provenance.

During his audiences with the pope and other Vatican officials, Taylor also protested the deportation of French Jews and Nazi brutality and argued that the Soviet Union would grant religious toleration if it were admitted to the family of nations—a condition the Vatican had placed for its support of Lend-Lease to the Soviet Union. But it was the pope's reply to Taylor's memorandum, possibly drafted by Vincent McCormick, S.J., an American resident in Rome, that was most significant. The pope stated that he had "never thought in terms of peace by compromise at any cost."[80] Thus, Pius XII seemed to anticipate the demand for "unconditional surrender" that Churchill and Roosevelt proposed at Casablanca in January 1943, but had done so without knowledge that Taylor's memorandum had emanated from the leadership of the NCWC.[81]

Once back in the United States, Taylor then assisted the NCWC in drafting the pastoral letter of the bishops, "Victory and Peace," issued on November 14. The United States, they wrote, was "associated with other powers in a deadly conflict" against those nations that were "united in waging war to bring about a slave world." Such a "conflict of Principles," they argued, made "compromise impossible." After quoting from Roosevelt's response to Mooney's promise of the hierarchy's support of the war effort the previous December, they went on to show the compatibility of Christian principles and American law as the basis for social reform, not only domestically, but also internationally. By this time, firm evidence for the Holocaust was coming into the United States, so the bishops expressed both their sympathy for the people "in all countries of the world where religion is persecuted" and their "revulsion against the cruel indignities heaped upon the Jews in conquered countries." Lest there be any American self-righteousness, however, they also called for the "acknowledgement and respect particularly for our colored fellow citizens," who "should enjoy the full measure of economic opportunities and advantages which will enable them to realize their hope and ambition to join with us in preserving and expanding in changed and changing social conditions our national heritage."[82] The bishops thus outlined a program for postwar social action.

While at the Vatican, Taylor had also discussed having the Allies spare civilian populations. Behind the Vatican position was the question of sparing Rome. On December 7, Spellman discussed the issue with Roosevelt, but recognized that the United States could make no guarantee of sparing Rome.[83] Within seven months, this would become a bone of contention with the bishops and drive a wedge between them and the president.

In the meantime, as military ordinary, Spellman had been wanting for some time to visit American troops abroad. Roosevelt, however, asked him to await his return from Casablanca. On February 4, 1943, the two met at the White House and Roosevelt promised to place at his disposal all the resources of the armed forces. The next day, Mussolini removed Count Galeazzo Ciano, his son-in-law, as foreign minister and named him ambassador to the Holy See. By this stage, McCormick reported a growing Italian sentiment for peace.[84] On February 6, Cardinal Maglione cabled Spellman asking him to come to Rome during his visit to the troops. Roosevelt approved Spellman's trip to Rome and had the State Department arrange for Carlton J. H. Hayes, the ambassador to Spain, to arrange with Italian authorities for a safe conduct.[85]

Spain was one place where American and Vatican policy coincided. Franco had received substantial aid from Hitler during the Spanish Civil War. Now both the Vatican and the United States wanted to keep him from joining the Axis. Straining relations between the United States and Spain was the alliance with the Soviet Union. Perhaps to prove that the alliance did not mean American sympathy with Communism, Roosevelt had appointed Hayes, a Catholic, as ambassador. And what better way to explain the American policy than through a Catholic archbishop? At the same time, incidentally, the nuncio or papal ambassador to Spain was Gaetano Cicognani, the brother of the apostolic delegate to the United States hierarchy. On February 9, Spellman left New York by clipper through Bermuda to Lisbon amid rumors that he was carrying a secret message from Roosevelt to open negotiations with Italy. On February 12, he arrived in Madrid. After visiting Hayes, he was invited to meet with Franco, to whom he explained that the Soviet Union had signed the Atlantic Charter and had no desire to expand its territory or impose its government on any nation. As history would attest, he was far too optimistic on this point, but he informed Roosevelt that any residual sympathy of Franco and the Spanish for the Axis was due solely to fear of Communism.[86]

Although some Italian officials opposed Spellman's visit to Rome, he arrived on February 20 for an 11-day series of meetings with the pope. Unfortunately, he confided neither to his diary nor to his official biographer, Robert I. Gannon, S.J., what he discussed during his visit.[87] The Italian archives, however, indicate widespread speculation that he was following up on Taylor's visit the previous September and may have been trying to develop a strategy to separate Italy from Germany. The British were more concerned that he was accepting the Vatican argument against the British expulsion of Vatican diplomats and the incarceration of Italian missionary priests in North Africa. Whatever the facts, Spellman soon found a way of proving to the British that he enjoyed Roosevelt's confidence.

On March 3, Spellman had returned to Spain to resume his visit with American forces. By this time, Churchill was concerned not only about his stance in regard to the Italian missionaries but also whether he would meet alone with Charles de Gaulle, whom the British wished to keep isolated. On March 17, Spellman had just said Mass for troops on St. Patrick's Day, when he received word of the death of Cardinal Arthur Hinsley of Westminster. Spellman decided he would attend the funeral, which was delayed so he could be present. The British government not only assisted in his travel arrangements but also determined that Churchill should meet with him. On March 19, he left for London on a mail plane. "It was awful," he recorded, "cold & lumpy and I had no covering. It was a long ride to England."[88] On March 23, he gave one of the absolutions at the funeral.[89] The next day, he had lunch with Churchill and his wife. In the report to his Cabinet, Churchill asked, "Are you a Short-Snorter?" and he "produced his credentials, which were in due form." The "Short-Snorters" had derived from the meeting between Churchill and Roosevelt on the North Atlantic. Shortly after, Roosevelt sent Churchill a dozen new dollar bills that he and Harry Hopkins had signed. Churchill and King George then signed them and returned them to Roosevelt for distribution to his inner circle, in which Spellman clearly had a place. For that matter, despite their differences over the imprisonment of Italian missionaries, Churchill seems genuinely to have liked his American visitor.

Spellman had originally intended to continue on to the Far East, but he had to cut short his trip. On July 19, the Americans bombed Rome. This precipitated a crisis in the relations between the Holy See and the United States and between the bishops and the president. On May 19, Pius XII had written Roosevelt pleading that he recognize the sacred character of the city and spare the civilian population. On June 16, Roosevelt responded that he appreciated the pope's concern for the civilians of Rome, for "Americans are among those who value most the religious shrines and the historical monuments of Italy." But, he continued, they were "likewise united in their determination to win the war which has been thrust upon them and for which the present government of Italy must share its full responsibility." He, nevertheless, promised that bombing would be limited, as much as possible, to military targets and assured the pope that American aviators had been informed "as to the location of the Vatican and have been specifically instructed to prevent bombs from falling within the Vatican City."[90] In the meantime, Cicognani had sought the American hierarchy's intervention. In Spellman's absence, he had turned, for unknown reasons, to Cardinal Dennis Dougherty.

On June 30, with a copy of Roosevelt's letter in hand, Dougherty wrote the president. He reminded Roosevelt that the British had conspicuously sought not "to offend" Moslem or Hindu "religious susceptibilities" by bombing their holy places. Yet, Anthony Eden had declared that the Allies might have to bomb Rome. Not only did it seem that the world's Catholic population of "between 350 and 400 millions" was "to be treated worse than Moslems and Hindus," but "Catholics would resent universally and bitterly the destruction of the Holy City," the residence of the pope. After recounting Rome's significance for Western culture, Dougherty asked how it could "be convenient for military purposes [to bomb Rome] if all the Catholic soldiers under the banners of the Allies will be disaffected?" In particular, he noted that Catholics were serving in the American forces out of proportion to their numbers, but numerous Catholics served also in the forces of Great Britain, Canada, Australia, and South Africa. It did little good to guarantee that Vatican City would be spared, for many papal offices were located in Rome. Hence, the bombing of Rome "would be like making mince meat out of a man's body and leaving his head intact." Dougherty concluded his letter by stating "it is providential" that Roosevelt was "the head of our nation during this war, because you know that among your best friends are Catholics, who have stood by you, and intend to stand by you." He now besought the president to communicate with Churchill that Rome was not to be bombed.[91] Roosevelt made no response until July 21, after the first bombing of Rome, when he cited for the cardinal the letter he had sent to the pope upon the invasion of Sicily.[92]

Cicognani realized that Dougherty was not the best prelate to intervene with the president, but only after the cardinal had written did he ask Mooney to negotiate with the president in the name of the hierarchy. But military events were moving too fast. On July 10, the forces of the United States, Great Britain, and Canada stormed the shores of Sicily to establish the first Allied foothold on European soil. Roosevelt immediately cabled the pope that the troops had "come to rid Italy of Fascism and of unhappy symbols and to drive out the Nazi oppressors who are infesting her." In an effort to assuage fears of the bombing of Rome, he pledged to respect the neutrality of Vatican City and of other papal territories outside the city:

> There is no need for me to reaffirm that respect for religious beliefs and for the
> free exercise of religious worship is fundamental to our ideas. Churches and
> religious institutions will, to the extent that it is within our power, be spared
> the devastations of war during the struggle ahead. Throughout the period of
> operations the neutral status of the Vatican City as well as of the Papal
> domains throughout Italy will be respected.[93]

Roosevelt's recognition of "Papal domains throughout Italy" would create
further tension between the Holy See and the United States, after the
Americans bombed the papal villas at Castel Gandolfo.

But the bombing of July 19 had an immediate effect. On July 26,
Mussolini submitted his resignation as premier. The new goverment of
Marshall Pietro Badoglio immediately made overtures through the Vatican to
Washington to declare Rome an open city and to begin negotiations for an
Italian surrender. While the Italian government was still waiting to hear the
Allied conditions for declaring Rome an open city, however, American planes
again bombed the city on August 13. Two days later, Badoglio declared
Rome an open city.[94]

When Spellman returned to Washington in early August, he deferred
meeting with any government officials, and, instead, conferred with
Cicognani. Both Mooney and Hurley had already voiced their concern that
the United States had taken a moral risk in the first bombing of Rome.[95] In
the meantime, Pius XII decided not only to write again to Roosevelt about the
bombing of Rome but also to send a personal emissary, Count Enrico
Galeazzi, to the president and to mobilize the hierarchy to intervene with the
president. By this time, the Vatican concern was that the continued bombing
of Rome would drive the people toward Communism. On August 23,
Cicognani notified Spellman, Mooney, and Stritch of the Vatican's desire to
have the bishops and laity demonstrate their concern about the bombing.
Each, however, together with Dougherty, had already made statements and
feared that any further expression of concern would make them appear
opposed to Roosevelt's policy. In the midst of these negotiations, Roosevelt
summoned Spellman to meet him at the White House on September 2 with
Churchill. They discussed not only the bombing of Rome, but also
Roosevelt's plans for postwar Europe. While the president thought that any
further bombing of Rome would be unnecessary, it would depend on military
exigencies. But the military situation continued to change. Even as Roosevelt
and Spellman were meeting, General Montgomery was crossing the straits of
Messina to begin the invasion of Europe. On September 8, Badoglio
announced Italy's surrender, but German troops immediately entered Rome.

The Vatican was now in an even more precarious position. It now changed its strategy for dealing with Roosevelt and withdrew Galeazzi's instructions.[96]

On September 15, the date on which Galeazzi had originally been scheduled to meet with Roosevelt, Spellman, Mooney, and Stritch met with the president. They prepared a memorandum noting, among other arguments, that the Germans had spared Athens and Cairo. In a passage that may have indicated the influence of Dougherty, they reminded the president that "military measures which offend the religious sense of so many citizens in so many nations may have consequences fatally prejudicial to the interests we all have at heart in the making of the peace and to national and international collaboration necessary to that blessed end."[97] In response, Roosevelt proposed a free zone of 20 miles around Rome, provided the Germans respected it. "It be O.K. if he keeps his promise," Spellman recorded with little enthusiasm.[98]

For the next few months, however, the American bishops and their people faced a dilemma. On the one hand, they wanted to respond to the pope and work to spare the Eternal City. On the other, they were afraid of upsetting the *modus vivendi* they had with their fellow citizens by protesting the bombing. On November 8, the administrative board of the NCWC met in Washington to discuss what actions the bishops could take on the Holy See's behalf, and then Spellman, Mooney, and Stritch conferred with Cicognani. On November 11, the bishops at their annual meeting expressed their devotion to the Holy See and pledged to continue informing public opinion and the government to guarantee the safety of the Vatican. But they said nothing about the bombing. The Holy See, however, wanted more. In December, Maglione asked that Spellman, Mooney, and Stritch again meet with Roosevelt to have him guarantee the 20-mile free zone and to convene the hierarchy to consider the gravity of the situation. It would be impossible with the difficulties of wartime transportation, Cicognani informed Maglione, to reconvene the hierarchy. The three archbishops, moreover, thought it better to approach Roosevelt through highly placed laymen, lest any White House statement seem to emanate from their influence.[99] This was the official reason for the archbishops' hesitancy to approach Roosevelt that Cicognani reported to his Vatican superiors. But there is also some suspicion that they thought they had lost their influence with the president.

The relations between the bishops and the White House were strained yet more with the bombing on four occasions of the papal villa at Castel Gandolfo on February 1 and 10, May 31, and June 4, 1944. The first bombing brought a letter of protest from Cicognani to the State Department. The second brought Spellman into public opposition to the president. On February 20, he wrote a strong letter to Roosevelt stating:

> After my several talks with you and my repeated assurances to the Holy Father of our desire to show him every respect, I feel that I must do something to

comfort him, and others who reverence him and are pained to see his home at Castel Gandolfo bombed by our airmen, and the while the Vatican states that "no German soldier has been admitted within the borders of the neutral Pontifical Villa and that no German military whatsoever are within it at present." There are only helpless and homeless people refuged there.

Spellman felt compelled to make a public statement on the matter "lest many people think me failing in my duty," unless the president could "see some other action that can be taken."[100]

Spellman gave Roosevelt little time to come up with "some other action." On February 22, he celebrated the annual memorial Mass for the Knights of Columbus in St. Patrick's Cathedral. In his address, he deplored

the fact that the armed forces of our country have attacked the territory of a neutral state, thereby violating rights which are among those for which America is waging war. We have the word of the Pope, expressed by the Apostolic Delegate to the United States, that no Germans were there or had ever been allowed there. In the winning of the war, let us keep not only the respect of others but also our own self respect. I also hope and pray that, as Britain once spared the Holy City of Mecca, military ingenuity will overcome "military necessity," which would destroy the Eternal City of Rome, the citadel of civilization.[101]

These were strong words from the bishop who for almost 10 years had counted the president among his friends. Mooney, too, joined in the chorus of criticism, but he restricted his emotions to a private letter. Making no mention of the bombing of Castel Gandolfo, he focused on keeping Rome an open city. The "pressure of considerations advanced in the name of military necessity," he avowed, in a short time might "lose their extenuating force in view of the accusing finger raised in every pillar that would stand amidst the new made ruins of Rome.... These are strong words," he admitted, but he felt "so deeply that the judgment of plain-thinking men would, on reflection, be against those who even allowed themselves to be trapped by Nazi cunning or provoked by Nazi malice into wreaking destructions on the shrines and monuments of Rome.... Nazi provocation would serve only to highlight our lack of cleverness," he continued "or our failure to rise above Nazi standards of cultural appreciation and religious reverence."[102] The threat of further bombing of Rome and the actual bombing of Castel Gandolfo caused a serious breach in the relations between Roosevelt and the American bishops, but it was soon overcome.

On June 4, 1944, the date of the fourth bombing of Castel Gandolfo, Allied troops liberated Rome. Roosevelt immediately dispatched Taylor to see the pope, who, in turn, immediately summoned Spellman, who was on the point of making another visit to the troops. Before departing, Spellman won Roosevelt's guarantee that the city would not become a military base but would be used only for the recreation of the troops in the surrounding area.[103] On July 28, he was back in Rome for the first of several meetings with the pope in between trips to be with the troops. During this time, he was, incidentally, offered the post of secretary of state.[104] Again, he intended to go on to India and China to visit the troops, but, on September 10, he received a cable from Leo Crowley, American foreign economic administrator, to return immediately. Spellman replied that Mooney or Stritch could well act in his place. But trouble was brewing. On October 5, Crowley cabled him again. Both Roosevelt and Pius XII wanted him back in New York.[105]

The emergency arose from the policy of the Allied Control Commission, the virtual government of Italy, which was charged with distributing rations to the Italian people, now reduced to about one-fifth of their prewar consumption. Since the previous May, the War Department had blocked the NCWC's War Relief Services from sending volunteers to Italy for relief work. Late in August, Crowley convinced Roosevelt to send a memorandum to the War Department authorizing four priests to go to Italy, but it was ignored until the president sent a second memorandum almost a month later. Soon after he returned to the United States, Spellman met with Crowley and Ready and then had lunch with Roosevelt and Harry Hopkins. He found that the president was apparently uninformed about the Italian situation. But there is no evidence that he was responsible for bringing about any change in the situation.[106]

From the available evidence, Spellman's lunch with Roosevelt on October 18, 1944, was the last contact between the president and any member of the hierarchy. In November, Roosevelt was elected to an unprecedented fourth term, but by April 1945, he had died. He had initiated his contact with the hierarchy in the person of Mundelein to gain Catholic support for his domestic policies in the New Deal. But the Vatican, and particularly Pacelli, had been rebuffed during World War I. It was concerned about building a bridge to the president as Europe moved toward World War II. Spellman, accordingly, was the principal figure in working for some form of diplomatic relations between the Holy See and the United States. During his first two terms, Roosevelt, therefore, initiated his contact with the Catholic community through Mundelein and then accepted the overtures on behalf of the Vatican from Spellman. But always until 1941, there was the question of Coughlin. Here the president seemed largely to ignore the role of the NCWC in preference to using his personal relationship with Mundelein, aided, apparently under Pacelli's pressure, by Spellman. Once the war broke out, he recognized the significance of the NCWC and Mooney as the chairman of the administrative board, but still he knew that Spellman had the ear of Pacelli, now Pius XII. The cordial relations between the president and the hierarchy ultimately ran upon the shoals of the problem of the bombing of Rome. Here he apparently failed to see the religious sensitivities of the American hierarchy and its Catholic people. Whether he was misled by some of his advisers or simply had to respond to military necessities, he confronted a problem analogous to what Wilson had faced in regard to the Irish problem. What had begun in 1933 as a close alliance between Roosevelt and American Catholics ended in 1944 with the feeling among Catholic prelates that the president subordinated the interests of Catholics to transitory military expediency influenced by British policy.

### ABBREVIATIONS

AANY     Archives of the Archdiocese of New York

AACi     Archives of the Archdiocese of Cincinnati

ADSS     *Actes et documents du Saint siege relatifs a La Seconde Guerre Mondiale*, ed. Pierre Blet, Angelo Martini, Robert Graham, and Burkhart Schneider, 11 vols., Vatican, 1965–85

ASV      Archivio Segreto Vaticano

NA       National Archives

### NOTES

1. James P. Gaffey, *Francis Clement Kelley & the American Catholic Dream* (Bensenville, IL: The Heritage Foundation, Inc.,1980), I, 151–155. For the difficulties in the Chicago succession, see Gerald P. Fogarty, S.J. (ed.), *Patterns of Episcopal Leadership* (New York: Macmillan Publishing Co.,1989), pp. xxxiii–xxxv. While Kelley is the principal source for why Mundelein was chosen for Chicago, the apostolic delegation files in the Vatican archives say nothing about his being considered for Buffalo.

2. Woodrow Wilson, *History of the American People*, quoted in Dragan R. Zivojinovic, *The United States and Vatican Policies, 1914–1918* (Boulder, CO: Colorado Associated University Press, 1978), p. 19.

3. Quoted in James Hennesey, *American Catholics: A History of the Roman Catholic Community in the United States* (New York: Oxford University Press, 1981), p. 223.

4. John Tracy Ellis, *Life of James Cardinal Gibbons: Archbishop of Baltimore, 1834–1921* (2 vols.; Milwaukee: Bruce Publishing Co., 1952), II, 231–232. See also ASV, AA.EE.SS., Guerra Europa, II, fasc. 1–7, 10a, Gasparri to Bonzano, Dec. 12, 1916 (draft), 10, Bonzano to Gasparri, Washington, Jan. 5, 1917.

5. Hennesey, *American Catholics*, p. 225.

6. Lansing's response to the pope is in ASV, AA.EE.SS., Guerra Europa, IV, fasc. 12, document 124.

40 G E R A L D  P.  F O G A R T Y

7. Ellis, *Gibbons*, II, 243–246. See also L. Bruti-Liveratie, "Santa Sede e Stati Uniti negli anni dell grande guerra," in Giorgio Rumi *Benedetto XV e La Pace—1918* (Brescia: Morcelliana, 1990), pp. 138–141.
8. Ellis, *Gibbons*, II, 250–252.
9. ASV, AA.EE.SS, Guerra Europa, I, fasc. 1–7, "Viaggio Mgr. Pacelli 1917," Pacelli to Gasparri, Munich, May 26, 1917. Pacelli's source of information was the archbishop of Cracow.
10. Ibid., XII, 18: Emperor Karl to Benedict XV, Dec. 23, 1917.
11. Bruti-Liberati, p. 145.
12. Zivojinovic, *The United States*, pp. 147–149, 169. Here and elsewhere, Zivojinovic must be used with caution, especially in his suggestion that Gibbons was willing to use British diplomatic channels to present his ideas to the Vatican. See also Gerald P. Fogarty, *Vatican and the American Hierarchy*, from 1870 to1965, (Stuttgart: Anton Hiersemann Verlag, 1982; Collegeville, MN: Michael Glazier, 1985), p. 210.
13. ASV, AA.EE.SS., Guerra Europa, VII, 3, Bonzano to Gasparri, Washington, Oct. 28, 1918.
14. Ibid., Wilson to Benedict XV, Washington, Oct. 17, 1918.
15. Ibid., Bonzano to Gasparri, Oct. 28, 1918.
16. Ibid., Benedict XV to Wilson, Nov. 8, 1918 (draft).
17. Ibid., 2, Pacelli to Gasparri, Munich, Oct. 16, 1918.
18. Ibid., XV, fasc. 23c, Mercier to Gasparri, May 14, 1919.
19. Quoted in James Hennesey, *American Catholics: A History of the Roman Catholic Community in the United States* (New York: Oxford University Press, 1981), p. 227.
20. Harold J. Ickes, *The Secret Diary of Harold L. Ickes* (New York, 1954), II, 349–350.
21. Edward R. Kantowicz, *Corporation Sole: Cardinal Mundelein and Chicago Catholicism* (Notre Dame, IN: University of Notre Dame Press, 1983), p. 218.
22. FDRL, PPF 321, Mundelein to Roosevelt, Chicago, Apr. 26, 1933.
23. George Q. Flynn, *American Catholics and the Roosevelt Presidency, 1932–1936* (Lexington, KY: University Press of Kentucky, 1968), p. 38. Kantowicz gives the date as May 17.
24. Archives of the Archdiocese of Philadelphia, Dougherty to Bernardini, Philadelphia, May 7, 1935 (copy).
25. AACi, McNicholas to Mooney, Cincinnati, Feb. 28, 1936; see also Leslie Woodcock Tentler, *Seasons of Grace: A History of the Catholic Archdiocese of Detroit* (Detroit: Wayne State University Press, 1990), p. 326.
26. Quoted in Flynn, *American Catholics*, pp. 184–185.
27. AACi, McNicholas to Mooney, Cincinnati, Feb. 28, 1936 (copy).
28. AACi, Mooney to McNicholas, Rochester, Mar. 5, 1936. For a more detailed treatment of this exchange, see my *Vatican and the American Hierarchy*, pp. 244–245.
29. Charles J. Tull, *Father Coughlin and the New Deal* (Syracuse: Syracuse University Press, 1965), pp. 143–144.

30. AANY, Spellman Diary, Sept. 25, 27, 1936.

31. Ibid., Sept. 28, 1936.

32. FDRL, PPF 321, Farley to Roosevelt, New York, Oct. 23, 1936.

33. Ibid., *The Times* (Chicago), Sept. 15, 1936.

34. Tentler, p. 325.

35. Francis L. Broderick, *Right Reverend New Dealer John A. Ryan* (New York: Macmillan, 1963), pp. 225–228.

36. FDRL, PPF 628, Hayes to Roosevelt, New York, Nov. 6, 1936.

37. Ibid., Keagan to Roosevelt, New York, Nov. 5, 1936.

38. AANY, Spellman Diary, Oct. 18–29, 1936. See Marcus Sheldon, *Father Coughlin: The Tumultuous Life of the Priest of the Little Flower* (Boston: Little, Brown, 1973), p. 131.

39. John B. Sheerin, *Never Look Back: The Career and Concerns of John J. Burke* (New York: The Paulist Press, 1975), pp. 217–218.

40. FDRL, PPF 321, memo for McIntyre, Oct. 26, 1936.

41. Fogarty, *Vatican and the American Hierarchy*, pp. 248–249.

42. George Q. Flynn, *Roosevelt and Romanism: Catholics and American Diplomacy, 1937–1945* (Westport, CT: Greenwood Publishing Group, 1776), p. 13.

43. "Die Fuldaer Bishofskonferenz von der Enzyklika 'Mit brennender Sorge' bis sum Ende der NS-Herrschaft," in Dieter Albrecht (ed.), *Katholische Kirche im Dritten Reich* (Mainz: Matthias-Grünewald, 1976), pp. 66–67.

44. *New York Times*, May 21, 26, June 2, 1937. For the German reaction, see Politisches Archiv des Auswartiges Amts, R 103248, Kardinal Mundelein.

45. FDRL, PPF 321, Mundelein to Cicognani, Chicago, Oct. 5, 1937 (copy).

46. Ibid., Mundelein to Roosevelt, Chicago, Oct. 6, 1937.

47. AANY, Pacelli to Spellman, Rome, Nov. 26, 1937.

48. AANY, Spellman to Pacelli, n.p., Jan. 7, 1938 (draft).

49. AANY, Pacelli to Spellman, Rome, Feb. 26, 1938.

50. Fogarty, *Vatican and the American Hierarchy*, pp. 251–252.

51. FDRL, PPF 4727, Roosevelt to Mooney, July 16, 1937 (copy); Mooney to Roosevelt, Detroit, July 30, 1937.

52. AANY, Spellman diary, Sept. 9, 1938.

53. Ibid., Oct. 12, 19, 21, 1938.

54. FDRL, PSF 58, Phillips to Roosevelt, Rome, Nov. 10, 1938, with enclosed memorandum for the State Department.

55. George Q. Flynn, *Roosevelt and Romanism: Catholics and American Diplomacy, 1932–1945* (Westport, CT: Greenwood Press, 1976), p. 100.

56. AACi, McNicholas to Tardini, Cincinnati, June 29, 1938 (copy).

57. Cordell Hull, *The Memoirs of Cordell Hull* (2 vols.; New York: Macmillan, 1948), I, 713–715.

58. AANY, Spellman to Maglione, New York, Oct. 25, 1939. Curiously, Roosevelt seems to have made no allusion to the congressional legislation of 1867 cutting off funds for a mission to the Papal States. Repeal of this legislation in 1983 was the first step toward establishing diplomatic relations in 1984.

59. AANY, Cicognani to Spellman, Washington, Nov. 28, 1939.

60. AANY, Cicognani to Spellman, Washington, Dec. 2, 1939.

61. AANY, Cicognani to Spellman, Washington, Nov. 28, 1939 (copy); there is also a draft in Spellman's own hand.

62. AANY, Spellman Diary, Dec. 7, 1939.

63. Cicognani to Maglione, Washington, Dec. 23, 1939, Pierre Blet, Angelo Martini, and Burkhart Schneider (eds.), *Holy See and the War in Europe: March 1939–August 1940*, trans. Gerard Noel (London: Herder Publications, 1968), I, 327–329.

64. FDRL, Taylor, memorandum for Taylor, Feb. 11, 1940.

65. FDRL, PSF 185, Stritch to Spellman, Milwaukee, Jan. 20, 1940. See also Fogarty, *Vatican and the American Hierarchy*, pp. 263, 266.

66. Fogarty, *Vatican and the American Hierarchy*, pp. 270–271.

67. Hugh J. Nolan (ed.), *Pastoral Letters of the United States Catholic Bishops* (Washington: NCCB/USCC, 1983), I, 416–418.

68. Ibid., 419–421.

69. Flynn, *American Catholics*, pp. 29–62.

70. The most recent and detailed analysis of Hurley's relationship with Welles and of this episode is Charles R. Gallagher, "Patriot Bishop: The Public Career of Archbishop Joseph P. Hurley, 1937–1967," unpublished Ph.D. dissertation, History Department, Marquette University, 1998, pp. 235–255.

71. Fogarty, *Vatican and the American Hierarchy*, p. 272.

72. Ibid., 272–273.

73. Ibid., 273–274.

74. AACi, Mooney to McNicholas, Detroit, Oct. 29, 1941.

75. Nolan, *Pastoral Letters*, II, 28–35.

76. Ibid., 36–37.

77. Tentler, *Seasons of Grace*, pp. 340–342; Fogarty, *Vatican and the American Hierarchy*, pp. 276–278.

78. Incidentally, Archbishop Filippo Bernardini, nuncio to Switzerland and former professor at the Catholic University of America, was also in Rome at the same time, Schwiezerishex Bundesarchiv, 2001 (H) 1969/121 B.80 B. 22.21.Vat. Bernardini. There is, however, no evidence the two ever met.

79. NA, RG 59, DS 212.866A/245B, draft attached to Welles to Roosevelt, Washington, Sept. 4, 1942; ADSS, V, 717–722.

80. Pius XII to Taylor, Vatican, Sept. 22, 1942, ADSS, V, 692–694.

81. Fogarty, *Vatican*, pp. 284–286, 291.

82. Nolan, *Pastoral Letters*, II, 38–43.

83. Ibid., 288–289.

84. James Hennesey, "American Jesuit in Wartime Rome: The Diary of Vincent A. McCormick, S.J. (1942–1945)," *Mid America: An Historical Review* 56 (1974), pp. 35–38.

85. Cicognani to Maglione, Washington, Feb. 6, 1943, Actes, VII, 218; Feb. 7, 1943, p. 221.

86. Fogarty, *Vatican*, p. 291.

87. Robert I. Gannon, *The Cardinal Spellman Story* (Garden City, NY: Doubleday, 1962), p. 204.

88. AANY, Spellman Diary, Mar. 17–19, 1943.
89. AANY, Spellman Diary, Mar. 21, 23, 1943.
90. Roosevelt to Pius XII, June 16, 1943, in ADSS, VII, 430–431.
91. FDRL, PPF 2922, Dougherty to Roosevelt, Philadelphia, June 30, 1943.
92. Ibid., Roosevelt to Dougherty, July 21, 1943 (copy).
93. Roosevelt to Pius XII, July 10, 1943, in ADSS, VII, 479–480.
94. Fogarty, *Vatican and the American Hierarchy*, pp. 294–299.
95. ADSS, VII, 637n.
96. Fogarty, *Vatican and the American Hierarchy*, pp. 301–302.
97. Mooney, Stritch, and Spellman to Roosevelt, Sept. 15, 1943, attached to Cicognani to Maglione, Washington, Sept. 21, 1943, ADSS, VII, 648–650.
98. AANY, Spellman Diary, Sept. 15, 1943.
99. Fogarty, *Vatican and the American Hierarchy*, pp. 304–305.
100. FDRL, PPF 4404, Spellman to Roosevelt, New York, Feb. 20, 1944.
101. AANY, attached to Spellman to Roosevelt, New York, Feb. 20, 1944 (copy).
102. AANY, Mooney to Roosevelt, Detroit, Feb. 23, 1944 (copy).
103. AANY, Spellman Diary, July 4–5, 1944.
104. AANY, Spellman Diary, Sept. 28, 1944.
105. AANY, Spellman Diary, Sept 10, Oct. 4, 5, 10, 12, 1944.
106. Fogarty, *Vatican and the American Hierarchy*, p. 308.

# PART 2

# CATHOLIC FRIENDS/ CATHOLIC FOES

## THE NEW DEAL AND AMERICAN CATHOLICISM

CHAPTER 3

# JOHN A. RYAN, THE NEW DEAL, AND CATHOLIC UNDERSTANDINGS OF A CULTURE OF ABUNDANCE

ANTHONY BURKE SMITH

JOHN A. RYAN HAS LONG SERVED AS AN IMPORTANT EXAMPLE of Catholic engagement with modern American social and political thought.[1] However, a dimension of Ryan's work that has been little explored is his relationship to the rise of consumer culture. Given his commitment to the New Deal project of raising the income and standard of living of America's wage-earners, Ryan in fact offers an important avenue to consider how Catholics understood the transformation of modern America into a mass consumer society and the emergence of a culture of abundance.

Historians such as Gary Gerstle and Steven Fraser, Alan Brinkley, and Lizbeth Cohen have shown how the New Deal played a central role in establishing a consumer society in twentieth-century America—a coalition of labor, enlightened businessmen, liberal intellectuals, and the state found common purpose in reforming capitalism and providing workers with access to the material abundance of the industrial economy.[2]

Scholars have explored a range of historical actors including intellectuals, workers, social scientists, politicians, and state officials in tracing the relationship between the New Deal and consumer society, but Catholics have remained largely absent from this reassessment in historical interpretation.

As scholarly focus in the New Deal has shifted from consideration of the age of reform to issues of mass society and consumerism, where do Catholics, long acknowledged as an important group within the New Deal coalition, fit?[3]

More specifically, to what extent did Ryan's thought offer a Catholic sanction, implicit or otherwise, to a consumer culture in America? Or did Ryan's social reformism indicate a more unstable, contradictory relationship with the culture of abundance that the New Deal order helped realize in twentieth-century America? In this chapter I explore Ryan's thought as a Catholic perspective of modern consumer society. I argue that Ryan's sanctioning of the importance of consumption in economic life did represent an acceptance of a modern, wage-earner, industrial order but that his understanding of abundance was mediated by traditional Catholic assumptions that made his agenda of reform quite distinct from a consumerist vision of society.

There can be no gainsaying Ryan's support for the New Deal. From early in Roosevelt's presidency through the mid-1930s when Ryan went on the radio to critique Father Coughlin, to very late in his life when Ryan summarized Roosevelt's legacy by stating, "he did more for those who stood most in need of social justice than any other man who ever occupied the White House," Ryan was a steadfast advocate of FDR and the New Deal.[4] Ryan believed that Roosevelt's policies were the best hope for alleviating the misery of the Depression and for putting America on a more sound economic and social order.

Informing much of this support for the New Deal was Ryan's belief that the Depression had been caused by underconsumption. Thus a language of consumerism runs throughout much of his reflections on the New Deal and the Depression. Recovery and reform would not be achieved, he believed, until wage earners enjoyed greater access to the abundance of American industrialism. Savings and overinvestment had led to a distorted economy where wealth existed in the hands of the few and the majority of Americans were unable to absorb the excess productivity. Besides embracing the language of consumption and the modern discourse of economics, Ryan demonstrated, in his thought, a real commitment to increasing the wages of American workers in order to enjoy a decent living wage and a comfortable standard of living.

At times sounding like Stuart Chase and Rexford Tugwell, both champions of the underconsumption theory, Ryan believed that the economic problems confronting the nation lay in the underdeveloped power of wage earners to consume.[5] For Ryan, "The fundamental and enduring cause of our slow industrial recovery is the lack of purchasing power in the hands of millions of our people who would buy enormous qualities of goods if they had the money."[6] Again, in 1934, Ryan asserted, "the rational and human remedy [to the Depression] is to rearrange our industrial system so that all will be employed in producing the goods that will provide the means of an abundant life for every member of every social class."[7] Similarly, in June, 1939, Ryan wrote, "What we need now is not more capital investments but a better distribution of purchasing power, so that those who need to consume more will have the means to do so and thus bring about full use of our productive plants and full employment for our working men."[8] Ryan's social thought therefore expressed a belief that increased consumption and the sharing of the material abundance of American productive forces were the solutions to the inequalities of industrial capitalism.

In his autobiography written in 1941, Ryan outlined what he believed to be the proper means of addressing unemployment. These included raising the minimum wage, reducing interest rates, creating public works projects, and collecting higher taxes on incomes and excess profits.[9] These proposals were largely fiscal and suggest that Ryan's thought, like that of many New Dealers as Alan Brinkley has shown, moved, after the late 1930s, away from a less active, industrial policy-oriented state toward a compensatory-oriented vision of the state that rested on increasing and sustaining American's ability to consume.

Indeed, the diminished expectations that Ryan had for the New Deal by the end of his life in the mid-1940s is clear in a letter he wrote to Roosevelt in 1944. In it Ryan corrected the president who had written him saying "much has been accomplished, but much remains to be accomplished." Ryan instead suggested "greater stress upon the former than the latter." He singled out three pieces of social legislation that he believed embodied "great gains for social justice" superior to all other reforms in the nation's history. These were the National Labor Relations Act, the Social Security Act, and the Fair Labor Standards Act.[10]

Therefore, the theme of underconsumption running throughout much of Ryan's writings, his support for the New Deal, and his acceptance of a less active, more fiscal state suggests the importance of a consumerist logic in his thinking. Yet Ryan's use of a language of consumption and his understanding of abundance were mediated by the traditional moral and cultural assumptions of Catholic social teaching of Leo XIII and Pius XI, particularly in the two social encyclicals, *Rerum Novarum* and *Quadragesima Anno*. Indeed, Ryan's thought combined modern economics, progressive concerns for efficiency, and a traditional Catholic vision of an organic society characterized by mutual obligation and responsibility.

The result was a support for the New Deal and an understanding of modern industrial life quite distinct from other liberal and progressive interpretations of what the New Deal offered. Abundance, which Ryan recognized was the result of America's industrial productivity, was construed through the lens of a corporatist vision that identified the common good in terms of limits, restraints, and moderation. The boundlessness of American industrialism should not lead to a rich and vital compensatory private realm as many enlightened business liberals imagined.[11] Nor did a living wage, in Ryan's estimation, sanction an expansive vision of consumption as many labor advocates championed.[12]

Indeed he believed that while workers deserved a living wage, there were also limits to abundance. He felt there were limits to how much comfort, recreation, food, and housing one should enjoy. "Experience warns us," he wrote in 1931, "that without capacity for sacrifice we get nowhere and achieve nothing. We cannot have the power to do unless we have the power to do without."[13] His was a vision shaped by traditional concepts of character, restraint, virility, and moderation.

Indeed, Ryan was explicitly critical of the consumerist ethos of modern society that privileged liberation from moral restraint and self-expressiveness. He dubbed this the "happiness morality" with its rejection of absolute moral standards in favor of relativist notions of value, its sanctioning of divorce and companionate marriage, its emphasis on experiences over objective moral truth.[14]

Furthermore, Ryan associated the new ethic with constant creation of artificial needs. It had authorized the idea that:

> mass production will make happiness general because it will provide indefinitely increasing luxuries and will arouse new wants for other luxuries when popular demand fails to take away all the goods that must be sold if the productive machinery is to be kept going.[15]

Similarly, he believed that "the true and rational doctrine" dictates "that when men have produced sufficient necessaries and reasonable comforts and conveniences to supply all population, they should spend what time is left in the cultivation of their intellects and wills, in the pursuit of the higher life."[16]

Ryan's championing of a living wage and liberal social reform therefore needs to be seen in the context of his understanding of culture, which stressed the virtues of restraint, moderation, self-control, and cultivation.

Nowhere is this understanding more evident than in Ryan's thought on birth control. As far back as 1907, in an essay entitled, "The Fallacy of 'Bettering One's Position,'" Ryan wrote of the "enervating self-indulgence," and "materialistic conception of life" that characterized people, largely middle class and upper class in his perspective, who practiced birth control.[17] He thus did not envision, as many Americans increasingly did, the private realm as an arena for individual autonomy and self-expression.[18]

Ryan devoted numerous occasions to writing about birth control.[19] In 1934 he went before the subcommittee of the Senate Judiciary Committee to oppose the Hastings Birth Control Bill. He reiterated his long-standing belief that supporters of birth control promoted policies that diverted attention from the real issues confronting poor families, namely that of reforming capitalism. Social justice and birth control were, in Ryan's eyes, "mutually exclusive methods of human betterment."[20]

Just how strongly Ryan connected opposition to birth control and authentic social reform is evident in his declining an invitation from the Committee on Unemployment, a liberal group chaired by John Dewey, to speak at one of its conferences. Ryan wrote that the other speakers would stress the "relationship between birth control and national recovery... [and] the proposition that the unemployed and the destitute should themselves bear the burden of their sad economic condition by restricting the number of their children. Of course this tends to shift the blame and divert attention from our economic organization and its responsibility for the inability of the poor to bring up a normal family decently."[21]

But beyond the issue of birth control, Ryan's cultural values of moderation, restraint, and respecting limits informed his support for the New Deal. His thoughts on economics and social issues as well as on culture share a Catholic suspicion of modern culture and an understanding of society founded upon mutual obligations and responsibilities. Restraint and moderation curbed the excesses of individualism, and government regulation of the market tamed the predatory and greedy character of capitalism.

Thus Ryan explained the New Deal as ushering in an era where "[i]nstead of unrestrained competition, we have regulated competition." Similarly, he wrote, "[t]he profit motive will continue to function but it will not enjoy unlimited scope."[22] Ryan championed the NRA because it would "prevent business men from receiving excessive profits."[23] His philosophy of economic restraint and limits, reflecting the Catholic corporatist tradition, were reflected in his praise for the codes and other regulatory features of the NRA that he hoped would "become permanently embedded in our political and industrial system." Ryan added that the "greatest obstacle to the attainment of social justice is the inability of men to perceive their industrial obligations and their unwillingness to fulfil [sic] these obligations."[24]

Similarly, Ryan argued in 1942 that limiting wealth through higher taxation was legitimate in order to "impose boundaries upon the right and use of ownership."[25] Along the same lines, Ryan boldly asserted that after the war, "capital must be content with less," and "labor should receive a greater share of the national income and capital a smaller share than was the case up to 1943."[26]

That Ryan believed there were limits to profits, that capital needed to be content with less so that labor could have more—as opposed to everybody getting more—suggests that he saw the social realm in complementary terms to that of the personal—characterized by restraint in order to achieve the common good for all. Indeed, running throughout Ryan's work is the belief that the common good entailed, not so much an ever-expanding material abundance, but assurances that the basic needs of all people, for shelter, work, and family, were met.

Ryan's liberalism existed alongside a range of Catholic perspectives on society and economics ranging from Father Coughlin's strident populism to Dorothy Day's gospel-inspired personalism.[27] Equally important, Ryan's agenda for social reform competed with those of others, including advertisers, labor advocates, politicians, the state, and mass culture, to gain the allegiance of Catholics. Indeed, understandings of modern abundance competed with each other. While in some regard these understandings, manifesting particular social interests, overlapped to forge a culture of consumption, they were by no means identical. Beneath the surface of commonality lay diverging impulses. Ryan's social Catholicism may have sought to identify Catholicism with the New Deal order, but his liberalism had two sides: one embracing the politics of reform, the other resisting the consumer culture it spawned.

### NOTES

1. Francis L. Broderick, *Right Reverend New Dealer John A. Ryan* (New York: MacMillan Co., 1963); David O'Brien, *American Catholics and Social Reform: The New Deal Years* (New York, Oxford University Press, 1968); Joseph M. McShane, S.J., *"Sufficiently Radical": Catholicism, Progressivism, and the Bishops' Program of 1919* (Washington, DC: The Catholic University of America, 1986).

2. See, e.g., Steve Fraser and Gary Gerstle, *The Rise and Fall of the New Deal Order, 1930–1980* (Princeton: Princeton University Press, 1989); Lizbeth Cohen, *Making a New Deal: Industrial Workers in Chicago, 1919–1939* (New York: Cambridge University Press, 1990); Alan Brinkley, *The End of Reform: New Deal Liberalism in Recession and War* (New York: Vintage Press, 1996). See also Christopher Lasch, *The True and Only Heaven: Progress and Its Critics* (New York: Norton, 1991), pp. 424–439. For the classic interpretation on the culture of abundance, see Warren I. Susman, *Culture as History: The Transformation of American Society in the Twentieth Century* (New York: Pantheon Books, 1984).

3. The classic liberal history of the New Deal is Richard Hofstadter's *The Age of Reform* (New York: Vintage, 1955). The influence of Hofstadter can be seen in Broderick's and O'Brien's accounts of Ryan and Catholics and the New Deal.

4. John A. Ryan, "Roosevelt and Social Justice," *Review of Politics* 7 (July, 1945): 296.

5. See for instance, Stuart Chase, *The Economy of Abundance* (New York: MacMillan Co., 1934); Rexford Tugwell, *The Battle for Democracy* (New York: Columbia University Press, 1935).

6. Ryan, "What About Industrial Recovery?" *Catholic Action* 17 (March, 1935): 7.
7. Ryan, "Fallacious Arguments of the Birth Controllers," *Catholic Action* (April, 1934): 10.
8. Ryan, "Economic Reorganization in the U.S.," *Catholic Action* 21 (June, 1939): 15.
9. Ryan, *Social Doctrine in Action: A Personal History* (New York: Harper & Brothers, 1941), pp. 239–240.
10. Ryan to Franklin D. Roosevelt, June 17, 1944, Franklin D. Roosevelt Presidential Papers, PPF 2406, Roosevelt Library, Hyde Park, NY.
11. See Steve Fraser, "The 'Labor Question,'" in Gerstle and Fraser, 55–84. See also Lary May's discussion of Eric Johnston in Lary May, "Movie Star Politics: The Screen Actors' Guild, Cultural Conversion, and the Hollywood Red Scare," in Lary May (ed.) *Recasting America: Culture and Politics in the Age of Cold War* (Chicago: University of Chicago Press, 1989), pp. 125–153.
12. See Laurence Glickman, *A Living Wage: American Workers and the Making of Consumer Society* (Ithaca: Cornell University Press, 1997).
13. Ryan, *Questions of the Day* (Boston: Stratford Co., 1931), p. 269.
14. Ryan, "The New Morality and Its Illusions," *Catholic World* 131 (May, 1930): 131.
15. Ibid., 132.
16. Ibid., 242.
17. Ryan, "The Fallacy of 'Bettering One's Position,'" *Catholic World* 86 (November, 1907), pp. 150–151.
18. On the redefinition of the private realm in early twentieth-century America as a dynamic sphere of expressiveness and freedom, see Lary May, *Screening Out the Past: The Birth of Mass Culture and the Motion Picture Industry* (Chicago: University of Chicago Press, 1980).
19. See e.g., Ryan, "The Case for Birth Control," in *Declining Liberty and Other Papers* (New York: MacMillan Co., 1927), pp. 307–329; Ryan, "Birth Control," in *Questions of the Day*, pp. 268–273; Ryan, "The New Morality," particularly, p. 132; Ryan, "Monsignor Ryan on Present-Day Evils," *Catholic Action* 22 (October, 1940): 6.
20. Ryan, "Fallacious Arguments," 10.
21. Ryan to Benjamin Marsh, January 23, 1934, File 2, Collection 11, John A. Ryan Papers, Catholic University of America Archives.
22. Ryan, "Aims of the New Deal Explained," *Catholic Action* 16 (May, 1934): 14.
23. Ryan, "New Deal and Social Justice," *Commonweal* 19 (April 13, 1934): 657.
24. Ryan, "Organized Social Justice," *Commonweal* 23 (December 13, 1935): 175.
25. Ryan, "Right of Private Property is No Exemption from Ethics," *America* 68 (October 24, 1942): 62.
26. Ryan, "Labor and Economic Construction After the War," *Vital Speeches* 9 (February 15, 1943): 268; Ryan, "Labor After the War," *Catholic Digest* 7 (April, 1943): 23.
27. See O'Brien, *American Catholics and Social Reform*.

CHAPTER 4

# AL AND FRANK

## THE GREAT SMITH–ROOSEVELT FEUD

### ROBERT A. SLAYTON

IT WAS ONE OF THE GREAT TRAGEDIES OF TWENTIETH-CENTURY AMERICAN politics. In 1936, Al Smith, born and raised a Democrat, had joined the right-wing Liberty League and was giving a major speech on the radio. This oration, one of the most famous denunciations of Franklin Roosevelt and the New Deal of the decade, accused the new administration of having given in to left-wing elements: "Just get the platform of the Democratic Party, and get the platform of the Socialist party, and lay them down on your dining-room table, side by side ... get a heavy lead pencil, and scratch out the word 'Democrat' and scratch out the word 'Socialist' and let the two platforms lay there." To Smith, the results would be obvious, as was the problem: "This country was organized on the principles of a representative democracy, and you can't mix socialism or communism with that" (parenthetically, he added, "that is the reason why the United States Supreme Court is working overtime throwing the alphabet out the window three letters at a time"). By this time his anger could not be contained, despite the fact that he was reading from a prepared speech: "It is all right with me. It is all right with me if they want to disguise themselves as Norman Thomas or Karl Marx, or Lenin, or any of the rest of that bunch, but what I won't stand for is allowing them to march under the banner of Jefferson, Jackson or Cleveland." Rising to a fiery finale, Smith had a "solemn warning." His audience must realize, "There can be only one capital—Washington or Moscow." Even more, "There can be only one atmosphere of government, the clear, pure, fresh air of free America or the foul breath of communistic Russia. There can be only one flag, the Stars and Stripes, or the red flag of the godless union of the Soviet."[1]

The standard historians' explanations for the Smith–Roosevelt feud all depend on rather superficial, transitory factors. Matthew and Hannah Josephson claimed that it came from the fact that FDR refused to offer Smith a position in the state government or hire aides like Bob Moses or Belle Moskowitz. Other historians cite Smith's resentment at losing the nomination in 1932, a year when the Democrats were sure to win. Others argue that by this time Smith had become rich, that he had sold out his past.[2]

While there are important elements of truth in all these accounts, the problem is that they fail to explain a rift this deep. Men like Smith, who grew up on sidewalks where the Democrats were not a party but an act of faith, do not bolt, especially do not bolt publicly, and in particular, do not bolt publicly when the party and all their friends are enjoying triumph. The argument that there were personality differences, or that Al was just mad because Franklin would not retain his advisers, seems accurate, yet far too small an explanation for a break this drastic. What, in fact, really caused Smith to turn so forcefully on his heritage? The answer goes to the core of Smith's soul, speaking to lessons learned on the streets as a boy, and to the most devastating event in the man's life.

Al Smith was the quintessential product of New York City, and like all good New York stories, this one begins with a neighborhood. He grew up in the old Fourth Ward, about where the Brooklyn Bridge launched itself across the East River. Originally Irish, by the time of Smith's birth and childhood the area had become a port of entry for a variety of ethnic groups, including Italians, Jews, Russians, Greeks, and Syrians. Thus, the world Al Smith grew up in has been depicted in all biographical accounts as a model of working-class European diversity in a typical urban neighborhood. Residents were hardworking folk, and the section was reasonably safe and stable. The reality, however, was that the neighborhood was considerably more diverse than this.

Take, for example, the matter of race. It is physically far closer from Smith's house to Chinatown, than it was from his home to the legendary docks. Few of the biographies mention this. Then there is the Bowery, which began at Chatham Square, about half a block from Smith's home. Every account of New York—except those featuring Smith—highlights this section as the home for the city's underground culture. Daniel Czitrom wrote, "After 1850 the Fourth Ward...eclipsed...the Five Points as the section of New York most associated with poverty, crime, and vice." He titled his article on Smith's beloved section, "The Wickedest Ward in New York."[3]

In addition, this was one of the city's centers for homosexual activity, something else that Smith and his biographers seem to have missed. According to George Chauncey, in *Gay New York*, the waterfront and the Bowery were the leading rendezvous spots for New York's homosexual population. Al Smith did not see any of this. This may seem strange, but, in fact, Smith was acting according to the basic rules of New York, and most other American cities.

Cities are dense and diverse places, filled with people of different backgrounds and different understandings of life. In order to keep some sort of peace, urban residents developed a system of segmented neighborhoods. People remained on their own side of the tracks, among their own, and minded their own business. This meant that you would be with people who saw things the same way you did, who followed the same rules and ethics you did, who honored and practiced your customs, your morals, your religion, and your language. All of this built a tremendous bond of trust, a sense that you could rely on one another.

The people on the other side of the street were also in a sense your neighbors; they weren't bad, they were just different. You respected them, but there was relatively little contact, except in such formalized situations as the exchange of goods or services. You did not expect to depend on them the same way, but neither did you feel you had to fight them; frequently they were separated by urban boundaries like a street or a park. In this way conflict was minimized; Smith's world was predicated on Robert Frost's belief that "good fences made good neighbors." This concept, in turn, explains a lot about Al Smith.

First, it makes clear why Smith and the scholars who wrote about him, missed the world of the "Bloody Fourth." Simply put, using the guidelines of segmentation, Smith happily ignored what was going on in other locations, no matter how close geographically, and went about his business within his own world. As Frances Perkins put it, "although he grew up in the slums, he hadn't noticed them much."[4]

It also meant that Smith was rather a trusting soul; segmentation had dealt with the conflicts, and you were surrounded by your own, people you could trust. Frances Perkins once observed that Al Smith was always on the surface, had little in the way of guile and deceit; as she put it, he "had very few reserves."[5] Al Smith never lost these values, and made them the cornerstone of much of his life in politics. This was possible because of one other aspect of his worldview, namely an incredibly naive sense of America.

Al Smith was hardly a well-traveled gentleman; in 1922, he said that for months at a stretch he rarely got above Canal Street, only a few blocks away. Thus, his understanding of America was based on some rather meager sources. As a young man, for example, he attended the Buffalo Bill Cody Wild West Show, with its images of heroic cowboys and the romantic, nationalistic drama of the so-called taming of the west.[6]

His school books did not help, either. All of these primers were devoted to sentimental patriotism, with an emphasis on great men. And what else did he read? Throughout his life one of his standard lines was that the only book

he had ever read was *The Life and Battles of John L. Sullivan*. Published in
1883 by Richard Fox Publications, the slim volume had many of the same
characteristics as the magazine that Fox had founded and made famous, the
*Police Gazette*. Like that tabloid, *Life and Battles* was filled with adolescent
male fantasies of a bountiful and glorious country that raised champions.

Smith took these lessons to heart, and combining them with his own
success story (dropping out of school in the seventh grade, Smith went on to
become governor and presidential hopeful), Smith developed a positive,
simplistic view of America. Walter Lippman said that Smith "believes in the
soundness of the established order and the honesty of its ideals."[7]

Al Smith took this knowledge and combined it with his understanding
of neighborhood segmentation, to come up with a unique concept of
American politics. The American people were basically good, just like the
folks on the Lower East Side. Since the latter practiced a positive form of
segmentation, so must the former. This lead, in turn, to two other amaz-
ing conclusions: first, that Smith truly understood the American people;
and second, that they could be trusted implicitly when it came to politics.
This is what he must have meant when, in 1922, he told the *Evening World*,
"I've met a lot of people from all over the country outside New York
and I've found them fundamentally the same kind of people I was raised
with," a remarkable statement indeed.[8] This theory would take him far,
but would eventually collide with two of the most monumental events
in twentieth-century U.S. politics: the election of 1928 and the rise of
Franklin Roosevelt.

In 1928 Alfred E. Smith received the Democratic nomination for
president. In the course of his campaign, he discovered a vision of America
that shattered his preconceived notions of a simple and healthy heartland.
While the cause of his defeat is still a matter of debate, many scholars, led
by Allan Lichtman, now argue that the primary reason why Smith lost the
election was anti-Catholic prejudice. Whatever the interpretation, it is clear
that he ran into a horrible buzz saw of hate. Dr. Mordecai Ham of the
First Baptist Church of Oklahoma City, the city's largest congregation, told
his followers, "If you vote for Al Smith, you're voting against Christ and
you'll all be damned." The Reverend Bob Jones announced that he would
"rather see a saloon on every corner... than see the foreigners elect Al Smith
President." Robert Schuler, a Los Angeles minister,[9] wrote, "Al Smith is
distinctly Rome's candidacy. It has been fostered by Tammany, for years
recognized as an active ally of Rome. It is headed by Rome's active chamberlain to the Pope... If America desires a President born and raised in a foreign
atmosphere, politically trained and promoted by a foreign political
machine... that man may be had by electing Al Smith..." If that wasn't
enough, Schuler warned Americans that if Smith was elected, the public

school system would be destroyed, all Protestant marriages would be annulled, and all their children would become bastards. He also pointed out that Lincoln, Garfield, and McKinley had been killed by Romanists.[10]

A number of interesting claims were made, and usually believed. Mrs. J. L. Swint wrote Franklin Roosevelt that her neighbor told her, "If Gov. Smith is elected President, the *Pope's son* will be his secretary" (emphasis in original). Mrs. Swint asked her "how many sons the Pope had, and their occupations." The *American Standard* headlined, "Rome Suggests That Pope May Move Here," and also informed readers that Calvin Coolidge had been appointing many Roman Catholics. J. H. Fletcher, "Kligrapp" or secretary of the Bay Shore, Long Island chapter of the Klan, wrote, "This fight is not only a battle against Rome, but against all the evil forces in America, cutthroats, thugs, the scum from the cesspools of Europe, etc."[11]

The Ku Klux Klan went all out, distributing literally millions of items. One piece, a flyer for a book by Tom Watson that exposed the evils of Catholicism, used the top third of the page for a series of images under the headline, "Will It Come to This?"; these depicted scenes such as a priest throwing a baby into a fire; torture that appears to include vivisection; a priest whipping a woman as she is burned at the stake; and the hanging of numerous Protestants from a single tree, a harbinger of things to come. Franklin Roosevelt estimated that the printing and postage bills of the *Fellowship Forum* alone ran between two and five million dollars.[12]

The Klan did more than print flyers. The Birmingham, Alabama chapter responded to Smith's nomination at the Democratic national convention by holding a rally. A dummy representing the governor of New York was brought in, while the crowd yelled, "Lynch him!" A Klan official then slit the figure's throat, pouring mercurochrome down the chest to simulate blood. Other Klansmen then fired revolver rounds into the image, after which a rope was thrown around its neck and it was dragged around the hall as members repeatedly kicked the wounded effigy.[13]

This was an attack on every aspect of America that involved diversity and modernism. Bishop Alma White of the KKK was the author of *Heroes of the Fiery Cross*, written in 1928 at the height of the presidential campaign. The Bishop asked, "Who are the enemies of the Klan? They are the bootleggers, law-breakers, corrupt politicians, weak-kneed Protestant church members, white slavers, toe-kissers, wafer-worshippers, and every spineless character who takes the path of least resistance." While she referred to Smith as "the papal Governor of New York," she also was sure to point out, "Among the forces threatening America are the great Hebrew syndicates that have acquired a monopoly of the motion-picture industry. These conscienceless, money-mad producers have no worthy ideals, either of dramatic art or virtue. Playing with sex themes, they are so depraved as to give the public any thrills they dare, for profit. They are destroying the moral standards of America and educating our youths in vice."

Every commentator was stunned. Frances Perkins, campaigning in Maryland, the oldest Catholic settlement in America, encountered what she described as "some of the most terrible fantastic prejudices and dreadful yarns that I ever heard...I had pointed out to me...the estate which had been purchased for the Pope and where the Pope was coming as soon as Smith was elected...It was pointed out to us. They knew it for a fact." Marvin Jones, a Texas Democrat, went into a drug store in his home town of Amarillo and was asked if he was going to vote for Smith. Jones, a good party man and a liberal to boot, said that, yes, he was most definitely going to vote for Smith. He asked how others felt, and the owner replied, "We've been fighting that bunch for 2,000 years. Do you think I'm going to turn the government over to them?" John W. Davis, the Wall Street lawyer who had been the party's candidate in 1924, gave a radio address supporting Smith; he got a letter telling him, "Your talk went over big with Micks but rotten with the most intelligent minds of America..." It was signed, "a 100 percent American."[14] Toward the end, Lillian Wald wrote a friend about "the organized bigotry, the like of which I have never seen. I feel as if some poison gas had spread over us, and that our democracy will suffer from this for many years to come."[15]

For Al Smith, 1928 was the pivotal event of his career. Everything in the past was the buildup, the preparation for this moment. Everything after that would represent decline. Frances Perkins said, "He was a lost soul after that...there was great sadness over Al."[16] But it was not just sadness; there was also anger. And a lot of this anger, a lot of this bitterness, was aimed at the American people. Al, in his innocence, felt supremely betrayed by them. In 1928 Al Smith found out that America was not like the Fourth Ward, that not only did it not honor the rules of urban segmentation, but that it could be vile.[17]

But Al could not express this. He had mouthed the homilies of democracy for too long. A crucial outburst came in 1929, as wreckers were tearing down the old Waldorf-Astoria Hotel to build the Empire State Building, which Al would head. Shortly after his autobiography appeared, he went over to watch the destruction. His comments, afterwards, to a friend, revealed deep emotions: "In the banquet room where I've spoken so many times...," Al commented, "it was pathetic. Those great gold and brass moldings and decorations...that I supposed were really costly—nothing but gilded plaster. And the chandeliers! They looked magnificent hanging, but on the floor—just junk."[18] This was Al Smith's new vision of America: a shallow facade of pretty glitter covering a reality of "pathetic junk." A facade, moreover, that had cruelly deceived and hurt him. Al Smith would need a symbol for that newly discovered concept of America, and he would find it in the career of Franklin Delano Roosevelt.

Regarding Franklin Roosevelt, Smith's feelings had always been mixed. The Governor recognized some of the political potential of this young man and liked him. Eleanor had even led Democratic women in the 1924 and 1926 campaigns for governor. Tempering this was Smith's view that Franklin was young, immature, and flighty. This was not surprising, given that Al had worked his way up the ladder the hard way, with guts and brains, while Roosevelt had been born with a silver spoon and a silver name. Joseph Proskauer said that in 1920 "none of us took him seriously," and Robert Moses referred to Roosevelt, whom he detested, as "window dressing." Colonel Edwin House, Woodrow Wilson's personal adviser felt that, "Smith looks on Roosevelt as sort of a Boy Scout . . . doesn't really think of him as an equal."[19]

For Al Smith, there was one other factor that exacerbated this belief terribly. Smith was a totally dedicated public servant. He perceived the job as consuming, and horribly destructive of one's health. Despite the fact that Smith had a robust physique, and that there is no indication of any congenital weakness or disease,[20] he was constantly ill, constantly exhausted; his correspondence is studded with accounts of frequent minor illness brought on by exhaustion. As a result, Smith conceived of the job as a killer, as one that only an individual possessed of strength and stamina could stand up to.

What then, in an age far less enlightened as to the abilities of those with handicaps, did Al think of a man who wrote to Bob Moses in 1924, "I fear I cannot get to your office as it is so difficult to manage on crutches"? The story of the 1924 Democratic Convention is that of the triumphant return of Franklin to national politics, with the "Happy Warrior" speech. But did Al notice the effort it took, notice how difficult the task, how cumbersome were the braces? The cumulative result of all these factors was that Smith began to take a paternal attitude regarding the young man from Hyde Park. Franklin was perceived by Smith as a child: loved and cared for, played with and sometimes indulged, but never respected. Louis Howe, with remarkable insight, stated simply, and accurately, "Smith considered Franklin a little boy."[21]

This complex relationship was revealed in a unique, angry exchange of letters in 1927 and 1928. Franklin had been asked by Smith to head the Taconic Park Commission. This brought him into direct conflict with Robert Moses, Parks Commissioner, who hated FDR. Moses did everything in his power to make the job miserable, from cutting budgets to denying Louis Howe's salary. Eventually Roosevelt had had enough. On December 14, 1927, he finally wrote Smith, "I only took this job at your request and because it was you." He was proud of his own record and the Commission's: "the work accomplished during the past year . . . has been carried on in an economical manner and the Commission has nothing to apologize for." But enough was enough: "I know all about the need of cutting appropriations. Try just for once making the cut on somebody else—I decline the honor." An exchange of letters followed, with the Commission, lead by Roosevelt, protesting its total emasculation. Finally, Franklin had had it; on January 30, 1928, he wrote "Dear Al" a letter that began, "This is wholly personal and confidential; the enclosed is the official letter of the Commission." Having clarified his intentions, Roosevelt then wrote, "When all is said and done, I wasn't born yesterday. You see I have been in the game so long that I now realize the mistake I made with this Taconic State Park Commission was in not playing the kind of politics that our friend Bob Moses has used." Later on, after detailing some of Moses' abuses, Roosevelt warned, "Just one other point. You and I have not got a 'meeting of the minds' on what the... Commission exists for."[22]

Smith responded on February 3, 1928, addressing his letter to "Dear Frank," the first sentence acknowledging receipt of the letters. Immediately after, however, Smith began an intensely personal statement: "I know of no man I have met in my public career who I have any stronger affection for than for yourself. Therefore, you can find as much fault with me as you like. I will not get into a fight with you for anything or anybody." Notwithstanding this sentiment, however, the Governor pressed on: "But that does not prevent me from giving you a little tip and the tip is don't be so sure about things that you have not the personal handling of yourself. I have lived, ate, and slept with this park question for three-and-one-half years. I know all about it and I know the attitude of the legislative leaders to the whole thing. I fought and battled with them in the regular session ... When I told you ... that the legislative leaders would not stand for these appropriations, I was telling you what I knew to be a fact and you were guessing at it." He then proceeded to explain the situation, and his position in some detail.[23]

The letters are remarkable for their passion; nothing else even remotely like them exists in the files. Roosevelt is asking to be treated with honesty and openness, in other words, like an adult. When he is not, he is, he claims, justifiably angry. But Smith will have none of this characterization. His letter reads like a lecture to a child, moving from affection to sternness. Franklin was clearly the object of deep emotion, but at the same time, Smith clearly felt that the young man "had milk on his chin."[24]

These visions in turn had a powerful impact on the 1928 New York State Democratic gubernatorial nomination. The traditional story is that Roosevelt was chosen over many of his own objections, having declared that he was not a candidate. Party leaders, however, led by Smith, needed the upstate patrician. Roosevelt refused to take their calls, but finally, they turned to Eleanor to get him on the phone, which she did, but put Smith on instead. Al told Franklin that he was the only man who could carry the state, and that he would balance the ticket. Most accounts claim that at one point Smith said, "Frank, I told you I wasn't going to put this on a personal basis, but I've got to." Roosevelt accepted, and everyone seemed happy. Eleanor telegraphed her husband, "Regret that you had to accept but know that you felt it obligatory; good luck, much love." Franklin himself was swell-headed, writing his Uncle Frederic Delano a few days later, "There is no question that at the time the convention was in a hopeless quandary—there was no one else to satisfy all parts of the State."[25]

While this account is totally accurate, and reflects the public record as it exists today in all historical accounts, it leaves out the details of other crucial meetings. In the Private Files of the Jim Farley Papers at the Library of Congress, there is a memo recounting a series of conferences beginning in August, "when we met to take up the name of the man to be nominated to succeed Smith." These sessions, in other words, took place several months before the events narrated above.[26] At the first meeting, Farley noted "All agreed that inasmuch as Smith was a Catholic that a non-Catholic be named." His choice was Franklin Roosevelt, and he presented it to the group. Smith's reaction to this was strong. He "threw it out on the theory that it was a mistake to attempt to nominate a man in his physical condition. He stressed the great amount of work attached to the Governorship and said Roosevelt could not be expected to do it." According to Farley, "It was apparent that Smith wanted Lehman." Following this there were two other meetings to discuss candidates. Nothing was resolved at the next session, but at the third one, Smith was still supporting Lehman, while others were pushing Wagner. Smith seemed to be looking for a candidate, any candidate but the obvious choice. When George Olvany, reigning head of Tammany Hall, "insisted that Wagner would not run . . . Smith replied that he would not take NO for an answer until he had talked to him." "Considerable discussion of candidates" followed, with Smith holding out for Lehman. Finally, after "all recommendations were thrown out," Farley "made a motion that we communicate with Roosevelt and ascertain whether or not he would accept the nomination and the motion was unanimously carried." The final line of the memo reads, "Smith had to accept it." Years later, when Ruth Proskauer Smith asked her father why, if he hated FDR so much, they had nominated him for governor and put him on the path to the White House, he replied, it was a "purely political deal."[27]

Thus, as the 1928 campaign began, Smith was running with a man he did not understand. Eleanor Roosevelt wrote, "In many ways Governor Smith did not know my husband." Far more devastating, he woefully underestimated Franklin's abilities and skills, an opinion that would not change.[28]

R O B E R T   A .   S L A Y T O N

Problems blossomed after Franklin took office in Albany. Al had discovered a new position for himself, the power behind the throne. He told Franklin not to worry, that he could spend most of his time down in Warm Springs, while Al and Lieutenant-Governor Herbert Lehman ran things; in fact, he need not return till the end of the Legislative Session.[29]

Even worse was to come in the next presidential season. By 1932 Smith felt that it should be, must be his year, the year he would smash the opponents who had hurt him so badly four years before. Belle Moskowitz told Frances Perkins, "He's entitled to it and he feels entitled to it...the Democratic Party should run him again and it is his right to be run again."[30] By the time of the Democratic convention in 1932, James Michael Curley began to tell his friends that "Smith had changed since 1928. he had lost the common touch." But Smith had only lost his innocence and spontaneity and spunk, as he had lost his vision of America.[31] And the ultimate target of that frustration, that anger, that sadness, was Franklin Delano Roosevelt. Smith had wanted to become president, as a chance to redeem himself and to overcome the bigots of 1928, as a chance to end the sadness. And all of this was denied by FDR, whom he considered a lesser man, really, in fact, no more than a child.

In 1932 Franklin Roosevelt achieved the goal Al Smith never attained: inauguration as president of the United States. Within a little more than 100 days, he was not just the president, but also a national hero. To Al Smith, this was the worst conceivable insult, the final betrayal. The American people had rejected him, a self-made man and real hero of the American creed; and turned to someone he considered inferior, an adolescent, a cripple, a fop who had never had to work a day in his life. And by 1936 even Smith's people, the urban immigrants, were lining up to support Roosevelt in record numbers. Franklin was the final, ultimate symbol of the fraud that was the American spirit, the supreme manifestation of the shallowness that had destroyed Al's life. It was only fitting and appropriate that this would be the greatest target of his rage as well.

### NOTES

1. Alfred E. Smith, "The Facts in the Case" (Washington, D.C.: American Liberty League, January 25, 1936), pp. 13, 14, 18–19.
2. Mencken is quoted in Richard O'Connor, *The First Hurrah* (New York: G. P. Putnam's Sons, 1970), p. 175.
3. Daniel Czitrom, "The Wickedest Ward in New York," *Seaport* XX (Winter 1986/87), pp. 20–26; Jimmy Durante and Jack Kofoed, *Night Clubs* (New York: Alfred Knopf, 1931), pp. 51, 89, 92.
4. Frances Perkins interview, Book 1, p. 93, CUOHC.

5. Frances Perkins interview, Book 3, pp. 344, 352, 356–357, CUOHC.

6. *New York Evening World*, October 17, 1922.

7. Richard Lynch, *Alfred E. Smith—An Anthology* (New York: Vantage Press, 1966), p. 9; Walter Lippman, *Men of Destiny* (New York: Macmillan Company, 1928), p. 4.

8. *New York Evening World*, October 20, 1922.

9. This Schuler was no relation to the present-day minister, Robert Schuler of Orange County, according to the information office at his headquarters, the Crystal Cathedral.

10. Allan Lichtman, *Prejudice and the Old Politics* (Chapel Hill: University of North Carolina Press, 1979); David Burner, *The Politics of Provincialism* (New York: Alfred Knopf, 1968), p. 203; Andrew Sinclair, *Era of Excess* (New York: Harper and Row, 1962), p. 285; Robert Schuler, *Al Smith, A Vigorous Study* (Los Angeles: J. R. Spencer, 1928), pp. frontpiece, 54–58, unnumbered pages.

11. Mrs. J. L. Swint to Franklin Roosevelt, no date, Box 4, Democratic National Committee Papers, FDRL; George Graves to Patrick Cardinal Hayes, March 1, 1928, Box 29, George Graves Papers, New York State Archives; *The American Standard*, *House of Death*, and *Gate of Hell* are all in the "*Book of Horrors*" in the Rare Book Room, Columbia University; Caroline Bond to John Roach Straton, August 20, 1928, Box 12, John Roach Straton Papers, American Baptist Historical Society; J. H. Fletcher to John Roach Straton, August 20, 1928, Box 12, John Roach Straton Papers, American Baptist Historical Society.

12. *Fellowship Forum* and *The Tocsin* are in the "Book of Horrors," Columbia University, Rare Book Room; Kenneth Davis, *FDR: New York Years*, p. 67.

13. "Dubious Compliments," *Outlook* (July 25, 1928), p. 484.

14. Frances Perkins interview, Book 2, pp. 579–580, and Marvin Jones interview, pp. 375–376, CUOHC; John W. Davis Papers, Box 57, Sterling Memorial Library, Yale University.

15. Lillian Wald to Henry Farnum, October 22, 1928, Box 5, Lillian Wald Papers, New York Public Library; interview with Ernie Chapman.

16. "Al Smith and Wendell Willkie," *Commonweal* 41 (October 20, 1944): 4; article by Charles Stewart, October 24, 1931, vol. 2, Empire State Building Scrapbooks, Empire State Building Collection, Drawings and Archives, Avery Architectural and Fine Arts Library, Columbia University; Interview with Alfred E. Smith, IV; Frances Perkins interview, Book 3, p. 35 and Book 2, p. 698, CUOHC; Richard O'Connor, *The First Hurrah* (New York: G. P. Putnam's sons, 1970), p. 237.

17. Marvin Jones interview, p. 383, and Frances Perkins interview, Book 2, pp. 701–702, both in CUOHC; Speech by Robert Wagner at the Al Smith Dinner, October 16, 1963, Wagner and LaGuardia Archives.

18. The only account of this crucial conversation appears in O'Connor, *First Hurrah*, pp. 233–234.

19. Joseph Proskauer interview, p. 23, CUOHC; Lash, *Eleanor and Franklin*, pp. 322–323; Frank Freidel, *Franklin D. Roosevelt: A Rendezvous with Destiny* (Boston: Little, Brown, 1990), p. 51; Page Smith, *Redeeming the Time* (New York: Penguin Books, 1987), p. 319.

20. This conclusion came not only from a careful reading of written sources, but was also based on a number of interviews, especially with family members, who could recall no stories of congenital illness.

21. Quoted in Murray, *103rd Ballot*, p. 287.

22. Louis Howe to Joseph Wilson, October 19, 1926, Folder 200–276, Alfred E. Smith Official Correspondence, New York State Archives (hereinafter referred to as AESOC); Franklin Roosevelt to George Graves, ca. November 1926, Folder 200–276, AESOC; George Graves to Franklin Roosevelt, November 30, 1926, Folder 200–276, AESOC; Franklin Roosevelt to Alfred E. Smith, December 14, 1927, Folder 200–242, AESOC; Franklin Roosevelt to Alfred E. Smith, December 30, 1927, Folder 200–276, AESOC; Alfred E. Smith to Franklin Roosevelt, January 23, 1928, Folder 200–276, AESOC; Franklin Roosevelt to Alfred E. Smith, January 30, 1928, Folder 200–276, AESOC; Franklin Roosevelt to Alfred E. Smith (private correspondence), January 30, 1928, Folder 200–276, AESOC.

23. Alfred E. Smith to Franklin Roosevelt, February 3, 1928, Folder 200–276, AESOC.

24. This was the phrase my father always used when I was talking about things that I knew nothing about.

25. Telegram from Eleanor Roosevelt to Franklin Roosevelt, October 2, 1928, Box 9, Franklin D. Roosevelt Papers, 1928 Campaign, FDRL; telegram from Breckinridge Long to Franklin Roosevelt, Box 89, Breckinridge Long papers, LC; Franklin Roosevelt to Frederic Delano, October 8, 1928, Box 10, Franklin D. Roosevelt Papers, 1928 Campaign, FDRL.

26. The Farley memo is in Box 37, Private Files, James Farley Papers, LC.

27. Interview with Ruth Proskauer Smith.

28. Roosevelt, *This I Remember*, p. 51.

29. Freidel, *Roosevelt: Rendezvous with Destiny*, p. 56; Frances Perkins interview, Book 3, pp. 27, 63 and Book 2, pp. 718–719, CUOHC; Roosevelt, *This I Remember*, p. 50.

30. Frances Perkins interview, Book 3, p. 335 and George Van Schaick interview, p. 26, both in CUOHC; interviews with Anthony Smith and Governor Hugh Carey.

31. James Michael Curley, *I'd Do It Again* (Englewood Cliffs, New Jersey: Prentice-Hall, 1957), p. 231.

# CHAPTER 5

# CALIFORNIA CATHOLICS AND THE GUBERNATORIAL ELECTION OF 1934

## STEVEN M. AVELLA

ONE OF THE MOST CONTROVERSIAL AND NETTLESOME Catholic figures of the Roosevelt era was Father Charles Coughlin of Royal Oak, Michigan. Clearly, his popularity and the wide listenership to his weekly radio broadcasts created anxiety within the Roosevelt White House and presented a problem to be "managed." During the 1936 elections, as the Radio Priest moved into a more confrontational role with the administration, the appearance that he was speaking in the name of the church alarmed certain members of the American hierarchy. Among them was Archbishop John J. Mitty of San Francisco, who expressed misgivings about Coughlin's visits to the state in a letter to his counterpart in Los Angeles, Bishop John J. Cantwell. Cantwell dismissed Coughlin's ability to seriously affect the outcome of the 1936 California vote, and tried to put the matter in perspective by noting: "Speaking about Father Coughlin, I may say that his activities have not caused half the anxiety that the campaign of Upton Sinclair generated a couple of years ago. At that time, I had many applications from good friends to intervene." He concluded, "It all ended up satisfactory."[1]

Upton Sinclair's quixotic bid for the governorship of California has been the subject of a good deal of serious research.[2] His conversion back to the Democratic party in 1933, and his victory over two regular Democrats in the August 1934 gubernatorial primary, represents a case study of the kinds of politics bred by desperate times. Sinclair's nomination, along with the successes of Charles Coughlin, Huey Long, and Francis Townsend, was one of many "firebells in the night" for the Roosevelt administration, suggesting that the New Deal's reform and recovery efforts had not gone far enough.[3] For historians of American Catholicism during this era, it provides yet another example of the kind of delicate line they had to walk in staking out their own political position. Catholic leaders would be among the most trenchant critics of the abuses of the capitalist system and some of the strongest supporters (and beneficiaries) of President Roosevelt's relief and reform efforts. Yet at the same time, they had an abhorrence of radicalism and anything that remotely resembled either state socialism or atheistic communism. A version of this larger national story was played out in the 1934 California gubernatorial election, which pitted former socialist and Catholic critic Upton Sinclair against a conservative, even reactionary Republican, Frank Merriam. Sinclair, who had been a bitter critic of organized religion, recognized certain affinities between his ideas for economic recovery and elements of Catholic social teaching and he apparently had Catholic supporters. This examination of the role of Catholics in the 1934 election hopes to contribute a regional variation on the larger theme of the church's role in the political and social life of the nation during the Roosevelt era. Additionally, it offers some additional information about the realities of Roosevelt era politics in the American West.[4]

Upton Sinclair was a well-known name in American literary and political life.[5] Most Americans knew him then, as they do today, for his famous book *The Jungle*, which detailed the horrors of the Chicago stockyards and was a stimulus to pure food and drug reform. Since 1904, Sinclair had been a committed Socialist (with a brief hiatus during World War I), and had devoted his considerable writing talents to promoting various party causes. His sometimes wicked pen took on virtually every bastion of established society from higher education to religion. After a flirtation with a communal project in New Jersey, Sinclair moved to California in 1916 and settled into the easy life of Pasadena, where he committed himself with equal passion to vegetarianism and tennis—as well as to writing and political activism.[6] In 1923 he was arrested at a waterfront strike at San Pedro for trying to read the Constitution to a group of strikers on an empty lot. By 1933 he had written forty-seven books including a utopian novel, *I, Governor of California and How I Ended Poverty: A True Story of the Future*. In this futuristic account of California from 1933 to 1938, he laid out the details of his plan to alleviate the Depression that was already beginning to strangle the state's economy. Known by its acronym EPIC (End Poverty in California), Sinclair's blueprint revolved around the central socialist tenet of government ownership of the means of production and included cooperative farms on state-purchased agricultural lands, a plan to purchase failed factories and use state monies to employ the unemployed in them, and a California Authority for Money that would issue bonds to buy lands, factories, and scrip, which would serve as a medium of exchange among the cooperatives. "Production for use" would be the mantra of the hundreds of EPIC clubs that popped up all over California and the phrase became a shorthand for Sinclair's constellation of ideas and proposals. Sinclair had allowed his name to be used as the Socialist Party candidate for the House of Representatives in 1920, for the Senate in 1922 and for governor in 1926 and 1930. In September 1933, at the behest of some friends, he changed his party registration to the Democratic Party and announced his intention to run for the governor's office.

Sinclair's progressive, and some would say radical agenda, found a more receptive electorate in 1934 for the Depression's impact on the California economy had been disastrous. Farm income, still the mainstay of California's economy, sank in 1932 to half of what it had been in 1929. The building boom, which had also fueled the state's growth, ground to a screeching halt as the number of building permits shrunk to less than one-ninth of what they had been in 1925. Most ominously, 1,250,000 Californians were on public relief in 1934, one-fifth of the state's population.[7] In Los Angeles County, which would be the cornerstone of Sinclair's primary victory, one of every seven persons was on the dole. So dire was the poverty that many Californians had turned to barter as a way to sustain themselves during the crisis. The spontaneous generation of a number of cooperatives attracted scores of impoverished citizens—75,000 in Los Angeles alone—signaling a serious breakdown in the economy.

Adding to the general distress, serious labor unrest hit California's agriculture and ocean trade industries. Public tension was raised considerably by a Longshoreman's Strike spearheaded by labor radical Harry Bridges who had revivified the broken down International Longshoreman's Association.[8] Beginning in May, dock workers in all the Pacific Coast ports went on strike, joined later by several other seafaring unions. Labor violence erupted on July 5, 1934, along San Francisco's Embarcadero and Acting Governor Frank Merriam dispatched the national guard to restore order. In retaliation, labor organized a general strike for four days in July. The spiraling unrest brought active intervention by the Roosevelt administration, which compelled arbitration on both sides and ultimately gave the union the power over hiring that it desired. Meanwhile, equally serious agricultural disputes erupted between growers and workers in the rich agricultural valleys of the state.

Given this chaotic state of affairs and the general lack of enthusiasm for the incumbent governor, Frank Merriam, one could agree with the assessment of historians James Rawls and Walton Bean, who have observed, "Almost any reasonably presentable New Dealer could probably have been elected governor of California in 1934."[9] But Upton Sinclair was not that man.

For although he aroused a dormant Democratic party and energized it as never before, the simple fact was that he was far too inept a campaigner and altogether too vulnerable to attacks from his ideological enemies.[10] His candidacy had the effect of stimulating the creation of a powerful coalition of opposition forces that considered Sinclair a menace and committed itself to doing whatever it took to prevent him from going to Sacramento. But all this was in hindsight. In late August 1934, the prospects for a Sinclair victory in November burned bright.

In the wake of his stunning primary victory , Sinclair made a bid for White House support. In early September 1934, he made the pilgrimage to Hyde Park with hopes of securing a much-needed Roosevelt endorsement. For a time, it appeared that an endorsement might be forthcoming as both Harry Hopkins and James Farley initially urged support for Sinclair's candidacy. However, internal discussions within the administration shifted to the view of Comptroller of the Currency, and California political consultant, J. F. T. O'Connor (himself once considered for the California governorship), who insisted that neutrality was the safest policy. Sinclair, it was reasoned, was too divisive and polarizing a figure and might not be easily controlled if he won the governor's chair.[11] White House ambivalence sent a strong signal to state Democratic panjandrums who also withheld critical support from the nominee. Matters grew worse for Sinclair when Roger Haight, a San Francisco attorney, also entered the race under the banner of the Commonwealth party. Haight gave Progressive warhorses, like *Sacramento Bee* editor, C. K. McClatchy, an alternative to Merriam, whom he loathed and Sinclair, whom he considered to be impractical and dangerous.[12] Undercut by state Democrats and the White House, and finding his election clout weakened by the presence of Haight in the race, Sinclair was left exposed to a campaign of intense opposition from some of the major power-houses of California political life, including real-estate agents, fruit growers, movie studios, and the forces of organized religion who dreaded the possibility of a Sinclair governorship.[13]

Sinclair gave his enemies plenty to work with, and even distort, as operatives of well-financed committees, such as Clem Whitaker and Leone Baxter of "Californians Against Sinclairism," revealed the Democratic candidate's "hostility" to the American way of life by culling damning extracts from the voluminous writings of the loggorhetic Sinclair. His opponents struck a gusher of damaging material in a pamphlet Sinclair had written in 1918 entitled *The Profits of Religion*. Every religious denomination in the state would take offense at the contents of this work. Sinclair's earlier attacks on religion would haunt him throughout the campaign. Aroused Protestant ministers, such as pistol-packing preacher Martin Luther Thomas, relentlessly assailed Sinclair via pamphlet, pulpit, and radio.[14] Others used their Sunday sermons to educate voters about the record and words of the candidate. The culmination of these church-inspired efforts produced a unique outpouring of ecumenism on November 2, 1934, a few days before the general election, when a large anti-Sinclair/pro-Merriam rally, replete with special pageant produced by Aimee Semple McPherson, was staged at the Los Angeles Shrine Auditorium.[15]

As outraged as many Protestant groups were, the group that came in for the most serious criticism in Sinclair's writing were Catholics. George Creel, who had had a few of the anti-Catholic writings of his early career dredged up and used against him in the primary campaign, noted in a letter to James Farley after the State Democratic convention, "The Republicans will play up Sinclair's connection with Communist organizations, but above all, they will concentrate on the distribution of his book, '*The Profits of Religion.*' It is the vilest and most violent attack on every known denomination, particularly the Catholic and it is bound to hurt him."[16] Catholics were indeed offended, but their reaction was much more complex than Creel assumed.

## CATHOLICS IN CALIFORNIA: A PROFILE

With a history stretching back to the earliest days of the Spanish encounter, Catholics had been a part of California life since the outset. In 1934, their total number stood at around 877,000 out of a total population of six million and constituted roughly 14 percent of the state. This was down from 1928 when they numbered 786,000 and were about 17 percent of the state's total population.

Yet, even with a shrinking percentage of the state's populace, Catholicism had a "niche" in California life. This was due in part to the state's Catholic Hispanic history, which had left its imprint on place names and the visible symbols of a romanticized past, the fabled missions. Interestingly, the missions became an important marketing icon during the great land boom of the 1880s, as real-estate operators, the Southern Pacific railroad, and even fruit packers deliberately used a romanticized version of the famous centers of evangelization to lure newcomers to the state.[17] Equally important, Catholic citizens had been an active and vigorous component of the state's political and social life from the onset of its existence under American auspices. Similar in many respects to the experience of Catholics in the Midwest, Catholics in California were "present at creation" and consequently suffered few of the liabilities and social stigmas that their co-religionists had endured in the East. For example, Catholic office holding, one symbol of acceptance, was a reality from the outset. The first American governor of the state, Peter Burnett, was a Catholic convert, and high offices such as senators and local legislators were held by devout Catholics throughout the state's history.[18] Even today, two Catholics are vying for the governorship of the state. But to speak of California with any degree of precision, it is important to take into account the real differences between the northern and southern portions of the state.

Traditionally, Catholicism had been strongest in Northern California, especially in the city of San Francisco, where Catholic hegemony had been an established fact for decades. From its earliest days San Francisco had a respectable and regular Catholic press, schools, and orders of religious men and women who operated hospitals and protective institutions.[19] These institutions reflected the size of the Roman Catholic population and were its base in affecting the political and social culture of the city. From the outset the city elected Roman Catholic mayors and city officials, and one of the leading figures of its history was Father Peter C. Yorke, a controversial but powerful figure, who dominated Catholic life in the city from the 1890s through the 1920s.[20]

In the Southland the situation was different. The great land boom of the late nineteenth century brought scores of Midwestern Protestants to Southern California, overwhelming its earlier Catholic ambience and replicating a kind of Protestant heartland south of the Tehachapis.[21] However, evidence suggests that Catholics were making a comeback in the region, especially in Los Angeles County. Catholic numbers in the Southland were rising steadily. In 1928, the Diocese of Los Angeles/San Diego numbered 299,350 Catholics. By 1934, the number had climbed to 313,106. It is of particular importance to the subject of this chapter to note that the Catholic presence in Los Angeles County was growing, demonstrated by the fact of parochial expansion. In 1928, there were 116 Catholic Churches in the city. By 1934, the number had climbed to 134. Eventually Los Angeles would outdistance her northern neighbor ecclesiastically and in 1936, Roman authorities elevated Los Angeles to the status of an archdiocese, a special ranking that put it on an even ecclesiastical par with San Francisco—the only time that has ever been done in a single state of the American union.

It is not easy to ascertain the predominant political affiliation of California Catholics. One might assume that the political affiliation of California Catholics was with the Democratic Party and this might be borne out by the strength of the party in the Bay Area, where Catholics were numerically stronger. However, California was a staunchly Republican state until the 1950s and regularly awarded its highest offices to GOP candidates. Probably the fairest characterization of the Catholic political affiliation was made by a columnist for the Los Angeles *Tidings*, who observed, "sincere Catholics are members of all parties and are to be found supporting all candidates. The so-called Catholic vote, while usually appealed to on religious grounds, is just the same, very democratic, it splits in all directions."[22]

This analysis seems to be validated by any number of examples. Two Catholics that can illustrate the point are the state's sole Democratic senator for much of the twentieth century, former mayor of San Francisco, James Duvall Phelan and Joseph Scott, a loyal Republican and perhaps California's most prominent Catholic layman, who had nominated Herbert Hoover at the 1928 convention.[23]

Because they were so well accepted and integrated into the political and social life of the state, Catholics were unorganized as an electoral force in California politics for much of the state's history. Moreover, even the Catholic bishops of the state were slow in developing the techniques of lobbying for their concerns in state politics.[24] However, as historian Mark Hurley relates, this was beginning to change. Evidence of this is found in the fact that one year prior to the gubernatorial election there had been a very divisive ballot proposition election in which Catholics renewed earlier efforts to repeal the taxation of private schools. The initiative, Proposition Four, had gone down to crashing defeat in a campaign that highlighted outbursts of anti-Catholic invective by Proposition Four's opponents.[25] Yet, despite the loss, Hurley contrasts the 1933 campaign with an earlier effort in 1926 by noting, "The support of Proposition 4 [the ballot initiative to end the taxation] was, in contrast to the 1926 campaign, quite extensive and organized."[26]

## DID SINCLAIR HAVE CATHOLIC SUPPORT?

By 1934, the single largest problem in California was not taxation of public schools, but the devastating effects of the Depression. These conditions helped bring about a major shift to the Democratic Party in California, especially in Los Angeles County.[27] It was this fact that secured the nomination for Sinclair, for in the primary he drew 214,404 votes in Los Angeles County out of nearly 400,000 cast. He did not cross-file as was permitted under California law and so these represented all Democratic votes. No statistical data exists that measured Sinclair's votes in relation to religious affiliation. Moreover, in the dire economic conditions of Los Angeles County, real questions could be raised as to whether denominational affiliation really mattered, at least in the primary election, for as *Tidings* columnist Patrick Henry observed, "the election will be decided upon the pocketbook issue. This is how elections have been decided since democracy found its voice at the polls."[28]

What we do know, however, is that Los Angeles County appears to have had a fairly large percentage of the churches in the entire Diocese of Los Angeles/San Diego, and, one might legitimately surmise, an equally substantial number of the 331,000 Catholics listed in the *Official Catholic Directory* for 1934.

Making allowance for the fact that some of these institutions served very small constituencies (ethnic groups or small chapels), we see that the majority of the Catholic churches in the confines of the Diocese of Los Angeles were within the boundaries of Los Angeles County. In 1934, the Diocese of Los Angeles consisted of Imperial, Los Angeles, San Bernardino, Orange, San Diego, Santa Barbara, and Ventura Counties. There were in the diocese a total of 221 churches with resident priests and 67 missions served by visiting clergy. Of these 221 churches, Los Angeles City had 87 churches and an additional 47 were in county locations, making 134 in all. This means that well over half of the Catholic population resided in Los Angeles County. An admittedly crude but simple deduction would be that a portion of Sinclair's support came from the numerous Roman Catholics living in the county.

We also know that Catholics supported the Sinclair candidacy, because Sinclair's enemies said so. One source was Father John Dunne, the editor of the Los Angeles Roman Catholic diocesan paper, the *Tidings*. Dunne, a trenchant critic of the Democratic candidate, admitted in an editorial, "There are a number of Catholics who are supporters of Sinclair and up to the present at any rate, it would be a very grave injustice to even doubt their sincerity as Catholics."[29] Similar evidence is found in the correspondence of Archbishop Edward Hanna of San Francisco for the year 1934. One correspondent, who called on the prelate to assist in the "positive defeat" of "this insane radical, Upton Sinclair" noted that some Catholics were considering voting for Sinclair, and wondered if Hanna could "ascertain if something cannot be done to inform some well-meaning but mis-guided Catholics, warning them of the great dangers which threatens our Commonwealth if they vote for the wrong candidate?" She also noted that three of the city's Catholic Churches had refused to accept anti-Sinclair pamphlets because Hanna had not given permission.[30] One letter representing another point of view came from a journalist who had been handed an anti-Sinclair leaflet at Old St. Mary's Church. Protesting that he did "not much care who is elected Governor," the correspondent nonetheless expressed disdain "about the use of the Catholic Church by a hack politician [Merriam] and his financial backers."[31]

## SINCLAIR REACHES OUT

Whatever the breadth or depth of Sinclair's support among California Catholics, he and his operatives believed it was worth the effort to build bridges to them based on what he perceived were common ideas and visions about the future of California. In this regard, as with his willingness to bargain and deal with Democratic regulars over the nature of the party platform, Sinclair clearly was a man who was in the process of transforming himself and his image when he "converted" to the Democratic Party in 1933.

Clearly he knew that he had a "religious problem" created by his analysis of religious faith in *Profits*. During the primary season he sought to repair the problem by courting groups of Congregational and Methodist clergymen who threw open their churches to his meetings and who provided some assurance that Sinclair really did believe in God. He also seized the moment of Democratic rival Justus Wardell's confusion of him with the character Elmer Gantry in novelist Sinclair Lewis's work of the same name, to deny that he had stood on a platform in Kansas City with watch in hand and "wickedly invited Almighty God to strike him dead" (a scene from the novel).[32] During the campaign he would remind supporters that his 1922 book, *They Call Me Carpenter*, "reveals Sinclair's pious reverence for Jesus Christ."[33] It is difficult to know if he really believed his efforts would erase the harshness of his written words. What is evident however, was that he thought he had a real shot at influencing Catholics to become part of his efforts.

Even before he won the primary, his chief mouthpiece, the *Epic News*, kept up a steady flow of information about the campaign and seemed to give special attention to the attitudes of the churches, Catholics in particular. For example, the *News* reported approvingly the activities of a Catholic Action week in April 1934, which included among other events, the consecration of Robert Emmett Lucey as the bishop of Amarillo, Texas. It reported on some of the sessions, offered quotes from Apostolic Delegate Amleto Cicognani and Father Raymond McGowan of the NCWC, and noted, with appreciation, that "the conference discussed the industrial breakdown with striking fearlessness and frankness. Church leaders without apology, condemned the piracies of 'rugged individualism' and demanded social reconstruction that will end poverty in the modern world. Laymen applauded."[34] A few issues later, a boxed quote from Pope Pius XI's encyclical *Quadragesimo Anno* appeared stating, "It is patent that in our days not alone is wealth accumulated but immense power and despotic economic determination is concentrated in the hands of a few, and that those few are frequently not the owners but only the trustees and directors of invested funds who administer them at their good pleasure."[35]

Another "find" of the Los Angeles Catholic Action Conference was a speech given by Father J. M. Campbell, director of the Rural Life Conference of the Archdiocese of Dubuque, who spoke on parish credit unions, a form of cooperative, and was an acknowledged expert in home subsistence farming— production for use. Sinclair's campaign seized on some friendly comments Campbell had made to Sinclair's supporters who rushed up to him after the talk.[36] Campbell would later repudiate the association with Sinclair.

However, even during the primary season when his campaign was picking up steam and winning support from some Roman Catholics, Sinclair was aware of trouble on the horizon stemming from *Profits*. "The thing they intend to make the most use of—they have already begun in San Diego and Los Angeles and San Francisco—is my book, *The Profits of Religion*. You will find isolated passages poking fun at the devices whereby some religious groups have been getting money from the poor. These passages may hurt the feelings of Catholics, Episcopalians, Christian Scientists, Mormon, and Theosophists—hurt them so greatly that they will prefer to live in poverty the rest of their lives rather than to vote for the author of *The Profits of Religion*." While he averred that he would not change much if he had to do it over again, he did admit: "Some of these words are very harsh, and some of them I would cut out if I were re-writing the book today."[37] What he said in this controversial tract would hurt him seriously in the election campaign.

### THE PROFITS OF RELIGION

*The Profits of Religion* was first published in early 1918 and went through at least six editions, with the last revision taking place in 1931. It was one of a series of volumes in which Sinclair's acerbic pen skewered capitalism and its various supporting institutions. *Profits* was an especially vitriolic attack on organized religion, subtitled "A Study of Supernaturalism as a Source of Income and a Shield to Privilege." Its pages are a popularized version of age-old rationalist attacks on religion, written in the punchy language of the muckraker. Sinclair dismissed the supernatural claims of organized religion with derision and characterized their activities as nothing more than a pernicious fraud perpetrated on the unsophisticated and downtrodden for the accumulation of wealth on the part of churchmen, the maintenance of unjust social and economic arrangements for the rich and powerful of all times and cultures, and which constituted a detriment to the ability of men and women to think for themselves and to determine policies and economic arrangements that would ultimately benefit them. Perhaps to titillate his readers, Sinclair added a whiff of sexual innuendo, repeating, in essence, many of the same accusations leveled at celibate clergy and religious orders that one read in some nineteenth-century anti-Catholic literature such as Maria Monk's *Awful Disclosures*.

Sinclair reserved his bitterest invective for "The Church," namely the Roman Catholic Church. He attacked Catholic practices and teachings on the universal scale, but also provided multiple examples of how the Catholic Church in America worked in tandem with the powers of corporate influence to secure its own financial well being (and especially the high life-styles of the major clergy) while giving spiritual legitimation to the oppression of the capitalist system.

Reading his prose years later, it strikes one that he seemed to know instinctively what Catholics loved dearly and just how to ridicule it to best effect. Hence, early in the tract, under a heading entitled "Slave Regina" (a deliberate slur on the Marian anthem Salve Regina), he mocked a brochure carrying a picture of the Virgin Mary that was distributed as part of a fund-raising operation for the Catholic University of America. When the prayer card suggested that gifts could be given in the name of deceased relatives and friends (mass stipends), Sinclair railed against what he thought was the implicit suggestion that a failure to contribute would mean that those deceased would be in hell.

> In the days of Job it was threats of boils and poverty that the Priestly lie maintained itself, but in the case of this blackest of all Terrors, transplanted to our free Republic from the heart of the Dark Ages, the wretched victims see before their eyes with the glare of flames, and hear the shrieks of their loved ones writhing in torment through uncounted ages and eternities.[38]

Sinclair also attacked the other Catholic prayer forms and especially ridiculed indulgences,

> The Catholic religion was founded before the Tibetan, and is less progressive; it does not welcome mechanical devices for saving labor. You have to use your own vocal apparatus to keep yourself from prayer . . . Thus each time you say "My God and my all" you get fifty days indulgence; the same for "My Jesus Mercy," and the same for "Jesus my God I love Thee above all things." For "Jesus, Mary, Joseph," you get 300 days—which would seem by all odds the best investment of your spare breath.[39]

Sinclair attacked Catholic association with such "malefactors" as Republican Marcus A. Hanna and Speaker Joseph Cannon, the resolution of the friar's dispute in the Philippines, the efforts of Catholics at preventing birth control information from traversing the mails and the sale of contraceptives, and the presence of Catholics on police forces and the subsequent cover-ups of priestly crime (usually moral failures). Despite his later protestations to the contrary, he seemed to have a special animus toward the Roman Catholic faith. Again, leafing through a popular prayer manual, his revulsion with the whole Catholic system could hardly be restrained as he read the titles of the prayers.

> I cannot bear to read them [the prayer titles], hardly to list them. I remember standing in a Cathedral "somewhere in France" during the celebration of some special Big Magic. There was brilliant white light, and a suffocating strange odor, and the thunder of a huge organ, and a clamor of voices, high, clear voices of young boys mounting to heaven, like the hands of men in a pit reaching up trying to climb over the top of one another. It sent a shudder into the depths of my soul. There is nothing left in the modern world which can carry

the mind so far back into the ancient nightmare of an anguish and terror which was once the mental life of mankind, as these, Roman Catholic incantations with their frantic and ceaseless importunity. They have even brought in the sex-spell; and the poor, frightened soldier-boy, who has perhaps spent the night with a prostitute, now prostrates before a holy Woman-being who is lifted high above the shames of the flesh, and who stirs the thrills of awe and affection which his mother brought to him in early childhood.[40]

Most relevant to his political aspirations was this attack on the bishop of Los Angeles, the seat of his strongest political strength in the state:

It is not too much to say that today no daily newspaper in any large American city dares to attack the emoluments of the Catholic Church, or to advocate restrictions upon the ecclesiastical machine. As I write, they are making a new Catholic bishop in Los Angeles, and all the newspapers of that graft-ridden city herald it as an important social event. Each paper has the picture of the new prelate, with his shepherd's crook upraised, his empty face crowned with a rhomboidal fool's cap and enough upholstery on him to outfit a grand opera company. The Los Angeles "Examiner" the only paper with a pretense to radicalism, turns lose its star-writer—one of those journalist virtuosos who will describe you a Wild West "rodeo" one day, and a society elopement the next, and a G.O.P. convention the next and always with his picture, one inch square, at the head of his effusion.... To read him now you might think he had been reared in a convent...

Sinclair then took aim at Cantwell's speech, delivered to his archenemies the Los Angeles Merchants and Manufacturer's Association.

How the Shepherd of Jesus does love the Merchants and Manufacturers! How his eloquence is poured out on upon them! You represent, gentlemen, the largest and the most civilizing secular body in the country. You are the pioneers of American civilization . . . I am glad to be among you; glad that my lines have fallen in this glorious land by the sunset sea, and honored to meet in intimate acquaintance the big men who have raised here in a few years a city of metropolitan proportions.

As if this indictment were not severe enough, he twisted what was probably Cantwell's gentle appeal for a more humane capitalism into an affirmation of the rich, "How will men obey you, if they believe not in God, who is the author of all authority."[41]

As noted earlier, Sinclair later regretted that he wrote "too damned much" and sought to mend some of his fences with organized religion by stressing that his social and economic ideas to some extent dovetailed with their own. As mentioned earlier, he regularly reminded readers of a work he had written in 1922, *They Call Me Carpenter*, which stressed, as did *Profits*, Jesus's "proletarian" beginnings. He even wrote a prayer stressing the fatherhood of God and the brotherhood of man "O God My Father/God My Friend, and God My Guide to Poverty's End."[42] However, he seemed to try hardest with Catholics whose social teaching seemed, at least on the face of it, to resonate with ideas such as production for use and endorsed the idea of cooperatives.

## SINCLAIR COURTS CATHOLICS

All through the election campaign, Sinclair would make efforts to alert thoughtful Catholics to the fact that his ideas were not all that radically different from the official teachings of their Church on matters of social justice. To shore this up, he sought to align himself with one of the most popular Catholic spokesmen in the country, Father Charles Coughlin. After departing Hyde Park with what he thought was Roosevelt's backing, he made a special stop at the Shrine of the Little Flower in Royal Oak, Michigan, where Coughlin reigned supreme. Coughlin at this point was on the verge of recommencing his radio programs, shut down for the season, and was, according to his biographer, at something of a crossroads in his relationship with FDR. He continued to support the president and spoke in favor of the New Deal, but privately he was beginning to have his doubts about the efficacy of the Roosevelt program and the usefulness of the two-party system to deal with the systemic problems of the collapsed American economy.[43] It was in this context that Sinclair appeared at his doorstep on the way back West and the two men had a meeting that Sinclair related to *Epic News*,

> Father Coughlin was cordial. He said he is heart and soul for the program of production for use. He said he had been studying it hard and was going to broadcast it. He asked me to recite the rest of the program to him, and this I did; and he approved every detail one after another. He gave me authorization to say that he approved our program entirely.

Sinclair was especially enthused that Coughlin seemed to confirm that there had been a change in Catholic social thinking over the past years (spearheaded by Pope Leo whom Sinclair had lambasted in *Profits*) and noted to his diary. "Father Coughlin starts broadcasting again in the latter part of October and we ought to try to get one of these programs put through into California, even if we have to pay for it ourselves."[44] Sinclair's operatives regaled for a time in Coughlin's "endorsement" and the tacit promise of a supportive radio broadcast on production for use from the Radio Priest and cast about for other Catholic support, which may have come to them from self-identified Catholics in EPIC clubs throughout the state and from other sources.

## CATHOLIC OPPOSITION

But even as Sinclair was attempting to distance himself from his earlier harsh statements about the Catholic faith and was openly courting the most powerful Catholic voice in America, the forces opposing him were moving into high gear to stop his march to the governorship. Almost simultaneously with the release of pamphlets and newsreels denouncing the Democratic candidate, a Catholic press campaign against him began as well. Although no apologist for "laissez faire" capitalism, Bishop John Cantwell of Los Angeles probably needed little prodding from the various visitors who importuned him to denounce Sinclair and enjoin his flock to do the same.[45] However, consistent with his practice in other public matters related to politics, he did not comment publicly on the campaign nor were there any diocesan directives mandating which way Catholics should vote—such meddling would probably have been discouraged by the apostolic delegate and would have been counterproductive. However, there was no doubt about Cantwell's opinion of Sinclair. What he was reluctant to express publicly was made known through the editorial policy of his diocesan organ, the *Tidings*. The guiding force of the paper at the time was Tipperary-born John Dunne who had been a priest since 1927 and editor since 1931.[46] Dunne preached weekly through his own personal column "El Rodeo." A critic of the New Deal and an isolationist in the foreign policy debates of the 1930s, Dunne was no unabashed admirer of Roosevelt, and left the paper after World War II began. No doubt acting at Cantwell's behest, but also from his own suspicions of leftist politics, Dunne was scornful of the candidate's efforts to mend the breach with Catholics. He was especially not amused by what he considered to be the superficial efforts of politicians to appeal for the support of Catholic voters by stressing some personal tie to the Church (such as a relative who was a priest or a nun). Dunne sardonically wrote "that does not work so well any more. Nowadays, they dish up a blob of platform sandwiched between two slices of encyclical and hungry or not you are supposed to swallow it for the love of God and the good of the church." Dunne proclaimed official neutrality in the campaign, but warned readers "you do not have to swallow the hook of any Catholic politician just because he has baited it with a large hunk of encyclical."[47] However, Dunne was anything but neutral and revisited the subject of Sinclair on several occasions during the fall campaign. Seeking to persuade Catholics who supported Sinclair, he wisely avoided questioning their motives, but left no doubt that the author of *Profits* was not fit to hold public office. He even added to the length of his "El Rodeo" column in late October to specifically refute the charges against Bishop Cantwell leveled by Sinclair sixteen years before in *Profits*.[48] Occasionally, his columns drew blood. For example, after he tweaked Father Coughlin for receiving Sinclair and allegedly telling him that most priests don't really understand Catholic social teaching, the Radio Priest publicly disavowed any support for Sinclair.[49] *Epic News* was so antagonized by Dunne's swipe at Coughlin that they departed from their normal policy of highlighting the positives of church issue to fire back at Dunne by quoting the priest's own words; "With regard to the candidacy of Mr. Sinclair, and despite the efforts of some Catholic politicians, the Church will have nothing to say. In going to vote let the good of the state be your guide."[50]

Dunne's antipathy to Sinclair was echoed to some degree by his colleague on the *Tidings* staff, Patrick Henry. A skilled journalist, and trained in editorial writing, the Irish-born Henry had been with the paper since the 1920s. Henry clearly did not like Sinclair, but walked a fine line between his disdain for the candidate and an outright endorsement of the capitalist excesses that caused the Depression. "Mr. Sinclair's plan is state socialism in a fancy dress. It appeals to desperate people, which includes those who have lost heavily and are struggling to hang on to what is left as well as those who lost everything and live upon the dole."[51]

The *Tidings'* anti-Sinclair position no doubt had some effect on its readers. However, its limited circulation (ca. 45,000 and some of that bulk parish subscriptions) circumscribed its effect on the larger Catholic body in the Los Angeles area. For those who did not (or could not afford) to subscribe to the diocesan paper, the secular dailies, especially the *Los Angeles Times* began and kept up a drumfire of opposition targeting Catholics. In a tacit acknowledgment of the growing significance of Catholic voters, and taking advantage of the disdain of Bishop Cantwell for the candidate, both the anti-Sinclair committees and the newspapers kept up a steady flow of quotes from *Profits* intended specifically to provoke members of all religious faiths, but especially Catholics, and to turn their votes to Merriam or Haight. Beginning on Sunday, September 23, 1934, the *Los Angeles Times* began running boxed sections containing quotes from Sinclair's writings. The very first one was devoted to "Sinclair and Religion" and was targeted at a "typical" family who would have gone to church. In all, forty-two columns would be printed using quotes from Sinclair's writing. Virtually every Sunday of the campaign (along with some on weekdays) readers of the *Times* received a steady dose of Sinclair's antireligious feelings.[52] Indeed, of the forty-two columns, ten, or about a fourth, were given over to "exposing" him on the religious question, and most of them were aimed at Catholics.

Supplementing the newspaper, Catholics in the Southland were specifically targeted by United for California with a pamphlet "Upton Sinclair on the Catholic Church." It carried a series of the most offensive quotations from *Profits* and concluded with a bold question: "Will you turn California Over to the Mercies of Upton Sinclair?" Thousands of these pamphlets were circulated throughout the state and mailed to Catholic pastors.[53]

## NORTHERN CALIFORNIA

Shifting north, where Sinclair's support was considerably weaker, efforts appeared to be just as intense to undermine whatever support Sinclair had among Catholics. Like Cantwell in the south, Archbishop Hanna made no official pronouncements and issued no guide to voters, but his feelings were expressed through the official newspaper, *The Monitor*.[54]

By contrast with its counterpart in Southern California, the San Francisco Catholic weekly, *The Monitor*, devoted less ink to either the primary or general election, but nonetheless expressed its concerns about the candidacy before its reading public. Choosing to address the socioeconomic issues raised by Sinclair, rather than his feelings about organized religion, the *Monitor* ran a lengthy six-issue column reprinting Hilaire Belloc's treatise on the Redistribution of Property, entitled "The Restoration of Property."[55] In the introduction, the editor expressed the hope that "these articles [offered] the best and most practical available thesis by which to give our people a better plan of economic life than those offered by the Communists, the Utopians, the Socialist-Democrats and the laissez faire spokesmen for big business."[56] Embracing the Chesterbelloc position between extreme laissez faire and socialism, the articles argued for the creation of a "Distributist or Proprietary State," which would preserve human freedom while making possible a more equitable distribution of the ownership of the means of production. "This is the kind of State we should and could have in California. Unless it is worked for, some messy substitute will be foisted on us."[57]

The articles appear to have evoked little response, one pastor calling the newspaper to complain that the articles were "somewhat long and a bit heavy for people who have not had the advantage of higher education." Another priest commented that people without property were unlikely to be convinced by the arguments presented: they would vote for candidates who promise "that if they are elected, the wealth of the rich will be confiscated by taxation and the poor will be taken care of by the State."[58] In a rejoinder, *The Monitor* attacked Sinclair's ideas, without naming him—decrying a bureaucratic state as a diminution of freedom.[59] Only in the paper delivered one week before the general election did *The Monitor* open up a full-throated attack against Sinclair, when it published on its front page an article that bitterly attacked Sinclair, reprinted from *The Western Catholic* of Quincy, Illinois.[60]

Meanwhile two Northern California–based organizations mobilized to hit Catholic voters with a strong anti-Sinclair message. One was the "Non-Sectarian Voters League of California," chaired by the owner of San Francisco's posh Hotel Manx, Harvey Toy. Toy and his colleague, San Francisco attorney Paul Fratessa, generated a pamphlet entitled "So the People May Know That Upton Sinclair is opposed to ALL the established churches." The pamphlet included a promise of "documentary evidence of the mental state of a candidate for governor who may endanger California's social, political and economic security," and consisted of damning quotes from *Profits*.[61] With the pamphlet they also sent a letter to 505 pastors of Catholic Churches in California and an offer to provide additional copies. The initial results of the mailing were so disappointing to Fratessa that he wrote a personal note to Archbishop Edward Hanna's private secretary, John Lally, complaining that he had received requests from only twenty pastors. He pressed Lally to "see if someone can send out a letter from your office, not officially, stating that we were mailing under separate cover a number of these pamphlets and request pastors to have the men of the parish distribute them to those with whom it will do the most good." Fratessa warned, "If the apathy of pastors persists until election day, Sinclair will be our next governor."[62] Lally's reply is not extant.

Another San Francisco–based group, "The Catholic Laymen's League Against Religious Intolerance," also emerged during the campaign, comprising, to a large extent, members of the San Francisco Councils of the Knights of Columbus. The executive secretary , John F. Holland, was a former Grand Knight of California Council 880, headquartered in San Francisco, and had served as a state secretary and treasurer. The organization's letterhead included a lengthy list of prominent San Francisco Catholic laymen, including Judge Matt I. Sullivan, and members of other councils of the Knights of Columbus.[63] Holland denounced Sinclair and ended the standard quotes from *Profits* with this dire warning, "Either you are for Sinclair and his program or you are against it. There is no middle ground. If you are against it, then be militantly against it."[64] It is not known how many people really worked on these committees, how they were funded, and how representative they were of "mainstream" Catholics. Nonetheless, their efforts appeared to be validated by a series of embarrassing repudiations of Sinclair by Catholic leaders whose sympathy and support he had claimed.

## CATHOLIC "DEFECTIONS"

Sinclair attempted to refute Catholic attacks while still keeping the door open to Catholic support. However, while some Catholic spokesmen may have shared some of his critique of capitalism and looked favorably on some of his remedies for the economic crisis, they did not want their names or reputations associated with the candidate. As a result, Sinclair suffered a series of embarrassing rejections at the hands of Catholics whose support he had presumed and trumpeted in *Epic News* as proof that he was not antireligious.

The first "defection" came from the pen of Father Campbell of Ames, Iowa, whose words at the Catholic Action Conference were quoted so approvingly by *Epic News* the previous spring. Splattered prominently over the front page of the *Tidings*, Campbell vigorously denied that he had endorsed Sinclair's candidacy and the assertion reported in *Epic News* that he had characterized Sinclair "to be a man of sound thinking." He accused Sinclair's supporters, who had approached him after his Los Angeles talk, of "wishful thinking" if they sought to construe his comments as support for the Democratic candidate. He asked for the "widest publicity" for his statement, and Dunne readily complied.[65]

Even more damning was the letter of Charles Coughlin to Dunne in response to the editor's September 21,1934 editorial upbraiding the Michigan priest for "supporting" Sinclair. On October 1, 1934, Coughlin wrote a public letter to Dunne disavowing any support for Sinclair and mildly chiding the *Tidings* for believing the Democratic candidate's version of the meeting. Said Coughlin, "Mr. Sinclair called at my home. Naturally, I treated his as any other stranger would be treated with the hospitality which he deserved. I am so ignorant, however, that I have not read any of his books and I am so provincial that I have not even read his *EPIC* program."[66] Coughlin's personal secretary followed up on this denial with a telegram to Joseph O'Connor, State Knights of Columbus Official, which announced, "Father Coughlin does not mix in Michigan politics let alone California politics, consequently any politician using his name is doing so without authorization." This telegram was gleefully reported in the October 9 edition of the *San Francisco Chronicle*.[67]

Struggling to recoup from the Coughlin defection, *Epic News* ran another Catholic piece favorable to the Sinclair movement found in the popular *Church Extension* magazine. The Chicago-based *Extension* was the chief organ of the Catholic Church Extension Society, which sponsored and supported Catholic missionary presence in the "home-missions," that is, in the rural areas of the country. Writing in the October 1934 issue, editor S. A. Baldus noted the controversy stirred up in the California gubernatorial election and wrote a carefully worded article that did not actually endorse Sinclair, but noted the elements of his platform and the opposition it received from "hide-bound Conservatives and Bourbons—this is, those who never learn anything." Baldus suggested that Sinclair's candidacy highlighted the fact that "people are aroused, as never before. They are avid for a change from the old order of things which has brought them so little good and heaped on them an abundance of misery." Although Baldus expressed some hesitation for Sinclair's philosophical approach to these issues, the tone of the article was more positive and open than negative. He concluded his short piece by urging *Extension*'s readers to read some of Sinclair's books.[68] When Baldus began to receive clippings of his words in *Epic News* (and perhaps cancellations to *Extension*) from outraged California readers, he penned a harsh protest to Sinclair, which he copied to the editors of the Catholic newspapers. Lashing out at Sinclair for the "despicable act" of quoting him out of context, Baldus left no doubt as to how he felt about Sinclair and the EPIC program. To California correspondents who inquired about his opinions of EPIC he replied:

> As regards Mr. Sinclair's platform, his campaign pledges and promises, I think they are simply crazy. If I were a resident of the State of California, not only would I vote against Mr. Sinclair, but I would work for his defeat. As I see it— it would be a calamity if he were elected; and a catastrophe would result if he attempted to carry out his absurd Utopian schemes.[69]

Sinclair kept up his efforts to woo Catholics to the bitter end, announcing in late October the addition of a "Father Philip" to "the Democratic forces seeking to elect Upton Sinclair." *Epic News* reported on the padre, whose last name was not given, "Father Philip asserts that Upton Sinclair's Christianity is beyond question as Sinclair proposes to make the Fatherhood of God and the Brotherhood of Man a reality in the modern world."[70] These efforts were in vain, for as J. F. T. O'Connor reported to Marvin McIntyre in the White House, "he has opposing him practically the United Protestant and Catholic Churches, as well as most of the Jewish people."[71]

## CONCLUSION

O'Connor's prognostication of defeat came true. Sinclair lost the election by a vote of 1,138,620 (48.7%) to 879,537 (37.6%), and 320,519 (13.7%) for Haight. Commentators noted the relative close finish of the election when one took into account the power of the collective forces arrayed against him.

Was the attack campaign of both secular and Catholic forces successful in contributing to Sinclair's defeat? Without a doubt. It is fair to assume that the pamphlets and press reports of Sinclair's *Profits* crystallized opposition to him and even changed the minds of those who voted for him in the primary. Sinclair himself noted this anecdotally in his postmortem of the election, *I Candidate for Governor, and How I Got Licked* in which he relates a conversation of Franklin Hichborn, a well-known investigative journalist, with two Portuguese fishermen. "They had registered Democratic, and voted for me in the primary," Sinclair notes, "but were going to vote for Merriam in the finals. 'They say that if we vote for Sinclair, the Virgin will be angry.' "[72] Other Catholics, like San Franciscan Florence Bickmore, were less pious. As she wrote to her archbishop, "Mr. Sinclair is not the proper party to elect to office."[73] In San Francisco County, Sinclair lost decisively winning only 86,764 votes to 112,778 for Merriam and 21,352 for Haight.

In Los Angeles County, Sinclair's electoral base, the votes gave Merriam 406,617 to 362,749 for Sinclair and 87,969 for Haight. Here Sinclair's earlier strength seemed to have held, suggesting that his supporters in the primary had not withered even among Catholics. Again, continued Catholic support for Sinclair in the general election is suggested by the editorials written by Dunne and Henry after the election. The *Tidings* resisted any temptation to crow over Sinclair's defeat (a considerable achievement when one notes Dunne's sarcasm in certain editorial matters) and even attempted to calm passions in its postmortems on the tumultuous and frenetic campaign. Dunne shifted gears and scorned those who tagged Sinclair's devotees as "communists": "Would it not be better if it were taken for granted that those who differ from us have the interest of their country equally at heart, and then fight out the difference cleanly? As it is, people persist in the foolish and harmful practice of branding all those who differ from them as Communists."[74] Henry opined, "Mr. Sinclair was not defeated upon the merits of his economic program alone. He might even have withstood the opposition to his record as a Socialist and a radical, but his books, especially those on religion, turned the tables against him."[75]

Cantwell was relieved. Writing to a priest friend back in Ireland, he said, "Mr. Upton Sinclair, who made his money writing filthy things about religion in general, was running for Governor of the State of California. Fortunately, he was beaten."[76] Yet even though the candidate was defeated, he left in his wake a rejuvenated California Democratic party that would capture the governor's chair four years later and produce a new, more liberal force in California politics that would have a decisive influence on the state. California would grow dramatically in the years ahead and its local politics would take on a greater national significance. The Catholic Church would grow in numbers and institutional visibility as well, especially after World War II. Symbolically, the archbishop of Los Angeles would be given a cardinal's hat in 1953, and the archdiocese he headed would one day become the largest in the United States. Catholic Californians would begin to take advantage of their swelling numbers by pressing ballot initiatives in the 1950s that removed taxation from private schools—a victory that had eluded them for years. The 1934 gubernatorial election may have been one step along the way in this process of political maturation. Perhaps there is some significance to the fact that a Catholic has sat in the California's governor chair since 1999.

## NOTES

1. John J. Cantwell to John J. Mitty, September 16, 1936, Archives of the Archdiocese of Los Angeles [hereafter AALA].
2. The most recent work about the campaign is Greg Mitchell, *The Campaign of the Century: Upton Sinclair's Race for Governor of California and the Birth of*

*Media Politics* (New York: Random House, 1992). Campbell writes a day-by-day account of the campaign integrating the details of the election with biographical and other material so as to give a rather richly detailed background to all the events. More straightforward accounts of the campaign include the following: Charles E. Larsen, "The EPIC Campaign of 1934," *Pacific Historical Review* 27 (May 1958): 127–147; Donald L. Singer, "Upton Sinclair and the California Gubernatorial Campaign of 1934," *Southern California Quarterly* 56 (Winter 1974): 375–406; Richard Antognini, "The Role of A. P. Giannini in the 1934 California Gubernatorial Election," *Southern California Quarterly* (Spring 1975): 53–86; Leonard Leader, "Upton Sinclair's EPIC Switch: A Dilemma for American Socialists," *Southern California Quarterly*, 62 (Winter 1980): 361–385; Fay M. Blake and H. Morton Newman, "Upton Sinclair's EPIC Campaign," *California History* 63 (Fall 1984): 305–312; George G. Rising, "An Epic Campaign: Upton Sinclair's California Gubernatorial Campaign," *Southern California Quarterly* 79 (Spring 1997): 101–124. See also Michael P. Rogin and John L. Shover, *Political Change in California: Critical Elections and Social Movements, 1890–1966* (Westport, CT: Greenwood Publishing, 1970), pp. 112–152; R. D. Delmatier, C. F. McIntosh, E. G. Waters, *The Rumble of California Politics, 1848–1970* (New York: John Wiley & Sons, 1970), pp. 272–281.

3. Alan Brinkley, *Voices of Protest: Huey Long, Father Coughlin and the Great Depression* (New York: Alfred Knopf, 1982).

4. Two representative works highlighting the West and the Roosevelt administration are Richard Lowitt, *The New Deal and the West* (Bloomington: Indiana University Press, 1984) and Thomas Joseph Sitton, "Urban Politics and Reform in New Deal Los Angeles: The Recall of Mayor Frank L. Shaw" (unpublished Ph.D. dissertation, University of California Riverside, 1983).

5. Helpful biographies of Sinclair are John Yoder's *Upton Sinclair* (New York: Frederick Ungar, 1975); Leon Harris, *Upton Sinclair, American Rebel* (New York: Thomas Y. Crowell, 1975); William Bloodworth, Jr., *Upton Sinclair* (Boston: Twayne, 1977); and Dieter Hermes, ed., *Upton Sinclair: Literature and Social Reform* (New York: Peter Lang, 1990).

6. Kevin Starr's colorful account of Sinclair's lifestyle and the 1934 campaign can be found in *Endangered Dreams: The Great Depression in California* (New York: Oxford University Press, 1996), pp. 121–128; 137–155.

7. James J. Rawls and Walton Bean, *California: An Interpretative History* (6th ed.) (San Francisco: McGraw Hill, 1993), p. 308. See also William H. Mullins, *The Depression on the Urban West Coast, 1929–1933* (Bloomington: Indiana University Press, 1991) for a discussion of conditions in San Francisco and Los Angeles and *The Great Depression and the West*, a special issue of the *Journal of the West* 24 (October 1985).

8. John Kagel, "The Day the City Stopped," *California History* 63 (Summer 1984): 212–223. See also, Frederic Clair Chiles, *War on the Waterfront*, (unpublished Ph.D. dissertation, University of California, Santa Barbara, 1981).

9. Rawls and Walton, *California*, p. 313.

10. Sinclair's part in reenergizing the moribund California Democratic Party is attested to by Rogin and Shover, *Political Change*, pp. 124 ff. See also Delmatier et al., *The Rumble*, pp. 230 ff.

11. J. F. T. O'Connor Diary, August 29, 1934, microfilm, Bancroft Library, University of California, Berkeley. For additional information about O'Connor, see Alice Jane Johnson, *The Public Career of J. F. T. O'Connor* (unpublished M.A. thesis, University of North Dakota, 1956).

12. McClatchy, who controlled papers in Sacramento, Fresno, and Modesto, exercised enormous clout in the Central Valley and was not initially disposed to support Haight. He wrote to his friend Franklin Hichborn regarding the election, "You state that it looks now as though Merriam would receive the Republican nomination and Sinclair the Democratic, and that the only loophole would be to support Haight. I thought so at one time too; but I have changed my mind when I found out that Haight is really the protege of that notorious scamp, the Rev. Robert Shuler [a strong Prohibitionist whom McClatchy opposed] ... Now I will not support any Shuler alias. If Merriam and Sinclair receive the nominations, I think I will have the McClatchy newspapers editorialize principally upon the glorious California weather." McClatchy to Hichborn, July 24, 1934, Franklin Hichborn Papers, Special Collections, University of California, Los Angeles. McClatchy later changed his mind and many of Haight's votes came from the coverage area of the McClatchy papers.

13. The California press was universally hostile to Sinclair. The *Los Angeles Times*, which Sinclair had attacked for years, was the candidate's chief antagonist. In the north, Michael deYoung's *San Francisco Chronicle* and William Randolph Hearst's *San Francisco Examiner* were bitter foes. As noted previously, the powerful McClatchy newspapers dismissed Sinclair and, refusing to support Merriam, threw their support behind Progressive Roger Haight who remained in the race. Movie studios, especially Republican Louis Mayer, spared no expense in attacking the Democratic candidate, even to the filming of staged "people on the street" interviews with hired Hollywood actors both denouncing Sinclair, or speaking in fake Russian accents suggesting similarities between the Soviet system and EPIC. A political consulting firm under journalist Clem Whitaker, established in 1933, was engaged by George Hatfield, Republican candidate for lieutenant governor. With the help of Leone Baxter, the group formed an association called the "California League against Sinclairism," which spearheaded a campaign, especially in the north, to attack Sinclair by assiduously combing through his writings and plucking out passages that were calculated to offend and alarm. The League pumped out hundreds of anti-Sinclair materials, which were in pamphlet form or editorials that local presses gladly inserted.

Yet another anti-Sinclair organization developed under the auspices of C. C. Teague, one of the state's wealthiest farmers, who helped to bankroll "United for California" an anti-Sinclair group to promote a campaign in print and on radio. Working with "United" was the West coast office of the Lord and Thomas Advertising firm. Each of these groups tarred Sinclair as a dangerous radical, a "menace" and as a force inimical to the values and standards of Californians. This approach depicted him as a wild-eyed radical that threatened to undermine the capitalist system and an enemy of every other feature of American life and culture—including and especially religion.

14. Thomas was pastor of the Metropolitan Federated Church in Los Angeles. A copy of his widely circulated *The Unmasking of Upton Sinclair* can be found in OF, File 1165, "Sinclair, Upton," Franklin D. Roosevelt Papers, Franklin D. Roosevelt Library, Hyde Park, New York [hereafter FDRL].

15. "Churchmen Aid Merriam," *Los Angeles Times*, November 2, 1934; "Church Rally Urges Defeat of Sinclair," *Los Angeles Evening Herald and Express*, November 3, 1934. Representatives of all the chief religious groups were represented. Among the luminaries were Martin Luther Thomas, who delivered the main address, and Aimee Semple McPherson, who staged a pageant called "America Adrift" or "The Enemy Within." Representing the Catholics was layman Joseph Scott.

16. George Creel to James Farley, September 21, 1934, Franklin D. Roosevelt Paper, PPP 2346. Creel apparently had indulged in a bit of Catholic-bashing in his own earlier writings—a fact gleefully exploited by one of his other Democratic rivals, Justus Wardell, who repeated them in a letter to every priest and mother superior in the state. See James E. Waddell to Louis McHenry Howe, June 14, 1934, OF 300, California, T-W, Democratic National Committee, 1933–45, PDRL.

17. James J. Rawls, "The California Mission as Symbol and Myth," *California History* 71 (Fall 1992): 343–360; 449–451.

18. A random sample of Catholic office holders of note in California history include Governors Peter Burnett, John G. Downey, and Edmund G. Brown (Senior and Junior) along with U.S. Senators David Broderick, Stephen Mallory White, and James Duvall Phelan. John Francis Neylan was head of the powerful Board of Control under Progressive Governor Hiram Johnson, and San Francisco had "Blind Boss" Chris Buckley as well as Mayors Eugene Schmitz and Joseph Alioto.

19. Douglas Firth Anderson notes the powerful influence of Catholicism in the Bay Area by noting the marginalized status of mainline Protestantism. Douglas Firth Anderson, " 'We Have Here a Different Civilization': Protestant Identity in the San Francisco Bay Area, 1906–1909," *Western Historical Quarterly* 23 (May 1992): 199–221.

20. For Yorke's career see Joseph Brusher, *Consecrated Thunderbolt: Father Yorke of San Francisco* (Hawthorne, N.J.: Joseph F. Wagner, 1973).

21. For the displacement of Los Angeles' Catholic community see Michael E. Engh, S.J., *Frontier Faiths: Church, Temple, and Synagogue in Los Angeles, 1846–1888* (Albuquerque: University of New Mexico Press, 1992), pp. 165–186.

22. "Commentaries," *The Tidings*, November 9, 1934.

23. Here the difficulties in pinning down the depth of the individual's Catholic identity emerge as well. Phelan was a generous benefactor of the church, but somewhat indifferent about his other religious duties. Scott by contrast

was very devout and active in a number of Catholic organizations. See James Walsh and Timothy J. O'Keefe, *James Duval Phelan and Villa Montalvo*, (Saratoga: Villa Montalvo Association, 1993), p. 176 and G. Patrick Ziemann, "Joseph Scott, President of the Board of Education in the City of Los Angeles, 1907–1912" (unpublished M.A. thesis, Mount St. Marys College, 1977).

24. Issues of concern to California Catholics involved matters that touched many of their social welfare and educational institutions. Catholics appeared to have a very limited voice in shaping debate on education, orphanages, hospital regulations, and charity work—all matters in which they had vital interests because of their involvement. This conclusion is drawn from an examination of the political activity of the priest involved in charity work in the Archdiocese of Los Angeles, Monsignor Thomas Dwyer, and, as well, the correspondence of Bishop Robert Armstrong with San Francisco Archbishops Edward Hanna and John J. Mitty. Armstrong, as the bishop of Sacramento was often queried by legislators and other state bureaucrats about Catholic concerns and felt reluctant to commit on some issues since he could only speak for himself and not his brother bishops. Many legislative matters were handled on an ad hoc basis by the San Francisco diocesan attorney, Garrett McEnerney. Eventually, the Catholic dioceses would come together to agree on a more coordinated and vigorous lobbying effort.

25. Mark J. Hurley, "Church–State Relationships in Education in California," (Ph.D. dissertation, The Catholic University of America, 1948), p. 120.

26. Details related to Proposition 4, the effort to repeal taxation on schools are in Hurley, "Church–State Relationships," pp. 119–133.

27. Rogin and Shover, *Political Change*, pp. 124–141.

28. "Commentaries," *The Tidings*, November 9, 1934.

29. "El Rodeo," *The Tidings*, October 5, 1934.

30. Rose A. Guillemet to Edward Hanna, October 25, 1934, Archives of the Archdiocese of San Francisco (hereafter AASF).

31. John Sullivan to Edward Hanna, October 21, 1934, AASF.

32. Carey Mc Williams, "Upton Sinclair and His E.P.I.C.," *New Republic* 80 (August 22, 1934): 39–41.

33. "They Call Me Carpenter," *Epic News*, October 1, 1934.

34. "Catholic Action Group Hits Greed," *Epic News*, May 1934.

35. "Wealthy Few Enslave State, Says Pope Pius," *Epic News*, May 28, 1934.

36. "The Parish Credit Union," *The Tidings*, May 11, 1934.

37. "Expected Attacks on Epic Begin," *Epic News*, June 4, 1934.

38. Upton Sinclair, *The Profits of Religion* (taken from Internet www.infidels.org, "Slave Regina," Library: Historical Documents).

39. Ibid., "God's Armor."

40. Ibid., "God's Armor."

41. Ibid., "Holy History."

42. The full text of the prayer can be found in "The Week," *The New Republic* 80 (November 7, 1934): 350–351.

43. Charles Tull, *Father Coughlin and the New Deal* (New York: Syracuse University Press, 1965), pp. 59–60.

44. "Sinclair Diary Records Trip East," *Epic News*, September 17, 1934.
45. Cantwell's biographer characterizes him as "a man of progressive but restrained views on most public issues. Whenever possible he avoided and advised others to avoid the 'tendency to extremes.'" Francis J. Weber, *Century of Fulfillment: The Roman Catholic Church in Southern California, 1840–1947* (Mission Hills, California: The Archival Center, 1990), p. 474. It is important to note that Cantwell considered J. F. T. O'Connor, FDR's Comptroller of the Currency and California political consultant, to be a good friend. O'Connor was a devout Catholic and a member of the Knights of Columbus. He was occasionally entertained at the episcopal mansion in Los Angeles and from time to time interceded for Catholic issues within the administration. For example, he assisted Bishop Michael Gallagher of Detroit, Father Coughlin's Ordinary, with some financial problems with the First National Bank of Detroit. He also met with the Radio Priest and discussed currency issues. O'Connor's diary records in copious detail various meetings and daily affairs, including his regular attendance at Mass. There is no evidence that he was in direct contact with Cantwell during the 1934 election. For Cantwell's relationship with O'Connor and O'Connor's intercession on behalf of the Diocese of Detroit, see, J. F. T. O'Connor to Cantwell, April 24, 1933, Letter 6687, AALA; John M. Doyle to Cantwell, November 19, 1934, Letter 6825, AALA. O'Connor's diary records two meetings with Coughlin in October 1934, held to listen to the priest's complaints about the Treasury Department. The second meeting included Jesse Jones, head of the Reconstruction Finance Corporation, with whom Coughlin had some disagreements. See citations for October 9 and 10, 1934, O'Connor Diary, microfilm, Bancroft Library, University of California.
46. Sister Mary St. Joseph Feickert, S.N.D., "The History of the Tidings, Official Organ of the Archdiocese of Los Angeles, 1895–1945" (unpublished M.A. thesis, Catholic University of America, June 1951) copy in AALA.
47. "El Rodeo," *The Tidings*, September 21, 1934.
48. "El Rodeo," *The Tidings*, October 26, 1934.
49. "El Rodeo," *The Tidings*, September 21, 1934.
50. "Priest Scouts Sinclair Menace," *Epic News*, October 1, 1934.
51. "Commentaries," *The Tidings*, September 7, 1934.
52. The Sinclair columns in the *Los Angeles Times* devoted to attacking him on the issue of religion were, "Sinclair and Religion" (September 23); "Sinclair on Christianity" (September 27); "Sinclair Parodies Christ" (September 30); "Sinclair on Catholics" (October 1); "Sinclair on the Knights of Columbus" (October 4); "Fools, Knaves, Charlatans" (October 5); "Sinclair on Christ" (October 7); "Sinclair and the Clergy" (October 14); "Sinclair on Mormonism" (October 31); "The Church and Prohibition" (November 2).
53. A copy of the pamphlet can be found in OF 1165, "Sinclair, Upton," FDRL.
54. Hanna had ties to the Roosevelt White House and had been the president's choice to chair the mediation board of the Longshoreman's Strike. His general approach to social matters was similar to Cantwell's and most Catholic prelates of his time, namely he held no brief for capitalist abuses and believed and

spoke about the key elements of papal social teaching. There is no evidence of contact with administration officials during this period, but no doubt he was approached as his counterpart in Los Angeles to speak out against Sinclair. However, special circumstances in San Francisco make it difficult to state with absolute certainty what "official" thinking was on the Sinclair matter. Archbishop Hanna was apparently in failing mental and physical health during these days. Since 1932, he had been served by a coadjutor bishop, John Joseph Mitty, who had been transferred to San Francisco in 1932. Mitty took no stand on the matter that could be found in archival sources.

55. The dates of these issues are *The Monitor*, August 11, 1934; August 18, 1934; August 25, 1934; September 1, 1934; September 8, 1934; September 15, 1934.

56. "The Restoration of Property by Hilaire Belloc," *The Monitor*, August 11, 1934.

57. "Belloc and the Distributists," *The Monitor*, August 14, 1934.

58. "The Coming Election," *The Monitor*, August 25, 1934.

59. "The Coming Election," *The Monitor*, August 25, 1934.

60. "Editor of Catholic Paper Warns California Against Voting for Upton Sinclair," *The Monitor*, November 3, 1934.

61. A copy of this pamphlet is found in OF File 1165, "Sinclair, Upton," FDRL.

62. Paul Fratessa to John Lally, September 26, 1934, Chancery Files, Folder "S" 1934, AASF.

63. Many of these names were included in the officer member list found in Peter Conmy, *Seventy Years of Service: History of the Knights of Columbus in California, 1902–1972* (Los Angeles: California State Council of the Knights of Columbus, 1972), pp. 295–296; 301–303.

64. Copy of this pamphlet in OF 1165, "Sinclair, Upton," FDRL.

65. "Fr. Campbell Denies He Endorsed Upton Sinclair," *The Tidings*, September 28, 1934.

66. Dunne reprinted this letter in its entirety in "El Rodeo," *The Tidings*, October 12, 1934.

67. "Sinclair Aid Repudiated by Coughlin," *San Francisco Chronicle*, October 9, 1934.

68. "Straws in the Wind," *Extension Magazine* 29 (October 1934): 16–17.

69. S. A. Baldus to Gordon O'Neill, October 22, 1934, "S" File, 1934, AASF.

70. "Catholic Priest Joins Campaign," *Epic News*, October 22, 1934.

71. J. F. T. O'Connor to Marvin McIntyre, November 2, 1934, OF 300, California 0, 1933–37, FDRL.

72. Upton Sinclair, *I, Candidate for Governor, and How I Got Licked* (Berkeley: University of California Press, 1934, 1994 repr.), p. 70.

73. Florence Bickmore to Edward Hanna, October 29, 1934, AASF.

74. "El Rodeo," *The Tidings*, November 9, 1934.

75. "Commentaries," *The Tidings*, November 9, 1934.

76. Cantwell to Rt. Rev. Msgr. Welch, December 4, 1934, Cantwell Papers, Letter #7047, AALA.

# CHAPTER 6

# THE PRACTICAL PERSONALISM OF THE CATHOLIC WORKER AND THE PRAGMATIC POLICIES OF THE NEW DEAL

FRANCIS SICIUS

HISTORIANS HAVE LITTLE DIFFICULTY DRAWING CONTRASTS between the New Deal and the Catholic Worker movement. The Catholic Worker embraced an anarchistic, decentralist, and anticapitalist philosophy, which clearly stood as a contradiction to the New Deal effort to preserve liberal democratic and capitalist values. Both these movements, however, are more complex than the generalizations made about them, and closer investigation reveals that they shared much in common, if not in results, at least in motivation and philosophy.

Comparisons begin with the men who were the architects of their respective movements. Franklin Roosevelt and Peter Maurin were contemporaries, born within four years of each other. One was a patrician from upstate New York, the other a peasant from southern France, yet they shared many similarities. They both came from family traditions and values that had a great influence on their personality and intellect. Although they both spent the major part of their lives in urban areas, they each believed that the land could serve as a catalyst for social and economic change. Both men preferred the spoken to the written word, and each had an ability to put complex economic issues into very simple and understandable language. In an early fireside chat, for example, while discussing the consequences of declining profits for workers, Roosevelt's words appear amazingly similar to those in one of Maurin's *Easy Essays*. Roosevelt explained to his listeners:

> If all our people have work and fair wages and fair profits, they can buy the products of their neighbors and business is good. But... if you take away the profits of half of them, business is only half as good. It doesn't help much if the fortunate half is very prosperous. The best way is for everybody to be reasonably prosperous.[1]

Peter Maurin, in a variation of the same theme, wrote:

> To enable the poor to buy
> is to improve the market.
> To improve the market is
> to help business.
> To help business is
> to reduce unemployment.[2]

Maurin and Roosevelt also shared a strong sense of social justice and both believed that the depression was not simply a period of market adjustment but that there was something intrinsically wrong with the social and economic order of things. Both wanted to change the direction in which the world was going; one entered politics, the other chose to be a teacher and agitator, and both acted out their chosen roles on the stage provided by the Great Depression.

The decade of the 1930s provided one of the most fecund eras of social thought the country has ever experienced. One product of this fertility was the Catholic Worker Movement, which based its ideals on the thoughts and teaching of Peter Maurin. Maurin was born in 1877 in the small farming village of Oultet, near the town of Mende in the Languedoc region of Southern France. Maurin liked to say he had peasant roots, but actually the term "peasant" had lost its original meaning by the time Maurin was born. His family had, for centuries, owned the land, which they continue to work.[3]

Maurin passed his early years influenced by the reforms of the Third Republic launched in 1874. Laws passed by the new government allowed him to attend free of charge the new school, St. Privat, run by the Christian Brothers in Mende. He also came under the influence of the worker priests and other Catholic social movements that emerged in this era in response to accusations made by the Third Republic that the Church had abandoned its commitment to social justice.[4] At the age of 15, Maurin entered the novitiate of the Christian Brothers where he spent five years. During this experience he cultivated his pedagogical instincts, which would characterize his later life.

After spending the next few years as a Christian Brother teaching in a number of different cities, he left and began to work for Christian social movements among the poor of Paris. There he came to know Charles Peguy and other Catholic intellectuals of that era. Another person familiar to Maurin at the time was Marc Sangnier who founded a reform movement and newspaper, which called for an economic restructuring, based on the social teachings of the Church.[5] While Maurin labored among the poor in Paris the economy of France deteriorated. Unwilling to become one of the destitute that he served, Maurin accepted the invitation extended by the Canadian government to all able bodied and landless young men throughout Europe to come to the new Province of Saskatchewan and homestead. In 1909, at the age of 32, Peter Maurin found himself on the land once again. Unfortunately, he chose what historians have described as the hardest of economic times for farmers in this area, and his experiment on the land ended in disaster.[6]

Penniless and once again landless, Maurin took to the rails, crossed the border into the United States, and for the next 25 years, he worked as a laborer, sometimes achieving the comfort of the lower middle class, sometimes living in abject poverty using an empty coal bin for a bedroom. Finally in 1927, at the age of 50, as a result of a lifetime of reading, working in various levels of the economy, and reflecting on the meaning of those experiences, Maurin went through a great intellectual and spiritual transformation. He had been living a rather comfortable life as a translator and tutor in upstate New York, when suddenly, he abandoned this life, and began working on a farm converted into a Catholic boys camp near Mt. Tremper. He spent his free time reading, writing out his thoughts, and traveling to New York City, where he began his one-man revolution to transform society.

During his intellectual development in the 1920s, Maurin began to adapt many of the ideas of the French Personalists who derived their concepts from an earlier generation of French Catholic thinkers who were also known by Maurin. Because he often cited the French Personalists, Maurin is credited with introducing this intellectual tradition into the United States. Although this characterization provides a neat place for him in the flow and order of historic facts, it does not clarify the depth of Maurin's thinking. In Europe, Personalism remained an abstraction, but Maurin's plan, at least in his mind, was a practical approach to problems of unemployment and social inequity created by modern capitalism. The "Personalist" label is useful, however, because it provides a means of connecting the thought of Peter Maurin to that of the New Deal.

Personalist influences, of varying degrees, existed in America in the 1930s, and they contributed, to some degree, to a number of New Deal policies.[7] Yet historians rarely include Personalism in the orbit of modern American ideas.[8] Despite the disinterest of most historians, the Personalist idea, as an expression of disdain for political and economic structures as they were evolving in the early twentieth century, had a significant following. Those who adopted Personalism saw it as a protest against all materialist philosophies, including fascism, communism, and bourgeois capitalism. Personalists did not advocate supremacy of the spiritual over the material (despite accusations to the contrary, they did not want to return to the Middle Ages), but rather they sought to bring these two dimensions of human personality into greater harmony. They admitted that great material progress had been made in the nineteenth and early twentieth century, but at a spiritual cost: destroying social harmony, setting poor against rich, worker against capitalist, and nation against nation. Many early fascists also condemned the rise of destructive competition in the new age of materialism, but fascists sought to resurrect what they called "spiritual values" in either the nation state or, as in the case of Jose Antonio, a revitalized organizational Church. The guiding social principle of the French Personalists did not exist in the state or in the organizational Church, but rather in the newly emerging Catholic image of the Mystical Body of Christ, a theory elaborated by the German theologian Karl Adam, which became recognized as a Church doctrine in 1943. This doctrine defines the Christian community as members of a single body and reminded them that the actions of one part of the body impact the whole. It was a call to a new human solidarity based on the spirituality of Christ, calling all Christians to an aroused and revitalized social conscience.[9] Personalists believed that a truly just society must proceed from the premise that each person, as a spiritual and material reflection of creation, merits dignity.

In Europe, this idea remained relegated to the salons of intellectuals such as Jacques and Raissa Maritain. In the United States, through the work of Peter Maurin, Personalism took to the streets, and its influence filtered into various arenas of thought, including the New Deal. Although seen as unrealistic by many, Peter Maurin's program seemed to him to be very practical. Personalism did not call for a mass political movement, but rather for individual action. Maurin began his one-man revolution talking wherever he could, from a Rotarian meeting in Upstate New York, to a worker rally in Union square. He also spoke and developed friendships with John Moody, of Moody Investment Corporation, with historian Carlton Hayes of Columbia University, and with others who, from Maurin's perspective, could exert political, economic, or intellectual influence on a badly flawed system. The most significant reference point for Maurin's practical Personalism was the historic Catholic Church. There was a time in the history of the Church, Maurin wrote, when it organized social welfare for the community. For the poor, there were daily meals; for the homeless, there were houses of hospitality. Given the current economic crisis, it was time, Maurin believed, to resurrect this social model. The Church needed to be reminded, Maurin wrote, of its historic role on issues of social justice. For Maurin, it was time for scholars to rediscover the history of the Church so that the social message could become the "dynamite" it was meant to be. He lamented the fact that the Catholic Church had also been swept up in the rush for material prosperity, and in doing so had diminished its commitment to social justice. It was time, he concluded, to "turn parish domes into parish homes."[10]

From 1927 until 1933, Maurin's message was rarely heard by more than the few unemployed workers who listened for entertainment in Union Square or by the random professor or economist whom he happened to buttonhole. Dorothy Day, whom he met in 1932, changed all that. Day, a writer and former socialist turned Catholic, took Maurin's message of Catholic social thought, added her own concerns about the emerging class struggle, and published a paper called the *Catholic Worker*. Within a year, the paper boasted a circulation of 50,000, and Catholic Worker study groups or houses of hospitality flourished in most major cities in the country. What attracted thousands of people to the *Catholic Worker* was not Maurin's sophisticated social analysis nor the prospect of great political success, but rather his attempt to define a philosophy that went beyond the modern materialist synthesis. It called for an end to destructive competition and for a new economic communitarianism based on humanity's shared spirituality. The fascists had appropriated and distorted the idea in Europe, but in the United States, it attracted a number of young intellectuals at the opposite end of the 1930s political spectrum, some of whom would become part of, or at least influence, early New Deal thought.[11]

The myriad of ideas that permeated the White House in the early years of the New Deal shared certain stipulations a priori. First, they had to express a preference for social solidarity over competition; second, they had to work for a fairer distribution of the wealth of the country; and finally, they had to be practical. The New Deal justification for social solidarity emanated from the concept of nation. For Peter Maurin, similar commitments arose from the more universal concept of the Mystical Body of Christ. Although they started from different premises, both groups (Personalists and New Dealers) arrived at similar conclusions.

Like Maurin, Franklin Roosevelt was a pragmatist, and he was willing to experiment with almost any idea that promised to put equity and prosperity back into the economic system. In his quest, he often came surprisingly close to many of Maurin's economic assumptions. Three examples of New Deal theory and practice that come into confluence with Personalist politics are the National Recovery Act (NRA), the Works Progress Administration (WPA), and the Rural Farm Homestead movement.

Although the Catholic Worker movement could not propose a program so grand in scale as the NRA, the spirit that motivated Roosevelt to formulate the NRA gathered a great deal of support from the Catholic Worker philosophy of communitarian Personalism. In his "Forgotten Man" radio address in 1932, Roosevelt pointed out that success in the World War had come from mobilizing the nation's economic and social resources from "bottom to top not top to bottom." Roosevelt pointed out that it was once again time to put faith "in the forgotten man at the bottom of the economic pyramid."[12] This statement was directed specifically against those who still adhered to the trickle-down school of economics, and Roosevelt wanted the people to know that his administration would not follow the same timeworn policies.

Peter Maurin also advocated the "bottom-up" approach to economic rebuilding. In response to New Deal proposals he told the 50,000 readers of the *Catholic Worker*:

> Save Industry is the cry
> Put business on its feet
> and all will be well
> as it was in the past
> We are beginning to learn
> That to put big business on its feet
> does not necessarily put
> the forgotten man on his feet.[13]

Maurin's Personalism led him to the strong belief that a corporate system of labor and management was far superior to an adversarial relationship. "Workers want to co-operate with the businessmen," he maintained, and he believed that there should be associations of Catholic employers as well as employees "indoctrinated with the same doctrine."[14]

Maurin's cooperative vision found substance in Roosevelt's NRA. In a Jefferson Day speech in 1932, as a presidential candidate, Roosevelt declared,

> I plead not for class control but for a true concert of interests. The plans we make for this emergency, if we plan wisely and rest our structure upon a base sufficiently broad, may show the way to a more permanent safeguarding of our social and economic life to the end that we may in a large number avoid the terrible cycle of prosperity crumbling into depression. In this sense I favor economic planning not in this period [of depression] alone but for our needs for a long time to come.[15]

A month later, Roosevelt stated "we are at the threshold of a fundamental change in our popular economic thought. In the future," he predicted, "we are going to think less of the producer and more of the consumer. The millions who are in want will not stand by silently forever while the things to satisfy their needs are in easy reach."[16] These seeds of thought, which germinated during the first campaign, provided a framework for the NRA, after his election.

Roosevelt described the NRA as the most important and far-reaching legislation ever enacted by an American Congress. In his radio address announcing the NRA, he stated that it was not time "to cavil or to question," but rather a "time for patience and understanding and cooperation." Many historians feel that Roosevelt depended on World War I models for this economic recovery plan. The rhetoric is certainly similar, and the appointment of General Hugh Johnson as the leader of NRA also calls for such a conclusion.[17] However, there was a spirit of concern for the person, and a sense of the solidarity of the human community, which could be defined as an active pragmatic Personalism typical of the Catholic Worker movement. Roosevelt himself used Personalist language in Wisconsin in 1934 when he told a crowd that the purpose of the New Deal NRA was to "cement our society rich and poor, manual worker and brain worker, into a voluntary brotherhood of free men standing together, striving together for the common good of all." The *Catholic Worker* quickly picked up on the spirit guiding the NRA. In an article supporting the plan, the paper noted that many have drawn similarities between the NRA and wartime mobilization of industry, but these people, the *Worker* concluded, "are not familiar with Church teachings on modern economic systems."[18]

There were those who became uncomfortable with Roosevelt's rhetoric in defense of the NRA. Many feared that it sounded too much like the experiments in corporate government occurring in Europe.[19] After observing the New Deal experiment in social legislation for a little over a year, the *Nation* magazine concluded, "The New Deal in the United States and the new forms of economic organization in Germany and Italy are merely the latest and most extreme manifestations of a tendency for nations and [people to] demand a larger measure of security than can be provided by a system of free competition."[20] But as the Catholic Personalist Peter Maurin pointed out, concern for the "common good" is a "Catholic doctrine. We don't need a new doctrine [such as fascism]." Maurin wrote, "We need the technique of the first Christians. What was practical for them ought to be practical for us."[21] Concern for the entire human community, and for creating an economy that puts resources and products within economic reach of everyone, existed in the minds of Personalists such as Mounier and their predecessors such as Peguy and Sangnier long before any fascist state existed in Europe. The fact that the fascists had appropriated these Personalist concerns does not make these ideas fascist, and if the New Deal shared anything with fascism, it was the appropriation of Personalist ideas on cooperative use of economic resources. In reaction to similarities being drawn between fascism and Personalism, Emmanuel Mounier, the movement's founder declared, "We denounce fascism [as] a true enemy of . . . spirituality." Mounier pointed out that, in order to bend personal will, fascism used "Pseudo humanism, pseudo spiritualism, and the most ambiguous mystique: the cult of race, the nation or the State, of the will to power . . . in order to control and bend the will of people. In the last analysis," he concluded that fascism represented a new and more destructive phase of materialism.[22]

As provisions of the NRA became clearer, the Personalist *Catholic Worker* told its 50,000 readers that they were becoming "more and more enthusiastic about the NRA." They pointed out that this New Deal Program represented an "effort to arouse people to a cooperative effort in opposition to the old code of competition and unbridled individualism. Never before, the *Catholic Worker* noted, has such an effort been made by government . . . We can only work and pray that the Government will succeed."[23] The *Worker* also warned its readers to be vigilant in protecting the NRA, which, as they pointed out, was "being attacked from all sides," capitalist as well as Communist.[24] And when the Supreme Court nullified the New Deal experiment in cooperative economics, the *Catholic Worker* protested and noted that "the Communist party and big business are jubilant over the finish of the NRA."[25]

Arthur Schlesinger, Jr., a historian of the New Deal, may never have described himself or the president as a Personalist, but he certainly identified those characteristics in NRA legislation. In commenting on its verdict in the court of history, Schlesinger considered the source of NRA suffering to be,

> in part because the people who have written about it have taken the classical model of the competitive market as the baseline from which to offer judgement. This dismissal of NRA has become an historian's and economists cliché. It is no doubt futile to suppose that this verdict can now be altered. Yet NRA was surely neither so rigid nor so ominous an undertaking as has been conventionally depicted. Its ends—economic stabilization and social decency—were necessary and noble.[26]

NRA legislation, which replaced the destructively competitive spirit of raw capitalism with a sense of cooperation, demonstrated an attempt to open a new frontier in American economic planning and thought. Perhaps Schlesinger is correct in his conclusion that the NRA will never be viewed favorably by "objective" history. However, if Schlesinger is also accurate in concluding that the NRA began from the premise that social decency was necessary and noble, then from the Personalist or subjective perspective, the NRA should also be remembered as a bold but unfulfilled experiment in economic planning.

Another example of the confluence of Catholic Worker and New Deal thought was the Four Arts Program. Of the initial $2 billion appropriation for the WPA, designed to provide work for some of the millions of unemployed, $27 million was earmarked for unemployed artists, actors, musicians, and writers. During its existence, the Four Arts Program employed over 40,000 creative artists at its peak.[27] Of course, the bulk of WPA money went to provide basic jobs that could somehow be identified as promoting the public good. However, fixed within the legislation was an attempt to remedy the problem noted by Personalists, that work in a capitalist system had denied the person "his true daily bread: the development of an interior life in the heart of communitarian life." Such a life would initiate aesthetic improvements as well, the Personalists pointed out, and "Art must become once again mixed with the day to day life of everyone."[28]

Programs such as the NRA and the WPA illustrate that within the New Deal there existed a will to move away from the classic models of capitalism toward a more human and Personalist economy. These experiments hint at a confluence of New Deal and Catholic Worker philosophies, but the clearest and most concrete example of harmony between the economic vision of some New Dealers and the Catholic Worker is provided by the New Deal's rural farm legislation. Despite its urban roots, a "Back to the Land Movement" always remained central to the Catholic Worker plan. Peter Maurin did not believe that the industrial capitalist system would ever have the capacity to support the entire workforce, and Franklin Roosevelt agreed with this observation. The president felt that even if the recovery of production reached the peak levels of 1929, there would still be unemployment in the cities.[29] Schlesinger pointed out that Roosevelt wanted to strike a better balance between urban and rural population, and between subsistence farming and parttime factory work. Before his inauguration, Roosevelt spoke privately of putting a million families back on the land and into subsistence farming. During his first months in office, he told Senator George Norris, "I would like . . . a bill which would . . . allow us to spend $25 million this year to put 25,000 families on farms at an average cost of $1,000 a family." He asked Norris to talk it over with some of "our other dreamers" on Capitol Hill. Apparently there were enough "dreamers," since Congress appropriated $25,000,000 for what Senator Bankhead of Alabama called "the model for a new basis of American society."[30]

The New Deal Rural Farm Program also provided the opportunity for direct and documented contact between New Dealers and Catholic Workers. There are a number of clear paths between the two ideas. Columbia University, for example, through their faculty, had a foot in the New Deal and at least a toe in the Catholic Worker movement. The Columbia University faculty formed the core of Roosevelt's Brain Trust and on the

Catholic Worker side, Columbia historian Carlton Hayes knew Peter Maurin and even participated in a number of his roundtable discussions. Parker Thomas Moon, another Columbia professor who had written a book on French Catholic Social Thought, also visited the roundtable discussions of the Catholic Worker movement. The possibilities for cross-fertilization of ideas seem apparent if not specific. The only documents that provide clear evidence of Catholic Worker/New Deal dialogue are a few letters written to the *Worker* from Carl Taylor, a Columbia professor, and also the Chief of the New Deal's Rural Farm Program. In December 1937, Taylor wrote to Peter Maurin and thanked him for an interesting and enjoyable visit to the *Catholic Worker*. He asked Maurin if he could explain "in concrete terms their farming commune experiment," and also for the best book he could recommend on the philosophy of Personalism. After a visit to the *Catholic Worker*, and conversations with its members, Taylor came to the same conclusions as this monograph, that there were many expressions of New Deal economics that had an affinity with the economic thought of the Personalists.[31]

In the precarious economic world of the 1930s, many people dreamed of a new postcapitalist economic structure. It was an environment that allowed practical government bureaucrats to call themselves dreamers, and dreamers such as the Catholic Workers to call themselves realists. Soon after Taylor's visit to the *Catholic Worker*, the era of experimentation and dreaming ended. The terrible and threatening reality of fascism overshadowed all dreams of social economic redemption. The United States, as well as the rest of the world, felt the terrible threat of Adolph Hitler and his Nazis who had appropriated just enough of the idealism of the 1930s to hypnotize an entire generation of people desperately searching for community and economic security. Hitler took these basically good instincts and transmogrified them into the awful German fascist state, which distorted the universality of community into a racist and paranoid fascist state, and promised an economic security based on a world of German masters and Russian slaves. It was clear to most that Hitler's fascist state represented the most horrible threat to civilization in human memory.

Many New Dealers who had been earnestly searching for alternatives to liberal capitalism had to abandon their quest, as it became obvious to them that liberal capitalist democracy, with all its faults, represented the only system that could successfully challenge the Nazi threat. Ideals were tossed aside for a just and necessary struggle. World War II greatly diminished the Personalist impulse in political America. John Cogley, a Catholic Worker radical in the 1930s who turned into a postwar liberal, acknowledged that it was the harsh reality of fascism that brought an end to the idealism of the 1930s.[32] James Farrell has pointed out that Personalism as an idea returned after the war but only on the margins of American thought.[33] Even before the war, the *Catholic Worker* noted that the heady days of radicals entertaining government decision-makers were over. In a front-page editorial in February 1939, the *Catholic Worker* reported that they could no longer support New Deal policies, especially in the area of foreign affairs. "It is a painful duty to criticize one whom we have learned to love for his sense of charity and whom we have learned to respect for the wonderful way in which he handled the internal affairs of the country during its most trying economic years," the article began. It went on to praise Roosevelt for his great courage, but it revealed that a significant break with the *Catholic Worker* had occurred over the belligerent policy the president was following in Europe.

As war became inevitable, Catholic Worker Personalism drew that movement further from the mainstream and into a very narrow passage of pacifism. Taking this path split the movement, and also drove the Worker movement out of its tenuous place on the edge of the mainstream of American political thought. After the war, Personalism, which had reached its most influential political hearing during the early New Deal era, would settle into the fringes of the intellectual tradition in this country.

The era of the 1930s, when Personalists and New Dealers saw common goals and means, remains a tribute to the underlying idealism of government in those days. Personalists supported the early New Deal because they recognized that the government had a concern for the dignity of the person that went beyond political phrase making. It is significant that Roosevelt, in seeking support for the Homestead Act, asked Norris to seek out some fellow "dreamers" for support. The word fits the New Deal era, which if the conclusions of this chapter are correct, might be described as the last time in American history that the humanists outnumbered technicians in government, and the dignity of the person took precedence over the significance of the economic statistics.

## NOTES

1. Rexford Tugwell, *FDR: Architect of an Era* (New York: MacMillan Company, 1967), p. 101.
2. Peter Maurin, *Easy Essays* (New York: Catholic Worker Press, 1975), p. 40.
3. Jean Baptiste Maurin, interview by author, Oultet, France, July 11, 1998.
4. Maurin interview, Arthur Sheehan, *Peter Maurin: Gay Believer* (Garden City N.J.: Doubleday, 1959), p. 76.
5. Sheehan, p. 61.
6. Ibid., p. 78; W. A. Mackintosh, *Prairie Settlement: The Geographic Setting* (Toronto: Macmillan and Co. Ltd., 1934), p. 176.

7. James J. Farrell, *The Spirit of the Sixties: The Making of Post War Radicalism* (New York: Routledge Press, 1997), pp. 9–13.
8. John Hellman, *Emmanuel Mounier and the New Catholic Left 1930–1950* (Toronto: University of Toronto Press, 1981), pp. 5–9.
9. Ibid., p. 7.
10. Peter Maurin, *Catholic Radicalism: Phrased Essays for the Green Revolution* (New York: Catholic Worker Books), p. 6.
11. One example is Edgar Brightman who while a student at Boston University in the 1930s developed a comprehensive Personalist philosophy. In his book *Moral Laws* (1933) Brightman "tried to develop a social ethics of personalism." Brightman became a conscientious objector in World War II, and after the war it was his presence at Boston University that convinced the young Martin Luther King, Jr., to attend classes there. See: Farrell, p. 13.
12. Samuel Rosenman, ed., *The Public Papers and Addressees of Franklin D. Roosevelt* (New York: Random House; MacMillan; Harper; 1938–50), I, 631–632.
13. Maurin, *Easy Essays*, p. 26.
14. Maurin, *Easy Essays*, p. 71.
15. Rosenman, I, pp. 631–632.
16. Ibid., I, pp. 645–646.
17. Arthur Ekirch, *Ideologes and Utopias: The Impact of the New Deal on American Thought* (Chicago: Quadrangle Books, 1969), pp. 98–99; and Arthur Schlesinger, *The Coming of the New Deal* (Boston: Houghton Mifflin Co., 1959), p. 176.
18. *The Catholic Worker*, September 1933, p. 1.
19. Ekirch, *Ideologes and Utopias*, p. 178.
20. *The Nation*, August 1934.
21. Maurin, *Easy Essays*, p. 35.
22. Hellman, *Emmanuel Mounier*, p. 75.
23. *Catholic Worker*, September 1933, p. 1.
24. Ibid., November 1933, p. 1.
25. Ibid., April 1935, p. 1.
26. Schlesinger, *The Coming of the New Deal*, p. 175.
27. Ekirch, *Ideologes and Utopias*, p. 152.
28. Hellman, *Emmanuel Mounier*, p. 82.
29. Schlesinger, *The Coming of the New Deal*, pp. 362–363.
30. Ibid., p. 363.
31. *Catholic Worker*, January 1938, p. 8; Dorothy Day, *Biography of Peter Maurin*, pp. 111–116 (unpublished manuscript, St. Thomas University Archives, William Miller/Catholic Worker papers).
32. John Cogley, "Pacifists," *Commonweal* 59 (October 23, 1953): p. 54.
33. Farrell, *The Spirit of the Sixties*, p. 14.

CHAPTER 7

# FATHER FRANCIS E. LUCEY AND PRESIDENT FRANKLIN D. ROOSEVELT

## A NEO-SCHOLASTIC LEGAL SCHOLAR'S AMBIVALENT REACTION TO THE NEW DEAL

AJAY K. MEHROTRA

### INTRODUCTION

ON SUNDAY JANUARY 31, 1960, THE REVEREND FRANCIS E. LUCEY, regent of the Georgetown University Law Center, delivered the Red Mass Sermon at St. Matthew's Cathedral in Washington D.C.[1] Speaking before a full audience of public officials that included Vice President Richard Nixon, Chief Justice Earl Warren, and Associate Justices William Brennan and John Harlan, as well as prominent lawyers and members of the legal academy,[2] Lucey celebrated the annual opening of the judicial year by discussing the importance of the "Catholic Natural Law Doctrine."[3] One month earlier, Professor John Herman Randall, Jr., the Woodbridge Professor of Philosophy at Columbia University, had asked in a letter written to *The New York Times* just what Catholic thinkers meant by the "natural law" of morality.* Responding to Professor Randall's inquiry, Lucey outlined his view of law and morality in his sermon, entitled "The Catholic Natural Law Doctrine and Its Relation to Civil Law."[4]

For Lucey and other Catholic lawyers, Scholastic natural law could not be divorced from civil law. With the teachings of St. Thomas Aquinas reverberating in his mind, Lucey declared in his sermon that society "quite easily recognizes fundamental principles that are easy references from the principle of 'do good and avoid evil.' "[5] Indeed, to the Catholic natural law philosopher these fundamental principles were an innate part of the human condition. "They are so intimately connected with the perfection of man's nature," preached Lucey, "that they are said to be universal, perpetual and immutable. While man remains man, they will universally apply."[6] Armed with this backdrop of fundamental, universal principles, humankind could, with the aid of reason, develop a just and fair civil law. "In developing a body of ethical law or even civil law," proclaimed Lucey, "the Catholic natural law philosopher is always using reason against a particular framework of reference, namely ... the spiritual nature of man's soul, its creation by God, its capacity to know, freedom of the will, the duty to act for the perfection of his being, all those elements which constitute the dignity, equality and independence of the individual."[7]

For Lucey, such talk about the absolute nature of human dignity, equality, and independence was not just an exercise in philosophical pontification, but the bedrock upon which this nation had been founded.

> We here in America sometimes forget that our United States owes its existence to a rebellion against a constituted but tyrannical authority and its oppressive legislation. We at times forget that those who brought this great civil society into existence justified their rebellion on a higher law, natural law. "God-given inalienable rights" in the Declaration of Independence was not just a pious ejaculation. The founding fathers fought and suffered for the higher law. Many of their relatives and compatriots died for it.[8]

As a Catholic lawyer preaching before a bar and bench dominated by Protestants, Lucey's reference to the Founding Fathers and the American tradition of natural law was tinctured with the psychological and social concerns of American Catholicism. Long regarded as outsiders to the "American" way of life, Roman Catholics in the United States often searched for signs of ethnic legitimacy. To assuage Catholic concerns of minority alienation, and to rebut the anti-Catholic sentiments of the Protestant majority, Thomistic scholars like Lucey did not hesitate in tracing the ancestry of American democracy back to the natural law tradition or in identifying contemporary American political policies with Scholastic teaching.

To many American Catholics, especially elite spokesmen like Lucey, the 1932 presidential election of Franklin D. Roosevelt and the subsequent socioeconomic reforms of the New Deal marked the beginning of a new era of American Catholicism. For the New Deal represented not only a social and economic reform movement that corresponded to the teachings of the papal encyclicals, it was seen, more importantly, as an opportunity for American Catholics to contribute to the political dialogue that would shape the future of American society.

Yet, despite having a common origin in the official teachings of the Church, Catholic social thought during the New Deal years varied widely.[9] At one end, there were those liberal-minded Catholic leaders such as John A. Ryan and Cardinal George Mundelein, who supplied unwavering support for Roosevelt's programs. At the other end were impatient and vitriolic critics such as Father Coughlin and Al Smith, who viewed New Deal policies as a betrayal of Catholic doctrine. The middle ground between these two antino-mies was occupied by progressive yet cautious Catholic thinkers such as Lucey who sought to link Catholic notions of social justice and charity with New Deal legislation while preserving the sanctity of natural law precepts against the moral skepticism and empirical positivism of New Deal pragmatism. The aim of this chapter is to place Lucey's Catholic social theory, particularly his neo-Scholastic jurisprudence, within the greater framework of twentieth-century American thought. By exploring Lucey's views on legal education, his opposition to Justice Oliver Wendell Holmes, Jr., and his critique of "liberty of contract" jurisprudence, this chapter argues that, in many ways, Lucey and likeminded neo-Scholastic scholars can be seen as the mediators between two distinctively separate historical eras. By occupying the middle ground between the dogmatic ideologue Coughlin and the liberal reformer Ryan, Lucey also inhabited the liminal space between traditional and modern notions of jurisprudence. In so doing, Lucey helped usher in what Alan Brinkley has called the "reconstruction of New Deal Liberalism"—the shift in the history of American political economy from a notion of "reform liberalism" to "compensatory liberalism,"[10] from a structural critique of capitalism to a resigned acceptance of Keynesian policy-making.

## BETWEEN RYAN AND COUGHLIN: LUCEY'S MIDDLE WAY

Although Father Lucey delivered the 1960 Red Mass Sermon in the twilight of his career as a legal educator,[11] the address concisely embodied the spirit of his Catholic social theory and jurisprudence. From his early years as a teacher, to his long-standing tenure as regent of Georgetown Law, Lucey often evoked the natural law tradition and the influence of theology on American democracy. In his lectures and publications he reminded listeners and readers that it was the clergy who were responsible for molding early common law, and that it was a group of Founding Fathers, steeped in natural law, who laid the cornerstones of American democracy.[12]

As David O'Brien has demonstrated, Catholic leaders and spokespersons throughout the 1930s and 1940s equated Catholicism with American democracy.[13] Harking back to the revolutionary period, the Catholic historian, Father Moorehouse F. X. Millar, for example, wrote a series of essays in 1928 arguing that "sound" democratic ideas, including those of the American Revolution, stemmed from Catholic Thomistic thought.[14] Likewise, the philosopher Father Patrick J. Roche argued that the Declaration of Independence "ancestry was Catholic and its principles ultimately derived from the Schoolmen."[15] Even non-theologians made the connection. William Franklin Sands, writing in the partisan journal, *Commonweal*, declared in 1941 that "the positive and definite American philosophy of life" was "drawn directly from the Catholic philosophy of life."[16] Addressing their perceived status as interlopers in the Protestant origins of American history, Catholics went to great lengths to convince non-Catholics and themselves that they were truly "American." By discovering the roots of American democracy in the groundwork of Catholic theology, they believed they could prove that, despite their religious beliefs, they could be loyal to the president as well as the pope.

Although Lucey never explicitly attached a Catholic connotation to the natural law tradition of the Founding Fathers, his references to the "God-given rights" of the Constitution and the Founding Fathers' belief in, or recognition of, natural rights echoed the same anxiety and social insecurity that confronted other Catholics.[17] Moreover, Lucey attempted to alleviate Catholic concerns by focusing on the contemporary connections between natural law and American politics, particularly the Catholic roots of President Franklin Roosevelt's New Deal.

Lucey, however, was not alone in making this association. Many Catholic thinkers at the time pointed to the social encyclicals of Popes Leo XIII and Pius XI in interpreting the reform measures of the New Deal as embodiments of Catholic social teaching.[18] The Church's lessons to renounce economic individualism, to help the weak and defenseless, and to use the state as a means of establishing social justice for the common good, seemed to them to be an integral part of the New Deal's social legislation. Indeed, at least initially, Catholic intellectuals greeted the New Deal with nearly unanimous enthusiasm. Father John A. Ryan of Catholic University remarked that Roosevelt's actions were epochal, and the most Reverend W. D. O'Brien wrote that the "Almighty God raised up FDR—Apostle of the New Deal."[19]

As has been well documented, the Catholic support for Roosevelt and the New Deal was not, however, completely unanimous.[20] Reverend Charles Coughlin, priest of the parish of Royal Oak, Michigan, and national radio personality, and Al Smith the 1928 Democratic nominee for president, and the first Roman Catholic to run for president, both denounced Roosevelt as a Communist turncoat. Erstwhile supporters of the New Deal, Coughlin and Smith broke away from the Democratic Party in 1936 to form the National Union for Social Justice.[21] As one of the founders of the Union party, Coughlin, who for years vacillated in his support for Roosevelt, concluded that he would "not support a New Deal, which protects plutocrats and comforts Communists."[22] Similarly, Al Smith, speaking before the conservative American Liberty League likened Roosevelt's Democratic party to the Communist Third International.[23]

Lest one, however, confuse Lucey's advocacy of natural rights with an anti–New Deal stance, Lucey carefully, albeit implicitly, endorsed increased government regulation. Addressing those groups, such as the Liberty League and Father Coughlin's moribund Union party, who regarded the New Deal as undemocratic and pro-totalitarian, Lucey went to great lengths to disassociate himself from those Catholics disaffected by the New Deal. He wrote that though the increased government intervention of the New Deal meant "more restrictive laws, [i]t does not however require destruction of individual rights, whether in the form of civil liberties or property rights, or loss of control of government by the people."[24] With the proper philosophy of law, namely natural law, government could regulate for the common good without abandoning the innate rights of the individual. "Proper restriction of rights versus complete loss of rights"[25] was, for Lucey, the central issue.

## BUILDING AN INSTITUTION: LUCEY'S VISION OF A CATHOLIC LAW SCHOOL

Like many social theorists of the time, Lucey was seeking to forge a middle lane between the paths of what he called "exaggerated individualism" and social collectivism. But as a Catholic leader he believed that any effective middle way could not eschew the importance of the natural law tradition. Imbuing Catholic lawyers and jurists with this moral imperative was thus an important mission for Lucey the educator. His steps to transform Georgetown Law into a nationally recognized Catholic law school, and his emphasis on the importance of a natural law jurisprudence in the school's curriculum were not only the result of Lucey's Catholic upbringing and training as a Jesuit; they also demonstrated Lucey's desire to preserve the Catholic faith and culture. Although the law school had always had a Catholic complexion, Lucey directed a major transformation in the law school's culture from the genteel Catholicism associated with English progenitors to a newer Catholicism, that of immigrants from Ireland, Italy, and Central Europe.[26] Indeed, Lucey's own experience as the child of Irish immigrants raised in Boston's Catholic subculture and educated at Jesuit schools, certainly played a part in his identification with New Deal policies that benefited a Democratic constituency and the immigrant working class.

Appointed in 1931 as only the second official regent in the history of the Georgetown Law School,[27] Lucey took over in the midst of the Great Depression, at a time when the law school's own solvency became precarious. Nevertheless, under Lucey's stewardship, the school witnessed a rehabilitation and expansion of the physical plant,[28] reforms in admission requirements[29] and the curriculum,[30] and a marked increase in the quality of the faculty.[31]

Father Lucey's long-enduring commitment to Georgetown University and the Catholic Church originated from his abiding parochial education and the familial influences of his uncle, Reverend Patrick Lucey. Born on August 2, 1891, in Malden, Massachusetts, Francis Edmund Lucey was the fourth of eight children of first generation Irish American immigrants. Lucey spent the first 10 years of his life in the Boston suburb of Malden, but it was not until he moved to Weaverly, Minnesota, where he lived with his Uncle Pat, that the young Frank Lucey began to think about dedicating his life to the Society of Jesus.[32] Having spent five critically formative years with his uncle in Minnesota,[33] Lucey returned to Malden in 1906, where he enrolled in the Boston College Preparatory High School, a devoutly Jesuit-run institution. After graduating as Valedictorian of his high school class,[34] Lucey entered the novitiate in 1909 and two years later, at the age of 20, he took his first vows at St. Andrew-on-Hudson in upstate New York. From there he went on to earn bachelor and masters degrees in philosophy from the Jesuit Training School, Woodstock College in Woodstock, Maryland.[35] From Woodstock, Lucey embarked on his career as an educator, first teaching at Loyola High School and Fordham University in New York City, and then returning to Woodstock College as a professor in 1921.[36]

Lucey's association with Georgetown University followed soon afterwards. Ordained in Georgetown University's Dahlgren Chapel in 1923,[37] Lucey spent several years teaching Metaphysics and Ethics at Loyola College in Baltimore, and again at Fordham, before his appointment in 1928 as professor of Logic, Metaphysics, and the History of Social Thought at Georgetown College. At that time, Lucey also began work on his doctorate in sociology, which he received from Georgetown in May 1931.[38] Later that same year, Father Lucey, the young, recently appointed college professor, succeeded Father Thomas B. Chetwood as regent of the law school.[39] Although Lucey became regent of the law school without having any formal legal training, shortly after his appointment as regent he enrolled at the law school, and in 1941 he graduated with an LL.B.[40]

From his earliest connections with the law school, Lucey was concerned with the place of morality in legal education. Indeed, Lucey had, in addition to his college course load,[41] taken on the role of teaching jurisprudence at the Law Center since October 1929, well before he was appointed regent. For Lucey, jurisprudence was the most important subject in a law school,[42] and the one course more than any other that belonged in the first-year curriculum.[43] "In short, the course has to be a sort of Comparative Philosophy of Law," wrote Lucey, "if it is to be an effective, broad, and deep foundation for the study of Civil and International Legal systems."[44] As a Catholic law school, Georgetown had the added responsibility "to teach each course against a background of Natural Law"[45] so as to inculcate each student with a "knowledge of legal ethics and the principles of morality" that is necessary to meet "the obligations to God and fellow man."[46] Yet Lucey realized that dogmatic teaching of natural law would only hinder the true objective of an ideal jurisprudence class. Such a class must teach "the prevailing antagonistic philosophies of Law that exist in America today, as well as some of the philosophies which preceded these," wrote Lucey. "Any intelligent and effective influence which our graduates will have on the law of tomorrow will flow almost as much from their knowledge of adverse philosophies as from their knowledge of Scholastic philosophy."[47]

Although Lucey began teaching jurisprudence at the law school prior to 1931, the full effect of his commitment to mold Georgetown into a nationally recognized, Jesuit law school was not realized until he became regent. In addition to the Scholastic and physical reforms he initiated, Lucey enhanced the reputation and prestige of the Georgetown Law Center by developing alumni allegiance,[48] and establishing the administration's financial support for the *Georgetown Law Journal*.[49] Lucey knew that if Georgetown was to become the leader of a morally and religiously informed jurisprudential movement, as he had envisaged, it would require the financial support of its alumni and a national forum that could broadcast its morally inspired learning.

## THE ATTACK ON HOLMES AND LEGAL REALISM

But even with alumni support and a prominent journal, Lucey and the law school did not attract much attention from the leaders of legal education until 1941 when Lucey stepped up as one of the vicars of the American neo-Scholastic movement.[50] Lucey had become regent during the heyday of legal realism—the modernist movement among elite law professors that challenged the orthodoxy of classical legal thought by promoting the use of "value-neutral," social science methodology in the study of law. As the legal historian Ted White has noted, legal realism was, in fact, a pervasive part of New Deal thinking.[51] But for Catholic legal scholars, such relativism encouraged what Lucey called "pragmatic pantheism," and was thus an affront on the rational absolutism that guided scholastic teachings. For centuries theologians had referred to the medieval and Thomist ideals of the unity of religion and life, the natural and the divine, as a defense against secular reform. Lucey and other Catholic leaders revived neo-Scholastic thought as a powerful and cohesive set of beliefs that could be used to confront the modern, secular culture associated with legal realism.

In 1941, Lucey initiated the high watermark of the neo-Scholastic movement by defending the absolutes of his natural law philosophy against the epistemological and moral relativism of the late Justice Holmes and his legal realist descendants, many of whom came to occupy key positions in the New Deal bureaucracy.[52] Throughout his jurisprudence lectures in the 1930s, Lucey admonished the social engineering of legal realism as an amoral abandonment of natural rights. It was not, however, until the early 1940s that Lucey felt confident enough to publish his attacks on Holmes and realism. By then, many Catholics had become disenchanted by the late New Deal programs, especially in the realm of foreign policy, where recognition of Russia and indifference to the religious persecution of the Mexican Revolution were seen as a return of the bigotry that continued to haunt American Catholics. Moreover, the specter of totalitarianism in Europe at this time galvanized many American Catholics into believing that communism and social revolution were imminent.

Lucey played on these fears as he attacked the pragmatism of Holmes and the realists. Writing at a time when Holmes was widely regarded as the "hero of legal realism,"[53] and as an America icon of mythical proportion, Lucey criticized Holmes as "an agnostic, if not an atheist, a sceptic [sic] and experimentalist," whose philosophy was not "consonant with democracy, with fundamental rights, with the dignity of the individual."[54] Applying his training in theology and philosophy, Lucey singled out modern pragmatism as "the theme song of the Nazi storm troopers."[55] Nazism, for Lucey, was a "false philosophy of life, law and government, a philosophy that divorces itself from the moral dignity of man," one that leads to "the deification of the state and social interests, claims and demands."[56] The judicial philosophy of legal realism and its father, Justice Holmes, according to Lucey, was not far off. Holmes, "the so-called great liberal, had no patience with the jurisprudence of the founding fathers, . . . no belief in absolute values nor the importance and dignity of the individual,"[57] wrote Lucey. Because totalitarianism and the modern philosophical fashions rejected the principle of moral necessity, "[a]ny sharp analysis of pragmatism, utilitarianism, Hegelianism, or realism, as applied to law discloses one inescapable consequence, namely, might makes right."[58] Lucey, of course, would have nothing to do with a philosophy that abandoned moral oughts in favor of majority force.

Quoting liberally from Holmes' essay *Natural Law*,[59] Lucey drew a direct analogy between the philosophies of Nazism and Holmesian realism—an analogy that captured the attention of many legal scholars. David Burton, for example, has written, just "[a]s the Nazis had relied on force as the ultimate justification for their actions, so the Jesuit was at great pains to identify the place of force in Holmes' version of natural law."[60] Indeed, Holmes did embrace and perpetuate the functional approach of judicial pragmatism. For this he was vilified by Lucey and others as the universal skeptic whose ideas were leading the United States toward the totalitarian state and the precipice of a second world war.

Lucey's rejection of Holmes did not, however, occur from the start of his career as an educator. Instead, Lucey's disdain for the late justice developed in stages and with some reluctance. During the late 1920s and early 1930s, Lucey, like so many others, admired Holmes as a defender of civil liberties. His opinions and dissents in cases involving personal liberties "seemed to express in epigrams a heart that welled with understanding and deep solicitude for the dignity of the individual and especially for the less fortunate," wrote Lucey. "They appeared to express and champion the spirit of our democracy."[61] Yet something about Holmes's underlying philosophy left Lucey uncertain about his admiration, piquing his curiosity to read and reread all of Holmes's works. Through careful research and diligent examination, Lucey discovered a "philosophical skeleton of life and law, of man and morals, that was horribly deformed."[62]

After the publication of the first attack on Holmes, Lucey continued his assault with a second essay, "Natural Law and American Legal Realism," published the following year in the *Georgetown Law Journal*.[63] In between the publication of the two articles, Lucey's ammunition against Holmes greatly multiplied, as Holmes's private letters to his longtime friend and British jurist, Fredrick Pollock, became public.[64] With added fodder as the impetus for a second salvo, Lucey's attack became relentless. Although Lucey's second article focused more on legal realism than Justice Holmes, all that was wrong with realism was attributed back to the universal skepticism and pragmatic instrumentalism of Holmes. In turn, Lucey's writings on Holmes and realism engendered an acrimonious debate among lay and Catholic legal scholars, a debate that would ultimately signal the end of the orthodox and traditional view of legal theory and herald the beginning of a modern, realist jurisprudence.

The debate over the social consequences of Holmesian realism continued unabated during World War II. But by this time the socioeconomic reforms championed by early New Deal liberals of all religious denominations had come to an end. The structural critiques of capitalism initiated by the early New Deal, the ones often identified as consonant with the papal encyclicals, had been replaced by a war organization effort and a system of political economy that seemed to be self-sustaining. In the realm of legal theory, an analogous transformation was taking place. The earlier critique of *Lochner* era jurisprudence, initiated by Justice Holmes' dissent in the famous 1905 case, no longer seemed necessary.[†] Classical liberalism's faith in the laissez faire policy of "liberty of contract" had been repudiated, or so it seemed. With a social and economic welfare state in place, Catholics now feared conglomeration of state power.

Lucey stood at the center of this legal and political transition. Though he had skewered Holmes and the realists only a few years before, his Catholic faith in social justice and the common good had always required him to repudiate "liberty of contract" much like his realist foes. But his residual conservatism had also compelled him to fear social revolution; thus, while he embraced the modern regulatory state, he resisted the loss of human independence. Without singling out President Roosevelt or his New Deal programs, Lucey enunciated his paradoxical position in his commencement address before the 1943 law school graduating class. Lucey addressed the group of young lawyers with a history lesson on the rise and fall of "freedom of contract."[65] Tracing the rise of freedom of contract from the decay of feudalism and the advent of the industrial revolution, Lucey stated that "an exaggerated emphasis on freedom of contract" was an illusory panacea.[66] "Freedom of contract it was believed—made all men equals," proclaimed Lucey. "But freedom of contract did not work as anticipated."[67] The inevitable disparities of civil society, especially "the disparity of bargaining position," exacerbated the inequality between individuals. "Freedom of contract, and the stern obligation of the law to hold men to their bargains," Lucey said, "reduced millions to a status not far above that of former serfs and villeins, a status thought to have been dead and buried."[68]

To assure the burial of "the status of serf and villein," and to heed the Thomistic call for social justice, an "*intranational* social revolution" had commenced—a revolution of "successive steps taken by legislation and judicial law making to correct the evils of unbridled freedom of contract."[69] Lucey continued his praise for the modern regulatory state and its concomitant reliance on positive liberty through state action. "[L]abor legislation, the securities exchange acts and workmen's compensation laws" were just a few of the successive steps "clearly directed at protecting the weaker party contracting for labor or goods."[70] In addition, the social revolution entailed, according to Lucey, a shift in dependence from other individuals to the positive state. "Whereas formerly the individual depended on the justice and mercy of other private individuals or groups," Lucey stated, "now he depends on his government." This added dependence on the state, in turn, required a vast and complex government machinery of federal commissions and administrative agencies that Lucey heralded as a return to the splendor and dignity of "the ancient legislative, judicial, and executive branches of our government."[71]

Although Lucey celebrated the rise of the modern regulatory state as a much-needed correction to the excesses of freedom of contract, his residual conservatism eyed the expansion of legal novelties with much trepidation. Like many Catholics, for that matter like most liberals, Lucey contemplated the limits of state action. Fearful that "[d]elegated power is always apt to be abused," Lucey reminded the recent graduates of the natural law fundamentals Georgetown so earnestly stressed. In analyzing social and legal novelties, the trite fundamentals of the natural law were, for Lucey, the critical and ultimate touchstones. As he instructed the class of 1943:

> My suggestion is: when in doubt go back to fundamentals for your guide. Ask yourself: Does the legal novelty help to protect or enhance the dignity of man as an individual and as a social being? Does it truly benefit the family? Does it safeguard man's independence and his service of God? Does it serve to increase his intellectual and moral stature? At times the answer must await the functioning. If the legal novelty will clearly destroy or endanger any of those trite fundamentals I know it is dangerous. The aviator must have his star or his radio beam to find his way in the darkness. When he loses contact with them, anything can happen.[72]

According to Lucey, the trite fundamentals of the natural law, the absolute respect for human dignity and independence, were stars and radio beams that no morally minded aviator entrusted with the role of guiding the state should be without.

Although Lucey did not, at least in his commencement address, explicitly praise Roosevelt as such a morally minded aviator, his references to "*intranational* social revolutions" corresponded to the bold, new intellectual agenda that the New Deal established during the 1930s. Indeed, President Roosevelt's New Deal was working well within the natural law tradition because it focused on "the dynamic peace and prosperity of society" while preserving the innate decencies of humankind. American Catholics could be proud, according to Lucey, because their social philosophy not only influenced the founding of the nation, it also guided the politics of the day.

## CONCLUSION

It is only with the benefit of hindsight that one can argue that Lucey's paradoxical position was reflected in the greater political, legal, and economic thought of the times. Lucey's simultaneous attempt to embrace and resist the New Deal and legal realism can thus be seen as a pivotal point in the history of twentieth-century legal and Catholic social thought. This paradoxical position is indicative of the difficulty of building a stable site within the realm of a contested terrain. It demonstrates how defending one's teachings and ideas may have unintended consequences; how a defense of natural law may also lead to a realist renunciation of liberty of contract; how protection of individual liberty can also allow for the rise of the modern state, and how a measured critique of reform can usher in a new and different liberal order.

## NOTES

* John Herman Randall, Jr., "Defining 'Natural Law." *New York Times*, December 14, 1959, p. 30.
† *Lochner v. New York*, 198 U.S. 45, 75–76 (1905) (Holmes, J., dissenting).
1. "Sermon on Natural Law Preached at Red Mass," *Washington Post*, February 2, 1960, B3.
2. Justice William Brennan not only attended the Mass, he later requested that Lucey send him several copies of the sermon. Correspondence with Brennan, February 10, 1960, Francis E. Lucey Papers, Special Collections Division, Lauinger Library, Georgetown University, Washington, D.C.
3. Francis E. Lucey, " The Catholic Natural Law Doctrine and Its Relation to Civil Law," Lucey Papers, Georgetown University.
4. Ibid.
5. Ibid.
6. Ibid.
7. Ibid., 6.
8. Ibid., 3.
9. David J. O'Brien, *American Catholics and Social Reform: The New Deal Years* (New York: Oxford University Press, 1968), p. 213.
10. Alan Brinkley, *The End of Reform: New Deal Liberalism in Recession and War* (New York: Vintage, 1996).
11. One year later, in 1961, Lucey at the age of 70 was retired to the position of regent emeritus, relieving him of his administrative duties as regent. *Res Ispa Locquiture* (law school alumni publication) 6/61, vol. 14, no. 1, p. 5.
12. Francis E. Lucey, "Holmes–Believer in Democracy?" *Georgetown Law Journal* 39 (1951): 523–524.
13. O'Brien; see also Edward Purcell, *Crisis in Democratic Theory: Scientific Naturalism and the Problem of Value* (Lexington: University of Kentucky Press, 1974).
14. Moorehouse F. X. Millar, "The Origins of Sound Democratic Principles in Catholic Tradition," *Catholic Historical Review* 14 (April, 1928) (quoted in Purcell, *Crisis in Demoratic Theory*), p. 170.
15. Patrick J. Roche, "Democracy in the Light of Four Current Educational Philosophies" 12 (1942), quoted in Purcell, *Crisis in Democratic Theory*, p. 170.
16. William Franklin Sands, "What is an American?" *Commonweal* 438 (February 21, 1941) (quoted in Purcell, *Crisis in Demoratic Theory*), p. 171.

17. Lucey took on the charge that the Founding Fathers may not have believed in God: "It is irrelevant to point out that some of the Founding Fathers may not have subscribed to God-given natural rights. The real point is that all knew that people believe in natural rights and that there is no surer way of starting discord and rebellion than by an invasion of those rights." Lucey, "Holmes—Believer in Democracy?" 552.

18. George Q. Flynn, *American Catholics and the Roosevelt Presidency, 1932–1936* (Lexington: University of Kentucky Press, 1968), pp. 22–26.

19. Ibid., 40.

20. See, Alan Brinkley, *Voices of Protest: Huev Long. Father Coughlin, and the Great Depression* (New York: Knopf, 1982).

21. See, William E. Leuchtenburg, *Franklin D. Roosevelt and the New Deal. 1932–1940* (New York: Harper and Row, 1963), pp. 181–182. In the 1936 presidential election, Coughlin and Smith offered Representative William Lemke of North Dakota as their Union party's presidential candidate. Lemke polled only 882,000 votes, as FDR was reelected by carrying every state save two—Maine and Vermont.

22. Arthur M. Schlesinger, Jr., *The Age of Roosevelt: The Politics of Upheaval* (Boston: Houghton Mifflin, 1960), p. 25.

23. On January 25, 1936, at a Liberty League banquet at the Mayflower Hotel in Washington, D.C., Smith essentially pinned the communist label to the New Deal as he proclaimed "[t]he young brain-trusters caught the Socialists swimming and they ran away with their clothes." For a more detailed account of the Liberty League, see generally, George Wolfskill, *The Revolt of the Conservatives, a History of the American Liberty League, 1934–40* (Boston: Houghton Mifflin, 1974).

24. Francis E. Lucey, "Natural Law and American Legal Realism: The Respective Contributions to a Theory of Law in a Democratic Society," *Georgetown Law Journal* 30 (1942): 533.

25. Ibid., p. 533.

26. Daniel R. Ernst, *The First 125 Years: An Illustrated History of the Georgetown Universitv Law Center* (Washington, DC: Georgetown University Law Center, 1995), p. 95.

27. Ibid., 102. In 1931 Lucey replaced Father Thomas B. Chetwood as regent mainly because Lucey had a better understanding of the importance of the lay community to the history and future of the law school.

28. Refurbishment of classrooms and offices began in the early 1930s and the commitment to plant and equipment growth continued for decades as Lucey acquired for the Law School several adjoining buildings that were remodeled into dormitories and a new library. *Res Ipsa Loquitur*, May 1951, vol. 3, no.1, p. 9.

29. In response to alumni pressure to raise standards and the Association of American Law Schools' demands for more stringent requirements, Lucey and the Executive Faculty Committee agreed that beginning in the fall of 1936 "applicants for the Georgetown University Law Center would need an under-graduate degree." Ernst, *First 125 Years*, 103.

30. Ibid.

31. Lucey was instrumental, for example, in acquiring James Scott Brown, former secretary of the Carnegie Foundation for International Peace, to teach international law. *The Hoya*, June 12, 1933, vol. 1, no. 1, p. 3. Sharing Lucey's view of law and morality, "Dr. Scott [was] widely known because of his insistence that International Law can not and must not be separated from international morality." Lucey was able to implement such changes because of his unique role as regent. Like many other Jesuit law schools where the regent functioned as the de facto dean, Georgetown's Regent Lucey handled those duties that would be ordinarily managed by the aging Dean Hamilton: supervising the physical expansion, curriculum reform, and the recruitment of faculty. Lewis C. Cassidy, "A Critique of Catholic Legal Education, 1937," Special Manuscript Collection, Harvard Law School Library, Cambridge, MA, mimeograph copy, p. 3. Although regents of Jesuit law schools were appointed merely as liaisons between the law school deans and the presidents of the university, many regents were able to usurp the responsibilities and duties of their deans on their way to controlling the future of their respective institutions (p. 15).

32. Ernst, *First 125 Years*, 101.

33. "Later Father Lucey would relate that it was his experience with 'Uncle Pat' in Minnesota that firmly implanted in him the thought of serving God." James R. Theirry, *A Partial History of the Georgetown Law Center*, Special Collections Department, Edward Bennett Williams Library, Georgetown University Law Center, Washington, D.C., 25 (citing Lucey Interview, November 7, 1968).

34. ibid., 4.

35. *Res Ipsa Loquitur*, May 1960, vol. 12, no. 2, p. 1.

36. *Res Ipsa Loquitur*, October 1961, vol. 14, no. 1, p. 6.

37. *Woodstock Letters*, vol. 52, p. 430.

38. Theirry, *A Partial History*, 5. Although Lucey is not mentioned in the 1931 Graduation Bulletin as having received his doctorate in Sociology, official transcript records of his tenure at Georgetown state that he did, indeed, earn his Ph.D. in sociology in May 1931. See, official transcript, Lucey Papers.

39. *Res Ipsa Loquitur*, October 1961, vol. 14, no. 1.

40. Not surprisingly, Regent/student Lucey received excellent marks from the professors who were also his fellow faculty members. Only Prof. Huard was brave enough to give him a low grade. "Official Transcript," Lucey Papers.

41. Lucey taught Logic and Metaphysics at the undergraduate college and the History of Social Thought at the graduate school. *Res Ipsa Loquitur*, October 1961, vol. 14, no. 1, p. 12.

42. Lucey correspondence with Rev. Timothy Sullivan, August 16, 1962, Lucey Papers.

43. Lucey memo to Prof. James Hayden of Georgetown, August 11, 1958, Lucey Papers, Folder #218. Lucey also believed "that a short course should be added in third year where students who have practically finished their course could really apply the Jurisprudence they have learned." Lucey correspondence

with Prof. Robert W. Foster of the University of Louisville School of Law, March 20, 1952, Lucey Papers, Folder # 218. But Lucey realized the difficulty of adding "a couple more hours of Jurisprudence to an already over-crowded schedule."

44. Lucey, correspondence with Rev. Sullivan.

45. Lucey, memo to Prof. James Hayden. To further the application of natural law to the teaching of more general law school classes, Lucey recommended that each law professor be given a handbook—prepared by a lawyer theologian—that expounded on the ethical problems associated with the individual courses.

46. Preliminary Report of Proposed Program for Orientation, Lucey Papers.

47. Francis E. Lucey, "The Place and Scope of Jurisprudence in the Law School Curriculum," Lucey Papers.

48. Lucey initiated the publication of an alumni magazine originally entitled *The Law School Hoya*, and now known as *Res Ipsa Loquitur* to foster greater communication with alumni. He also revived the District of Columbia Alumni Association to keep alumni informed of law school developments and to "provide an impetus for a nation-wide organization of alumni." Theirry, *A Partial History*, pp. 6–7.

49. As a guest speaker at the 1936 Georgetown Law Journal banquet, Lucey explained the many reasons why he believed the school should support the law journal: "The reason that the school is eagerly willing to support the Journal financially as well as academically is not merely because it supplies such valuable experience for the men serving the staff, nor because it broadcasts the fame and prestige of the school, but most of all because the quality of the work on the journal is such a goal and an inspiration to the general student body," *The Hoya*, vol. 17, no. 27, May 13, 1936, p. 8.

50. Purcell, *Crisis of Democratic Theory*, 164.

51. G. Edward White, "From Sociological Jurisprudence to Legal Realism," in *Patterns of American Legal Thought* (1978), pp. 122–143.

52. Francis E. Lucey, "Jurisprudence and the Future Social Order," *Social Science* 16 (July, 1941). Although this article was indeed the first attack on Holmes by a Thomistic scholar, the first general scholar to come out against Holmes was Boyd H. Bode. But as David Burton has explained, Bode's critique of Holmes originated from the political Left rather than the Right, as he argued that Holmes' position was not revolutionary enough. "What it offers is, in the last analysis, but a continuation of the old tradition that right conduct consists in conformity to a pre-existent standard. Standards are repudiated for no other purpose than to set up in their place certain arbitrary and accidental preferences to rule over us by divine right." In place of these preferences, Bode called "for the emancipation of the moral life and not a perpetuation of its servitude" by using intelligence. Bode, "Justice Holmes on Natural Law and the Moral Ideal," *International Journal of Ethics* 29 (July 1919), pp. 397–404 (cited in David H. Burton, "Justice Holmes and the Jesuits," *American Journal of Jurisprudence* 27(14) (1982): 32, 34).

53. Burton, "Justice Holmes," 32.

54. Lucey, "Jurisprudence," 212.

55. Ibid., 213.

56. Ibid., 211.

57. Ibid., 213–214.

58. Ibid., 213.

59. Oliver Wendell Holmes, Jr., "The Natural Law," *Harvard Law Review* 32 (1918): 41.

60. Burton, p. 34.

61. Lucey, "Holmes—Believer in Democracy?" p. 524.

62. Ibid., 524.

63. Francis E. Lucey, "Natural Law and American Legal Realism: Their Respective Contributions to a Theory of Law in a Democratic Society," *Georgetown Law Journal* 30 (1942): 493.

64. Edward Purcell thus errs in suggesting that the publication of the Holmes–Pollock letters led Lucey to initiate his attack on Holmes. Purcell, *Crisis in Democratic Theory*, at 167–168. But Lucey's first public assault on Holmes—his reading of the paper, "Jurisprudence and the Future Social Order," came in March 1941, months before the publication of the Holmes–Pollock letters. This explains why Lucey's initial article cited only Holmes "Natural Law" essay and Shriver's collection of Holmes's papers, and why the second essay is filled with quotes from the Holmes–Pollock collection. Lucey, "Jurisprudence and the Future Social Order."

65. Lucey, "Commencement Address," June 6, 1943, Lucey Papers.

66. Ibid., 2.

67. Ibid., 3.

68. Ibid., 3.

69. Ibid., 4 (emphasis my own).

70. Ibid., 4.

71. Ibid., 4.

72. Ibid., 7.

CHAPTER 8

# RELIGIOUS LIBERTY IN AMERICAN FOREIGN POLICY, 1933–41

## ASPECTS OF PUBLIC ARGUMENT BETWEEN FDR AND AMERICAN ROMAN CATHOLICS

PHILIP CHEN

THE IDEA OF RELIGIOUS LIBERTY HAS ALWAYS BEEN LINKED to the thought and execution of American foreign policy from the very early days of the Republic. Its importance has waxed and waned over the course of history, fueled at times by the enthusiasm of missionary organizations, later on by the interest of immigrants in the religious conditions in their former home countries, and often fundamentally by the principle of human rights. The drive to protect religious liberty internationally is still with us today, and it is important to consider the ways in which others in the past have grappled with its conceptual issues and policy implications.[1]

### THE QUESTIONS

In examining the larger issue, this chapter considers some responses to four international episodes linked explicitly to the question of religious freedom. These four cases are (1) U.S. diplomatic recognition of the Soviet Union (1933); (2) Mexican anticlericalism (1934–35); (3) Spanish Civil War (1936–38); and (4) Nazi Germany and Soviet Lend-Lease (1939–41).[2] I suggest three central questions to keep in mind when considering the cases: (1) Why should religious liberty be taken into account in the conduct of foreign policy? (2) What do we mean by religious liberty? What sorts of abuses constitute violations of religious liberty? (3) What kinds of policies and under what circumstances should the United States pursue the protection of religious liberty internationally? In attempting to answer these questions, this chapter outlines some of the major sorts of public reasoning that surrounded the issue of religious liberty in American foreign policy, as put forward by two prominent Roman Catholic periodicals, *America* and *Commonweal*, and as compared with the public views of FDR. By examining the development of concepts and arguments from 1933 until the end of 1941, I describe the ways in which the idea of religious liberty intersected with foreign policy over the course of Roosevelt's first two terms.

## WHY LOOK AT PUBLIC ARGUMENTS?

The dominant cultural norm in the United States has been and is today generally in favor of some sense of religious liberty. This liberty is often reflected in the belief that an individual has the right to be able to worship, within reason, any way he or she wishes to do so. To be seen as against "religious liberty," or its other linguistic siblings—religious freedom, freedom of worship, freedom of conscience—is undesirable often for both personal and political reasons. Politicians, policy-makers, and those engaged in public debate are thus constrained by this societal norm in advocating policies that may sometimes, on its face, appear to violate it.

This is where public reasoning emerges. In the context of this chapter, individuals or groups were often pressed to present public reasons why, in each particular case, the United States ought to intervene (or not intervene) in order to protect religious liberty. In addressing my case studies, one way to grapple with this question is to compare and contrast Roosevelt's views with those of articles in *America* and *Commonweal*. While this is certainly not an exhaustive survey of all Catholic opinion, it provides one good indicator of what types of influential Catholic arguments were circulating in the public arena. *America* and *Commonweal* were often cited during this period as influential Catholic periodicals. When trying to convey to Franklin Roosevelt the sense of American Roman Catholics on the issue of diplomatic recognition of the Soviet Union, Father Edmund Walsh of Georgetown sent him editorials from the two weeklies suggesting that the opinions represented "the feelings of the majority of American Catholics."[3]

To illuminate how these arguments played out in practice, let us turn to the case studies. I present them in chronological order and as the arguments develop, I shall try to show how they build and respond to each other. Where possible, assumptions are made explicit and contradictions exposed.

The conclusion at the end summarizes the lessons and suggests how these might help in approaching the question of religious liberty in foreign policy today.

## SOVIET RECOGNITION

As a starting point, consider the case of the extension of diplomatic recognition to the Soviet Union by the United States in 1933. The background to this dates back to the days of World War I. At that time, President Woodrow Wilson had staunchly refused to recognize the Soviet regime in the hopes that he could deprive it of enough legitimacy and material that it would crumble. In so doing, he set a new American standard for diplomatic recognition. Instead of granting recognition to governments ostensibly in control of a country, the United States would consider whether or not that government had a legitimate right (in moral terms) to rule.[4] *Commonweal*, on May 5, 1933, suggested that opposition to recognition should simply be fought on the issue of religious liberty. The Soviet war on religion was very clear: regular suppression of worship together with the incarceration or execution of clergy and believers horrified Americans.[5] In its words, recognition after 14 years of "a social order guilty of persecution in the worse sense" would be "to endorse a spiritual tyranny."[6] It supported this position because the "war on religion" was a "suppression of the fundamental rights of the Christian conscience."[7] *America* buttressed this by claiming that recognition did imply moral approval of a regime. Resorting to an analogy, one editorial read: "Diplomatic recognition does not greatly differ, after all, from the recognition that is customary in polite society. While neither implies approval in every detail, men do not invite known murderers and thieves to their homes."[8]

This type of categorical moral argument, however, was not completely persuasive. After all, reality is more complicated than strict moral commands often acknowledge, especially in politics. In many cases, moral imperatives become tempered, depending on the other competing moral values at stake. In this case, national interest was implicitly cited as a reason for granting recognition. Proponents stated that commercial benefits could bolster the economy. *America* acknowledged: "Governments are not infrequently forced to do not what they would but what they can, and so must choose the lesser evil, and tolerate the improprieties which flow from it."[9] This statement revealed some leniency toward application of moral imperatives to the realm of policy. But under what circumstances would *America* tolerate a situation full of "improprieties"? One might argue this way: putting forward the idea of trade benefits resulting from recognition of the Soviet Union was a powerful argument in light of the international economic depression.

Roosevelt was elected, primarily, because he promised to deal with grave economic crises facing the country. The survival of the nation, arguably, was at stake and any means to revive the economy could be viewed favorably. Could the state of the economy be a mitigating factor?

These issues explain, to some extent, why *Commonweal* and *America*, week after week, attacked the idea of economic benefits resulting from recognition. They undercut the rosy economic promises by saying the U.S.S.R. had no money or goods with which to trade.[10] One article baldly declared "there is little doubt that today's economic depression is caused in great part by the existence of the Soviet regime in Russia."[11] What these arguments tried to do in part was to eliminate reasons that could be posed as mitigating factors to the moral issue of religious liberty.

This strategy hinged on other parts of the question as well. Another pro-recognition argument claimed Soviet cooperation necessary to deter Japan in the Far East. Japan, having invaded Manchuria and now threatening China, had thrown into disarray the balance of power in the Far East, sparking war anxiety.[12] *America* countered this by relying upon post-Versailles Wilsonian skittishness with Old World "balance of power." One article that opposed using recognition as a tool for deterring Japan, concluded "neither justice nor charity between nations can be urged if human rights are to be subordinated to political expediency."[13] Still, another emphasized the inherent untrustworthiness and threat of the Soviets in that they supported local Communist parties in America in organizing to overthrow the U.S. government.[14]

The recognition controversy did not reveal very much about Roosevelt's own public position on the issue. He dodged nearly every press conference question posed on recognition during 1933. He realized that pushing for recognition meant having to answer difficult questions on the relationship between recognition and religious liberty.[15] This was the standard implicitly set by Wilson and tacitly accepted by the country at large for nearly a decade and a half. The only major address that seemed to touch on the topic obliquely was his October address to the National Conference of Catholic Charities. There, he suggested that "spiritual values count in the long run more than material values." He continued, "Those people in other lands... who sought by... law to eliminate the right of mankind to believe in God... have... discovered... they are tilting in vain against... religion."[16] But this told people very little other than that Roosevelt thought that religion was some sort of unstoppable force, and that he, Roosevelt, was probably in favor of religion.

However, the social and political context of the debate over recognition was such that more elaborate answers in public were not necessary. FDR could push the policy agenda toward recognition. The eventual settlement itself was tame; the Soviets agreed that Americans in the U.S.S.R. would be given free exercise of religious worship. They would not be persecuted or hampered on the basis of religion. They could conduct religious services, but the use of buildings was to be regulated by Soviet laws. Religious instruction for children could only be conducted in private.[17] In the official agreement, Maxim Litvinov, the Soviet representative, insisted that the religious rights granted already existed in the Soviet legal code, and he cited the relevant provisions. This seemingly was to underscore the point that none of the concessions given were really "concessions" but just clarifications.

In the end, Roosevelt could claim he did his best to secure religious liberty and worship for Americans. In reality, the agreements circumscribed a very narrow definition of religion—one confined to religious ceremony and services, almost entirely in private and as individuals.[18] In this sense, the Soviet regime granted the Americans little more than what Soviet citizens themselves received, although in fact, one could argue that at least Americans were not subject to the religious persecutions that Soviet citizens experienced. But the public aspects of religion—education of children, communal worship, and religious organization—were mostly denied to Americans residing in the U.S.S.R. as well.

The American Catholic press as a whole did not penalize Roosevelt for this result.[19] Instead, for example, it argued that the Soviet pledges to preserve American religious rights in the Soviet Union constituted the vindication of a human right "in the most thrilling diplomatic duel of modern times."[20] Another editorial ran, "Publicly to acknowledge a concession... to religion, would be a sign to the whole world that the defeat of the Russian [sic] atheistic war on religion has begun."[21] This position was patently inconsistent with the public reasoning forwarded prior to the recognition agreement and little justification was publicly made to reconcile this.

The outcome of the recognition case shows us that there was some consensus on the "floor" for consideration of religious rights: the rights of Americans in another country. It also shows that this floor involved a definition of religious rights that is primarily related to strict worship. Also, the moral imperative of religious liberty could be qualified under certain circumstances. Notice that what was not pushed strongly by FDR was the idea of state sovereignty, the idea that the Soviets had a right to decide for themselves how to regulate their internal affairs. For the implications of that argument, we turn to the situation in Mexico.

## MEXICAN ANTICLERICALISM

The Mexican case provides a better example of reasoning about the ties between religious liberty and intervention in foreign policy. Whereas in the case of Russian recognition, *America* and *Commonweal* defended a *status quo*

U.S. policy from change, in Mexico, their goal was explicitly to change the then current policy and advocate more forceful intervention. In the process, at times they broadened the *definition* of religious liberty and challenged some of the current notions of intervention.

The 1930s crisis in Mexico was a continuation of the most recent phase of Mexican church–state conflict, which had been developing rapidly over the previous 20 years. Many of the concrete issues in the dispute arose specifically from provisions of the Queretaro Constitution (1917), which set quotas on the amount of Catholic clergy.[22] Other restrictions provided for the exclusion of the Catholic Church from the educational system, enforcement of socialistic doctrine in the schools, and the imposition of government control on primary education.[23] Another virulent phase in Mexican anticlericalism erupted in 1934, when Mexican President Plutarco Calles sought to renew the drive against the Catholic Church. Throughout 1934, he called for the removal of clergy, whom he regarded as subversive and a conservative threat to the Revolution. By October 1934, the Mexican Congress was considering legislation to abolish all religious education.[24]

The starting point for U.S. policy in Latin America under Franklin Roosevelt was the Good Neighbor Doctrine. In his first inaugural speech, he had declared, "In the field of world policy I would dedicate this Nation to the policy of the good neighbor—the neighbor who resolutely respects himself and because he does so, respects the rights of others—the neighbor who respects his obligations and respects the sanctity of his agreements in and with a world of neighbors."[25] Subsequently, he signed in 1933 at Montevideo a convention on nonintervention.[26] Roosevelt hoped to reverse the image of the United States as an imperialistic great power in the region.

The Good Neighbor metaphor was meant to create the comfortable image of a community. The "neighborhood" became the community of states. The "neighbor who respects himself by respecting others" seems to indicate that neighbors know their boundaries. Neighbors do not inquire or involve themselves too deeply in each other's personal affairs.[27] It could also be seen as a reaction against one of the high tides of American intervention in Latin America, the Woodrow Wilson era. Under President Wilson's watch, the United States had become embroiled in the early phases of the Mexican revolution. The complicated maneuverings of that era, in which the United States had supported various "strong men" over others, had created a legacy of bitterness, especially after the landing of the Marines at Veracruz in 1914.

Naturally, the leading groups in the American Catholic community took the resurgent threat to the Catholic Church in Mexico very seriously. In order to argue that Americans should act to stop religious persecution in Mexico, it was necessary to attack the premise of the Good Neighbor Doctrine. In *America*, numerous headlines chastised the metaphor and drew analogies that revealed the Good Neighbor's limits. One editorial declared: "The good-neighbor policy has no sense if our neighbor is beating his wife... If the idea of that policy is to be good friends with the Government only, and to ignore the groanings of the Government's subjects, then we can only say that there is nothing new in the policy..."[28] Six months later, another editorial commented: "It is all right to be a 'good neighbor,'... but a good neighbor to what?"[29]

But Roosevelt insisted that nonintervention meant the U.S. government would not publicly criticize Mexico on the issue of religious liberty, for it was an internal matter. Many American Catholics, and those interested in the plight of religion in Mexico, interpreted this to mean that FDR denied the universality of religious liberty. They sought to press him on this question, and it placed Roosevelt in a difficult bind. On the one hand, he could be in political trouble if his attitude of nonintervention led people to believe he felt it was unimportant. Consequently, in response to a petition on Mexico sent by a number of House representatives, Roosevelt publicly declared that the Government believed in "freedom of worship not only in the United States, but also in other Nations."[30]

This admission, while fairly innocuous and platitudinous, did move Roosevelt down the next link in the logical chain. His statement on Mexico was made in reference to the growing movement among Catholic organizations such as the Knights of Columbus, together with some House and Senate members, to take up the religious issue. In February, Senator William Borah (R-Idaho), usually a strong isolationist, had introduced a resolution calling for the investigation of abuses of religious liberty in Mexico. The resolution noted, "American citizens of the Christian faiths have been outraged and reviled... [and that] ... such antireligious activity in Mexico is contrary to the traditions of freedom of conscience and liberty of religious worship, which are the cherished attributes of all civilized governments..."[31] It concluded that the Senate Foreign Relations Committee should conduct hearings on the situation in Mexico in order to determine "the policy of the United States in reference to this vital problem and in what way we may best serve the cause of tolerance and religious freedom."[32]

Roosevelt, however, continued to stand by his narrower definition of right: religious liberty may be in the abstract a fundamental right, but unless secured by prior agreement, it was not a means by which the United States could question another government's domestic legislation. To this point, he emphasized that no question of American rights and no complaints of their violation had been raised in Mexico. This revealed his approach: incremental, conservative, and case-by-case.[33]

*America* and *Commonweal* responded to this argument with a sleight-of-hand. They contended that religious liberty for Americans was necessarily violated in Mexico because the Mexican government had attacked clergy and worshippers, closed houses of religion, and banished religious instruction from schools. This, in theory, denied the opportunity for any American to worship in Mexico. Thus, American rights had been violated, even though no concrete case had arisen. One editorial put it: "Any Catholic American in Mexico going to Mass runs the risk, on coming out of church after Mass, of facing a firing squad armed with machine guns, as did a churchful of Catholics recently in Mexico City itself, among whom there *might just as easily have been some Americans*" (emphasis added).[34]

This pressure may have moved the president to make a speech further discussing aspects of religious liberty and its relationship to foreign policy.[35] This address at San Diego near the Mexican border weakened, in a subtle way, his position on nonintervention.[36] He declared first, "In the United States we regard it as axiomatic that every person shall enjoy the free exercise of his religion according to the dictates of his conscience." Then he admitted, "It is true that other Nations may, as they do, enforce contrary rules of conscience and conduct . . . but those policies are beyond our jurisdiction. Yet in our inner individual lives we can never be indifferent, and we assert for ourselves complete freedom to embrace, to profess and to observe the principles for which our flag has been such a lofty symbol."[37]

What Roosevelt did was attempt to hold both ends of the scale: on the one hand he pressed the state sovereignty argument and excluded official U.S. government action. On the other hand, he was reinforcing the legitimacy of the American Catholic interests represented by *America* and *Commonweal* in the press (and other interested organizations) to conduct their campaigns against the Mexican government. One net result was the pressure on Roosevelt to resolve the situation through back channel diplomacy. With the help of the National Catholic Welfare Conference and through Josephus Daniels, the U.S. ambassador to Mexico, FDR sought ways to persuade the Mexican government to ease the restrictions.

By the time the Mexican crisis left the front pages of discussion to be replaced by the issue of the Spanish Civil War, the public argument on the place of religious liberty in American foreign policy had evolved from its form in the debate over diplomatic recognition. First, the premise of state sovereignty in the Good Neighbor Doctrine still held, but its logic had been somewhat shaken. Roosevelt had conceded that individuals could not be indifferent to religious persecution, but the U.S. government must. This legitimized the protest, in some respects, and probably allowed for the increase of domestic political pressure against him on this issue.

## SPAIN

The Spanish Civil War followed straight on the heels of the Mexican crisis, giving little respite to the issue of religious liberty and its relationship to foreign policy. Spain in the 1930s faced significant political, social, and economic problems in modernizing. The removal of the monarchy and the creation of a republican government did not abate the country's instability. The election of 1936, that the Left won and that the Right took as their death knell, provided the immediate setting for the outbreak of the civil war. After the February election, fear and chaos reigned in the country. The religious situation, which concerns us here, was extremely precarious. From March through July, churches and other religious buildings were often looted and burned to the ground. Soon after May Day, six Catholic churches and schools were set on fire, while about 40 religious and lay people were attacked.[38] Often, it was unclear who was responsible for the destruction, but rightists "used the issue to attract moderates and people of modest means" who presumably were outraged.[39] The new government, whether due to reluctance or incompetence, was too feeble to stop the excesses.[40]

General Francisco Franco's revolt in July 1936 took place within this environment of chaos and confusion. Claiming to stand for traditional Spanish values and promising to protect religion from Communism and atheism, Franco at first appealed to those who sought to defend religious liberty. But the darker side of Franco soon appeared as his brutal military tactics, his apparent Fascist leanings, and his links with Hitler and Mussolini emerged. The dilemma for those protecting religious liberty was this: which side should American Catholic defenders of religious liberty support? The two previous cases had provided a simple conceptual framework. It was clear who was doing the persecuting, and one could criticize these regimes without worry. But Spain was different. It seemed to be a choice between a weak democracy, progressive in some areas, but bitterly against religion and an authoritarian, fascist state, supportive of the Catholic religion, yet opposed to many of the fundamental democratic ideals that Americans valued. *America* and elements of *Commonweal* split bitterly over the issue.[41] *America* argued that the permissive religious persecution was the responsibility of the government. On the one hand, if the leftist government, through deliberate negligence, failed to protect religious persons and property from being attacked by mobs, then it was just as guilty as if it had actively promoted violence and unrest.[42] On the other hand, if the government was simply incapable of restraining this destruction, then it should be replaced with a stronger government that could.[43] As the war continued, *America* assumed away many of the moral complexities of the situation. The chaos, they asserted, leading to permissive religious persecution, was the direct fault of the Communists who were infiltrating Spain. This was the first move in the Bolshevization of the country. Second, they assumed that the only choice in Spain lay between Communism and Fascism. In that choice, fascism (of the Italian variety) was preferable to Soviet-style communism. As one editorial read: "a collaboration with Fascism is possible...a collaboration with Communism is absolutely impossible for the Catholic Church."[44]

Some writers in *Commonweal* approached the issue warily and a bit more critically. Barbara Barclay Carter, in giving the perspective of anti-Franco European Catholics, expressed the deep concern of a Spanish Catholic who feared that "a victory of the Insurgents...would lay the country at the mercy of their financial backers, making social reform impossible, and binding Spain to the Fascist dictatorships, might well involve her in a world war."[45] George Shuster, in two articles that earned the ire of the editor of *America*, argued that "one's human affection for embattled priests and religion lead one to side with Franco; but one's love for the timeless mission of the Church leads one to believe that he may, after all, prove to be the greater of two evils."[46]

Despite the dilemmas that the issue of religious liberty placed on the question of the Spanish Civil War, there was a critical disjuncture between that debate and the question of what the U.S. role ought to be. The almost overwhelming sense emanating from both magazines was that FDR's plan to impose a weapons embargo and to remain solidly outside the conflict was the proper policy.[47] *Commonweal* asked, "What is the duty of Americans toward Spaniards in their present trouble?" The answer was humanitarian aid and prayer.[48]

This reflected the widespread political isolationism in the country and the fear of America being dragged into another world war. The international scene had become more unstable. The Spanish Civil War, the increased belligerency of Germany and Italy, Japanese aggression in the Far East, prompted the desire to avoid any steps that might lead to an American role in conflict. Moreover, pro-Franco American Catholics were aware that the practical effect of the American embargo was to aid the Nationalist cause by denying the Republicans a source of war material.

In this public dialogue with American Catholics, FDR found it easy to pursue the isolationist path with regard to Spain. A symposium on the policy of neutrality in *Commonweal* led its editors to "feel that in view of the present condition of world politics...the United States should for the time being be isolationist, at least to the point of not supplying anyone with arms in the immediate future." This policy, it argued, "is consonant...with the general base of pacifism which, from the moral point of view, is so essential for the modern world."[49] An earlier piece argued that it "seems almost impossible that Americans could seriously want to set our government up as the world's moral judge...and throw our military force with the 'good' to destroy the 'wicked.'"[50]

Roosevelt's rhetoric passed over the religious liberty issue. The pressure from isolationists such as Senator Gerald Nye in the Congress and from organizations throughout the country was clearly for the renewal of neutrality legislation and an embargo on the shipment of arms.[51] The year the civil war broke in Spain, 1936, was also a presidential reelection year. FDR tacked toward isolationism when he made his famous speech at Chautauqua, New York: "[S]o long as war exists...there will be some danger even to the nation that most ardently desires peace, danger that it also may be drawn into the war." He continued later, "I have passed unnumbered hours...thinking and planning how war may be kept from the United States of America."[52]

As the civil war continued, pressure mounted on Roosevelt to lift the embargo. But he and the State Department demurred and simply reiterated their policies. Much has been written about FDR's personal sympathy with the Spanish Republic, including the observation that this sympathy was negated by his fear of electoral reprisal by pro-Franco Catholics. Roosevelt had a further interest in following the policy of nonintervention set down by the British and the French. His New Deal policies were in full retreat, and the failure of the court-packing scheme placed his prestige in jeopardy. For many reasons then, FDR's public discourse on the Spanish Civil War was limited to emphasizing the fear of war and supporting an isolationist stance. It did not seem the time to push issues of religious liberty when world war seemed to be at stake.[53] The Spanish case shows us, in contrast to the first two cases, two things. First, it is very difficult to understand another country's internal religious situation, especially in cases of permissive religious persecution. Spain had a weak state that was anticlerical, and a significant portion of the horrific persecution (executions, arsons, and the like) was caused by non-state actors. How does one ascribe responsibility in this situation? One temptation was to ascribe total responsibility to the government.

Second, making religious liberty the central piece of criticism of another country is relatively easy when the stakes seem low. In the first case, one way or another, diplomatic recognition of the Soviet Union was not going to start a second world war. In the Mexican case, the United States was the hegemonic power and could have more leeway in imposing its views. But the Spanish case points to a more complicated paradigm. Surely, religious liberty was important, but the consequences of any U.S. action in the minds of many could have ignited an expanded war. This complicated calculus was not resolved, and thus there was a divorce between a discussion of the religious situation on its merits and the issue of the U.S. duty in resolving it.

## NAZI GERMANY AND SOVIET LEND-LEASE

The growth in power of Nazi Germany, the outbreak of war in Europe, and the subsequent Nazi invasion of the Soviet Union forced another critical debate on the issue of religious liberty in foreign policy. Both writers at *America* and *Commonweal* and Roosevelt realized that military aid to the Soviet Union was necessary to defeat Nazi Germany. However, both were constrained on the one hand by the precedents of their arguments in the previous three cases of religious liberty examined herein. Again, the moral problem of allying with the Soviet Union posed considerable difficulties. How could these constraints be overcome and a convincing publicly reasoned argument for Soviet aid be provided?

Within the context of his struggle to define a moral case against Nazi Germany, Roosevelt changed the way he saw the relationship between a state's internal religious policy and that state's foreign policy. In the first two cases especially, we saw FDR, through the concept of state sovereignty, argue that internal issues such as religious liberty were not the proper concern of the U.S. government. This did not mean that Americans, as individuals, ought to remain neutral. But his position remained silent on the links between religious liberty and foreign policy.

By decade's end, a different reasoning emerged. In 1939, FDR publicly noted that respect for religion meant respect for international order. "[W]here religion and democracy have vanished, good faith and reason in international affairs have given way to strident ambition and brute force." Earlier, he declared: "Religion, by teaching man his relationship to God, gives the individual a sense of his own dignity and teaches him to respect himself by respecting his neighbors."[54] Not only was religious liberty in other countries an indicator of their relative threat potential, but also religious free-dom itself constituted for Roosevelt, one of the four central liberties, one of the Four Freedoms so essential for a free, democratic society. Taking religious liberty into account in foreign policy simultaneously became both pragmatic for national security reasons and strongly moral for national values. In this sense, Roosevelt broadened its function. The entry of the Soviet Union into the war against Nazi Germany in the summer of 1941 only made clearer an apparent contradiction in Roosevelt's logic. If a state's repressive religious policy marked it as a threat to international order, then on what moral basis could the United States support the Soviet Union against Nazi Germany? How could he morally justify a policy of aid to a country that was commit-ting similar violations of religious liberty as the country he wished to fight against?

Roosevelt, realizing one of the problems he faced in trying to justify aid to the Soviet Union against Germany was this issue of religious liberty, made some unfortunate statements that suggested he was trying to square the circle. In one press conference, this exchange transpired.

> THE PRESIDENT: (Continuing) As I think I suggested a week or two ago, some of you might find it useful to read Article 124 of the Constitution of Russia.
> Q: What does that say, Mr. President?
> THE PRESIDENT: Well, I haven't learned it by heart...but anyway: Freedom of conscience...Freedom of religion. Freedom equally to use propaganda against religion, which is essentially what is the rule in this country, only we don't put it quite the same way. For instance, you might go out tomorrow onto the corner of-er-Pennsylvania Avenue, down below the Press Club, and stand on a soap-box and-er-preach Christianity, and nobody would stop you. And then, if it got into your head, perhaps the next day preach against religion of all kinds, and nobody would stop you.[55]

The problem with Roosevelt's characterization was that it did not reflect the realities of the religious situation in the Soviet Union.[56] *America* and *Commonweal* strongly attacked this FDR attempt to legitimize Soviet policies on religion. If Roosevelt was going to support Soviet Lend-Lease, two leading American Catholic magazines would not allow him to spread the illusion that it was because Soviet Russia had freedom of religion.

*Commonweal* editorialized explicitly: "What is religious freedom?" It condemned the formula of only "opportunity to worship God...according to individual preference." This common interpretation was what most people tended to regard the issue of religious liberty as representing. That formula, it asserted, "separates worship from act." True religious freedom meant, "that the Church be free to inform politics...[T]he privilege of worshiping freely, without the consequent privilege of acting in accordance with his worship, is no freedom at all, but a travesty."[57] This idea that religious liberty implied a certain amount of group freedom and public action was echoed in *America*. "Government must be made to understand [as Cardinal Hinsley said] 'that the practice of the Christian religion is something carried on in a Communion, that it is a social activity, the work of a society, and Christian religion is something carried on in a Communion, that it is a social activity, the work of a society, and not something pursued by individuals in isolation.'"[58]

Whereas Roosevelt had to find a way to rationalize Soviet practice, Catholic leaders in favor of some form of Lend-Lease had to contend with the papal injunction in the encyclical *Divini Redemptoris*, which had these strong, clear words: "Communism is intrinsically wrong and no one who would save Christian civilization may give it assistance in any undertaking whatsoever."[59] In the months from June to December 1941, *America* printed more articles and editorials seeking clearly to distinguish the Soviet regime from the Russian people, as well as the Russian nation from Communism. One such example was written by Msgr. Fulton Sheen: "The question of aid to Russia must begin with a distinction between Russia and Communism. Russia is not Communism." He continued later in the passage, "A philosophy of life is not identical with a people."[60] A subtler piece emerged in *Commonweal*. It ran: "These 180 million Russians we could not know until Hitler discovered them to our sight. It was not enough that they suffered the tyranny of their government... We could only condemn the theory on which their government acted. . . . It was necessary before we could think of the Russian people that their suffering should be related to our immediate hopes and fears and concerns."[61] These two articles were clear examples of individuals seeking to find ways around the discourse of the seemingly strict papal injunction. They turned to precedents to see how this injunction had been interpreted. The attempts in *America* and *Commonweal* mirrored the effort generally by the American Roman Catholic leadership to find ways around the papal language.[62]

Indeed, it proved a challenging task to present a position of support for aid to Russia without endorsing the Soviet regime. *America* insisted that the Nazi German government, by attacking the U.S.S.R., was doing so for its own evil purposes and not as a "holy crusader" against Bolshevism. Thus, it wrote: "[Hitler] is a scoundrel who in his country has the power and... the wish to persecute Christianity relentlessly."[63] Michael Williams at *Commonweal* concurred in his column that "Hitler is still our Enemy No.1." He continued, "...communism does not command the technical equipment for over throwing our form of government, our form of society, and destroying the cultural basis for Christian civilization to anything like the same extent as Hitler does."[64]

Clearly, FDR had the tempo of events on his side. After his failure to persuade the public that the Soviet Union had relented in its war on religion, he decided to push harder on the argument against the Nazi regime. In his Navy Day Address in late October 1941, Roosevelt revealed to the country a Nazi plan "to abolish existing religions—Catholic, Protestant, Mohammedan, Hindu, Buddhist, and Jewish alike. The property of all churches will be seized by the Reich. . . . In the place of the churches of our civilization, there is to be set up an International Nazi Church. . . . The god of Blood and Iron will take the place of the God of Love and Mercy."[65] By attempting to cast the Hitler regime in terms darker than Stalin's, FDR could win his argument by appealing to the plain fact that Hitler was the immediate threat.

Two months later, in December 1941, the United States would be at war, and much of the public argument would be swept aside in the rush for national defense. However, for this chapter's purposes, it is important to remember that the logic FDR laid down in 1939 linking religious liberty to international stability formed the basis of the philosophy underlying the United Nations and the current international human rights regime. FDR struck at the concept of state sovereignty, which he had upheld in the earlier Soviet and Mexican anticlericalism cases. The arguments and the logic put forth by *America* and *Commonweal* to justify aiding the Soviet Union against Nazi Germany are worth remembering, for again they reveal how previous discourse about religious liberty created obstacles that impeded Catholic leaders when they saw the need to pursue different policy objectives. Another way to look at the Soviet lend-lease debate is to see it as a development from the Spanish situation. In the Spanish case, the debate over religious liberty occurred without reference to the wider international implications of supporting the Francoist side. In the Soviet lend-lease case, religious liberty was weighed together with the recognized need to contain the larger threat of Hitler.

## SOME CONCLUSIONS

The four cases considered in this chapter offer some patchy answers to the questions that I posed at the outset. Certainly, however, three useful points might be fruitfully pointed out. First, during the 1930s, there was a definite growing trend to link the intrinsic value of religious liberty to more practical values such as national interest and security. This logic was pushed most forcefully by FDR during the late 1930s, after he reversed his stand on the concept of state sovereignty. Freedom of religion became an indicator of a state's likely behavior in the international system. This thought was echoed in *Commonweal* when it quoted Thomas Woodlock, an editor at the *Wall Street Journal*, who noted, "In those few short sentences in which the President reminded us that religion must be the source of democracy and international peace, the President went to the very heart of the troubles that vex the world today."[66] Second, on the question of "what is religious liberty" and when to recognize its violation, considerable confusion and flip-flopping occurred. The problem of definition and the tendency to expand or to contract it depending upon the policy goal desired created a lack of coherence. *America* demonstrated this in the Mexican case by arguing that even though no American complaints of religious persecution had been raised in Mexico, U.S. rights had been violated by the inherent nature of the Mexican policy. FDR, early on, tried to contract the sphere of religious liberty, restricting it to the implication of ceremonial worship. In Spain, there were elements of both directed persecution, such as in Mexico and the Soviet Union, and some elements of permissive persecution either through deliberate negligence or regime weakness. A tendency to oversimplify this problem on the part of *America*, for example, led to a distorted dilemma of Fascism versus Communism. The problem of permissive persecution and the situation in which the side supporting religious liberty is at odds with other democratic values paralyzed clear argument. Third, the cases demonstrate a massive abyss between the problem of international religious persecution and the implementation of policies to redress it on the part of the United States. Often there was very little meaningful discussion on the means necessary to remedy the problem of persecution. In the first case, it was unclear how not extending diplomatic recognition would prove constructive toward ameliorating Soviet religious policy. In the second case, little was said about what kind of intervention in Mexico would be sufficient to reverse its anticlerical attitude. The same issues applied to Spain.

The trends put into place during the 1930s on the issue of religious liberty in foreign policy are still with us, to a large extent, today. The linkage between religious liberty and national interest, and the use of the former as an indicator for international threat continues. We see this most clearly today in aspects of the debate over American policy with respect to China.[67] The problem of defining religious liberty and attributing responsibility for its violation also remains. Just as very little was known in the Spanish situation about the true nature of religious persecution, so too today it is difficult to pinpoint the exact contours of permissive versus deliberate religious persecution. Permissive persecution might call for a different set of policies than repression that is state-sponsored. Getting at that difference is difficult.

By tracing aspects of the public arguments over religious liberty involving FDR and the Catholic periodicals *America* and *Commonweal*, I have sought to flush out these ambiguities that are an eternal part of the challenge facing the issue of religious liberty in foreign policy.

## NOTES

1. From the early 1990s onwards, there has been a large domestic effort to highlight religious persecution overseas. This has resulted in the passage of legislation to sanction countries that violate a certain definition of "religious liberty." For the text of legislation, consult 105th Congress, 2nd Session, Senate Bill 1865, short title, "International Religious Freedom Act of 1998." See also H.R. 2431, "Freedom From Religious Persecution Act," 105th Congress. Passage of the legislation led to the creation of the U.S. Commission on International Religious Freedom, whose mandate is to monitor religious freedom worldwide and advise the president, the secretary of state, and the Congress. The Commission released its first report on May 1, 2000. See Office of International Information Programs, U.S. Department of State, website: http://usinfo.state.gov.

2. The dates are just general guides. In all of the cases, reporting and discussion on the religious situation in these countries were frequent throughout the course of the 1920s through 1940s. What I have done is to attempt to highlight the years in Roosevelt's first two terms in which some more notable or significant editorials, reports, and debates were published.

3. George Q. Flynn, *American Catholics and the Roosevelt Presidency* (Lexington: University of Kentucky, 1968), p. 140.

4. Peter G. Filene, *Americans and the Soviet Experiment* (Cambridge: Harvard University Press, 1967), pp. 89–90.

5. Richard Pipes details the antireligious campaigns of the Soviet government against many faiths during the 1920s in his book, *Russia Under the Bolshevik Regime*, (New York: Knopf, 1994).

6. *Commonweal*, May 5, 1933, 4.

7. Ibid., 4.

8. "On Recognizing Russia," *America*, October 28, 1933, 75.

9. "The Recognition of Russia," *America*, December 17, 1932, 251.

10. See *Commonweal*, August 4, 1933; *America*, April 1, 1933; April 29, 1933; August 5, 1933; November 25, 1933.

11. Leonid I. Strakhovsky, "Should Russia Be Recognized?" *Commonweal*, October 6, 1933, 527.

12. The evolution of the Far Eastern diplomatic situation in the 1920s and early 1930s is best described in Akira Iriye's *After Imperialism: The Search for a New Order in the Far East 1921–1931* (Chicago: Imprint, 1990). For how it played with Roosevelt, see Robert Dallek, *Franklin D. Roosevelt and American Foreign Policy* (New York: Oxford, 1979), pp. 28–30.

13. John LaFarge, S.J., "Soviet Sovereignty and Human Rights," *America*, May 13, 1933, 129–131.

14. R. F. Grady, S.J., "Russian Propaganda in the United States," *America*, May 27, 1933, 174.

15. George Q. Flynn notes that the Catholic Church in the United States had been vigorous in opposing recognition for many years. See chapter 7 of his book, *American Catholics and the Roosevelt Presidency*.

16. "Address to the National Conference of Catholic Charities," October 4, 1933, *PPA*, 1933, pp. 381–382.

17. Donald G. Bishop, *The Roosevelt–Litvinov Agreements* (Syracuse: Syracuse University Press, 1965), pp. 63–65.

18. To see how the agreements played out in practice, see Bishop's *The Roosevelt–Litvinov Agreements*, chapter 3.

19. Flynn suggests that this can be attributed to the fact that Catholics were "flattered by the unexpected hearing" given to their views by the President— see Flynn, *American Catholics and the Roosevelt Presidency*, p. 149.

20. Joseph F. Thorning, S.J., "What Russian Recognition Means," *America*, December 2, 1933, 200.

21. "Russia and Religion," *Commonweal*, November 24, 1933, 86.

22. Douglas J. Slawson, "The National Catholic Welfare Conference and the Mexican Church–State Conflict of the Mid-1930s: A Case of *Deja vu*," *Catholic Historical Review* 80 (January 1994): 59.

23. E. David Cronon, *Josephus Daniels in Mexico*, (Madison: University of Wisconsin Press, 1960), p. 83. Also Leo V. Kanawada, *Franklin D. Roosevelt's Diplomacy and American Catholics, Italians, and Jews* (Essex: Erasmus House, 1982), pp. 21–23.

24. Cronon, pp. 90–93.
25. Edgar B. Nixon, ed., *Franklin D. Roosevelt and Foreign Affairs*, vol. 1 (Cambridge: Harvard, 1969), p. 20.
26. Robert Dallek, *Franklin D. Roosevelt and American Foreign Policy, 1932–1945* (New York: Oxford, 1979), p. 83.
27. Nixon notes that "in a discussion of the Address with Professor Moley he [FDR] drew the analogy between the relations of the American Republics and the relations between a citizen in a small community with his own neighbors..." Cf. 21.
28. "What is a Good Neighbor?" *America*, April 6, 1935, 606.
29. "Good Neighbor to a Bad Neighbor?" *America*, October 12, 1935, 4.
30. Franklin D. Roosevelt, *Public Papers and Addresses* (henceforth, *PPA* with year attached) 1935, ed. Samuel I. Rosenman (New York: Macmillan, 1941), p. 305.
31. Senate Resolution 70, *Congressional Record*, vol. 79, 1338 (weekly edition).
32. Ibid., vol. 79, 1338.
33. A perfect example of this reasoning was FDR' s letter to the head of the Knights of Columbus, Mr. Martin Carmody. See *PPA*, 1935, 450 ff.
34. *America*, January 19, 1935, 342.
35. In 1935 in particular, Roosevelt was feeling political pressure from the Knights of Columbus to allow the Borah Resolution to move out of committee. See Christopher J. Kauffman, *Faith and Fraternalism* (New York: Harper and Row, 1982), pp. 303–305.
36. One way to interpret the San Diego speech is to see it as a fulfilment of a pledge that Roosevelt made to the Knights of Columbus to address publicly in a major speech the issue of anticlericalism in Mexico. See Douglas Slawson, "The National Catholic Welfare Conference and the Mexican Church–State Conflict of the Mid-1930s: A Case of *Deja vu*," *Catholic Historical Review* 80 (January 1994): 84
37. "Address at San Diego Exposition," *PPA*, 1935, 411.
38. Stanley Payne, *Spain's First Democracy* (Madison: University of Wisconsin, 1993), p. 317.
39. Payne, *Spain's First Democracy*, 288.
40. Payne suggests that there were elements of both reluctance and inability. In some cases, destruction of religious property was done by officials of the government, either acting on orders or on their own. Often times, the government and the police passively allowed the destruction. Other times, they were just incapable of stopping it.
41. J. David Valaik, "American Catholic Dissenters and the Spanish Civil War," *Catholic Historical Review* 52 (January 1968): 537–541.
42. John P. Delaney wrote: "Wittingly or unwittingly, by concerted design or before a show of force, the United Front regime slowly gave way to the forces of extreme Communism...to forces of anarchy that...forbid their fellow countrymen the most elementary rights to free speech and free worship...." *America*, August 22, 1936, 460.
43. As *America* put it: "The utter failure of the Left Republicans to maintain order, to protect churches and convents from arson and pillage, and to check

the drive of their allies toward a Red republic, has roused the army and the Right to insurrection." Laurence K. Patterson, S.J., "Right and Left Battle for Spain," *America*, August 8, 1936, 413.

44. "Further Reflections on the Spanish Situation," *America*, May 1, 1937, 77.
45. Barbara Barclay Carter, "European Catholics and Spain," *Commonweal*, March 5, 1937, 516.
46. George N. Shuster, "Some Further Reflections," *Commonweal*, April 23, 1937, 716.
47. Flynn, *Roosevelt and Romanism*, 51–52.
48. "Civil War in Spain and the United States," *Commonweal*, June 24, 1938, 229.
49. "Our Own Views on Neutrality," *Commonweal*, February 17, 1939, 452.
50. *Commonweal*, May 20, 1938, 85.
51. Dallek, *American Foreign Policy*, 127–132.
52. "Speech by Roosevelt, Chautauqua, New York, August 14, 1936," *Franklin Roosevelt and Foreign Affairs*, vol. 3, 377.
53. Richard P. Traina, *American Diplomacy and the Spanish Civil War* (Bloomington: Indiana University Press, 1968), pp. 223–228.
54. "Annual Message to Congress," *PPA*, 1939, 1–2.
55. Press Conference Number 771, September 30, 1941. *Complete Presidential Press Conferences of Franklin D. Roosevelt*, introduction by Jonathan Daniels (New York: Da Capo Press, 1972), vol. 18, 187–188.
56. For press reactions to this, see column by Walter Lippmann, "Russia, America and Mr. Roosevelt," *Washington Post*, October 4, 1941. Also, "Roosevelt Comment on Soviet Churches Seen Bid for Support," *Washington Star*, October 1, 1941; Arthur Krock, "What the President Said About Religious Liberty," *New York Times*, October 3, 1941. See also Dennis J. Dunn, "Stalinism and the Catholic Church During the Era of World War II," *Catholic Historical Review* 59 (October 1973): 404–428.
57. *Commonweal*, October 17, 1841, 603.
58. *America*, October 11, 1941, 14.
59. George Q. Flynn, *Roosevelt and Romanism* (Westport: Greenwood, 1976), p. 138.
60. Fulton J. Sheen, "Soviet Russia May Be Helped But Russia Must Be Reformed," *America*, October 18, 1941, 33.
61. "Russian Participation," *Commonweal*, August 8, 1941, 363.
62. This story is detailed best in Gerald P. Fogarty, *The Vatican and the American Hierarchy* (Stuttgart: Anton Hiersemann, 1982), pp. 271–276.
63. *America*, July 12, 1941, 378.
64. Michael Williams, "Views and Reviews," *Commonweal*, July 18, 1941, 303.
65. *PPA*, 1941, 440. For more on the Nazi plan, see John S. Conway, "A German National Reich Church and American War Propaganda," *Catholic Historical Review*, 62 (July 1976): 464–472.
66. "The President's Message, A Symposium," *Commonweal*, January 20, 1939, 341.
67. Much of the current legislation cited in note 1 is motivated by this issue of religious liberty in China and Sudan.

# PART 3

# SEARCHING FOR A NEW WORLD ORDER

## FDR, THE VATICAN, AND WORLD WAR II

# CHAPTER 9

# POPE PIUS XII AND THE MYRON TAYLOR MISSION

## THE VATICAN AND AMERICAN WARTIME DIPLOMACY

### JOHN S. CONWAY

PRESIDENT ROOSEVELT'S ANNOUNCEMENT ON DECEMBER 23, 1939, in the course of a Christmas broadcast, of his intention to appoint a personal representative at the Vatican aroused, as is well known, considerable controversy within the United States. Roosevelt's motives were essentially pragmatic, not religious. But his awareness of the dangers to the whole world, visibly heightened by Hitler's aggressive launching of war three months earlier, prompted him to seek ways to bring American influence to bear in wartorn Europe. The advantages were obvious in seeking to gain the Holy See's support in trying to achieve a quick end to hostilities and the restoration of peace. In addition, the Vatican was presumed to have sources of intelligence and contacts with other neutral states, which could be mobilized for Roosevelt's wider purposes.

In contrast to the furor in the United States, the response from Pope Pius XII was enthusiastic, and taken with uncharacteristic speed. From the moment of his election in March 1939, Pius had a very clear concept of his most pressing task, which was the need to prevent the outbreak or spread of war from once again engulfing Europe in the kind of disastrous suffering and conflict that he had witnessed so closely only 25 years earlier. Pius was well aware of the enormous damage to the Church's witness and credibility resulting from World War I. No effort must be spared to mobilize support for a morally convincing campaign to safeguard peace. Even though the outbreak of hostilities in September marked a striking defeat of Pius's initial and energetic efforts, nevertheless he was still convinced of the need to prevent any escalation and to make use of the Vatican's diplomatic network to alleviate suffering. The prospect of having Roosevelt's declared support for such aims was therefore most welcome.

Almost immediately, in his typical style of baroque circumlocution, Pius responded by declaring his hope that:

> When that day dawns—and We would like to hope that it is not too far distant on which the roar of battle will lapse into silence and there will arise the possibility of establishing a true and sound peace dictated by the principles of justice and equity, only He will be able to discover the path that should be followed who unites with high political power a clear understanding of the voice of humanity along with a sincere reverence for the divine precepts of life as found in the Gospel of Christ. Only men of such moral stature will be able to create the peace that will compensate for the incalculable sacrifices of this war and clear the way for a comity of nations, fair to all, efficacious and sustained by united confidence.

Whether Roosevelt would turn out to be a man of such a stature remained to be seen. But at a time of severe disillusionment, and with the prospects ahead ominously dark, the pope's eagerness to enlist the United States in this cause is understandable.

The evidence is clear that Pius XII, perhaps more than most other popes, had given considerable thought to the political aspects of his role and conduct as supreme pontiff. His whole training and experience had been that of a diplomat, and there can be no doubt that he saw his election to the papacy as summoning him to uphold the political-religious values of the Catholic Church in the open struggle against aggression, violent nationalism and racism, or revolutionary secular ideologies. He was well aware of the diminished efficacy of moral appeals against such dark forces, and the steady erosion of the papacy's powers of persuasion. Nevertheless, Pius was resolved to use his undoubted diplomatic talents in the service of international stability by upholding the ideal Christian standards of justice and peace. But just how this should be done presented constant dilemmas. As the escalation of hostilities took place in 1940 and 1941, to his very evident distress, Pius was more and more torn between the rival claims of his office. His ability to see the likely consequences of any particular course of action, particularly the disadvantages, undoubtedly deterred him from adopting any stance that could have incalculable, even disastrous, results not only for the cause of peace or for his own mission, but also for the whole church.

In Pius's view, the task of the Vatican was to prevent the descent of the world into another cataclysmic war, or if it nevertheless occurred, to provide an overarching forum for negotiating peace. The moral authority of Europe's oldest diplomatic entity, as well as that of the largest Christian community, had to be clearly committed to bringing hostilities to an end as quickly as possible by offering to serve as a negotiating vehicle for conclusive peace talks. An absolute prerequisite was to obtain or retain the confidence of the warring sides in the Vatican's neutrality. Without it there would be no chance of success. Hence Pius's deliberate decision to adopt an attitude of strict impartiality, and to reject the provocations and incessant pressures by one or other of the participants to have the Holy See endorse the justice of their respective crusades or to denounce their opponents' acts of aggression.

This was a stance Pius believed the United States would endorse and support. His belief was strengthened by the warm relationship he established with Roosevelt's choice as personal envoy, Myron C. Taylor. Taylor, although an Episcopalian of the same kind of unfervent variety as Roosevelt himself, was known to love Italy, and to uphold the anti-Communist patrician values of European civilization so esteemed in the Vatican. At the same time, he was already versed in the complexities of European diplomacy, having served as the American representative on the Intergovernmental Committee on Political Refugees at the ill-fated Evian Conference of 1938, which had shown clearly enough the limits of moral persuasiveness, and not only on the German government.

The close understanding that evolved between Pius and Taylor was therefore significant both personally and politically. Taylor was impressed by the pope's diplomatic subtlety and shrewd prudence. He was delighted to report to Roosevelt after his first audience in February 1940 that the pope had freely and voluntarily offered "very close collaboration with the President, through me, and daily access to the Pope day or night, whenever desired." For nearly two years, this bond remained, despite the increasing setbacks to their commonly understood pursuit, as Pius wrote to Roosevelt in August 1940, "of a golden era of Christian concord dedicated to the spiritual and mutual improvement of humanity."

There was little evidence of such Christian concord in the following months. Germany's astonishing victories, and Hitler's declared intention of remolding all of Europe on a Nazified racial pattern, sent shivers of alarm through the Vatican, and forced a scaling down of expectations that such a victor would be prepared to negotiate peace unless on his own terms. After Mussolini had been successfully seduced into joining in, the Vatican's influence was markedly affected. The pope grew more pessimistic. And the continued abstention of the United States seemed to presage the imminence of the Axis' total victory.

In these circumstances, the papal choices were bleak. To abandon the task of seeking to negotiate between the parties as an impartial peacemaker would not only have been an admission of failure, but a repudiation of Pius's entire previous career. But to seek an accommodation with the victorious Axis powers would have been equally unpalatable and fraught with dangers. A retreat into impotent silence until better times appeared would only have seemed cowardly. Despite the constant incitements of the warring powers to declare himself and God to be on their side, every occasion on which the pope urged moderation or offered assistance to the victims of the war, was deliberately or disdainfully spurned. Another factor that prompted prudence was the awareness that the Vatican was infiltrated by all sorts of agents who did not hesitate to spread defamatory reports abroad about the pope's alleged attitudes—so many in fact that the attempt to issue denials was abandoned. At the same time, the Vatican officials became alerted to the fact that their own codes for diplomatic communication were being monitored and even deciphered. Nonetheless the pope stood fast in his resolve to uphold the ideal of being a peacemaker whose services would, sooner or later, be required to bring about a restoration of international stability. In such an endeavor, he believed, at least until December 1941, the United States would also want to participate.

This common resolve was only made more complex following the German attack on the Soviet Union in June 1941. Despite urgings to bless this aggression as a laudable anti-Bolshevik "crusade," and despite their well-known anti-Communist antipathies, neither the pope nor the German Catholic hierarchy were prepared to do so. "We took special care," the pope later recalled, "notwithstanding certain tendentious pressures, not to let fall from Our lips, or from Our pen, one single word of encouragement for the war against Russia in 1941." For his part, however, Roosevelt was aware that the United States would face increased dangers if the Soviet Union were over-thrown. Paradoxically, therefore, circumstances dictated that the pope who hated Communism was obliged to keep silent, and the president who hated Communism was obliged to urge its cause.

In the United States, most Catholics were less far-sighted. They strongly condemned Communism and believed they had papal authority to do so. They were bound to be aroused by any moves Roosevelt might plan for assistance to the Soviet Union. In order to resolve this issue, Taylor was again dispatched to Rome in September 1941 to seek a compromise. To accommodate the president's wishes, Pius ordered instructions to be sent to the papal delegate in Washington that the encyclical of 1937 condemning Communism should be interpreted in a more lenient way, drawing a distinction between the errors of Communist theory and permissible support of the Russian people in their hour of need.

The pope was upheld in his faith in Roosevelt by Taylor's pointing to the commonality of aims as expressed in the Atlantic Charter of August 1941, "The objectives are based on the teachings of the New Testament, and call for spiritual leadership in opposition to the extremely pagan views and objectives of the Axis powers." No mention was made of the extremely pagan views of Stalin, nor of the entrenched hostility to the Vatican to be found in Britain, where the Foreign Office was scathing about the Holy See and about Pius— "the weakest Pope in the modern era"—and about their refusal to condemn the obvious crimes of the Nazis such as the bombing of British cities.

Such hopes for a just and lasting peace brought about by Pius's skilful diplomacy with the backing and power of the United States were shattered forever in December 1941. From then on, Roosevelt began to be as demanding as the other belligerents in calling for the Holy See to use its moral influence in the Allies' favor and even claiming that failure to do so "is endangering its moral prestige and undermining faith both in the church and in the Holy Father himself." Such sentiments from the State Department could only be regarded as a stab in the back. It is no wonder that the pope was obliged to become even more sibylline in his utterances.

Such unwelcome criticisms from a supposed "old and good friend" only added to the pope's woes as the brutality and horror of the war extended around the globe in 1942. The reports received every day from the Vatican's worldwide network of nuncios and delegates told of ever-increasing disasters and suffering inflicted not just on the military forces but also on countless civilians. Such news pained the pope grievously, providing proof of the terrifying lack of compassion in the hearts of the world's rulers. But the Holy See's resources to mitigate such horrendous circumstances were pitifully meager. It is hardly to be wondered at that the atmosphere of frustration and pessimism in the Vatican grew incrementally.

Surprisingly, in September 1942, the Italian government gave permission for Myron Taylor to pay his final wartime visit to the Vatican. But his interview with the pope must have been a difficult one, since this time he was instructed to seek to persuade Pius to give up his previous stance, and instead to accept the American view that a just and lasting peace could only be achieved by a massive and invincible use of force. Any hope for a quick cessation of hostilities through a negotiated peace would have to be abandoned. Even the promise that the United States would now join unprecedentedly in efforts to establish a international order could hardly outweigh the pope's fears that such an onslaught would involve the destruction of European stability and involve the specter of postwar chaos and/or Communist-provoked revolution.

These pessimistic apprehensions were only heightened a few months later by the Allies' public declaration of January 1943 that they intended to demand "unconditional surrender," a policy that was strongly deplored by the Vatican officials. Not only did it provide the Nazi leaders with a forceful propaganda advantage, but also it rendered still more nugatory the already fragile aspirations of the German resistance movement, on which the pope had placed unrealistic hopes.

The climax came later in 1943, after the fall of Mussolini when German troops seized control of Rome and encircled the Vatican's 108 acres. In this claustrophobic atmosphere, rumors were rife that the pope would be carried off into captivity, and the most significant papal files were hastily secreted under the marble floor of a papal chamber. Even if Pius himself faced the prospect of his forcible removal with considerable fortitude, the Holy See's powerlessness was only too evident. Even more disturbing was the clear sense of despair that the values of the Christian civilization so long upheld by the Church were being inexorably overwhelmed as the tide of war engulfed so many unfortunate populations.

It is in this context that the pope's response to atrocities of the Holocaust must be placed. At first, Vatican officials, like their counterparts in Western or neutral countries, were unwilling or unable to believe that mass murders of Jews were taking place. The Vatican was reluctant to accept unverifiable reports of horrendous events taking place in unreachable locations in Eastern Europe, and was still less able to evaluate their credibility. When Myron Taylor specifically inquired in September 1942 whether the Vatican would confirm that millions of Jews were being murdered in Poland, Cardinal Maglione could only say that they were unable to check the accuracy of such reports, but that the Holy See would not fail to intervene in favor of Jews whenever such a possibility existed. The dilemmas of distinguishing between fact and grossly exaggerated wartime propaganda continued.

The possibilities of intervention were in fact extremely limited, even where the evidence of suffering was undeniable. Diplomatic appeals to Berlin were returned unopened. The Germans refused to allow any papal representative to visit Poland. The Russians brusquely turned aside all interventions on behalf of residents in their territories. The British government would not allow its blockade to be lifted in order to bring foodstuffs to France or Belgium. The United States refused to increase the quotas allotted to European refugees. In sum, the pope's influence was far too slight to overcome the universal failure to realize the urgency of the Jewish plight. Nevertheless, in those cases where the Vatican had reliable information and when its interventions seemed likely to be heeded, the Curia acted forcefully. In Slovakia, Hungary, Bulgaria, and Roumania, its delegates took active steps to alleviate the plight of the threatened Jews, which succeeded in delaying, though not preventing, the deportations and other acts of degradation. Slovakia was a particularly grievous case, since its president, Josef Tiso, was also a Catholic monsignor. Despite strenuous representations from the Vatican in early 1942, the Slovak authorities persisted in their plans to deport all their Jewish subjects into German hands. This evidence of Slovak anti-Semitism, from president to people, aroused feelings not merely of frustration but of betrayal. As one of the Curia's senior officials bitterly commented in July 1942:

> It is a great tragedy that the President of Slovakia is a priest. Everyone knows that the Holy See cannot bring Hitler to heel. But who will understand that we can't even control a priest?

Nevertheless, as the situation grew even more critical, the Vatican's efforts continued. Their interventions in Hungary in 1944, after the Nazi seizure of that country, and the energetic but long-unrecognized relief endeavors of the Nuncio, Msgr Rotta, may be credited with rescuing at least a portion of Hungarian Jewry. In the light of history, such attempts seem pitifully inadequate. But while it is true that not enough was done, it is not true to state that nothing was done.

In subsequent years, after Pius XII's death in 1958, considerable criticism has arisen over his alleged failure to denounce the Nazi atrocities of the Holocaust in more forceful terms. The claim has even been put forward that, had he spoken with the voice of John the Baptist, he could have mobilized the forces of resistance or even obliged Hitler to abandon his plans. Pius is accused of being preoccupied with politics and the practical, with diplomacy and the temporal, and so overlooked or misjudged developments in the moral and spiritual realm. Hence his prudent silence is attributed to a failure of theological bravery and as such stands condemned as a grave dereliction of his Christian duty.

Behind such a sentiment lies, no doubt, a laudable view of papal responsibilities, but in the actual historical circumstances of World War II, this charge is surely misleading. For one thing, it greatly exaggerates the extent of potential papal authority, and as such is not far from wishful thinking. The evidence is now clear that the pope's power was not nearly as effective as these critics imagine, and indeed one wonders whether they would not accuse the pope of theocratic ambitions if such a power had been exercised in any cause other than their own. Certainly we can affirm that the pope was well aware that in urging support for the victims of the war, especially the Jews, he was addressing, even amongst his Catholic followers, men who are now branded as "eliminationist antisemites," but who, even without such exaggerations, felt no compulsion to heed his admonitions. Amongst German Catholics the rival claims of nationalistic and religious loyalties were only dimly realized to be incompatible. Any such papal appeals would have provoked even greater tensions, and the pope was fearful that Catholic loyalty would lose out. Amongst other East European Catholics, the virulence of anti-Jewish feeling was so deeply entrenched that the response would almost certainly have been damaging to the pope's overall moral authority and standing. And there can be no doubt whatsoever that all such denunciatory condemnations would have brought about savage reprisals by the Nazis against the very people the pope was trying to protect.

For his part, Myron Taylor, though he strictly avoided any reference to theological positions, may also have been guilty of exaggerating the extent of the Holy See's influence. That is why in 1942 he was so keen to enlist the papacy's support for America's unconditional war aims, even though he had previously expressed his appreciation of Pius's efforts to secure a negotiated peace. Although rebuffed, he still maintained his high regard for Pius's abilities, and advised President Roosevelt to continue such collaboration where possible. There is no reason to doubt the sincerity of his view, expressed in his resignation letter to Roosevelt at the end of 1944, that Pius XII "has indeed been a great spiritual ally and ranks with yourself, Mr President, in the galaxy of great men of these days." It is a flattering, but accurate, comment on Taylor's own attitude to the two leaders.

As for the wider issue, it is certainly legitimate to argue that the pope over-estimated the diplomatic influence of his office, or that, as events placed increasing obstacles to its exercise, he allowed himself to be more and more affected by the painful dilemmas of his position. No one familiar with the sources now available can doubt the difficulties of his predicament, or the virtual impossibility of calculating whether specific protests would result in more harm or good. As Pius wrote to Bishop Preysing in Berlin in April 1943:

> In constantly striving to find the right balance between the mutually contradictory claims of his pastoral office, the path ahead for the representative of Christ is becoming daily more overgrown, beset with difficulties and full of thorns.

A more cogent criticism of the papal stance, and of Myron Taylor's loyal support, is surely to be found not so much in the Vatican's alleged diplomatic or political shortcomings, but rather in the theological presuppositions that prevailed at the time. The pope's sympathy for the persecuted Jews and his distress at their plight was undoubtedly sincere. But there is no evidence that Pius or his officials ever considered the extent to which the traditional Catholic doctrine of antipathy toward Judaism, and its resulting practices of intolerance and discrimination, had contributed to the passivity of the Catholic population's response to the Nazis' anti-Semitic onslaughts. The strongly worded encyclicals of the 1920s and 1930s denouncing the aberrant ideologies of racism, totalitarianism, and anti-Semitism were genuine enough. But there is no indication of any willingness to revise the Catholic Church's teachings toward Judaism or to find any words of benevolence for the faith that had once been the cradle of Christianity. Another 20 years were to elapse before the Second Vatican Council in the 1960s promulgated a very different view, stressing the indissoluble bond between the two faiths, countering the age-old teaching of contempt, abandoning the mistaken triumphalism and exclusivity of the past, and affirming the common spiritual patrimony between Christians and Jews. Such moves toward a more sympathetic and sensitive approach, now to be found among both Catholics and Protestants, can be seen, in my view, as the most significant theological development of this century. The tragedy is that such steps were taken 50 years too late.

# CHAPTER 10

# CATHOLICS, JEWS, AND THE BOMBARDMENT OF ROME

## THE PRIORITIES OF PIUS XII DURING WORLD WAR II

### MICHAEL PHAYER

ROLF HOCHHUTH, INTRODUCING PIUS XII IN HIS FAMOUS PLAY, *The Deputy*, instructed the actor to capture the pope's "aristocratic coldness" and the "icy glint" of his eyes. Many of us, including, I suspect a good number of historians, have accepted Hochhuth's image of Pius as an uncaring and austere person. This characterization is baseless. Nevertheless, what I have to say here will probably not change many minds.

Although Hochhuth situated Pius in a fairly realistic historical setting in *The Deputy*, by and large he did not bring into play the pope's concern about the possible bombardment of Rome. Had he done so, his characterization of Pius would undoubtedly have projected an even more reserved and calculating person. My purpose here is to emphasize the importance that Pius XII placed on preserving Rome from bombardment. This objective had priority, even if Polish Catholics and European Jews, and in particular, Roman Jews, would suffer—indeed, die—for it. I suspect that Pius realized he could not posit the bombardment of Rome as his reason for not speaking out about the ongoing murder of the Jews precisely because the world would think him callous. Time will not permit us to review step by step the Vatican's responses to genocide during World War II. Here, I will take up three time periods— one at the beginning of the war, a second during its middle years, and lastly in 1944—to emphasize Pius's resolve to protect Rome and to illustrate the priority this resolution took over speaking out against the persecution of civilians.

## POLAND AND THE VATICAN DURING THE
## FIRST MONTHS OF THE WAR

At the beginning of the war, Pope Pius sought to remain neutral regarding the conflict itself while condemning moral abuses that accompanied it. Thus, while he did not comment on Germany's invasion of Poland or, subsequently, other European countries, he did condemn atrocities that took place in Poland. In an address to the College of Cardinals in December 1939, Pope Pius spoke out against atrocities perpetrated on the elderly, women, and children.[1] The Vatican also used its radio and press to inform the world in January 1940, of terrorization of the Polish people. The Vatican radio pointed out that part of Poland had been organized into a General Government into which Poles were being forced "in the depth of one of Europe's severest winters, on principles and by methods that can be described only as brutal." This was a reference to the Poles of the Warthegau area and the 750,000 Poles of the Polish Corridor area both of whom were dispossessed of house and home and driven into the General Government region. Once there, "Jews and Poles are being herded into separate ghettos, hermetically sealed where they face starvation while Polish grain is shipped to Germany."[2] The broadcasts, given in several languages, accused the Germans of wanton larceny and of depriving the people of their religious freedom by packing off their priests to concentration camps. Thereafter Vatican radio fell silent regarding Poland and the decimation of its populace.

Why had the Vatican changed course? According to the Holy See, silence spared Poles of greater atrocities. In May 1940, Pope Pius learned of "unbelievable atrocities" against Poles from an Italian consul who had to leave Poland. Three days later the pope told another visitor of his decision to keep silent in order to spare Poles from worse punishment.[3] Such a justification was preposterous, considering the tone of the supplications Pope Pius had received from church leaders in Poland. In fact, word came later from Poland objecting to this excuse, but the Holy See continued to use it later on during the Holocaust itself.[4]

The most likely reason for Pius's silence was fear of German retaliation against the Vatican rather than retaliation against Poles.[5] In 1940, the Vatican's cardinal, Eugene Tisserant, objected that the pope concerned himself too much with protecting the Vatican from bombing raids and too little with church problems.[6] In a conversation with the Italian minister of state, Roberto Farinacci, Hitler threatened to go so far as to destroy the

Vatican if it spoke out against the "battle of the German *Volk*."[7] Reference here seems to be to the dispossessing of Poles and the resettlement of Volksdeutsch from the Baltic Sea region onto Polish properties. After the January broadcast, the German ambassador to Chile requested that the nuncio there ask the Vatican to stop the radio addresses of Bishop Hlond about the disastrous conditions of Catholics in Poland.[8] Three days later cardinal secretary of state Maglione told the nuncio that the Vatican was disposed to stop the broadcasts in order to prevent the situation of Catholics in Poland from worsening. The actual reason, I argue, was not to make graver the situation of Catholics in Rome.

### ITALIAN JEWS AND THE VATICAN DURING THE MIDDLE YEARS OF THE WAR

Pope Pius's fears about Rome's aerial destruction became acute in 1942 and 1943. Aerial bombardment became possible for the allies after General Erwin Rommel's *Panzerkorps* had been pushed out of northern Africa, allowing English and American troops to cross the Mediterranean and occupy Sicily. Driving German forces from mountainous southern Italy proved a more difficult task, one that lasted from the summer of 1943 to the summer of 1944. During these months of acute danger, the Holy See communicated directly to President Franklin D. Roosevelt through his personal envoy to the Vatican, Myron Taylor, or to his *charges d'affaires* Harold Tittmann, no fewer than 34 times in an effort to forestall the bombing of Rome.[9] And, on more than one occasion, Pius warned the allies that he would protest publicly if they bombed the city of Rome.[10]

The problem facing Pius XII lay in the fact that he had failed to condemn German bombing of England during 1940 and 1941 but then spoke up against the bombing of civilians when the allies gained aerial superiority. Perhaps Pius's words of affection for German air raid victims resulted from the ferocity and duration of allied attacks after Marshal Hermann Goering's air force had become totally defenseless. Still, by expressing sympathy and concern for Germany's bombed out churches after not having regretted the Nazi destruction of Coventry Cathedral in England, the pope had made a serious tactical mistake.[11]

In October 1942, when U.S. envoy Taylor attempted to extract a promise from Winston Churchill not to bomb Rome, the prime minister refused to commit himself. Pius continued to hope that he could get President Franklin D. Roosevelt to persuade the English not to bomb Rome, but Taylor delicately pointed out that this might be difficult: "I am not clear," he told Monsignor Montini, "whether the Holy See has condemned the bombing of London, Warsaw, Rotterdam, Belgrade, Coventry, Manila, Pearl Harbor, and places in the South Pacific."[12] Early in 1943, Anthony Eden, addressing Parliament, stoked Pope Pius's anxiety when he said that "we have as much right to bomb Rome as the Italians had to bomb London. We shall not hesitate to do so to the best of our ability and as heavily as possible if the course of the war should render such bombing convenient and helpful."[13]

It exasperated observers, both inside and outside the Vatican, that the pope would be so concerned over what had not yet taken place and so little concerned over the ongoing murder of the Jews. In September, Myron Taylor told Montini that the "deplorable inhumanities in Germany against civilian populations are even more reprehensible than the attacks on all her neighbors whom she invaded."[14] British minister to the Holy See, Francis d'Arcy Osborne, put it to the Vatican secretary of state more bluntly on December 14, 1942: "instead of thinking of nothing but the bombing of Rome, [the Holy See] should consider [its] duties in respect to the unprecedented crime against humanity of Hitler's campaign of extermination of the Jews."[15] Bishop Preysing, writing a few months later to Pius from heavily bombed Berlin, adopted the same perspective that Minister Osborne found lacking in the pope. "Even more bitter [than the air raids] faces us here in Berlin with the new wave of Jewish deportations that were put in motion just before the first of March [1943]." Preysing then asked the pope to speak out about the Holocaust.[16]

Six months later in October 1943, Pope Pius was confronted with the precise question that Bishop Preysing had put to him so pointedly— deportation of Jews versus aerial bombardment. The events that unfolded that autumn illustrate most clearly Pius XII's priorities when it came to the question of saving Jews or saving the city of Rome.

It was at that time that the Reich Security Main Office moved to deport the Jews of Rome to Auschwitz. On October 16, 1943, more than 1,200 Jews were temporarily incarcerated in the military college 600 feet from the Vatican. Of this group, about 1,000, including 896 women and children, were taken after two days to Rome's main railroad station where they were packed and locked in freight cars. Five days later the train, without food, water, or toilets, arrived in Auschwitz too late for detraining. After another night, the Jews detrained in the morning at Birkenau and passed immediately through Mengele's selection. About 200 were sent to work; the rest were immediately gassed and cremated.[17]

No events placed Pope Pius in greater physical proximity to the Holocaust than those that occurred in October in Rome. Not surprisingly, the judgment of many historians against the pontiff has revolved around the drama of the Roman Jews. There are three reasons for this: well before the roundup of the Jews, the pope knew that they were going to be seized but failed to warn them; the incident occurred in the immediate vicinity of Vatican City;

and, after the Jews had been deported, the pope failed to condemn Germany for its barbarity. Time does not permit us to review in any detail the events surrounding the October roundup of Roman Jews, but we must at least consider Pope Pius's actions during this time since they bear on the question of Rome's bombardment.

The Vatican's response to the October 16 catastrophe, muted and delayed, was couched in several considerations. Since thousands of Jews remained at large in Rome after the roundup, the German ambassador, Baron Ernst von Weizsacker, advised the Vatican not to protest the detention of the Jews for fear that this might trigger a second, more intensive hunt. But such a protest would have had other potentially dire consequences for the Vatican and for the Holy Father himself. The possibility that Hitler would take the pope captive was taken seriously by the diplomatic staff in Rome, including the Germans themselves, and according to his housekeeper, Sister Pasqualina Lehnert, by Pope Pius himself.[18] Two other possibilities probably seemed more likely and of greater importance to the pope. A strong protest against the seizure of the Jews would have irritated Hitler to such an extent that recriminations most likely would have followed. These would have taken the form of the Germans using the city of Rome as a center of resistance against the approaching Allied armies with the consequence of heavy aerial and artillery bombardment, or of a German attack on Vatican City itself. Clearly, a protest against the October roundup would have had serious consequences both for the Vatican and for the Jews in hiding.

While it would be speculative to affirm which consequence weighed most heavily in the pope's considerations, we know what action the Vatican took after the roundup. On October 19, one day after the freight train packed with Jews left Rome for Auschwitz, the Vatican publicly acknowledged, as Hitler's Foreign Minister Ribbentrop had requested sometime before the October roundup, that German military behavior in occupied Rome toward the Vatican had been correct and civil. Second, Pius requested additional German forces in Rome to control Communist insurgents.[19] And, still on the nineteenth, the Holy Father pressed the American *charges d'affaires*, Tittman, to give assurances that the Allied forces would not bombard Rome and wrote President Roosevelt an emotional letter of complaint on account of a recent bombing.[20] Pius held up Germany's good conduct in Rome to Tittmann and contrasted it with Allied bombings. In spite of the roundup of the Roman Jews and the murder of millions of other Jews about which the Vatican was well informed, Ambassador Weizsacker could report to Berlin that Germany was winning the propaganda war in the Vatican against the Allies.[21]

In the end, nothing came of anything the Holy See said about the fateful days beginning on October 16, 1942. Having known in advance what would befall the Roman Jews, the pope said nothing to forestall it. Afterward, he said nothing to condemn it. On October 25–26, 10 days after the roundup of the Jews, an obfuscated statement appeared in *L'Osservatore Romano*, which the German ambassador told his home office not to fret about. On the same day that the article appeared in the Vatican paper, Tittmann notified the State Department that the Holy See's anxiety over German violation of its neutrality had given way to optimism.[22] Pope Pius's diplomacy had succeeded in protecting Rome from the Germans.

## PIUS XII REASSERTS A MORAL VISION LATE IN THE WAR

The successful landing of Allied forces near Rome at Anzio Beach in January 1944, would have assured that Rome itself would have fallen victim to aerial and artillery bombardment had not German occupation troops withdrawn from the city in deference to the holy father. A few weeks earlier, Italy's puppet Fascist regime issued a directive to provincial administrators ordering that all Jews be sent to concentration camps. *L'Osservatore Romano* protested, calling the order unchristian and inhuman both with regard to Mosaic and converted "Jews." To expose women, children, the lame, and the elderly to the harsh conditions of a concentration camp was a violation of the laws of God.[23] Not since the atrocities against Poland at the beginning of the war had the Vatican spoken so bluntly. An American nun living in Rome, who kept a diary during the war years, took no note at all of the Vatican's veiled demur of October 26, but characterized the December 3 article as a "strong protest."[24]

The following day the Italian Fascist press responded, asserting that Jews were alien foreigners and as such subject to concentration camp detention. *L'Osservatore Romano* did not back off. On December 5, the Vatican paper objected that the Fascists had offered no satisfactory answers to the criticisms the Vatican had made earlier. Why, *L'Osservatore Romano* asked, did Fascists consider Jews born in Italy national enemies and aliens? What legal right did the state have to confiscate their property? Rather, *L'Osservatore Romano* insisted, the Fascists must obey public law according to which the state lacked the jurisdiction to change the status of an Italian-born citizen. Again, the Vatican asserted that in no event should the elderly, women, children, and the ill be subject to detention.[25]

Now why would the Vatican protest strongly in December of 1943 against a detention order, but not a few months earlier in October when the Jews were not only rounded up and incarcerated but also straightaway shipped off to Auschwitz in boxcars? The explanation lies most likely in the fact that Germany—actually the SS itself—was directly involved in the former incident but not in the latter.

A subsequent development in the summer of 1944 throws further light on the matter of the Jews and the Vatican. When Jews in northern Italy faced possible "resettlement," the papacy was asked to intervene. Pius, now "eager to cooperate in the endeavor to save Jewish lives," told Myron Taylor that he would urge Ambassador Weizsacker to press his government to desist from further deportations. "The pope declared that neither history nor his conscience would forgive him if he made no effort to save at this psychological juncture further threatened lives."[26] Now why would Pope Pius be "eager" to oppose Germany on behalf of Jews in August 1944, but not in 1943? Why would his conscience bother him in August 1944, but not in October 1943? The explanation lies again in the fact that in June 1944 the Germans had evacuated Rome and no longer posed a physical threat to the city or to the Vatican itself.[27]

<h2>CONCLUSION</h2>

Neither Germans nor other nationals, whether Jews or Gentiles, who came into personal contact with Pius XII would ever agree with Hochhuth's characterization of him as a heartless human being. On the contrary, he was found to be disarmingly charming. Nor was he cold and unemotional. He shed tears of sorrow for the severely bombed basilica of San Lorenzo in Rome and for murdered Jews of Europe as well.

Pope Pius's failure lay rather in the fact that he confined himself to a diplomatic role. Plying diplomatic waters allowed him to save the city of Rome and the Vatican from extensive damage. His motivation in doing this, Pius confided to Bishop Preysing, was to preserve Rome as the vital symbol of the center of the Christian world. Himself a Roman, Pius did not comprehend that the physical existence of the religious structures of Rome, such as the basilica of San Lorenzo, was not a fixture in the minds of Catholics around the world. Calling Pius's attention in 1944 to the continued seizure of Roman and Italian Jews, the British minister to the Vatican told the pontiff that it was "the opinion of a number of people that he underestimated his own moral authority and the high respect in which it was held by the Nazis because of the Catholic population of Germany."[28]

Once the imminent danger to the city of Rome had passed, Pius's anxiety fixed upon a second practical concern—Communism. After the battle of Stalingrad, Pius feared that Communism would spread throughout Europe and the world. Consequently, he first asked the Germans, then the Americans, to increase their presence in Rome so as to put down whatever Communist revolutionary attempts might arise during the frequent transitions of governmental power from 1943 to 1947. Driven by this fear, Pope Pius took misguided steps that, with the release in June 1998 of the U.S.

State Departments report on looted gold, threaten to discredit his pontificate altogether.[29]

Pius XII was a very capable secretary of state. Unfortunately, he lacked the moral vision of his predecessor that would have allowed us to remember him as a credible religious leader during the most turbulent and genocidal decades of our century.

### NOTES

1. Kazimierz Papee, ed., *Pius XII A Polska, 1939–1949* (Rome, 1954), p. 21. See British Library.

2. *The Persecution of the Catholic Church in German-Occupied Poland. Reports Presented by H.E. Cardinal Hlond, Primate of Poland, to Pope Pius XII, Vatican Broadcasts and Other Reliable Evidence.* Preface H. E. A. Cardinal Hinsley, archbishop of Westminster (New York: Longmans Green, 1941), pp. 115–117.

3. Burkart Schneider, *Plus XII* (Gottingen: Musterschmidt, 1968), pp. 46–47.

4. Owen Chadwick, *Britain and the Vatican during the Second World War* (Cambridge: Cambridge University Press, 1986), p. 81.

5. Bundesarchiv Abteilung Potsdam, Reichsministerium fur den kirchlichen Angelegenheiten, Wuhlisch, Amt des Generalgouverneurs, to the Auswartige Amt; Cracaw, March 14, 1940. This letter reports that permission for a priest in the General Government was denied because of hostile Vatican press and radio communications. I found no other incidents of retaliation resulting from Vatican news releases.

6. Manfred Clauss, *Die Bezeihungen des Vatikans zu Polen wahrend des II Weltkrieges* (Koln: Bohlau, 1979), p. 172. Clauss's source for this is Eberhard Jackel whose article "Zum Problem Rom—Offene Stadt" I have not been able to locate.

7. Clauss, *Die Bezeihungen des Vatikans zu Polen wahrend des II Weltkrieges*, p. 176.

8. Leon Papeleux, *Les silences de Pie XII* (Brussels: Vokaer, 1980), p. 165.

9. NA RG 59 740.0011, Boxes 2433–2435, 2439, 2441, 2448–2449, 2451–2454, 2457–2458, 2461–2463, 2465, 2467, 2469, 2470–2477. This number does not include other Vatican communications, also very numerous, about aerial attacks in other parts of Italy.

10. NA RG 982, microfilm reel 164; letter of the Apostolic Delegate to the United States, to Myron C. Taylor, Washington, D.C., June 15, 1943.

11. Papeleux, *Les silences de Pie XII*, 58–65.

12. NA Myron C. Taylor Papers, Informal Notes of Taylor for September 27, 1942; discussion with Mgr. Montini; see RG 59 740.001, Boxes 2433–2477.

13. NA RG 982, microfilm reel 165.

14. NA Myron C. Taylor Papers, Informal Notes of Taylor for September 27, 1942; discussion with Mgr. Montini; see RG 59 740.001, Boxes 2433–2477.

15. Chadwick, *Britain and the Vatican*, 216.

16. ADSS, 9, 127.

17. Susan Zuccotti, "Pope Pius XII and the Holocaust: The Case in Italy," *The Italian Refuge. Rescue of Jews During the Holocaust*, ed. I. Herzer, K. Voigt, and J. Burgwin (Washington, D.C.: Catholic University of America Press, 1989), p. 255. Chapter 6 of Zuccotti's book, *The Italians and the Holocaust* (New York: Basic Books, 1987), is the best account from the point of view of the victims, many of whom she has interviewed.

18. Albrecht van Kessel, "The Pope and the Jews," *The Storm over the Deputy*, ed. Eric Bentley (New York: E. P. Dutton, 1964), p. 75; Leonidas E. Hill III, "The Vatican Embassy of Ernst von Weizsacker, 1943–1945," *Journal of Modern History* 39, 2 (June, 1967): 150; and Sister M. Pasqualina Lehnert, *Ich durfte Ihm Dienen* (Würzburg: Naumann, 1983), p. 121. If the Germans had removed the pope from the Vatican, the entire diplomatic staff had resolved to accompany him into captivity; see NA RG 982, microfilm reel 176.

19. Zuccotti, "Pius XII and the Holocaust," 133.

20. Dan Kurzman, *The Race for Rome* (Garden City, N.Y.: Doubleday, 1975), pp. 83–84.

21. Leonidas Hill, III, ed., *Die Weizsacker Papiere, 1933–1950* (Frankfurt: M. Propyläen, 1974), p. 352.

22. Kurzman, *The Race for Rome*, 81.

23. *L'Osservatore Romano*, "Carita Civile," Dec. 3, 1943.

24. Jane Scrivener, *Inside Rome with the Germans* (New York: Macmillan, 1945), pp. 65–66.

25. *L'Osservatore Romano*, "Motivazioni," Dec. 5, 1943. For Jane Scrivener's comments, see, Scrivener, *Inside Rome with the Germans*, 65–66.

26. Michaelis, "The Holocaust in Italy and Its Representation in Italian Postwar Literature," *Remembering for the Future*, I, 395. Michaelis's quote is verified by the records of the U.S. Foreign Office; see FRUS I, 1123: The "Pope told Heathcote-Smith neither history nor his conscience would forgive him if he did not make this effort."

27. The Vatican was still not prepared in the fall of 1944 to condemn mass killings in Auschwitz and Birkenau. The Polish ambassador pleaded with the Holy See to intercede on behalf of those who were still to be murdered there, but he got nothing in reply other than a standard statement that "the Vatican is always ready to alleviate all misery due to war." See Papee, *Pius XII*, 94.

28. NA RG 84, Box 47, General Records 1944; 840.4–848 Balkans.

29. William Slany, *U.S. and Allied Wartime and Postwar Relations and Negotiations with Argentina, Portugal, Spain, Sweden, and Turkey on Looted Gold and German External Assets and U.S. Concerns About the Fate of the Wartime Ustasha Treasury* (Washington, D.C., 1998), pp. 141–156.

# CHAPTER 11

# TOWARD THE RECONSTITUTION OF CHRISTIAN EUROPE

## THE WAR AIMS OF THE PAPACY, 1938–45

### PETER C. KENT

THE ENDING OF THE COLD WAR AND THE DISSOLUTION of the Soviet Union at the beginning of the decade of the 1990s allowed for the reunification of Germany and the reintegration of the European continent, leading to east European memberships in the European Union and the North Atlantic Treaty Organization. The Holy See had participated in the first Conference on Security and Cooperation in Europe in Helsinki in the 1970s and had looked toward "the spiritual unity of Europe" as it was proclaimed by Pope John Paul II at Gniezno in 1979. The papacy placed itself at the center of the important developments of the late 1980s and the 1990s and was well prepared to play its role as the patron of the reemergence of Christian Europe.[1] The papacy had, in fact, waited since the end of World War II for this opportunity, deploring the division that had been forced on the European peoples by the Cold War. The aims of the Holy See during World War II had been focused on a postwar reconciliation of Christian Europe, in order to impede the spread of Soviet Communism. It had failed to achieve these aims, with the result that Soviet-style Communism remained a presence in Eastern Europe for 45 years. Only with the disintegration and decline of Communism in a new historical setting was it possible to achieve the aims that the Vatican had sought in an earlier period.

This chapter is designed to examine the definition and assertion of Vatican aims during World War II and to illustrate the efforts of the Roosevelt administration to cope with wartime criticism of its policies both from the Vatican City State and from the community of Roman Catholic voters within the United States. What is striking in the examination of Vatican war aims in this period is their static nature. The aims, which were defined by Pope Pius XII in 1939, shortly after the outbreak of war, were promulgated unchanged by that same pope in 1945 as the war was drawing to a close. And yet, the world had changed utterly in those six years. Not only had the Soviet Union worked as an ally of the British and Americans for four years in defeating the Axis powers, but many Germans and other Europeans had, at the same time, perpetrated unspeakable atrocities. None of this was acknowledged by the papacy with the result that it was not positioned to play any significant role in healing the wounds of the war, either in assisting people to cope with the presence of Soviet troops and Communist reform and revolution in central Europe or in dealing with the aftermath of the Holocaust. The issue of war aims serves both to demonstrate how detached the papacy was from the important issues of the war and, at the same time, to illustrate how that detachment was itself due to a blinkered and inflexible view of the world emerging from traditional European Catholic cultural values.

The death of Pope Pius XI in February 1939 brought his secretary of state, Eugenio Pacelli, to the papal throne as Pius XII just as Europe was heading toward a second Great War. In spite of the failure of Neville Chamberlain's appeasement policies, the new pope desperately sought to convene yet another meeting of the Great Powers in the summer of 1939 to resolve the Polish question. Pius XII feared the revolutionary destabilization of European society, which could result from war. Since 1917, the Holy See had been on its guard against the militant atheism fostered and promulgated by Moscow and, with the onset of the Great Depression, the Vatican despaired the increasing polarization of Europe, which linked the followers of Moscow and the Comintern together with liberal democrats in opposition to the growing menace of Fascism under the leadership of Adolf Hitler. This destruction of the European center had led Pope Pius XI, in March 1937, to denounce both the ideologies of Left and Right, the former through the encyclical *Divini Redemptoris* against Communist atheism and the latter through *Mit Brennender Sorge* against the dictatorship of the Nazis. In both cases, states and secular ideologies were charged with denying the free exercise of religion.

Once the war had started in September 1939, Pius XII recognized his duty to be ready to assist in fashioning a compromise peace. For this reason, he sought to give the impression of holding to a strictly neutral position between the belligerents by refusing to comment on the atrocities committed against Catholic Poland by the Germans and the Russians in 1939. In reality, however, the sympathies of the Vatican lay with the liberal democracies from the beginning, and the Pope was genuinely pleased when President Franklin Roosevelt named Myron C. Taylor as his personal representative to the pope in December 1939.[2]

One of the tasks of wartime diplomacy is to shape and sustain existing alliance systems. With Germany and the Soviet Union working together between 1939 and 1941, it was easy for the Vatican to provide quiet assistance to the Anglo-American cause as the war progressed. In 1940, the Pope sought, in collaboration with Roosevelt, to deter Benito Mussolini from dragging Italy into the war at Germany's side.[3] The German invasion of the Soviet Union in June 1941 posed a dilemma for the Vatican, however, since its two main antagonists were now on opposite sides of the conflict.

The Vatican response to the new shape of the war indicated well where its true sympathies lay, especially when the pope demonstrated his support for the Anglo-American cause by refusing to endorse Hitler's invasion of the Soviet Union as an anti-Bolshevik crusade. And yet, the Vatican was very uncomfortable with the new Western alliance with the Soviet Union. Following the German invasion of Russia, Roosevelt extended lend-lease aid to Stalin, but worried about a negative Catholic response to this action. The president was greatly relieved when the Vatican agreed in September 1941 that, while condemning Communism, it would be willing to see aid provided to the Russian people. Amleto Cicognani, the apostolic delegate in Washington, instructed the American bishops to issue a pastoral letter declaring that the 1937 anti-Communist encyclical, *Divini Redemptoris*, was "not to be applied to the present moment of armed conflict."[4] After the United States entered the war, Cicognani personally visited those bishops who had been most outspoken in their antiadministration views and warned them that the Holy See would be displeased at public statements that would "lessen in any way popular support of the policies of the administration."[5] Yet, Vatican support of the American and British alliance with the Soviet Union did have its limits and the pope was unwilling to make any direct gestures to Moscow, save some decrease in anti-Communist propaganda.[6]

A second function of wartime diplomacy is the definition of war aims. As the Vatican provided assistance to the Anglo-Americans in the war, it did so in the expectation that it would be able to influence the shaping and definition of the postwar world. Its war aims, however, did not adapt to the changing circumstances of the war, especially the significant military contribution of the Soviet Union, with the result that these aims bore less and less relationship to practical reality as the war progressed. Roosevelt, on the other hand, being concerned only with defining processes for international collaboration after the war, would not commit himself to any defined shape for the postwar. Nevertheless, the war aims of the Vatican, because they progressively came to be shared by members of the American Catholic community, could not be ignored by the American president.

In October 1939, Pius XII issued his inaugural encyclical *Summi Pontificatus*, in which he defined his preferred outcome for the war. In this encyclical he deplored the violence of the war and identified "the denial and rejection of a universal norm of morality" based upon the laws of God as being at the root of the problems confronting mankind in the modern age. Peace could only be established on a permanent basis if mutual trust existed and this would only be possible if Divine Law were to guide the work of civil authorities. The first test for the establishment of a secure peace would come at the moment of victory, which

> is an hour of external triumph for the party to whom victory falls, but it is in equal measure the hour of temptation. In this hour the angel of justice strives with the demons of violence; the heart of the victor all too easily is hardened; moderation and far-seeing wisdom appear to him weakness; the excited passions of the people, often inflamed by the sacrifices and sufferings they have borne, obscure the vision even of responsible persons and make them inattentive to the warning voice of humanity and equity. There is danger lest settlements and decision born in such conditions be nothing else than injustice under the cloak of justice.

Peace, therefore, must be built by the spirit, not by the sword, and must rest on a foundation of Christian morality.[7] The themes identified in *Summi Pontificatus* were reiterated by Pius XII in his subsequent messages during the course of World War II, particularly in his Christmas radio broadcasts. A lasting peace would result from a peace of reconciliation, which could reintegrate the European community.

The turning point in the war came with the German defeat at the battle of Stalingrad early in 1943. Thereafter, the Red Army began its advance toward the west. Meeting at Casablanca in January 1943, Roosevelt and Churchill sought to sustain the Russian offensive by assuring Stalin that they would fight until the unconditional surrender of the Axis powers. Dismissing the Anglo-American declaration as "idiotissima!" the pope felt that such a fight to the finish precluded the possibility of any negotiated peace. The result would be a bitter victory, leading to the political, social, and economic destruction of Italy and Germany. Such destruction of the core of Europe would only benefit the Communists.[8]

The pope believed that unconditional surrender imposed collective guilt on the German and Italian people and did not encourage either the Germans or the Italians to rid themselves of their Nazi and Fascist rulers in order to secure a compromise peace. In his address to the Sacred College of Cardinals on June 2, 1944, the pope "deprecated the confrontation of the German people with a choice between complete victory or complete destruction, since the dilemma would serve to prolong the war."[9] The pope assumed that the insistence on unconditional surrender was a particular interest of the Russians who wanted to prepare the way for a Communist takeover in Germany after the war. The leaders of German Catholicism, "the elements most necessary for the rebuilding of a Christian Germany," would be decimated, the pope believed, once they had been identified as part of the collaborationist German bourgeoisie.[10]

Papal concerns about the future of Germany and Italy were linked with more pressing concerns about the future of Poland once the victory at Stalingrad enabled the Russians to articulate their aims for Eastern Europe. In the spring of 1943, the Russians announced that they expected to move the eastern frontier of the Soviet Union to the west when the war was over, thereby annexing the eastern part of prewar Poland to the Soviet Union. At the Big Three meeting in Tehran in 1943, Churchill and Roosevelt, again paying the price for the unity of the Grand Alliance, supported Stalin's request and agreed to compensate Poland for its loss with lands taken from Germany in the west. At that same conference, it was agreed that Britain and the United States would invade Western Europe while the Soviet Union would liberate the east. Poland was to be left to the care of the Russians. Such an outcome would require some accommodation by the Poles, especially by the Polish government-in-exile in London, which broke off relations with the Soviet Union following the discovery of the bodies of Polish officers murdered by the Russians in the Katyn Forest in the summer of 1943.[11]

When Soviet troops entered prewar Polish territory in January 1944, the future of Poland became an issue of practical politics and the Holy See gave its support to the position of the London Poles. At the beginning of February 1944, this Polish government-in-exile outlined to the Vatican the dangers that they perceived were facing Poland in the event that it should fall under the control of the Communists. They called on the Vatican to "take all possible steps in order to prevent the spread of Communism in Europe."[12]

The Japanese attack on Pearl Harbor in December 1941 had brought American Catholics out of their traditional isolationism to give wholehearted support to Roosevelt's war effort. George Q. Flynn has explained how American Catholics, in defining their "theology of war," initially came to interpret the war as both just and holy and deserving of total victory. World War II was a significant turning point for American Catholics who, in spite of their diverse ethnic origins, proved their Americanism and were thereby integrated into the larger American cultural community.[13] Unlike the Vatican, American Catholics did not initially object to the prospect of unconditional surrender, since it was in conformity with their perception of the war as a moral crusade.[14] Poland was, however, another matter, especially when the politics of the Big Three toward Poland challenged principles that had earlier been defined in the Atlantic Charter.

President Roosevelt anticipated Catholic hostility to what had to be done in Poland and he sought to neutralize a negative reaction at the Vatican and among American Catholics. In September 1943, he told Archbishop Francis J. Spellman of New York that Russia would control Eastern Europe at the end of the war because it had too much power and deserved some reward for defeating the Nazi army.[15] On February 5, 1944, Roosevelt sent a direct warning to the Pope to expect that sacrifices would have to be made to obtain Soviet support for a peaceful world after the war. Because the Soviet Union had made a major contribution to the fight against Germany, it had "earned the right to participate in arrangements for peace." The United States expected postwar cooperation with Russia to continue and was actively working to lay the basis for such cooperation. Russia must be included in the postwar peace.[16]

In spite of the president's warning, the Holy See responded to the request of the London Poles with alacrity, becoming a key player in the Polish situation. On February 27, the apostolic delegates in London and Washington were instructed by Cardinal Luigi Maglione, Vatican secretary of state, to warn local Catholics and government officials of the danger inherent in a Communist occupation of Eastern Europe. Maglione believed that Catholic opinion could have a real impact on government policy in Britain and the United States.[17]

The instructions to Apostolic Delegate William Godfrey in London struck a favorable chord with Britain's Catholic community who remembered that World War II had started as a result of the 1939 invasion of Poland.[18] In the spring of 1945, Monsignor Bernard Griffin, the archbishop of Westminster, kept pressure on the government by making a speech on Poland, the object of which was "to hold the British Government to their promises to see that there should be a representative Government in Poland and that there shall be free elections."[19] American Catholics were similarly active on Poland's behalf, with the result that Roosevelt's foreign policy consensus started to come apart.[20]

Like Roosevelt, Stalin was also concerned about Vatican influence on the Polish situation and, in the spring of 1944, sought to establish some contact with the Holy See.[21] The intermediary selected by Stalin was Father Stanislas Orlemanski, a left-wing Polish American priest and the pastor of Our Lady of the Rosary Church of Springfield, Massachusetts. Orlemanski was a supporter of Roosevelt's policy of friendship with the Soviet Union and disliked the London Poles, who, representing the traditional governing classes of Poland, were always instructing Polish Americans on how to direct their prayers.

Since diplomatic relations had been broken between the London Poles and the Soviet government in the summer of 1943, it was necessary to fashion a Polish government that could be supported by the entire Grand Alliance and, consequently, in January 1944, Stalin proposed to the Americans that such a government might include representatives of the London Poles and the Poles in the Soviet Union along with three members of the Polish American community, including Father Orlemanski. In April 1944, Orlemanski, with Roosevelt's support, accepted Stalin's invitation to visit the Soviet Union. At the end of his meeting with Orlemanski, Stalin confirmed, both orally and in a signed document, that the Soviet government would never carry out a policy of coercion and persecution of the Catholic Church and that he was willing to join Pius XII in the struggle against religious persecution.

Orlemanski returned to the United States to find that the Polish American community and the American Catholic hierarchy were incensed at the gratuitous support that he had given to Stalin's policies. American government representatives, on the other hand, especially those closest to Roosevelt, were less critical. Joseph E. Davies, who had encouraged Stalin to make his peace with the pope in 1943, believed that the meeting was a "definite, if bizarre, Soviet overture to the Vatican."[22]

The Holy See was not impressed by the Orlemanski mission. They recognized that widespread public sympathy for the mission in the United States coupled with a division of opinion among American Catholics undermined the Vatican campaign to enlist American support for the London Poles.[23] Cardinal Maglione advised Cicognani that the Vatican had no intention of dealing with a discredited priest like Orlemanski and that, if Stalin gave proof through his actions that he was serious about respecting religious liberty and then wished to open diplomatic relations with the Vatican, he should do so through normal channels. That was the end of it as far as the Vatican was concerned.[24]

While Stalin was dealing with Orlemanski, the Americans tried to get the Vatican to encourage Stalin. Roosevelt believed that he could avoid domestic difficulties with his Catholic supporters if he could lessen the tension between Moscow and Rome.[25] In June 1944, Myron Taylor consulted with Ivan Maisky, the Soviet ambassador in London, and prepared a draft statement for Stalin wherein he would proclaim "complete freedom of religious teaching and freedom of worship in all Soviet territories." This draft was conveyed to Pius XII in an audience on July 12, when Taylor stressed the importance of Soviet support for the new United Nations Organization, which was expected to incorporate a guarantee of religious freedom in its charter.[26] The pope refused, however, to make cosmetic gestures for short-term gains and would not cooperate. The Vatican wanted practical demonstrations of religious liberty before they would respond to any gesture by Stalin.[27]

The Vatican stood firmly with the London Poles and, on July 28, 1944, the pope held an audience for Polish forces who were fighting in Italy, for their commanding officers, for the Polish ambassador to the Holy See, and for the former nuncio to Poland. He called for the "resurrection" of Poland and for reconciliation between Poles and Germans on the basis of Christian charity, suggesting that a renewal of hatred would only leave Poland at the mercy of the Russians.[28] The rising of the Polish Home Army against the Nazis in Warsaw in August 1944, offered Stalin a different way of dealing with the anti-Russian Poles. The Red Army halted outside Warsaw and allowed the Nazis to destroy the main forces of the Polish resistance. Nothing had come of Stalin's gestures to the Vatican, so, after the defeat of the Warsaw uprising, Stalin no longer sought Vatican support for the Soviet occupation of Poland.

By the end of 1944, with the war obviously drawing to a close, Pius XII used his Christmas message to reiterate his war aims. He saw Communist-inspired social revolution emerging from the victory of left-wing resistance coalitions throughout Europe and from the dominance of the Red Army in Eastern Europe. At the same time, he deplored the allied intent to force the unconditional surrender of Germany, which did not allow for any negotiated settlement with anti-Nazi Germans.

In his message, the pope outlined the conditions for a just peace. An effective peace settlement should include national self-determination, a ban on the use of war as an instrument for the settlement of disputes and the establishment of an international organization, "for the maintenance of peace and the timely repression of threatened aggression." More importantly, the settlement should embody a peace of conciliation that should neither detract from national sovereignty nor "impose any perpetual burden, which can only be allowed for a time as reparation for war damage." While those peoples to whose governments responsibility for the war could be attributable must "for a time undergo the rigors of security measures, they must be assured the promise of eventual association with the community of nations." The pope endorsed the punishment of war crimes for those "for whom supposed military necessity could at most have offered a pretext, but never a justification," but under no circumstances, should communities be punished for such crimes rather than individuals.[29]

In 1944, the American Catholic hierarchy found itself under pressure to take a public stand in opposition to the direction of Roosevelt's foreign policy. In April, Michael T. Ready, the general secretary of the National Catholic Welfare Conference (NCWC), the secretariat for the American hierarchy, was visited by William C. Bullitt, former American ambassador to Moscow and Paris, and told that "the time had come to oppose the apparent intemperate pro-Russian attitudes on the part of our highest Government officials." Bullitt said that the president and his closest advisers "felt helpless in the face of [a] well organized proRussian bloc in the Government" and he "bore down heavily on the Hopkins' influence and the pitiful incompetence of much of the personnel of the State Department." Bullitt's concern was that "the citizens of the United States must know that we are giving in on all fronts to Russia" and he sought through Ready "to gain the publicity and leadership of the Catholic Church against the rising Russian menace."[30] Further pressure on the NCWC and the hierarchy came in September from the Union of Slovenian Parishes of America and, in October, from the Coordinating Committee of American Polish Associations in the East.[31]

The American bishops met in mid-November 1944 to discuss the international situation. They believed that one of the main roles of the proposed United Nations organization should be to force the Soviet Union to respect the rights of individuals, the family, and religion. They criticized the assumptions underlying the plans for the United Nations, especially the dominant role to be assigned to the Great Powers. The postwar peace should be based not on power politics, argued the bishops, but on Christian principle, in which force would be subordinate to law. The administration was criticized for failing in its duty to stand by the Atlantic Charter, especially regarding Poland. The bishops indicated that the Catholic Church in the United States encouraged American involvement in world affairs to halt the spread of Communism.[32]

After the meeting, a letter was sent to President Roosevelt by the archbishops of Detroit, Chicago, and New York, expressing their support for Roosevelt's efforts "in making a just and enduring peace and in maintaining it through a sound and effective international organization," but warning that "it would be a catastrophe for the common good of all nations if the reconciliation of these differences and conflicts should be made at the price of justice." The bishops told Roosevelt that "a strong stand for justice in our relations with the Soviet Union is a postulate for our winning of the peace and for setting up an international organization which will command the support of our people."[33]

The spring of 1945 was a difficult time for the Holy See. In spite of earlier assurances by Roosevelt, the decisions taken by the Big Three at Yalta ran directly counter to Vatican support of the London Poles and to Vatican war aims, with the result that the Holy See found itself progressively isolated among the powers.[34]

Roosevelt knew the importance of assisting the Vatican and the Catholic community to accept whatever decisions might have to be made by the allied leaders when they met at Yalta. Accordingly, Roosevelt sent Harry Hopkins to Rome at the end of January 1945 to learn of the pope's concerns. The pope, pleased by this attention, told Hopkins of his fear of the consequence of a complete Russian victory for European equilibrium.[35] The Vatican was less pleased, however, when the outcome of the Yalta conference appeared to ignore the pope's fears. The pope had given loyal support to the London Poles and found himself in an untenable position as a result of the Yalta decisions, which abandoned the government-in-exile in London in favor of an expansion of the Soviet-sponsored Lublin Committee.[36] It appeared that the Great Powers were really turning over Eastern Europe to Russian imperialism.

Roosevelt sought to elicit some gesture from the Kremlin to allay expected Catholic disappointment with the results of Yalta. This was the reason for his taking the New York Catholic Edward J. Flynn to Yalta with him. Ostensibly Flynn intended to find out how the Soviet government was treating the church in general and the Roman Catholic Church in particular "with a view to reassuring American Catholicism on this point on his return."[37] He was also investigating whether any possibility existed for a rapprochement between the Vatican and the Soviet Union. Flynn went from Yalta to Moscow, where he had difficult and unsuccessful meetings with Soviet officials, including Foreign Minister Molotov, whom he advised that, because of the large number of American Catholics, Roosevelt would like a rapprochement of some kind between the Soviet Union and the Vatican.[38] From Moscow, Flynn traveled to Rome to report to the pope who dismissed any prospect of serious negotiation with the Russians.[39]

The Yalta Conference posed a severe challenge to Vatican war aims. Bolsheviks might be Bolsheviks but, in Eastern Europe in 1945, the Red Army held all the power. Should the Vatican hold firm to its principled stance and its support for the London Poles who no longer had the sanction of the Big Three and thereby lose whatever influence it might have had? Or, alternatively, should it at least seek to accommodate the Russians over the situation in Eastern Europe and try to save what could be saved?[40]

The two most senior officials of the Vatican Secretariat of State were divided on the correct course to follow. Monsignor Domenico Tardini, the undersecretary for Extraordinary Ecclesiastical Affairs, favored an uncompromising line in all dealings with the Soviet Union while Monsignor Giovanni Battista Montini, the substitute, favored compromise in order to be able to make contact with Catholics in the Soviet Union.[41] The issue was ultimately resolved by Pius XII, who supported Tardini's view, believing that any compromise with Russia would only make it more possible for the Russians to do what they wanted in Germany and make it less possible for the Vatican to protest.[42]

In his inflexibility, the pope was influenced by immediate personal concerns arising out of the Central European Catholic context, which had shaped him. Pius XII, one might say, was Italian by birth and German by adoption. In the spring of 1945, he was obsessed by worries about the future of Italy and Germany. He believed that Fascism and Nazism were deviant growths, which had been forced on reluctant populations. Once Italian Fascism and German National Socialism had been defeated and destroyed, the pope wanted to ensure that the Italian and German peoples would be welcomed back into the family of nations.

In Italy, the Lateran agreements of 1929 had reestablished and guaranteed the temporal power of the papacy. The agreements had been put to the test during World War II and, at no time during the war was the integrity of the Vatican violated either by the Axis or by the Allies, save by some Allied bombs that fell on the Vatican railway station. The first concern of the Holy See in the postwar period was to preserve the continuing validity of the Lateran Treaty and the temporal sovereignty of the Vatican City State. Much depended, however, on having a postwar government in Italy that would continue to respect the role of the Catholic Church. The pope recognized the influence of the Italian Communist Party in the resistance movement and feared that any Communist government could alter the contractual arrangements between Italy and the Vatican and put the institutional structure of the Church in peril.

The time of real danger would occur at the end of the war when popular misery could lead Italians to support parties offering radical social solutions. If Britain and the United States continued to treat the Italians as defeated enemies, rather than as cobelligerents, they might turn for support to the Communists and their Russian allies. Vatican officials used their friends in the United States, such as Archbishop Spellman of New York,[43] to get better treatment for Italy and to limit the suffering of the Italians by securing food and medical supplies from the Western democracies. The pope wanted the United States to keep its troops in Italy and to develop a plan for postwar Europe lest the lack of such a plan create "a most fertile field for Communistic activity throughout Europe."[44]

Pius XII was an Italian who had an affinity for all things German. He believed that he had a unique understanding of the Germans, a people whom he loved dearly. Eugenio Pacelli's most significant foreign diplomatic posting had been his term as apostolic nuncio to Bavaria and to Germany between 1917 and 1930. As a result of his experience, he understood well the bitterness of the Germans over their treatment after World War I. As papal nuncio, Pacelli was instrumental in negotiating concordats with Bavaria, Prussia, and Baden and he laid the foundation for the conclusion of a concordat with the German government itself in July 1933. He had also made a significant impact on the future development of the German Church. The hierarchy of that Church during World War II was largely Pacelli's creation since he had recommended most of the bishops for appointment during his term as nuncio. In Rome, when he became pope, many of Pacelli's personal assistants and advisors were German. The pope believed that, once the war was over and Hitler's government defeated, leading Nazis should be punished while the governance of Germany should be turned over to those Germans who had been the victims, and therefore the opponents of Nazism, foremost among whom would be the leaders of German Catholicism. The peace settlement should allow for the punishment of guilty men, but otherwise should treat Germany fairly and leniently and permit her, under new leadership, to return to her rightful place among the family of nations. Only in this way would a genuine and just peace be established.[45]

As the war drew to a close in the spring of 1945, the Vatican and the Catholic Church increased their criticism of wartime diplomacy, completely ignoring the critical role of the Soviet Union and the attempts of the Americans and the British to contend with it. Roosevelt's foreign policy support was crumbling. Barely three days after Roosevelt's death on April 12, the NCWC Administrative Board in Washington released a public attack on the Charter of the United Nations, designed to coincide with the opening of the San Francisco Conference. The bishops' statement reflected the war aims of the Holy See. Denouncing the United Nations Charter as "what is in effect only an Alliance of the Great Powers," the bishops lamented that certain provisions, such as the veto provision for the Security Council and the expansion of the powers of the Security Council at the expense of the General Assembly, had been decided upon in advance of the San Francisco conference by the Big Three and were not open for discussion. Great disappointment was expressed at the way in which the great powers had ignored questions of human rights, especially when they dealt with the Polish question at Yalta. "The peace of the world demands a free, independent, democratic Poland. It must not be that Poland become a puppet state under the domination and control of any foreign power."

The bishops hoped that justice would prevail when dealing with the enemy nations:

> Justice, indeed, is stern. It is not, however, born of hatred or vengeance, and prevails only when the mind is clear and calm. Moreover, the common good of the whole world must be kept in mind in dealing with these peoples. They must be freed from tyranny and oppression and they must be given the opportunity to reconstruct their institutions on the foundations of genuine democracy.

In the postwar period, democracy must gird itself to be constantly on guard against Marxian totalitarianism, "which herds the masses under dictatorial leadership, insults their intelligence with its propaganda and controlled press, and tyrannically violates innate human rights."[46]

In an encyclical issued at the same time as the NCWC statement, the pope renewed his call for a peace of reconciliation.[47] With the end of the European war in May, the Soviet press accused the pope, the Vatican, and the German Catholic Church of collaboration with the Nazis. The pope was provoked to respond on June 2 when he explicitly rejected the collective guilt of the German people for the crimes of the Nazi era. Pius XII explained that German Catholics had been among the earliest anti-Nazis and, therefore, should not be punished but should be entrusted with the construction of a new Germany. He hoped that the world had learned a lesson from the war and that it would no longer abuse and profane the family and "the domestic hearth," as was still being done by the Communists. Calling for a genuine peace where the rights of men and of religion would be respected by all, the pope warned against the alternative in "those mobs of dispossessed, disillusioned, disappointed and hopeless men who are going to swell the ranks of revolution and disorder, in the pay of a tyranny no less despotic than those for whose overthrow men planned."[48]

It was not surprising that the Vatican was disturbed by the decisions taken by the Allies at Potsdam in July 1945. Papal officials had grave reservations about making the Oder–Neisse frontier the western border of Poland, since this would dismember Germany and alienate such essentially German cities as Konigsberg and Breslau. The Vatican also had serious concerns about the expulsion of German populations from Polish and Czechoslovak territory since it felt that this was a blatant violation of the human rights of innocent people who were being wrenched out of their traditional communities.[49]

The war aims of the Holy See remained constant throughout the war, in spite of changing circumstances in Europe and the world. One might argue that the papacy was only calling for a peace based on Christian principles of love and reconciliation and that such principles were eternal and unchanging in any circumstance. Yet, this is belied by divisions of opinion within the senior officials of the Vatican Secretariat of State in 1945 over the principled course to follow in Eastern Europe. It is also belied by a recognition that Pius XII was himself obsessed by contingent concerns about the fate of Italy and Germany. Recent public debates about the Vatican's response to the Holocaust have indicated that there were alternative principled positions that could have been taken by Pius XII over the issue. By the same token, the war aims defined in October 1939 need not have remained as constant as they did in the context of the changing circumstances and fortunes of the war.

## NOTES

1. Peter Hebblethwaite, "The End of the Vatican's *Ostpolitik*," in Peter C. Kent and John F. Pollard, *Papal Diplomacy in the Modern Age* (Westport, CT: Praeger, 1994), pp. 253–261; Carl Bemstein and Marco Politi, *His Holiness: John Paul II and the Hidden History of Our Time* (New York: Doubleday, 1996).

2. Pius XII to Roosevelt, January 7, 1940, Ennio di Nolfo, *Vaticano e Stati Uniti, 1939–1952* (Milan: Franco Angeli Editore, 1978), p. 100.

3. George Q. Flynn, *Roosevelt and Romanism: Catholics and American Diplomacy, 1937–1945* (Westport, CT: Greenwood Press, 1976), p. 118.

4. Hansjakob Stehle, *Eastern Politics of the Vatican, 1917–1979* (Athens, OH: Ohio University Press, 1981), p. 212; Gerald P. Fogarty, *The Vatican and the American Hierarchy* (Stuttgart: Anton Hiersemann, 1982), pp. 269–278.

5. Flynn, *Roosevelt and Romanism*, p. 189.

6. Dennis J. Dunn, *The Catholic Church and the Soviet Government, 1939–1949* (New York: Columbia University Press, 1977), pp. 83–105; Stehle, *Eastern Politics of the Vatican*, pp. 220–224.

7. "Summi Pontificatus," Claudia Carlen Ihm, ed., *The Papal Encyclicals 1939–1958* (Raleigh: McGrath Publishing Co., 1981), pp. 5–22.

8. Taylor to Pius XII, November 28, 1944, *Actes et Documents du Saint Siege relatifs a la seconde guerre mondiale (ADSS)*, vol. XI, no. 446, pp. 631–632; Pius XII to Taylor, December 12, 1944, *ADSS*, vol. XI, no. 463, pp. 642–644.

9. Osborne (Holy See) to Eden, April 4, 1945, "Annual Report from the Holy See for 1944," Papers of the British Foreign Office (FO), ZM2608/2608/57.

10. This argument is made in a memorandum on "Soviet Policy and Tactics in Europe" prepared by Father Robert Graham, S.J., for the Social Action Department of the National Catholic Welfare Council, December 5, 1944, in Archives of the National Catholic Welfare Conference (NCWC), 1919–55, Box 8, Communism: General: 1943/45.

11. See John Coutouvidis and Jaime Reynolds, *Poland, 1939–1947* (New York: Holmes and Meier, 1986), ch. 4.

12. Godfrey (London) to Maglione, February 1, 1944, *ADSS*, vol. XI, pp. 106–108.

13. Flynn, *Roosevelt and Romanism*, pp. 189–197, 224; Fogarty, *The Vatican and the American Hierarchy*, pp. 3–312; Wilson D. Miscamble, "Catholics and American Foreign Policy from McKinley to McCarthy: A Historiographical Essay," *Diplomatic History* 4, 3 (Summer 1980): 233–240.

14. Flynn, *Roosevelt and Romanism*, pp. 202–203.

15. Flynn, *Roosevelt and Romanism*, pp. 217–218.

16. Tittmann (Holy See) to Pius XII, February 5, 1944, *ADSS*, vol. XI, no. 29, pp. 125–126.

17. Maglione to Cicognani (Washington), February 27, 1944, and Maglione to Godfrey (London), March 1944, *ADSS*, vol. XI, pp. 164–165, 195.

18. Godfrey (London) to Maglione, August 21, 1944, *ADSS*, vol. XI, pp. 501–502.

19. Griffin to Clancy, March 27, 1945, *ADSS*, vol. XI, pp. 723–724.

20. Flynn, *Roosevelt and Romanism*, pp. 218–219.

21. Maglione to Cicognani (Washington), February 16, 1944, *ADSS*, vol. XI, no. 40, pp. 139–140; notes of Montini, April 1944, *ADSS*, vol. XI, no. 143, p. 261.

22. Brother Berhard Donahoe, "The Dictator and the Priest: Stalin's Meeting with Father Stanislas Orlemanski," *Prologue* (Summer 1990): 169–183; Dunn, *The Catholic Church*, pp. 117–128; Stehle, *Eastern Politics of the Vatican*, pp. 225–232; Flynn, *Roosevelt and Romanism*, p. 220; Rizzo (Holy See) to Foreign Ministry, July 8, 1944, Archivio Storico, Ministero degli Affari Esteri (ASMAE), Rome, busta 71, Santa Sede 5—URSS.

23. Notes of the Secretariat of State, June 12, 1944, *ADSS*, vol. XI, no. 236, pp. 390–391.

24. Maglione to Cicognani (Washington), July 15, 1944, *ADSS*, vol. XI, no. 298, p. 464.

25. Andrea Riccardi, *Il Vaticano e Mosca, 1940–1990* (Bari: Editori Laterza, 1992), pp. 29–31.

26. Myron Taylor to Pius XII, July 12, 1944, *ADSS*, vol. XI, no. 292, pp. 453–456.

27. Notes of Tardini, July 12, 1944, Secretariat of State to Myron Taylor, July 13, 1944; notes of Tardini, July 14, 1944, *ADSS*, vol. XI, nos. 293, 296, 297, pp. 456–458, 460–463.

28. Rizzo (Holy See) to Foreign Ministry, July 28, 1944, ASMAE, busta 71, Santa Sede 5—Polonia.

29. Osborne (Holy See) to Eden, December 26, 1944, FO, ZM236/38/57; telegram from Osborne, December 30, 1944, FO, ZM5/5/57; Guerin (Holy See) to Bidault, December 28, 1944, Papers of the Ministere des Affaires Etrangeres (Q d'O), Paris, Z Europe 1944–49, Saint Siege 8.

30. Ready to Archbishop Mooney, April 17, 1944, NCWC, Box 8, Communism: General 1943/45.

31. Telegram to Mooney from Kaszubowski and Skoniecki, November, 1944, NCWC, 10, Communism: Poland: 1939–44.

32. Cicognani (Washington) to Tardini, November 19, 1944, *ADSS*, vol. XI, no. 438, p. 626; Hoppenot (Washington) to Foreign Ministry, November 25, 1944, Q d'O, B—Amerique 1944–52, EU 97; Flynn, *Roosevelt and Romanism*, pp. 221–222.

33. Archbishops to Roosevelt, December 13, 1944, NCWC, Box 10, Communism: Russia: 1944–45.

34. Cicognani (Washington) to Tardini, December 6, 1944, *ADSS*, vol. XI, pp. 640–641.

35. Telegram from Bourdeillette (Holy See), February 6, 1945, Q d'O, Z Europe 1944–49, Saint Siege 8; Rizzo (Holy See) to Foreign Ministry, February 20, 1945, ASMAE, busta 71, Santa Sede 5—URSS (1944); Osborne (Holy See) to Bevin, Annual Report from the Holy See for 1945, February 22, 1946, FO, ZM868/868/57.

36. Guerin (Holy See) to Bidault, February 19, 1945, Q d'O, Z Europe 1944–49, URSS 25.

37. Telegram from Halifax (Washington), March 14, 1945, FO, AN950/6/45.

38. Memorandum of Conversation, February 26, 1945, State Department Papers, U.S. National Archives, 861.404/3-1445; Osborne (Holy See) to Eden, March 27, 1945, FO, ZM2285/1600/57; Flynn, *Roosevelt and Romanism*, pp. 221–222; Riccardi, *Il Vaticano e Mosca*, pp 29–30.

39. Telegram from Guerin (Holy See), March 21, 1945, telegram from Bourdeillette (Holy See), March 30, 1945, Q d'O, Z Europe 1944–49, URSS 25; telegram from Osborne (Holy See), March 21, 1945, FO, ZM1701/1600/57; telegrams from Osborne (Holy See), March 23, 1945, FO, ZM1761/1600/57; and March 24, 1945, FO, ZM1788/1600/57; Osborne (Holy See) to Eden, April 12, 1945, FO, ZM2247/1600/57; Nester (Palermo) to Secretary of State, May 15, 1945, State Department, 761. 66A/5-1545.

40. These speculations are contained in a letter from Bronowska to Mikolajczyk, April 1, 1945, in FO, ZM2463/1600/57 of April 26, 1945.

41. Tardini to Myron Taylor, July 13, 1944, State Department, 121. 866A/9-146.

42. Telegram from Osborne (Holy See), March 28, 1945, FO, ZM1927/36/57.

43. Minute, August 24, 1944, ASMAE, busta 74, Santa Sede 5—USA (1945); Foreign Ministry to Holy See, February 21, 1945, ASMAE, busta 74, Santa Sede 5—USA.

44. Notes of Monsignor Carroll, July 3, 1944, *ADSS*, vol. XI, no. 271, pp. 428–430.

45. Guido Gonella, director of the Christian Democrat paper *Politica Estera*, and known as a mouthpiece of Pius XII, outlined this view as it applied to both Germany and Italy, in an article at the beginning of 1945. Q d'O, Guerin to Bidault, January 2, 1945, Z Europe 1944–49, St. Siege.

46. *Catholic Action*, May 1945; Flynn, *Roosevelt and Romanism*, pp. 222–223.

47. Osborne (Holy See) to Eden, April 19, 1945, FO, ZM2327/2327/57.

48. Osborne (Holy See) to Eden, June 4, 1945, FO, ZM 3216/38/57.

49. Telegram from Osborne (Holy See), August 10, 1945, FO, ZM 4263/4237/57 and Osborne to Bevin, August 20, 1945, FO, ZM 4651/4237/57.

CHAPTER 12

# DIPLOMACY'S DETRACTORS

## AMERICAN PROTESTANT REACTION TO FDR'S "PERSONAL REPRESENTATIVE" AT THE VATICAN

MICHAEL H. CARTER

AMERICAN PROTESTANT DENOMINATIONAL LEADERS responded with outrage and protest to Franklin Roosevelt's 1939 announcement that he would send Myron C. Taylor to the Vatican as his "personal representative with the rank of ambassador." Traditionally this flurry of Protestant activism has been alternately explained as an outburst of anti-Catholic bigotry or a valiant defense of church–state separation. An assessment of the personal histories of those who led the fight against the appointment and an examination of their rhetoric indicates that while concerns about threats from Roman Catholicism were often sincere, many Protestant leaders aspired to leverage the Vatican ambassadorship issue to reinvigorate recently failed efforts at ecumenical unity and political activism within the mainline denominations.

Two days before Christmas, 1939, President Franklin Roosevelt announced his intent to send a personal representative to Pope Pius XII to assist with refugee matters and coordinate mutual efforts for peace. Eleanor Roosevelt later described this action as one of the "wise preliminary steps in our preparation for war," but noted that "it created a certain amount of difficulty among some of our Protestant groups." In the first few weeks, this "difficulty" was expressed in a flurry of disparaging editorials and letters from a host of prominent American Protestant church leaders. Within the next few months the largest Protestant denominational assemblies passed stinging resolutions that condemned Roosevelt's actions and disparaged any form of diplomatic relations with the Vatican. The war inspired a sort of patriotic silence on the part of many critics, but a small corps of influential Protestants continuously sniped at the president and his "illegal ambassador." The controversy lingered into Harry Truman's presidency until it climaxed in 1951 when the attempt to appoint a permanent ambassador to the Vatican spawned more protest letters to the government than had previously been received respecting any other issue.[1]

Myron Taylor, FDR's "personal representative," was widely described at the time as an inoffensive Episcopalian who seldom visited the Vatican and accomplished little of diplomatic consequence. Indeed, during most of the war, hostilities prevented Taylor from being able to get to his post. Truman's proposed appointment of a permanent ambassador to the Vatican didn't even reach the Senate Foreign Relations Committee. Yet, this diplomatic relationship of such inconsequential international political achievement became for a brief while one of the most bitterly protested issues in American politics.

Traditionally, the vehement Protestant opposition to the ambassadorship has been explained as either a deplorable resurgence of anti-Catholic bigotry or a stalwart defense of American liberties and the separation of church and state. While both these divergent assessments bear a degree of truth, they fail to explain adequately the zeal with which American Protestants, and particularly liberals among them, organized to oppose the Vatican ambassadorship. An investigation of the personal histories of those who led the opposition to the ambassadorship and an examination of their arguments indicates that the Protestant response to FDR's "personal representative" may be more clearly understood within the context of the progressive Protestant crusades of the early twentieth century.[2]

The most prominent leaders of Protestant opposition to FDR's "personal representative" scheme had been active in the progressive Christian social gospel movement and brought many of the same sensibilities and methods to the fight against an American ambassador at the Vatican. Furthermore, the rhetoric of the debate indicates that many Protestant leaders understood the Taylor appointment amid the politics of Protestant identity and broader tensions between Protestantism and Catholicism within the United States. While anti-Catholic rhetoric was prominent throughout the debate, a quantitative assessment of the arguments marshaled against the ambassadorship indicates that neither bigotry nor sincere fear of pernicious Catholicism are sufficient to explain the Protestant reaction. The ecumenical aspirations of the Protestant opinion leaders who most strenuously opposed the ambassadorship, their personal communications, and the pattern of their arguments support the notion that many recognized that the ambassadorship issue provided a context in which the Catholic Church served as an adversarial other against which they might rally renewed Protestant political activism and interdenominational unity.

The most vigorous phases of the conflict over the ambassadorship occurred at the endpoints of the controversy, immediately after FDR's initial announcement of the appointment in early 1940, and in the winter of 1951–52 in response to Truman's plan to establish a permanent diplomatic post at the Vatican. Although the dispute reached its climax during Truman's presidency, continuities of the actors and their arguments may allow us to retrospectively explore the motives that drove Protestant opposition to FDR's "personal representative" plan by assessing the nature of the debate over its entire duration and examining the social background of the controversy.

The leaders of American liberal Protestant Christianity entered the twentieth century with a self-appointed mandate to transform America and the world, but the hopes of Protestant progressivism foundered amidst the failures of grandiose expectations in the 1920s. Denominational leaders who once felt themselves to be at the apex of American society soon found their influence and prestige diminished through growing secularism and general disillusionment compounded by the Fundamentalist controversies and the Great Depression. A host of prominent historians and sociologists have documented the travails of Protestant leaders during this troubled period in which the churches suffered a loss of preeminence akin to a "second disestablishment" in what Robert Handy definitively dubbed the "American religious depression." Nonetheless, most of these histories fail to trace the crusading ethos of American liberal Protestantism into subsequent decades. For example, Donald Meyer omits consideration of the ambassadorship controversy in *The Protestant Search for Political Realism, 1919–1941*, but his work significantly documents the influence of this period of disillusionment on several figures who became principal leaders in the ambassadorship debates.[3]

After the success of the temperance crusade, the collapse of the Interchurch World Movement and other such endeavors left many Protestant leaders both disillusioned and lacking in grand objects for their social activism. The crises of the Great Depression further frustrated many progressive aspirations. The combination of despair and financial difficulty impaired many churches' ability to mount substantial relief efforts for their communities. In response to such conditions and the widespread realization that "liberalism and reform were oversold" in the first decades of the twentieth century, many pastors began to "accept the role of spiritual agents rather than leaders or organizers of group care for the needy."[4] Furthermore, the New Deal supplanted church-based relief agencies in the fore of public consciousness. Despite the endorsement of progressive religious leaders, Roosevelt's New Deal was considered by many leading Protestants to be either a "profoundly secular movement of reform," or tainted by the hint of state absolutism.[5]

Additionally, much of FDR's New Deal conspicuously corresponded to the Catholic Bishops' 1919 *Program of Social Reconstruction*, whether by coincidence or design, and thus contributed to Protestant suspicions that the Catholic Church wielded undue influence on the Roosevelt administration. While Protestant leaders were reeling from their prior setbacks, the apparent ascent of the Roman Catholic Church made the declining influence of organized Protestantism all the more palpable. World War I proved to be a turning point for both Protestant progressivism and Catholicism in America.[6] The war provided the American Catholic Church with an eagerly embraced opportunity to demonstrate its institutional patriotism and "make manifest the loyalty of all Catholics, native and foreign born."[7] In the years after the armistice, the National Catholic War Council, later reconstituted as the National Catholic Welfare Conference (NCWC), began to publicly address broad social issues and became a widely recognized voice of Catholic opinion. The NCWC's national prominence and a broadly based new assertiveness in local affairs by Catholic clergy and laity led to an increasing concern among Protestants that the Catholic Church was growing in both numbers and confidence to become a substantial force in American society.[8]

Opposition to Al Smith's bid for the presidency in 1928 brought the political implications of Roman Catholicism to the fore of national debate. Despite the support of progressive intellectuals and even a few liberal Protestant leaders, Smith's campaign was opposed by a reinvigorated populist anti-Catholicism akin to the "no-Popery" promoted by the Know-Nothings and the American Protective Association of the nineteenth century. Indeed, Andrew Greeley has noted that "the Ku Klux Klan in the 1920s was more anti-Catholic in the North than it was antiblack." In this period, publishers churned out a bevy of alarmist treatises, which purported to warn Protestant Americans about the threats posed by Roman Catholicism. In *Catholicism and the American Mind*, Winfred Ernest Garrison claimed that there were "a very considerable number of issues upon which the Catholic Church has taken a definite stand" to which its members were beholden and warned of a Catholic "desire to impose upon the United States policies decided upon by Rome."[9]

While a host of liberal intellectuals and progressive Protestant leaders publicly decried the anti-Catholic bigotry that arose in response to Al Smith's presidential campaign, many still harbored their own suspicions about the Roman Catholic Church and its growing prominence in America. Liberal intellectuals became particularly alarmed by the growth of Fascism and totalitarianism abroad and began to argue that the Roman Catholic Church fostered dangerous authoritarianism. This concern became the core of a purportedly new and objective critique of the beliefs and practices of the Catholic Church, which distressed Protestants and concerned secular intellectuals developed in the 1930s. This respectable reiteration of earlier anti-Catholic themes set up the Catholic Church as an enemy common to Fundamentalists, Modernists, and atheistic intellectuals alike. What became known as the secular-liberal critique of Catholicism thus became an area of rapprochement both between the factions of the Fundamentalist–Modernist controversy and between American clergy and academics.

The secular-liberal critique emphasized the threat from Catholicism to the nominally Protestant bases of American democratic society. Critics disparagingly contrasted the hierarchical structure of the Catholic Church with the supposedly democratizing influence of Protestant congregational organizations and warned that Catholicism instilled authoritarian values. The Church's close association with foreign totalitarian regimes, particularly Spain under Francisco Franco, unsettled many critics who feared that Catholic political power might be similarly directed in the United States. Apparent Catholic bloc voting in northern cities further reinforced the notion that Catholics were beholden unto Rome for political direction and led many to fear that American Protantism was too splintered to successfully resist the expansion of Catholic influence. Free-speech partisans and academic critics also warned that the Catholic Church quashed the spirit of free inquiry and discourse necessary for both modern science and liberal democracy. These notions all had long-standing precedents in American anti-Catholicism, but in the 1930s these propositions were accepted as objective assessments of the dangers posed by a foreign church on American soil.[10]

The success of Catholic-endorsed legislation preventing the dissemination of birth control information in Massachusetts led many to conclude that Catholic political activism in the United States posed a real threat to classic American freedoms. Investigative reporter George Seldes's 1939 exposé *The Catholic Crisis* is properly considered to be the culmination of the prewar secular-liberal critique and the intellectual precursor of much of the anti-Catholic rhetoric invoked in the course of the ambassadorship debate. In *The Catholic Crisis* and his earlier writings for the *New Republic*, Seldes gathered older assertions into a broad catalogue of purported Catholic malfeasance including collaboration with Fascism, doctrinaire authoritarianism, media censorship, and devious workings within American politics. Liberal journals and the Protestant denominational press favorably reviewed Seldes's work and eagerly repeated his complaints in the course of the ambassadorship controversy.[11]

John McGreevy has recently argued that such anti-Catholicism should be considered, along with opposition to racism, Fascism, and Communism, as a defining feature of mid–twentieth-century American liberalism. Indeed, the *Christian Century* noted in 1937 that American liberalism had switched positions so drastically with respect to Catholicism that "the same temper which deplored the intolerance partly responsible for the defeat of Alfred E. Smith . . . must now itself combat the Catholic Church on several fronts." When FDR announced his intention to send an ambassador to the Vatican in late 1939, shared concerns about the purported evils of Roman Catholicism drew together anti-Fascist intellectuals, liberal Protestants, and conservative evangelicals in precisely such a conflict.[12]

On December 23, 1939, Franklin Roosevelt sent nearly identical letters to Dr. George A. Buttrick, president of the Federal Council of Churches in Christ in America, Rabbi Cyrus Adler, president of the Jewish Theological Seminary of New York, and Pope Pius XII, as representative leaders of America's principal organized religions. In each letter Roosevelt expressed his desire for peace and extended an invitation to the recipients to consult with him "from time to time" on matters of mutual concern. Only in the letter to Pius XII did he include any mention of a possible ambassadorship, noting "that it would give me great satisfaction to send to you my personal representative in order that our parallel endeavors for peace and the alleviation of suffering may be assisted." Shortly thereafter, the White House announced that FDR planned to send Myron C. Taylor, former chairman of US Steel, to the pope as his "personal representative with the rank of ambassador." Taylor was an Episcopalian vestryman, a friend of Cardinal Francis J. Spellman of New York and well received by the Catholic hierarchy.[13]

Early press coverage and the concurrent timing of Roosevelt's Christmas letters created an initial impression that all three recipients were both aware and supportive of the president's "personal representative" plan. Dr. Buttrick even sent a reply to Roosevelt in which he requested that the president convey his greetings to the pope. Following a brief meeting with Buttrick and Adler on December 27, the White House proudly announced that of over 400 telegrams received concerning the appointment, only four could be considered critical of the president's action. *Newsweek* declared "it is to be presumed that the spread of atheism has so united Americans of all sects who believe in the imperative need for a non-sectarian spiritual renaissance that Jews and Protestants, as well as the 21,000,000 Roman Catholics in the country, may be expected to regard the step as considerably more constructive than, say, the naming of a full-fledged ambassador to Soviet Russia in 1933." As subsequent events would demonstrate, both *Newsweek* and the administration were sorely mistaken.[14]

Indeed, just two days after the initial announcement, Dr. Louie D. Newton, editor of the *Christian Index* and pastor of Druid Hills Baptist Church in Atlanta, promptly posed a set of widely reprinted questions intended to force

FDR to acknowledge the illegality of Taylor's appointment. Roosevelt never directly answered these questions regarding the source of funding for Taylor's mission or its lack of congressional approval; instead White House officials replied evasively that the president was empowered to make whatever personal appointments he saw fit and that moreover the mission was merely a temporary expedient for peace. Protestant critics regularly repeated Newton's questions over the next several years with the intent of forcing the president to publicly admit that the appointment was unconstitutional and thereby bring the issue to closure, but to their repeated frustration no such statements were forthcoming.[15]

Two days after the *New York Times* published Newton's concerns, an official letter condemning the appointment was delivered to the White House on behalf of over 10 million Americans jointly represented by the Northern, Southern, and National (African American) Baptist Conventions. The letter dated December 30, 1939 was the first of many protests against the ambassadorship undertaken by the recently formed Associated Committees on Public Relations, a cooperative venture of the three aforementioned Baptist conventions that had convened earlier that year to coordinate Baptist efforts to promote church freedom in response to foreign totalitarianism and the expansion of government authority in the United States.[16]

On January 9, Roosevelt hastily summoned Rufus Weaver of the Baptists' Associated Committees to meet with him at the White House "within one hour" to discuss the Taylor appointment. Weaver later described a hurried half-hour session of "the president speaking for twenty-five minutes" and repeatedly insisting that the mission was "unofficial, temporary, and concerned primarily with the promotion of world peace."[17] Despite such assurances, as months passed critics became increasingly suspicious that this "temporary" mission would soon become a de facto permanent appointment. Indeed, as Taylor's assignment continued into the mid-1940s, critics charged that FDR had intended to sneak a permanent ambassadorship past the American public from the very beginning. Such notions were engendered in part by early reports that Taylor would be regarded as "the provisional ambassador to the Holy See" and that the Vatican expected that the appointment "might eventually prove a step toward resumption of diplomatic relations."[18] These suspicions were also fostered by the perception that Roosevelt had sent his concurrent Christmas letters to mislead the public about interreligious support for the appointment. Such mistrust of White House intentions became a regular feature of Protestant complaints about the ambassadorship, which persisted throughout the controversy and all the way through the Truman administration.[19]

An American Institute of Public Opinion (AIPO) survey fielded two weeks after FDR's announcement asked "Do you think the United States should send an Ambassador to the Court of Pope Pius in Rome, as it does to foreign countries?" The results indicated a slightly unfavorable initial public response to the matter with 43 percent disapproving of the appointment, 37 percent in favor, and 20 percent holding no opinion on the matter. In contrast to such numerically mild public disfavor, Protestant church leaders were almost unanimously opposed and quickly rallied to protest the appointment.[20]

*Christian Century* not only denounced the Taylor appointment, but also insisted that all true Protestant Americans must do the same. Dr. Buttrick of the Federal Council of Churches promptly wrote to the president and the *New York Times* to disavow any awareness or approval of the president's action that might have been implied by his initial cordial response to the president's Christmas letter. Nonetheless, after lengthy deliberation, Dr. Buttrick and the Federal Council, while opposed to a permanent appointment "as a violation of the principle of separation of governmental function and religious function," expressed approval for a mission that would be "temporary, unofficial, and centrally concerned with efforts for world peace." The *Christian Century* promptly accused Dr. Buttrick and the Federal Council of "betraying the Protestant position."[21]

This strong condemnation of Buttrick and others who wavered in their opposition to the ambassadorship may be understood in part as a result of the parallel insecurities and desires for Protestant unity on the part of Charles Clayton Morrison and other such veterans of previous ecumenical crusades. As editor of the *Christian Century*, Morrison had successfully transformed a struggling progressive organ of the Disciples of Christ into the most widely read journal of liberal Christianity. He was a broad ecumenist in the Disciples tradition, had been active in a host of progressive and pacifist inter-denominational organizations including the Fellowship of Reconciliation, and was deeply committed to contemporaneous efforts to forge Protestant unity. By 1940 his *Christian Century* was regarded not only as "the most influential Protestant magazine of its time" but as the "interpretive standard of the Protestant establishment." The *Century's* circulation was never much more than thirty thousand, but over one-quarter of the nation's clergy could be counted among its subscribers. This well-placed readership magnified the *Century's* editorial influence well beyond the reach of its nominal circulation and provided a ready market for pamphlet reprints, which *Century* issued for pastors to distribute to their congregations. Under Morrison's aggressive editorial guidance, *Century* became the recognized opinion leader for American Protestant opposition to the Vatican appointment.[22]

As denominational assemblies began their regularly scheduled meetings in the spring of 1940, resolutions mirroring the *Century's* editorial demands made their way through a host of conventions. In April 1940, the General

Conference of the Methodist Church adopted a typically strong statement of disapproval:

> The Roman Church has, in spite of admitted abuses, always succeeded in developing in exceptional individuals high types of saintliness, but she does not yet abate but one trace of her claim to totalitarian authority over all aspects of human life. Recent events reveal anew her purpose to press to the utmost even the most doubtful diplomatic advantages, especially in relation to the United States. We express our sincere appreciation of the oft-declared interest of the President of the United States on behalf of world peace, and we are ready to join with the Roman Catholic Church and with all other religious or secular organizations to promote world peace; but we do deplore and must firmly resist any union of church and state, and are and will be unalterably opposed to any establishment of diplomatic relations between the Vatican and the United States.[23]

The Methodists' statement is representative of such formal denominational pronouncements, and echoes the popular debate in its disparagement of the Catholic Church in conjunction with legal and political arguments against the appointment. In May, the Lutheran World Convention declared the appointment to be "unnecessary,... un-American," and "disruptive of American unity."[24] In the same month, the General Assembly of the Presbyterian Church in the United States (Southern) passed a resolution requesting that the President "terminate at the earliest possible date the unconstitutional relations established between our government and the Vatican."[25] After the three Baptist conventions similarly condemned the appointment the Associated Committees issued a 21-page brochure entitled *The Vatican Envoy*, which criticized the Taylor mission and reprinted an earlier declaration on church freedom from 1939.[26]

By June 1940, the editors of *Century* were proud to report that "hundreds of state, regional and local church bodies have passed resolutions demanding that the appointment be annulled." On the national level, *Century* boasted that "six leading Protestant denominations" with a combined membership of 18.25 million, "through their supreme governing assemblies have now registered their protest against the appointment of Myron C. Taylor as ambassador to the Pope."[27]

Despite such manifest displeasure with the appointment, condemnatory editorials, denominational resolutions, protest letters, and other manifestations of discontent diminished as 1940 progressed and U.S. involvement in the war appeared more likely. The Indiana Disciples (Disciples of Christ) meeting in May 1940 was among the first denominational bodies not to denounce the Taylor mission out of "a strong disinclination to condemn an action which might result in strengthening the hands of those who work for peace."

Nonetheless, the *Century* reported that the Disciples' action was "in no sense indicative of the convention's approval of American representation at Rome." The General Assembly of the Presbyterian Church in the United States (Southern) similarly adopted resolutions stating that it was "not advisable or feasible" to discuss the Vatican ambassadorship owing to "the crisis in Europe." Other denominational assemblies were less explicit regarding their intent, but most maintained a general silence on the issue until the end of World War II.[28]

With the exception of occasional sniping by *Century*, both Protestant and secular press coverage of the issue lapsed through the war due to both a lack of newsworthiness in the activities of the Taylor mission itself and the decline in domestic agitation. This decrease can be observed in figure 1, which shows the quarterly distribution of major magazine articles directly referring to the Vatican ambassadorship from its announcement through to its termination. Occasional discussions of the mission were prompted by the progress of the Allied campaigns in Italy, Taylor's continuing health problems, reports of his travel itinerary, and Vatican efforts to have Rome declared an open city, but the discussion lacked the initial vigor or vitriol until well into Harry Truman's administration.

Upon his assumption of the presidency, *Century* promptly reminded Harry Truman of the Vatican ambassadorship issue lest he "think that this violation of the principle of separation of church and state is unimportant." The editors

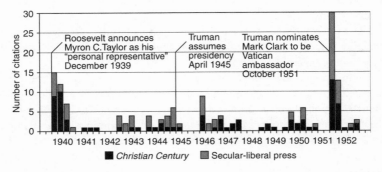

Figure 1.    Major magazine articles regarding the Vatican ambassadorship issue; total quarterly citations, September 1939–March 1953.

*Note:* The sample above includes all 170 citations from the *Reader's Guide to Periodical Literature* included under the headings "Roman Catholic Church: Diplomacy: United States" and "Catholic Church: Diplomatic Relations: United States" for the period noted. An additional 106 articles make reference to the ambassadorship and were coded for the analyses later in this chapter, but do not appear in the *Reader's Guide* categories above. Save for an increase in raw values, the distribution pattern is unchanged when these 106 articles are compounded to the figures above.

*Source: Reader's Guide to Periodical Literature* (New York: H. W. Wilson Co., 1938–53).

argued that since Franklin Roosevelt's death, the State Department could no longer hide behind the assertion that Taylor was FDR's "personal representative," and concluded, as they had throughout the war: "The Taylor mission ought never have been sent. It should now be recalled."[29]

Winfred Ernest Garrison, literary editor of the *Century* and author of the controversial treatise *Catholicism and the American Mind* described a 1947 meeting between the president and Protestant leaders in which Truman reiterated the temporary nature of Taylor's appointment and claimed, "I inherited this thing. I would not have done it this way." Despite such presidential assurances, Protestant critics charged that like his predecessor, Truman was dawdling and disingenuous regarding the duration and nature of Taylor's assignment. Furthermore, they argued that even if Taylor's purpose was to aid in the postwar peace settlements, the Vatican was explicitly hindering those arrangements, and therefore the American representative should be recalled. A few even argued that Taylor's continued presence in Rome would impair relations with the Soviet Union because the Vatican was even more stridently anti-Communist than the United States.[30]

While the Vatican ambassadorship lingered into the late 1940s with little newsworthy activity of its own, older concerns with Roman Catholicism returned to the fore of public debate. In 1946, *Century* published a special series of eight articles in which Harold Fey updated the secular-liberal critique in a conspiratorial expose provocatively titled "Can Catholicism Win America?" Fey, like Morrison, was a respected liberal Protestant pacifist and was well known for his work in a variety of ecumenical and progressive organizations including the Fellowship of Reconciliation and the American Civil Liberties Union.[31]

In "Can Catholicism Win America?" Fey argued that the Catholic Church was engaged in a broadly coordinated effort to take control of the United States through proselytism, media manipulation, and leverage of its ever-growing influence in government. He specifically decried the Vatican ambassadorship as both the product of coercive Catholic electoral power and an unfair institutional advantage that would further enhance the Catholic Church's ability to exert pressure on the federal government. The *Century* encouraged pastors to distribute copies of Fey's series to rally their congregations to the defense of American Protestantism and issued several press runs of the articles in pamphlet editions.[32]

Fey's series was not merely a regurgitation of the anti-Catholic propaganda of the 1930s and early 1940s, but a goad intended to bring Protestants back into action and renew the social, political, and apostolic vitality of the denominations. He overstated the malevolence of Catholic intent and the likelihood of a Catholic takeover to induce American Protestants to unite as an ecumenical community and encouraged the renewal of precisely the sorts of liberal home missions and social projects that had collapsed under Fey and his cohort in the 1920s and 1930s.

Charles Clayton Morrison responded shortly thereafter with his own complementary *Century* series entitled "Can Protestantism Win America?" in which he sought to organize those who had been stirred up by Fey's Catholic bogey and aspired to provide a plan for resurgent liberal Protestantism. In 1948, Morrison reedited these articles into a book length treatment, which he described as "a plea for Protestantism to be itself, that is, to be truly, consistently, unitedly, and militantly Protestant."[33] The Taylor appointment provided a clear focus issue around which Protestants could be militant and united, but despite continued concerns among Protestant leaders, for much of the public and clergy the ambassadorship matter became subsumed in the controversies regarding federal funds for education and the prospect of government assistance to Catholic parochial schools in the late 1940s.

The Supreme Court's 1947 decision in *Everson v. Board of Education*, which permitted New Jersey to continue reimbursing parents for bus fees they incurred while sending their children to parochial school, appeared to many Protestant activists as a first step to permitting government aid directly to Catholic schools. Duke K. McCall, executive secretary of the Southern Baptist Council described the court's decision as "the most unfortunate act on the part of any branch of our government in the memory of any now living."[34] Protestant denominational leaders and educators roundly decried the decision and in November 1947 rallied to form a new organization with the titular mandate to combat any further erosion of the separation of church and state. Protestants and Other Americans United for Separation of Church and State, usually abbreviated POAU, institutionally united many figures from the earlier anti-ambassadorship debate with other denominational and educational leaders. Although principally occupied with educational matters, POAU aggressively opposed the Vatican ambassadorship.[35]

The original leadership core consisted of familiar denominational and ecumenical leaders. Methodist Bishop G. Bromley Oxnam, a former coordinator for the Interchurch World Movement, served as the organization's founding president until he reduced his role to a vice-presidency so that he could attend to his principal responsibilities as president of the World Council of Churches. Edwin Poteat, then president of Colgate-Rochester divinity school and a former member of the Southern Baptist Social-Service Research Bureau, succeeded Oxnam as president of POAU. The executive committee included Louie Newton, who since his first letter against the Taylor mission had become president of the Southern Baptist Convention, Episcopal Bishop William Scarlett, John Mackay of Princeton Theological Seminary and Joseph Dawson, who succeeded Rufus Weaver as executive director of the Baptist Joint Committee on Public Affairs.[36]

Charles Clayton Morrison was particularly active in the early planning stages and served as a vice president of the organization. In a manner consistent with his emphasis on Protestant unity and the subsidiarity of interreligious ventures, Morrison is reported to have lobbied heavily to keep the phrase "Protestants and Other" prepended to the name of the organization. Morrison's influence overrode the desires of many early leaders, who preferred the more manageable and less contentious "Americans United for Separation of Church and State," to which POAU's official name was eventually shortened in 1972. Harold Fey, who was busy in 1948 as managing editor of the *Century*, was later commissioned to write the official history of the organization.

POAU's leadership declared the organization to be nondenominational and claimed no intent to "propagandize the Protestant faith or any other, nor to criticize or oppose the teaching or internal practices of the Roman Catholic Church."[37] Nonetheless, their 1948 founding manifesto went on to specifically condemn efforts to secure assistance for Catholic schools and described their opposition to the Taylor appointment as follows:

[The Roman Catholic Church] has made ominous progress in its strategy of winning for itself a position of special privilege in relation to the state. An ambassadorship to the papal head of the church, represented at the time it was set up as a temporary measure, has been in existence for seven years. President Truman in 1946 assured a Protestant delegation that it would be discontinued at an early date. But the powerful political pressure which the hierarchy is able to bring to bear against the fulfillment of this promise plainly makes it necessary that a strong and determined public opinion shall express itself in support of its fulfillment.

We are not deceived by the disguise under which the appointee to this ambassadorship was labeled as the President's personal ambassador...We hold that this ambassadorship constitutes an interlocking of the functions of church and state, which is contrary to the principle of their complete separation.

PROTESTANTS AND OTHER AMERICANS UNITED, speaking on behalf of an aroused body of American citizens, demands that this un-American ambassadorship to the head of a church be abolished. We resent, on behalf of all non-Roman churches, the privileged access to the ear of the state which this relationship creates. As patriotic Americans, we call upon all our fellow citizens who cherish the principle of religious liberty which is, implemented by the separation of church and state, to join us in condemning this unconstitutional entanglement of a particular church with the American state and in demanding its prompt abrogation.

PROTESTANTS AND OTHER AMERICANS UNITED proposes to carry on a campaign of enlightenment and mobilization of public opinion throughout the nation until the vital issue which has been raised by these violations and the threat of further violations has been decided by the voice of the people.[38]

In early 1951, POAU invited Paul Blanshard to serve as "special council" and arranged for him to deliver a flurry of speeches on behalf of the organization. Blanshard was a well-connected social gospel veteran who had been jailed for labor activism in 1919, was active with the Church League for Industrial Democracy in the 1920s, and was an occasional tennis partner of G. Bromley Oxnam. Blanshard had become recently famous for his critical writings of Roman Catholicism. His controversial series, "The Roman Catholic Church and Fascism," appeared in *Nation* in 1948 and was widely cited in other publications, including *Century* and *New Republic*. He subsequently edited these articles into *American Freedom and Catholic Power*, which ranked among the top 10 bestsellers of 1949.[39]

In January 1950, Myron Taylor formally resigned his ambassadorial post for reasons of personal health. The *Century* expressed cautious optimism that the resignation might be the end of the matter but throughout 1950 continued to warn against the dangers of American representation at the Vatican. The *Washington Post* and several Catholic publications endorsed the appointment of a permanent successor to Taylor but no official actions were announced for the next year and a half. On October 20, 1951, Harry Truman surprised friends and critics alike when he announced his intention to submit General Mark Clark to the Senate for confirmation as full ambassador of the Unites States to Vatican City State.[40]

In the process of attempting to appoint Clark, Truman managed to offend just about everyone involved. Indeed, the matter became such a debacle that Catholic historian Gerald Fogarty has even challenged Truman's seriousness in making the appointment. Nonetheless, Bishop Oxnam is reported to have considered Truman's intent to be as direct and stubborn on this as on any other issue. The public were reasonably aware of the issue in the month following Truman's proposal and about evenly split along denominational lines, as is indicated in tables 1 and 2 respectively. Such a distribution of opinion would not have been surprising at the time, but the administration seemed to be caught off guard by the vehemence of organized Protestant opposition in the ensuing months. Since Truman made the announcement only hours before the Senate had scheduled its adjournment for the session, no formal action by the Congress could be taken until January at the earliest and the matter was given plenty of time to simmer.[41]

Familiar charges burst forth immediately following Truman's announcement. Once again Protestant critics widely decried the president's disingenuousness, the illegality of an ambassadorship at the Vatican, and the totalitarianism of the Catholic Church.[42] Dr. Joseph Dawson, representing POAU and the Baptist Public Affairs Committee, described Truman's attempt to appoint an ambassador as "a frantic bid for holding machine ridden big cities in the approaching Presidential race" and "a deplorable

Table 1.   Awareness of the Vatican ambassador issue, November 1951

Have you heard or read anything about the naming of an American
ambassador to the Vatican in Rome?

|  | All respondents (%) | Protestants (%) | Catholics (%) |
|---|---|---|---|
| Yes | 60 | 58 | 65 |
| No | 40 | 42 | 35 |

*Source*: George Horace Gallup, *The Gallup Poll: Public Opinion 1935–1971*, vol. 2 (New York: Random House, 1972), Question 7a, Survey #482k, interview dates November 11–16, 1951.

Table 2.   Opinion regarding Vatican ambassador, November 1951

*Asked only of respondents answering yes to Question 7a (table 1)*
Do you think the United States Senate should or should not approve the
appointment of an ambassador to the Vatican?

|  | All respondents (%) | Protestants (%) | Catholics (%) |
|---|---|---|---|
| Should | 19 | 12 | 43 |
| Should not | 29 | 35 | 12 |
| No opinion | 12 | 11 | 10 |
| Total | 60 | 58 | 65 |

*Source*: George Horace Gallup, *The Gallup Poll: Public Opinion 1935–1971*, vol. 2 (New York: Random House, 1972), Question 7b, Survey #482k, interview dates November 11–16, 1951.

resort to expediency which utterly disregards our historical constitutional American system of separation of church and state."[43]

General Clark, Truman's nominee, was respected as a war hero in both the United States and Italy and was an otherwise reasonable choice for such an appointment, but many Texans blamed Clark's unchecked ambition and lax leadership for the unusually heavy casualties suffered by the 36th Texas Division while under his command during the war. Texas Senator Thomas Connally, then chairman of the Senate Foreign Relations Committee, was unsupportive of any Vatican ambassadorship scheme and furthermore perceived General Clark's nomination to be a direct affront to his constituents.[44]

Other senators, particularly those facing reelection in 1952, tried to avoid the issue so as not to risk offending the large and increasingly vocal portions of their constituencies who held strong opinions on the issue. Senators from states with large Catholic populations were notably silent, no doubt aware that church loyalty correlated highly with positions taken on the ambassadorship as indicated in table 2. A casual *Century* survey of senators conducted during the early weeks of the recess found some in open opposition to the nomination, most to be "prudently" evasive, and only one senator even mildly inclining toward support. Adding to the congressional tangle, General Clark refused to resign his military commission, and thus would require both Senate confirmation and a special exemption by the Congress from legal prohibitions barring military officers from concurrently serving as diplomatic agents.[45]

Meanwhile the Catholic Church made clear that it "would be more than pleased to have a diplomatic representative accredited to the Holy See," but the hierarchy made known that it would not accept another mere "personal representative." The pope himself was reported to be pleased with the selection of General Clark, but Truman announced the ambassadorial appointment to "Vatican City State" and not to the Holy See. The Catholic hierarchy felt this specification to be a severe affront to the supreme pontiff. Domestic critics were similarly unimpressed by this distinction, which they perceived to be legalistic dodge intended to get around constitutional difficulties with appointing an ambassador directly to the Roman Catholic Church.[46]

The *Century* again railed against the ambassadorship and promptly published a pamphlet edition of its feature editorial "in quantities which make circulation throughout your community possible at a minimum outlay" and thus provided "an unexcelled chance for constructive citizenship!" In addition to its own official letters and public statements, POAU sponsored Paul Blanshard on a whirlwind speaking tour against the appointment. The organization's official history notes that POAU organized "more than 120 huge public protest rallies" in late 1951, which it claims were influential in helping to quash the Clark appointment. While many of these may have simply constituted appearances by POAU endorsed speakers at the regularly scheduled Reformation rallies that many churches held in late October, POAU and *Century* nonetheless deserve considerable credit for mobilizing Protestant opposition to the ambassadorship.[47]

The *New Republic* reported in January 1952, that over 50,000 letters had been received by the Senate Foreign Relations Committee regarding the appointment with "scarcely more than 50" favorable to the idea. The success of Protestant leaders' agitation is evident in an extended description of the torrent of letters reported by *Newsweek*:

> Many were mimeographed; many were in the form of petitions. . . . It (the mail) consisted primarily of temperate discussion of the proper relationship between church and state, and there were very few expressions of Klan-type bigotry. There was evidence that many of the letters were a sort of church community enterprise, probably motivated as much by dutiful response to pastors as by burning personal convictions.[48]

In the face of mounting opposition, principally religious in origin, but occasionally personal in nature, Clark withdrew his name from nomination. No successor was named, the papal mission staff was transferred to the Italian consulate and the issue was dropped. Agitation predictably waned after the administration abandoned the prospect of a permanent ambassador to the Vatican. POAU returned to its focus on educational matters but continued to raise the issue throughout the 1950s and even demanded in 1960 that candidates Nixon and Kennedy announce their positions on diplomatic relations with the Vatican.[49]

At the climax of the controversy, the White House and Congress received more correspondence concerning the Vatican ambassadorship than had been sent regarding any previous issue. To understand this groundswell of Protestant protest it is necessary to consider the tactics and motives of the Protestant leaders who embraced the anti-ambassadorship crusade and the nature of the subject itself, which provided Protestant ecumenical activists with their most compelling and successful focus issue since the 1920s.

The relative fitness of the ambassadorship for directed Protestant political activism is readily apparent when the matter is considered in relation to other contemporaneous Catholic issues. Questions of undemocratic Catholic "otherness," often conflated with ethnic concerns, and fear that the Church acted as a foreign political power to subvert American democracy tended to dominate popular Protestant opinion of the Roman Catholic Church from the colonial era through the 1920s. Although prominent figures including Samuel F. B. Morse and Lyman Beecher had been affiliated with American anti-Catholic agitation throughout its history, populist mobs and unabashed bigotry permeated all such movements through the Al Smith campaign and came to taint even the most sincere liberal concerns in the 1930s. Even the progressive Protestant leaders who supported Al Smith couldn't dismiss their concerns with the political significance of Roman Catholicism, they simply dismissed the threat from Smith's own mild, non-doctrinaire Catholicism. For the majority of Americans concerned with the potential threats of Roman Catholicism, the 1928 election presented a relatively simple choice and a direct course of action—they could simply choose to vote against Smith.

In the aftermath of Smith's defeat, many of those who aspired to do something about the perceived Catholic menace became caught up in their own sophistication and desire for intellectual respectability as they strove to avoid the impression of mere anti-Catholic bigotry. Concurrently, the hardships of the Great Depression also limited the energies with which many Protestants could attend to the various issues associated with the Catholic threat. In the 1930s, amidst this milieu of complex arguments and economic difficulty, few Protestant laymen could be stirred to protest messy foreign matters involving the Catholic Church such as the Mexican crisis or the Spanish civil war.[50]

Notions of governmental financial support for Catholic parochial schools emerged as the dominant "Catholic issue" in the period of the ambassador-ship controversy. For decades critics had repeatedly argued that parochial schools hindered the Americanization of Catholic immigrants, fostered sepa-rateness, and taught undemocratic values, but broad consensus to act against Catholic schools was hard to come by in the 1930s. Even though a stable majority disapproved of government aid to Catholic schools throughout the era, "parochiaid" opponents were only able to mobilize large constituencies in the late 1940s, when the combination of the Supreme Court's *Everson* decision and Truman's proposals for federal education funding made the prospect of government aid to Catholic schools immediately relevant. Nonetheless, tangible mitigating concerns such as the child benefit notions invoked in the *Everson* opinion and implications for Protestant religious education may have mediated or diffused some of the opposition to Catholic school funding.[51]

Conversely, the Vatican ambassadorship seemed to many to be a rather removed and straightforward matter. While some critics of the ambassador-ship tempered their concerns out of pragmatic hopes that the Taylor mission might aid the purpose of peace in Europe or that the Vatican might be a useful ally against Communism, throughout the debate most opponents reduced the issue to a simple matter of church–state separation. Similarly, whereas school-funding issues directly touched the lives of millions of Americans, despite the broad implications claimed by its opponents, the ambassadorship was largely seen as a limited matter that personally involved only the pope, the president, and a few diplomats. Thus, those who may have been hesitant to oppose aid to their neighbors' schoolchildren felt no such restraint in opposing the ambassadorship.

The Vatican ambassadorship was also a strictly federal issue, while school funding involved many levels of government from local school boards through state and federal agencies. Parochiaid concerns were thus also confounded with issues of local determination and states' rights, which had both become major concerns during the expansive federalism of the New Deal and World War II. Moreover, unlike Catholic schools, the ambassador-ship was a new issue for most Americans and a legitimate matter of main-stream concern untainted by prior affiliation with fringe elements and the gross bigotry of the recent past. Reasonable people were therefore comfort-able to oppose the ambassadorship without the stigma of affiliation with the Klan or other extremist anti-Catholic elements.

The Vatican appointment thus constituted an issue ripe for focused activism. The matter was distinct, fairly easy to understand, and uncomplicated by mediating concerns. It was a prominent matter, yet its effects were understood to be distant from the lives of ordinary citizens, thus implying that rational people could expect that any negative consequences, which might result from the termination of the ambassadorship, would have a negligible personal impact on their lives. Last, there was a very low social cost associated with opposition to the ambassadorship; while cries of bigotry were occasionally leveled at the leaders of the movement, such charges were seldom attached to the bulk of ordinary citizens who opposed the appointments.

In a 1951 note to Bishop Oxnam, Harold Fey wrote that the ambassadorship controversy "offers Protestants the first opportunity we have had in a generation to speak with a united voice."[52] Indeed, by 1952, the protest against the ambassadorship became the first successful national Protestant ecumenical political movement since the 1920s. The traditional explanations of Protestant zeal as due to bigotry or attachment to church–state separation fail to account for the ecumenical emphases of the anti-ambassadorship movement. Although the movement's leaders were unable to maintain either activist intensity or intra-Protestant cooperation beyond the context of the ambassadorship controversy, the nature of their rhetoric indicates that many may have aspired to do so.

A quantitative comparison of the specific points of argument raised by the *Century* with those made in the secular-liberal press may help us to better understand the motivations of the ambassadorship debate from the Protestant position. To facilitate such an assessment 38 distinct points of argument made with respect to the Vatican ambassadorship issue have been traced through 144 citations from *Century* and 54 citations from the secular press represented by *Nation, New Republic, Harpers, American Mercury,* and *Atlantic Monthly.* These 38 arguments, assertions, and observations may be properly understood as *considerations* in the sense of the literature on political opinion salience, wherein each such consideration represents a distinct unit of information or point of argument intended to influence the opinions and actions of its recipients respecting specific political or social matters. These considerations widely range from specific complaints that the Taylor appointment lacked Senate approval as required under article 2, section 2 of the Constitution to broader charges that the Roman Catholic Church was manipulating the American political process to spurious personal attacks claiming that Myron Taylor was himself a fascist. Table 3 presents an overview of the categorical distribution of the major considerations regarding the ambassadorship that appeared in the *Century* and the secular-liberal press between January 1940 and January 1953.[53]

From the very beginning of the controversy, a wide array of arguments was lodged against the ambassadorship in order to mobilize the broadest

Table 3.   Considerations regarding Vatican ambassadorship

| Description | Code | *Christian Century* sample | Secular-liberal sample | Combined total |
|---|---|---|---|---|
| *Characterizations of the Roman Catholic Church* | | | | |
| Church collaborates with fascists | c1 | 25 | 25 | 50 |
| Church only wants its own interests | c2 | 29 | 11 | 40 |
| Catholic religious exclusiveness | c3 | 30 | 9 | 39 |
| Church is authoritarian | c4 | 23 | 16 | 39 |
| Church seeks undue power in U.S. politics | c5 | 22 | 14 | 36 |
| Church seeks postwar religious dominance | c6 | 11 | 3 | 14 |
| Church pressure or censors media | c7 | 8 | 5 | 13 |
| Church opposes free press | c8 | 7 | 5 | 12 |
| Church is devious | c9 | 8 | 3 | 11 |
| Church seeks financial establishment | c10 | 6 | 2 | 8 |
| Church seeks state enforcement of its moral laws | c11 | 6 | 2 | 8 |
| Vatican will spy on U.S. | c12 | 6 | 0 | 6 |
| Church seeks public money for parochial schools | c13 | 3 | 0 | 3 |
| Church wants to dominate world | c14 | 0 | 2 | 2 |
| Category total | | 184 | 97 | 281 |
| *Characterizations of the president* | | | | |
| President is devious | s1 | 33 | 6 | 39 |
| President is trying to court Catholic votes | s2 | 19 | 5 | 24 |
| President is lying, temporary mission will lead to permanent ambassadorship | s3 | 11 | 1 | 12 |
| Category total | | 63 | 12 | 75 |
| *Legal concerns* | | | | |
| Appointment violates separation of church and state (1st amendment) | 11 | 33 | 6 | 39 |
| Grants favoritism to Roman Catholic Church | 12 | 32 | 4 | 36 |
| Lacks Senate approval (article 2, section 2) | 13 | 13 | 1 | 14 |
| Public funds illegally aid the Roman Catholic Church through the Vatican mission | 14 | 2 | 0 | 2 |
| Category total | | 80 | 11 | 91 |
| *Protestant power* | | | | |
| Protestants must unite and oppose any U.S. ambassadorship to the Vatican | p1 | 22 | 4 | 26 |
| Protestants lose power as Catholics gain—zero sum | p2 | 3 | 0 | 3 |
| Category total | | 25 | 4 | 29 |

Table 3.   *(continued)*

| Description | Code | *Christian Century* sample | Secular-liberal sample | Combined total |
|---|---|---|---|---|
| *Utilitarian arguments* | | | | |
| Vatican intelligence not useful or available to U.S. | u1 | 9 | 5 | 14 |
| Taylor's mission not useful/a failure | u2 | 11 | 2 | 13 |
| Vatican is not a useful ally against U.S.S.R./Communism | u3 | 3 | 1 | 4 |
| Specific appointment is unnecessary. Rome embassy can handle any diplomatic needs | u4 | 1 | 2 | 3 |
| Vatican impedes U.S.–U.S.S.R. rapprochement | u5 | 2 | 0 | 2 |
| Vatican impedes postwar peace treaties | u6 | 2 | 0 | 2 |
| Category total | | 28 | 10 | 38 |
| *Domestic propriety* | | | | |
| Ambassadorship issue is too divisive domestically | d1 | 9 | 0 | 9 |
| Debate embarrasses U.S. Catholic hierarchy | d2 | 2 | 1 | 3 |
| Category total | | 11 | 1 | 12 |
| *Arguments in favor* | | | | |
| Vatican has useful information | v1 | 1 | 4 | 5 |
| Taylor's mission useful during war | v2 | 1 | 0 | 1 |
| Vatican helps peace process | v3 | 0 | 1 | 1 |
| Category total | | 2 | 5 | 7 |
| *Other considerations* | | | | |
| Secular media is pro-Catholic | x1 | 5 | 2 | 7 |
| Myron Taylor is a fascist/gives aid to fascists | x2 | 1 | 1 | 2 |
| Category total | | 6 | 3 | 9 |

*Note:* The full consideration coding bibliography and dataset are available upon request.

possible constituency against the appointment. Of these, disparaging characterizations of the Roman Catholic Church constituted by far the largest single class of arguments against the Taylor mission. In the course of the controversy such claims appeared in nearly two-thirds (63.8 percent) of the *Century's* articles, editorials, and letters that referred to the ambassadorship. Constitutional and procedural considerations that questioned the legality of the ambassadorship composed another substantial category argumentation levied against the appointment and appeared in over one-third

(36.1 percent) of the *Century*'s articles discussing the matter. Charges that FDR was intentionally misleading the public about the true nature of the appointment or pandering to Catholic votes constitute a third class of argumentation and appeared nearly as often in articles critical of the appointment as did substantive legal concerns in 1940. Similar charges against the Truman administration arose in 1945 and lingered through 1952.

In a manner akin to earlier ecumenical crusades, Morrison's *Century* particularly stressed the need for Protestants to unite if they were to successfully resist the ambassadorship and ominously described a zero-sum religious competition in which any Catholic gains represented direct Protestant losses. Conversely, the secular-liberal press was comparatively less concerned about the Catholic threat to the free exercise of Protestant Christianity and more concerned with the Catholic Church's relation to Fascism as may be noted in the balance of considerations in table 3. For each of the anti-Catholic propositions (codes $c1$–$c14$), the occurrence of each consideration in the secular-liberal sample is nearly proportional to the frequency in the *Century* articles except for those relating to the Catholic–Protestant religious balance (codes $c2$, $c3$, and $c6$), with which the secular-liberal press was somewhat less concerned, and the notion that the Catholic Church collaborated with fascists ($c1$), which the secular-liberal press substantially emphasized.

In addition to revealing a greater overall concern with Protestant–Catholic religious competition, the chronological distribution of arguments regarding the need for Protestant unity implies that Protestant activists were particularly attuned to the prospect of uniting their coreligionists through shared opposition to the ambassadorship from the very beginning of the controversy. Of the 22 incidences of such arguments in *Century*, precisely half appear within the first six months of 1940. Closer examination of the few secular-liberal press articles that include such exhortations for unity clearly indicates POAU's influence in the matter. All four incidences appeared during the Clark appointment debate at the explicit encouragement of POAU leaders and can be at least partially traced to an editorial favor to Paul Blanshard. Indeed the most substantial of these articles, "Down the Road to Rome," from the November 3, 1951 edition of the *Nation*, is essentially Bishop Oxnam's reiteration of the official POAU position.[54]

Comparing the distribution of the principal categories of considerations over time indicates that the *Century* began its assault on the ambassadorship with a broad barrage of arguments in the first few months of 1940 and then settled into an anti-Catholic pattern until Truman's presidency when concerns about the ambassadorship's legality and the president's handling of the affair returned to the discussion. The secular-liberal press began with criticisms of the ambassadorship in the context of broader anti-Catholicism, then, like the *Century*, adopted more legalistic concerns during the months surrounding Truman's attempt to appoint Mark Clark as a permanent ambassador. Figure 2 presents net emphasis scores for articles and editorials appearing in the *Century* and in the secular-liberal press that explicitly refer to either the Taylor mission or the proposed Clark appointment to the Vatican.

The notion that the effort to forge Protestant unity was indeed a principal motivation of the liberal Protestant critics of the ambassadorship is not inconsistent with the shift in argumentation emphasis noted in figure 2.

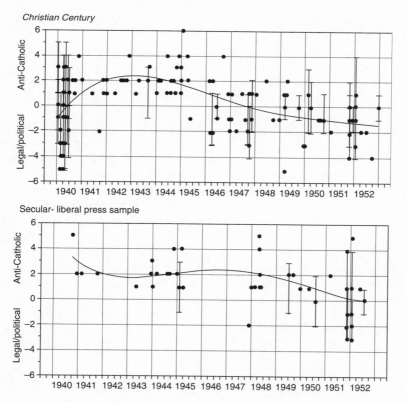

Figure 2.    Net argument emphasis by citation.

*Note:* Net emphasis is calculated by summing the specific points of argument made in each citation. Each anti-Catholic consideration is coded positively and each legal or broadly political argument is coded negatively. Table 3 lists the specific considerations that constitute each category. T-bars indicate the spread of arguments made in articles that include propositions from both anti-Catholic and legal or political categories. A fourth-order polynomial trendline has been included to aid visual interpretation of the moving average. The full consideration coding bibliography and dataset are available upon request.

If the motivation was principally anti-Catholic, then we might reasonably suspect that the argumentation would be more consistently skewed in that direction. Instead, the near balance of the distribution in the early months of 1940 and again in the latter 1940s and 1950s may actually represent the true balance of considerations in the debate. The skew toward anti-Catholicism during the war years may, much like the hesitancy of the Southern Presbyterians to condemn the Taylor appointment in May 1940, have been more a result of patriotic unwillingness to criticize the government in times of crisis than an indicator of a preponderantly bigoted approach to the issue. Without any of the otherwise common condemnations of the president, the otherwise typical level of anti-Catholic propositions in the period from 1941 through 1945 artificially skews the distribution from what may well be its true, vaguely legalistic equilibrium.

Cardinal Francis Spellman of New York complained in a famed speech in 1947 that Protestant lobbying for the termination of Taylor mission represented "the anti-Catholicism of unhooded Klansmen sowing seeds of dissension and disunion." Yet within Protestantism the effort was generally praised for its unifying effects. Ralph Lord Roy's 1953 survey *Apostles of Discord, a Study of Organized Bigotry and Disruption on the Fringes of Protestantism* noted that unlike other Protestant activist groups, "POAU's reputable leadership" had aspired to "avoid any concession to unreasoned hate" and "keep in check the less responsible elements." Roy furthermore praised POAU for holding together "an unusual combination of the right and the left, both theologically and politically," but tellingly revealed that "the only thing that could possibly hold together such divergent forces is the issue of 'Catholic power'—which they are all *against*."[55]

It is important to note that in Roy's formulation, anti-Catholicism is not an end in itself, but rather a means of holding together divergent Protestant constituencies. Roy's observation reinforces the notion that the liberal Protestant opponents of the Vatican ambassadorship recognized that the ambassadorship issue had the potential to reunify diverse elements of American Protestantism. From early in the debate Charles Clayton Morrison's *Century* editorials indicate his keen awareness of this prospect and his intent to leverage the ambassadorship issue to support his efforts at creating Protestant unity, even to the point of castigating those who were not sufficiently in line with the "Protestant position." Harold Fey incorporated the issue into his 1946 efforts to goad Protestantism back into social action and with some satisfaction noted in 1951 that the ambassadorship was the first issue on which disparate Protestant groups had spoken with a unified voice in over a generation. Tellingly, in 1947, Bishop Oxnam, who had been personally lobbying President Truman and was deeply involved in activism against the ambassadorship, noted that organized response to the issue had "done more to unite the religious groups of the nation than any single act in recent years."[56]

The liberal Protestants who led the crusade against the Vatican ambassadorship in the pages of the *Century* and on the speaking circuit with Protestants and Other Americans United did not merely target the appointment as a specific rupture of the wall between church and state, but aspired to reestablish their churches' political relevance and rebuild a broad spirit of Protestant ecumenical unity. The leaders of the fight against an American ambassador at the Vatican were unable to restore the unity and cooperation of the early twentieth century, but they briefly inspired one of the broadest and most vocal coalitions on any political issue in its time. While their arguments may at times have appeared to be motivated by bigotry or exaggerated fear, their disparagement of the Roman Catholic Church may be better understood as part of a process of redefining American Protestant social identity in reference to Protestantism's original adversary. Thus, the vehemence of the ambassadorship's detractors may have been motivated more by their own insecurity than by direct opposition to either FDR's personal representative plan or Truman's attempt to formalize relations.

## METHODOLOGICAL APPENDIX

For the quantitative discourse analyses of this chapter, *Christian Century* was selected as a representative of liberal American Protestantism due to its lead role in shaping broad Protestant opinion on the ambassadorship and other social issues as noted in the text. The *Readers' Guide to Periodical Literature* for the period from 1939 to 1952 classifies 85 citations to articles, letters, and editorials in the *Century* as directly relating to the Vatican ambassadorship. Further readings within the *Century* for the period in question yield an additional 59 articles, letters, and editorials that refer to the Vatican ambassadorship. The *Readers Guide* lists an additional 84 directly related citations from other periodicals. Of these additional citations, 22 are from the Catholic periodicals *Commonweal* and *Catholic World*.

Inspection of the readings yields 38 distinct arguments or assertions made with respect to the Vatican ambassadorship issue. All 144 citations from *Century* and 54 citations from the secular press were read and coded for the presence of these considerations. To assess the validity of article coding, a randomly selected subsample of the 198 citations used for the analyses were independently read and coded. A rate of agreement of 0.85 was achieved across all three readers. With the author's ratings considered as a control sample, a rate of agreement of 0.88 emerged between the two validation readers, a rate of 0.89 between the first reader and the control sample, and a rate of 0.93 between the second reader and the control sample. Examination of the consideration coding scores revealed a slight systemic bias toward reporting a higher incidence of anti-Catholic propositions among the validation readers relative to the control sample. Nonetheless, even if we assume the higher incidence of anti-Catholic propositions noted by the validation readers, the magnitude of the differences between these scores and the control sample are not inconsistent with the author's assertions regarding the overall distribution of considerations or the emphases of the controversy. Furthermore, the intercoder agreement on the presence of considerations not scored in the control sample was only 0.17. Accordingly, only the author's consideration coding of the articles (the control sample) is represented in the calculations that yield the percentages reported in the body of the chapter and the distributions cited in the tables and figures. The full consideration coding bibliography and dataset including validation scores, is available upon request.

## NOTES

1. Eleanor Roosevelt, *This I Remember* (New York: Harper, 1949), p. 209; "Illegal Ambassador to the Vatican," *Christian Century*, March 13, 1940, pp. 343–345; "Truman and the Vatican," *New Republic*, January 21, 1952, p. 7.
2. Catholic scholars have generally tended to consider the ambassadorship controversy only briefly and in the context of broader tensions between Catholics and Protestants in the United States. John J. Kane's 1955 study *Catholic–Protestant Conflicts in America* curiously omits any reference to the ambassadorship crisis that occurred just four years earlier and mentions Taylor's appointment only as possible evidence of an improvement in the standing of American Catholics prior to World War II. James M. O'Neill takes great pains to challenge many popular charges against the Catholic Church in his 1951 treatise *Catholicism and American Freedom*, but also largely ignores the ambassadorship issue. Lawrence Creedon and William Falcon similarly concentrate on the more general anti-Catholic attitudes of Protestant activists in their 1955 critique *United for Separation*. Andrew Greeley's more recent manuscript, *An Ugly Little Secret: Anti-Catholicism in North America*, simply lumps the ambassadorship controversy into a broader discussion of anti-Catholic bigotry. For their part, Protestant denominational scholars have tended to discuss the ambassadorship in similarly simplistic terms as a sideline issue to broader considerations of church–state separation principally rooted in concerns over the prospect of public funding for parochial schools. Glenn Igleheart characterizes the public conflict over the ambassadorship as a defense of the traditional Baptist position on the separation of church and state and provides a brief history of official denominational responses to the issue in "Southern Baptist Relationships with Roman Catholics." William Schmidt provides a similar description of Presbyterian concerns in "Roswell P. Barnes, Religious Freedom and an Ambassador at the Vatican." John Joseph Kane, *Catholic–Protestant Conflicts in America* (Chicago: Regnery, 1955), p. 214;

James M. O'Neill, *Catholicism and American Freedom* (New York: Harper, 1952); Lawrence P. Creedon and William D. Falcon, *United for Separation: An Analysis of POAU Assaults on Catholicism* (Milwaukee: Bruce, 1959); Andrew M. Greeley, *An Ugly Little Secret: Anti-Catholicism in North America* (Kansas City, MO: Sheed, Andrews and McMeel, 1977); Glenn A. Igleheart, "Southern Baptist Relationships with Roman Catholics," *Baptist History and Heritage* July (1990): 35–42; William J. Schmidt, "Roswell P. Barnes, Religious Freedom and an Ambassador at the Vatican," *American Presbyterians* Winter (1987): 259–274.

3. Robert T. Handy, "The Second Disestablishment (1920–1940)," in *A Christian America: Protestant Hopes and Historical Realities* (New York: Oxford University Press, 1984), pp. 159–184; idem, "The American Religious Depression, 1925–1935," *Church History* 29 (1960): 3–16; Samuel C. Kincheloe, *Research Memorandum on Religion in the Depression* (New York: Social Science Research Council, 1937); Martin E. Marty, *Modern American Religion: The Irony of it All 1893–1919*, vol. 1 (Chicago: University of Chicago Press, 1986); idem, *Modern American Religion: The Noise of Conflict 1919–1941*, vol. 2 (Chicago: University of Chicago Press, 1986); Eldon G. Ernst, *Moment of Truth for Protestant America: Interchurch Campaigns Following World War One* (Missoula, MT: American Academy of Religion distributed by Scholars' Press, 1974); Donald B. Meyer, *The Protestant Search for Political Realism, 1919–1941* (Middletown, CT: Wesleyan University Press, 1988).

4. Kincheloe, *Religion in the Depression*, 52; Marty, *The Noise of Conflict*, 254

5. Cushing Stout, *The New Heavens and New Earth: Political Religion in America* (New York: Harper & Row, 1974), p. 266.

6. Timothy A. Byrnes, *Catholic Bishops in American Politics* (Princeton, NJ: Princeton University Press, 1991), pp. 25–29.

7. Charles Shanabruch, *Chicago's Catholics: The Evolution of an American Identity* (South Bend: University of Notre Dame Press, 1981), p. 193, cited in Byrnes, *Catholic Bishops*, 25.

8. Thomas J. Shelley, "The Oregon School Case and the National Catholic Welfare Conference," *Catholic Historical Review* 75, July (1989): 439–457; Michael Warner, *Changing Witness: Catholic Bishops and Public Policy, 1917–1994* (Washington, DC: Ethics and Public Policy Center, 1995), p. 25.

9. Greeley, *An Ugly Little Secret*, 27; Winfred Ernest Garrison, *Catholicism and the American Mind* (Chicago: Willett, Clark & Colby, 1928), pp. 140–141; Paul M. Winter, *What Price Tolerance* (Hewlett, NY: All-American Book, Lecture and Research Bureau, 1928); Hiram Wesley Evans, *The Rising Storm: An Analysis of the Growing Conflict Over the Political Dilemma of Roman Catholics in America* (Atlanta: Buckhead Publishing Co, 1930).

10. Philip Gleeson, "Pluralism, Democracy, and Catholicism in the Era of World War II," *The Review of Politics* 49 (1987): 208–230; Greeley, *An Ugly Little Secret*, 28–35.

11. George Seldes, *The Catholic Crisis* (New York: J. Messner, 1939); idem, "Catholics and Fascists"; Conrad H. Moehlman, "Catholicism in

Politics: Review of *The Catholic Crisis* by G. Seldes," *Christian Century*, January 3, 1940, 17.

12. John T. McGreevy, "Thinking on One's Own: Catholicism in the American Intellectual Imagination, 1928–1960," *Journal of American History* 84, no. 1 (1997): 97–131, 98; D. A. Saunders, "Liberals and Catholic Action," *Christian Century*, October 20, 1937, 1293.

13. Franklin D. Roosevelt and Samuel Irving Rosenman, *The Public Papers and Addresses of Franklin Roosevelt: War and Neutrality*, vol. VIII (New York: Random House, 1944), p. 608; "Taylor Named Peace Ambassador by Roosevelt to Work with Pope," *New York Times*, December 24, 1939, 1, 6.

14. "Drs. Buttrick and Adler Call on President; Two Peace Leaders See 'All in Agreement,' " *New York Times*, December 28, 1939, 1, 3; "Ambassador Taylor," *Newsweek*, January 1, 1940, 13.

15. "Pastor Questions Roosevelt on Taylor Role; Seeks Clarification of Status at Vatican," *New York Times*, December 26, 1939, 32; Igleheart, *Baptist History and Heritage*, 37; "Unanswered Letter Asking Mr. Roosevelt to Clarify the Status of the Ambassador to the Vatican," *Christian Century*, March 20, 1940, 376–378; "Unsatisfactory Reply: President Roosevelt on the Status of Ambassador Taylor at the Vatican," *Christian Century*, April 10, 1940, 472–474.

16. "Baptists Protest Link to Vatican," *New York Times*, December 29, 1939, 6; C. C. Goen, "Baptists and Church–State Issues in the Twentieth Century," in *Civil Religion, Church and State*, ed. Martin E. Marty, Modern American Protestantism and Its World (New York: K. G. Saur, 1992), 109–136, 117–118.

17. Goen, *Civil Religion*, 118–119.

18. "Welcomed by Vatican," *New York Times*, December 24, 1939, 6.

19. "Vatican Embassy Fraud," *Christian Century*, April 3, 1946, 422–424; "Let the Senate Investigate," *Christian Century*, October 15, 1947, 1229; "Vatican Embassy Issue Enters Campaign," *Christian Century*, October 1, 1952, 1116.

20. Hadley Cantril and Mildred Strunk, eds., *Public Opinion, 1935–1946* (Princeton, NJ: Princeton University Press, 1951), p. 965. Interview date January 10, 1940.

21. "Injustice to the Federal Council," *Christian Century*, January 17, 1940, 102–103; Anson Phelps Stokes, *Church and State in the United States*, vol. 2 (New York: Harper, 1950), 109–111; "Betraying the Protestant Position," *Christian Century*, February 14, 1940, 208; "Does the Federal Council Disapprove," *Christian Century*, February 21, 1940, 238–239.

22. Meyer, *The Protestant Search*, 53–54; Dennis N. Voskuil, "Reaching Out: Mainline Protestantism and the Media," in *Between the Times: The Travail of the Protestant Establishment in America, 1900–1960*, ed. William R. Hutchison (New York: Cambridge University Press, 1989), pp. 72–92, 76–77; Stokes, *Church and State*, 99–100; Martin E. Marty, *Modern American Religion: Under God Indivisible 1941–1960*, vol. 3 (Chicago: University of Chicago Press, 1986), p. 203.

23. "Methodists Meet in Atlantic City," *Christian Century*, May 8, 1940, 613.

24. Ibid., 613.

25. Stokes, *Church and State*, 105.

26. Goen, *Civil Religion*, 119.

27. "Protestantism Goes on Record," *Christian Century*, June 26, 1940, 812.

28. "Indiana Disciples Approve Taylor," *Christian Century*, June 26, 1940, 829; "Southern Presbyterians Avoid Vatican Issue," *Christian Century*, June 5, 1940, 725; Stokes, *Church and State*, 105.

29. "What Is the Status of the Vatican Embassy?" *Christian Century*, May 23, 1945, 621.

30. Winfred Ernest Garrison, "Vatican Embassy: A Personal History," *Christian Century*, November 14, 1951, 1308–1310, 1308; "Vatican Embassy Fraud," *Christian Century*, April 3, 1946, 422–424; "What Is Delaying Mr. Taylor Now?" *Christian Century*, January 8, 1947, 37; "Pray and Watch," *Christian Century*, June 19, 1946, 774–776; "Mr. Truman: Recall Myron C. Taylor," *Christian Century*, December 4, 1946, 1460.

31. Harold E. Fey, "Can Catholicism Win America?" *Christian Century*, November 29, 1944– January 24, 1945; idem, *With Sovereign Reverence: The First Twenty-five Years of Americans United* (Rockville, MD: R. Williams Press, 1974), pp. 71–73.

32. Fey, "Can Catholicism Win America?" *Christian Century*, January 17, 1945, 74–76.

33. Charles Clayton Morrison, *Can Protestantism Win America?* (New York: Harper, 1948), p. viii.

34. Igleheart, *Baptist History and Heritage*, 37.

35. Fey, *With Sovereign Reverence*, 6; ibid., 21–22.

36. Ibid., 8–9; Robert Moats Miller, *Bishop G. Bromley Oxnam: Paladin of Liberal Protestantism* (Nashville: Abingdon Press, 1990), pp. 405–406; Creedon and Falcon, *United for Separation*, 10.

37. Fey, *With Sovereign Reverence*, 56.

38. Ibid., 60–62, emphasis in original.

39. Blanshard, *Personal and Controversial*, 213–214; idem, "Roman Catholic Church and Fascism," *Nation*, April 10–May 22, 1948; idem, *American Freedom and Catholic Power* (Boston: Beacon Press, 1949); McGreevy, "Thinking on One's Own," 97.

40. Myron C. Taylor and Harry S. Truman, "Myron C. Taylor Resigns as Personal Representative to Pope Pius XII: Letter to the President and His Letter of Acceptance," *US Department of State Bulletin*, January 30, 1950, 181–183; "Vatican Embassy Endorsed by Washington Post," *Christian Century*, August 30, 1950, 1012; Marty, *Under God Indivisible*, 200.

41. Gerald P. Fogarty, "The Vatican and the American Church Since World War II," in *The Papacy and the Church in the United States*, ed. Bernard J. Cooke (New York: Paulist Press, 1989), 121–140, 123–124; Miller, *Paladin of Liberal Protestantism*, 420.

42. G. Bromley Oxnam, "Down the Road to Rome," *Nation*, November 3, 1951, 368–370; "Ambassador at the Vatican?" *Christian Century*, November 7, 1951, 1272–1276.

43. "Undiplomatic Appointment," *Time*, October 29, 1951, 20–21.

44. Fogarty, "The Vatican and the American Church," 123–124; idem, *The Vatican and the American Hierarchy from 1870 to 1965* (Stuttgart: Hiersemann, 1982), p. 329; Roland Flamini, *Pope, Premier, President: The Cold War Summit that Never Was* (New York: Macmillan, 1980), p. 31; Creedon and Falcon, *United for Separation*, 11.

45. "Drop Nomination of Clark to Vatican," *Christian Century*, January 23, 1952, 91; Fogarty claims that Cardinal Spellman informed the Vatican in 1953 "that only nine out of ninety-six senators would have supported the nomination even if it had reached the senate floor." Fogarty, "Vatican and the American Church," 124.

46. Frank Freed, "Myron C. Taylor and the Separation of Church and State in America" (M.A. thesis, Stanford University, 1958), p. 85.

47. "Act Before Congress Acts (advertisement)," *Christian Century*, December 26, 1951, 1528; Fey, *With Sovereign Reverence*, 22; Marty, *Indivisible Under God*, 203–205.

48. "Truman and the Vatican," *New Republic*, January 21, 1952, 7; "Volume vs. Vatican," *Newsweek*, January 28, 1952, 24–28.

49. Fey, *With Sovereign Reverence*, 68–69.

50. McGreevy, "Thinking on One's Own," 108.

51. Cantril and Strunk, *Public Opinion, 1935–1946*, 187.

52. Miller, *Paladin of Militant Protestantism*, 420.

53. John R. Zaller, *The Nature and Origins of Mass Opinion* (Cambridge: Cambridge University Press, 1992), pp. 40–41.

54. Miller, *Paladin of Militant Protestantism*, 420–421; Oxnam, "Down the Road to Rome," 368–370.

55. "Vatican Envoy: Truman Dilemma," *US News*, February 10, 1950, 24–26; Ralph Lord Roy, *Apostles of Discord: A Study of Organized Bigotry and Disruption on the Fringes of Protestantism* (Boston: Beacon Press, 1953), p. 156; ibid., 150, emphasis in original.

56. Miller, *Paladin of Militant Protestantism*, 420; ibid., 414.

# CHAPTER 13

# THE DEPARTMENT OF STATE AND THE APOSTOLIC DELEGATION IN WASHINGTON DURING WORLD WAR II

## ROBERT TRISCO

RELATIONS BETWEEN THE AMERICAN GOVERNMENT AND THE HOLY SEE during World War II were not conducted only by the personal representative President Roosevelt appointed on December 24, 1939, Myron C. Taylor, who merely paid occasional visits to Rome, or by his charge d'affaires, Harold H. Tittmann, who took up residence in Vatican City after Italy declared war on the United States.[1] Relations between the Department of State and the Apostolic Delegation in Washington were also direct, frequent, and fruitful. In this chapter, a generally topical study will be presented with a focus on the apostolic delegate, Archbishop Amleto Giovanni Cicognani, who held that office from 1933 to 1958.

Friendly relations between the Apostolic Delegation and Sumner Welles, who had been undersecretary of state since 1937, were gradually developed before the war. Just before President Roosevelt released to the press on April 15, 1939, the cablegrams that he had sent to Hitler and Mussolini urging a peaceful settlement of the crisis in Europe, Welles telephoned Michael J. Ready, general secretary of the National Catholic Welfare Conference, and told him that "the President was anxious that the Papal

Delegate be informed of the communication and requested to petition the Holy Father's support of the appeal for a peace conference." As soon as Ready received copies of Roosevelt's message to the dictators, he took them to the apostolic delegate and informed him of his conversation with Welles.[2] The delegate then forwarded the message by cable to Cardinal Luigi Maglione.[3] The secretary of state replied that although the Holy Father was attentively following the president's endeavors in favor of peace, he was sorry that the Holy See's present relations with Germany did not permit it to intervene directly with Hitler. At the pope's order, Maglione had approached the Italian Government, but in view of its intimate collaboration with the Axis, he could not be hopeful.[4]

On May 10 Maglione informed Cicognani and the apostolic delegates or nuncios in a dozen other countries about the *demarche* he had made with the governments of France, Germany, Great Britain, Italy, and Poland for the double purpose of ascertaining and strengthening their peace intentions and, second, of calling a conference of the same powers. The first purpose was achieved, and the conference did not seem at the moment to be necessary because of an improvement of the general situation. The cardinal secretary had the impression of a detente in international relations. In a postscript for Washington, he asked Cicognani to bring the Holy See's action to Roosevelt's attention and to let him know that the pope had intended to request his good offices if the idea of the conference had been carried out.[5] On May 15, Cicognani conveyed the substance of Maglione's instruction, in the absence of Monsignor Ready, to the assistant general secretary of the NCWC, Howard J. Carroll, who on the following day secured an appointment with Sumner Welles and handed him the delegate's memorandum. Welles promised that the message would be given to the president that afternoon. Carroll also said that if Welles should wish to discuss the matter further with the apostolic delegate, the latter would be very happy to receive him and "would be most pleased to have lunch with him or visit the new Delegation, and that he would assure him there would be no publicity given to the visit. Welles expressed his gratitude, declared that nothing would please him more than such a visit, and observed" that he had little anxiety about publicity.[6] When Cicognani reported to Maglione that he had carried out his instructions, he added that the American press received from Rome news that the Holy See had communicated with the government of the United States through the Apostolic Delegation in regard to an international peace conference, but the secretary of state and the delegation had replied that they were unaware of such a step.[7] In a subsequent report to Maglione the delegate explained that his telegram regarding the news coming from Rome had been prompted by a request for information from the Washington correspondent of the London *Daily Mail* to the News Service of the NCWC and from an

American newspaper to the Stefani News Agency correspondent in Washington. As far as he knew, the news was not published in the United States.[8] It is noteworthy that at this early stage the delegate did not attempt to deal with the State Department directly but rather employed the general secretary of the NCWC or his assistant as an intermediary.

On June 29, 1939, Cicognani had Welles as his guest for lunch at the delegation. After the meal, Welles requested a private conversation with him and Monsignor Ready. In his memorandum of the discussion, Ready wrote: "Mr. Welles said he spoke to His Excellency at the request of President Roosevelt and the President was particularly concerned that all the forces for peace should work cooperatively to gain for society a much desired reign of peace amongst all nations." When Welles referred to Roosevelt's appeal to Hitler and Mussolini of April 14, 1939, suggesting a conference to explore "the friendly relations of nations," "the Apostolic Delegate replied that the President's communication of April 14 had been transmitted to the Holy See, as requested by the President through the United States Department of State; that the Holy See felt great difficulty in following up the message of April 14 because the governments addressed believed that they were unfairly singled out from amongst the nations." Cicognani also "spoke of the continuing difficulties the Holy See encountered in pursuing representations for peace but assured the Under Secretary that the President's desires as expressed on the present occasion would be reported to the Cardinal Secretary of State and brought to the attention of His Holiness."[9] Thus it is evident that the Department of State and the Apostolic Delegation were engaging in dialogue even before the conflict erupted in Europe.

Cicognani submitted Ready's memorandum to the cardinal secretary when he visited Rome in July and said that he had written it with Ready. He noted that Welles had added that the president in his earnest desire to cooperate for peace, would be honored and happy to receive timely suggestions from the Holy See.[10] It does not appear that Pius XII or his secretary of state perceived any way of taking advantage of this openness.

On October 24, 1939, when Archbishop Spellman had lunch with the president, they discussed the question of establishing relations between the American government and the Holy See for the pursuit of world peace. Roosevelt remarked, according to the report that Spellman composed afterwards for Maglione, "For the time being the relationship would consist of a mission of the United States Government to Rome accredited to the Holy See, without it being necessary that the mission of the Holy See in Washington should be recognized as an Apostolic Nunciature." Spellman entrusted his report to Cicognani for transmission to Maglione.[11] When the delegate performed this task, he commented: "Everything leads one to believe that the President would soon like to have a representative of his at the Holy See, especially in these times when many countries and a large part of humanity confidently turn their hopes for the return of peace to the Holy Father and also to the prestige of this great republic."[12]

Catholics in the United States and Rome, however, had to wait until December for the president to appoint a personal representative to the pope. On December 23, Cicognani cabled the news to Maglione, saying that by express desire of the president he was sending the statement that would appear in the American newspapers the next day.[13] On the same day the delegate forwarded the letter that Roosevelt had written in his own hand to Pius XII. The president had handed the letter to Spellman and Adolph A. Berle, Jr., assistant secretary of state, with instructions to deliver it to the apostolic delegate, who could telegraph it immediately to the cardinal secretary of state. Cicognani asked Spellman and Berle "to present to the President the warmest and most grateful congratulations for this decision," and he presented to Berle the annual Medal of the Holy Father, "which he was very pleased to accept."[14] In reply, Maglione instructed the delegate to express, through the good offices of Archbishop Spellman, the pope's deep gratitude for the sending of a representative with the rank of ambassador extraordinary in the person of Myron Taylor.[15] Not withstanding this appointment, the delegate continued from time to time to inform the cardinal secretary about public opinion in the United States.[16]

In September, Cardinal Maglione was disturbed by attacks of the newspaper *Regime Fascista* against the Holy See and the archbishop of New York. He directed Cicognani, therefore, to make the gravity of these base charges clear to the American press and to have the Catholics of the Archdiocese of New York manifest their solidarity with their shepherd and their sympathy for the Holy Father.[17] After consulting Spellman, Cicognani replied that according to the archbishop, the Fascist organ's calumnies were never mentioned in American newspapers, and it would be harmful to publish anything in the United States. Hence, Spellman asked the cardinal to suspend the instructions given to the delegate. The archbishop, however, protested formally to the Italian consul in New York, pointing out how harmful such attacks would be for Italian Americans.[18] The cardinal secretary, nevertheless, replied that it would be good if the Catholic press in the United States, inspired solely by religious motives, would deplore the fact that in a Catholic country such as Italy, where the press is strictly controlled by the government, a newspaper of a high Fascist authority was permitted to vilify the Holy See and the august person of the Holy Father.[19] Accordingly, Monsignor Ready did compose a protest on September 14; it was carried by the NCWC News Service under the heading "Vilification of Pope Pius, Holy See, by Fascist Editor, denounced by Msgr. Ready," and was reported by the press in general.[20] On September 24, the *Regime Fascista* renewed its attacks on the Holy See, the *Osservatore Romano*, and Archbishop Spellman, who was said to have been commissioned by American Jews to persuade the Vatican to entrust to them a monopoly for the motion picture propaganda on behalf of the Catholic Church. Maglione then ordered Cicognani to confer with Spellman to make opportune remonstrances, even publicly.[21] It seems that Cicognani and Spellman agreed to maintain silence.

Myron Taylor had gone to Rome in February 1940, and had remained for several months until he became ill and had to return to the United States for medical treatment in September. In January 1941, Maglione directed Cicognani, in unison with Spellman, to ascertain whether it was appropriate to try to learn the president's intentions regarding the eventual return of his personal representative and, if it was appropriate, to suggest that during Taylor's absence a substitute be appointed. Taylor's secretary, Harold H. Tittmann, had recently been appointed secretary in the American Embassy to the Quirinal.[22] Cicognani received this instruction just after he had a long and cordial conversation with the president on January 15, about which he then reported. Roosevelt had taken the initiative for this discussion; perhaps he was moved by Pius XII's letter of congratulations upon Roosevelt's reelection for a third term.[23] It appears that the delegate was being regarded more as a diplomatic representative of the pope. Only a month later was he able to inform Maglione that Tittmann would leave the American Embassy to the Quirinal and return to his former position but with the title of *charge d'affaires ad interim*.[24] In March, he finally received Pius XII's autograph letter to Roosevelt congratulating him upon his inauguration for the third term, and he forwarded it with his own letter in which he conveyed the felicitations and best wishes of the cardinal secretary of state.[25] In May, Cicognani reported to Maglione that Taylor, after having had lunch with the president, told the delegate that the president was fully satisfied with the present arrangement of relations with the Holy See, for while Tittmann was in contact with the Vatican, Taylor himself could easily see the president and relay any messages to the delegate, without arousing suspicions and reactions, so that the latter could transmit them to the Holy See.[26]

It was the delegate, however, who took the initiative in writing to Taylor about the audiences that Pius XII had granted, at their request, to Duke Aimone of Spoleto, second son of the Duke of Aosta, who was to be absentee sovereign of the nominal kingdom of Croatia created by the Axis after its conquest of the Balkans, and to Ante Pavelic, whom Hitler had appointed head of the small Croat state set up under German–Italian protection. Cicognani explained that the duke "was received simply as a Prince of the House of Savoy, and before any act regarding his position in the new Kingdom of Croatia took place." Pavelic was received "simply as a Catholic and private personage, without any of the ceremonial and formality usually observed for the audiences of heads of States or heads of diplomatic missions." The delegate was anxious to convince Taylor (and the American government) that "the Vatican significantly avoided everything that might" have had even the appearance of a lessening of its attitude of absolute neutrality and impartiality. On the next day, Taylor informed him that he had personally delivered a copy of Cicognani's memorandum to the president and to Sumner Welles, both of whom expressed their satisfaction. He also assured the cardinal secretary that no criticism of these audiences was made in the American press.[27]

A few weeks later Taylor, speaking for higher authorities, expressed to Cicognani the fear that the American bishops did not take into proper account the spiritual dangers threatened by the expansion of Nazism and that some of them favored Germany. The delegate replied that there was no statement of the bishops, collective or individual, from which any favoring of Nazism could be deduced, and he expounded this thesis at length. He admitted that Cardinal William O'Connell, archbishop of Boston, and Michael Curley, archbishop of Baltimore and Washington, whom Taylor had mentioned, had spoken in public against the armed intervention of the United States in the war, but he insisted that they had said nothing in favor of Germany; they were known for holding the common American feeling against the dictators. Cicognani asked Taylor to report his response to the higher authority, from which the complaint had come, and Taylor asked him to report their conversation to Maglione. He added that Spellman too had the impression of discontent in the higher spheres of the government with the attitude of the bishops and clergy regarding the government's international policy of supporting Great Britain in every way short of entering the war.[28]

A few days after the United States entered the war, Cicognani in a handwritten letter to Welles expressed his "fervent gratitude for the generous consideration" that the undersecretary had given "to this Delegation throughout the past years" and for Welles's "many and great courtesies," which had been "invaluable" to the delegate in the discharge of his duties. Sumner replied on the very same day, "It has been a privilege for me to be of service in the matters in which in recent years the Holy See and the Government of the United States have both been so deeply interested. It has been an additional satisfaction to cooperate in these matters with Your Excellency."[29]

### PRISONERS OF WAR

Meanwhile Cicognani had become active in striving to aid prisoners of war and to facilitate the transmission of information about them to their families.

On September 25, 1941, the papal Secretariat of State delivered a note to Myron Taylor at the moment of his departure from Rome, asking that representations be made by the United States Commission then in Moscow "to the competent Authorities there with a view to bringing about an understanding of the Holy See's charitable mission and a helpful cooperation especially to assure that prisoners in Russian hands might be afforded adequate religious and moral assistance." The secretariat also wanted the Commission to take steps "to assure an active participation of the competent authorities" in the work of the Vatican Information Bureau, which provided news of prisoners for their distressed families. Taylor was told that these charitable endeavors of the Holy See were prompted by a sincere desire to be of utmost assistance to men of all nations in those difficult and trying days of war and were not intended to interfere with or hamper in any way the undertakings of other organizations. Consequently, steps had been taken, the secretariat wrote, to provide for Russian prisoners the same services that were now being requested for prisoners in Russia.[30] Maglione sent Cicognani a copy and asked him to follow the initiative and to foster its desired outcome.[31]

Since this request produced no results, Maglione in December, after the United States had declared war on the Axis, asked Cicognani to inform him by cable whether it was possible to obtain through the American authorities lists of and news about Italian and German prisoners in Russia. The delegate replied on December 22 that he had renewed the Holy See's requests with urgency, but the American government had declared that it could do absolutely nothing.[32] In spite of that negative answer, Maglione made another attempt in January by speaking to Taylor's charge d'affaires at the Vatican, Harold Tittmann, and he asked the apostolic delegate to support this effort by renewing pressure in Washington, if he thought it wise.[33] In February, Tittmann transmitted to the Secretariat of State the reply that he had received from Washington:

> The warmest sympathy is felt by the Government of the United States for the motives inspiring the Holy See in its attempt to bring about some degree of alleviation of the sufferings resulting from the war. It regrets that, unhappily, the earnest and repeated attempts which it has heretofore made to obtain from the Soviet Union information of the nature that the Holy See desires were unsuccessful, and there seems to be no prospect that a favorable outcome would be likely to result from any further similar attempts.

The government suggested that the Holy See take up with the International Committee of the Red Cross at Geneva the possibility of cooperating with the Committee and of coordinating the activities of the Information Bureau of the Vatican with those of the official Central Information Agency that the Geneva Prisoners of War Convention provided for.[34]

In spite of this disappointing response, Maglione persisted. In March Cicognani wrote to Michael J. Ready, general secretary of the National Catholic Welfare Conference, that the cardinal wished to have "the whole question of obtaining information about prisoners in Russia" further studied, and trusted that "perhaps" the American government could induce the Soviet authorities to furnish news of the men in their hands, so that eventually a reciprocal exchange of information about prisoners of war could be established for the Eastern front, and thus some comfort and consolation could be brought to their families. He asked Ready to try to obtain information about the present status or eventual solution of the problem.[35] In April Cicognani cabled Maglione that he had repeatedly urged the undersecretary of state, Sumner Welles, to strive to obtain from Russia news of prisoners on the basis of reciprocity. He argued that only the government of the United States at that time could obtain such humane gestures, which were universally recognized by other belligerent nations. Up to that time, however, the Soviet government had resolutely refused news and lists of prisoners both to the International Red Cross and to the president of the United States, who, as Cicognani had learned confidentially, had written personally to Stalin. Welles, nevertheless, had promised to renew the attempt through the American ambassador in Moscow.[36] In reply Maglione immediately sketched for Cicognani a scheme by which the American government could transmit the desired information to the Apostolic Delegation in Washington, which in turn could transmit it to the Vatican Information Bureau; in return, the American government could transmit to the Russian government information that the Holy See would provide to the apostolic delegate. A beginning could be made by the exchange of lists of names and numbers of prisoners and addresses of their families. The Holy See already possessed several hundred names of Russian prisoners that it would gladly communicate. After that beginning, ways of providing sufficient spiritual and health assistance could be considered.[37] It was only on July 6 that Cicognani replied, saying that he had discussed the project at length with Welles. The American government had tried several times to persuade the Soviet government to accept the International Geneva Convention of 1929, and toward the end of June it had pressed the matter "with a high Soviet authority, probably Molotov" (who had recently been in the United States), presenting the Holy See's proposal. The response had been negative—no exchange of either lists or prisoners. Cicognani added that Russia seemed to prefer the International Convention of The Hague of 1907, in which it was not prescribed that a government permit visits to the camps. The American government had learned from much experience that without such visits the actual conditions in the camps in Russia could not be known.[38]

Finally, as Maglione informed Cicognani on October 19, 1942, Pius XII in a special memorandum delivered to Ambassador Taylor personally requested the president of the United States to exercise his unique influence with the Russian authorities to obtain some news about the prisoners in their hands, adding that the Holy See had taken an interest in the Russian prisoners and was ready to do more whenever it might be welcomed by the Russian authorities.[39] The last word on the subject was sent by the patient delegate to his superior on March 28, 1943. Cicognani wrote that every time the cardinal secretary of state had ordered him to seek information on prisoners of the Russians or means of exchanging news about them, he had promptly and with the greatest earnestness approached the government either personally or through Myron Taylor. Now the secretary of state, Cordell Hull, had communicated to him that he too had renewed such pressing demands through the American ambassador in Moscow, but the Russian government had not yielded to such requests, even those coming from President Roosevelt. Now it was not answering any requests at all. Therefore, the American government declared that it could not take new steps in this regard until it would have some indication that Russia was changing its attitude.[40]

Because of the intransigence of the Soviet government and the shifting theaters of military operations, the Holy See then turned its attention to North Africa. Cicognani was instructed to inquire about the possibility of the Vatican Information Bureau's functioning among the prisoners of war in that area, and on January 26, 1943, he replied to Maglione that the American government (presumably the Department of State), having consulted the War Department, regretted to have to reply that it could not comply with the Holy See's desire because of the many requests that the American officials in North Africa had to fulfil. It suggested that the Holy See interest the Red Cross, which had the means for that kind of international correspondence.[41] The cardinal secretary, however, was not content with that response. To resolve the difficulties involved, he directed Cicognani on February 7 to avail himself of the assistance of Archbishop Spellman and Ambassador Taylor and to show them that the Holy Father could not ignore the demands of Christian charity toward so many unfortunate persons who, lacking information about their dear ones and anxious about their fate, call upon his aid. Cicognani was to ask Spellman and Taylor to take new steps to have Roosevelt promote the Holy See's information service. Maglione assured the delegate that this service was not intended to work against any other similar service and could be advantageous to the humanitarian reputation of the United States and facilitate reciprocity for American prisoners and internees. The cardinal even proposed a plan for the functioning of the service in French North Africa.[42] The same thoughts were communicated to

Tittmann on the fifteenth after the *sostituto*, Monsignor Giovanni Battista Montini, had a conversation with him. Montini noted that Tittmann said that he was willing to favor the Holy See's desires, especially for the North African zone occupied by the Americans. Montini indicated to Tittmann the manner suggested by Cicognani to resolve the question in Algeria, that is, by giving charge either to the archbishop of Algiers or to a White Father.[43]

In extensive, informative notes or memoranda prepared by the Secretariat of State on March 1, 1943, for Archbishop Spellman, who was then at the Vatican, a final section was devoted to "Information Service for the United States of America." It was noted that many prisoners were being transferred from India and England to the United States, and it was stated: "It would be very convenient if the Apostolic Delegate in Washington could obtain from the competent authorities concessions and authorization similar to those guaranteed elsewhere to the Papal Representatives with regard to prisoners of war and civilian internees." The delegate would need to obtain lists of such persons with an indication of the state of each one's health; he would need to be authorized to act as a medium for the transmission of news to and from them in the form of short messages of a family character; lastly, he would need permission for periodic visits to prisoner-of-war camps for the purpose of spiritual and moral assistance. These concessions were said to be all the more urgent and necessary in view of the fact that the Italian authorities had already made arrangements facilitating the information service and other works of assistance being rendered by the Holy See to North American prisoners of war. In order that the information be transmitted to the Vatican in the fastest possible manner, it was recommended that the steps already taken for the establishment of telegraphic contact with Washington should be brought to a successful conclusion. It was also noted that to this end the apostolic delegate had been requested to study the possibility of an agreement with an American station, and preferably with Mackay Radio, which was already coordinating with Vatican Radio.[44]

As the hostilities in Tunisia were coming to a close, Maglione directed Cicognani by cable to communicate the outcome of the negotiations to obtain news of the Italian and German prisoners held there. He asked the delegate to emphasize the fact that numerous requests for information addressed to the Holy See remained without reply while the Vatican Information Bureau was communicating to the Apostolic Delegation in Washington and to the American chargé d'affaires, Tittmann, frequent notices about American prisoners.[45] Cicognani assured the cardinal that he had earnestly urged Undersecretary Welles to permit promptly the Vatican Information Bureau to function in North Africa and to transmit lists of prisoners of the Axis by telegraph. Welles promised to deal with both matters immediately, holding out hope of a favorable outcome.[46] In his memorandum of his conversation with Cicognani, Welles wrote: "I told the Delegate that I believed an understanding was being expedited with regard to this matter [the functioning of the Vatican Information Bureau for prisoners of war in North Africa, about which Cicognani had handed him a memorandum] and that I had no doubt that final word would be sent to him in the near future with regard to this question." Cicognani had also handed Welles a memorandum regarding "the possibility of the Apostolic Delegation in Washington obtaining information concerning Axis prisoners interned in prison camps within the United States." According to Welles's memorandum, Cicognani had "emphasized the fact that the Holy See was doing much to obtain information for American families with regard to American prisoners in Italian hands." The undersecretary added: "I told the Delegate that I would be very glad to ask that this question be taken up again and that the possibility of meeting the request of the Vatican be thoroughly explored."[47]

In reply to Cicognani's dispatch of May 24, Maglione suggested that the delegate interest Myron Taylor, giving the familiar reasons. He again requested permission to correspond by telegraph with the archbishop of Algiers or with some other ecclesiastic, even an American, who would be charged with organizing the service of compassion on the site. Cicognani replied that he would make use of Maglione's suggestions for more urgent requests. He had been interesting Taylor in the matter since the previous February. After an early reply that aroused the delegate's hopes, Taylor recently had told him that the matter was more complicated because various governments were controlling the place. Still, Cicognani promised to impress the pope's concerns on Taylor, who was to be in Washington the next day.[48]

The outcome was only a partial success for the delegate. The American government in June agreed that the Holy See might organize an information service in North Africa but only in regard to civilians, in keeping with the regulations of the local American authorities, and under American censorship. In regard to the prisoners of war held by the Americans, the government pointed out that in a short time they would be transferred to the United States; once they arrived, lists would be compiled, and the Apostolic Delegation would be permitted to make use of them for the usual messages. Having considered the proposal of transmitting the lists by telegraph, the government decided not to permit it because of the difficulty of control and the heavy burden on the telegraphic service; moreover, the lists were already transmitted to the government protector (Switzerland) and to the Red Cross in keeping with articles 79 and 77 of the International Convention of Geneva. Finally, Cicognani stated that prisoners of war, after arriving in camps in America, could use the forms provided by the Vatican Information Bureau, but the government begged the Holy See not to transmit their messages by radio; the delegate was to be limited to sending the lists by post.

Taylor, who conducted the negotiation, assured him that the government could not grant more.[49]

The cardinal secretary persisted, replying that His Holiness did not wish to believe that the American government could not grant more, in the light of its humanitarian statements, its repeated manifestations of friendly compliance, and the moral advantage accruing to it from the requested facilitations. Maglione, therefore, observed (1) that the Geneva Convention of 1929 in article 77 required the compilation of lists of prisoners in the briefest possible time, while the compilation of lists in America would certainly entail a further delay of some months; (2) the Geneva Convention did not seem to be in exclusive favor of determined entities (he obviously meant the Red Cross) but allowed the work of other relief associations; the Holy See, on the other hand, faithful to its mission, could not fail to respond to the countless and anguished requests addressed to it directly; (3) the transmission by telegraph at least of some names of prisoners for a limited number of words should not be difficult; and (4) the Holy See received favorable treatment from the Italian and Japanese to obtain lists of North American prisoners transmitted in large numbers and even by telegraph; in Japan especially the Holy See had to overcome considerable difficulties.[50] Two days later Maglione notified the delegate that the Secretariat of State was thinking of sending its attaché, Monsignor Walter Carroll, temporarily to facilitate the information service. He directed Cicognani to communicate this intention to the American government in order to obtain the necessary permission and to assist his mission.[51] Upon receipt of Maglione's instruction of June 28, Cicognani promptly wrote to Welles expressing the cardinal's ideas in suitable language and expanding on one point: "As for the strain on the telegraphic facilities of the United States, you are no doubt aware that Mackay Radio maintains direct contact with Vatican City, and we are prepared to file our messages with the broadcasting station directly, rather than through local telegraphic offices, thus obviating the need for any overland messages which might burden the country's telegraphic network."[52] The Secretariat of State also pursued its goal by addressing a note to Tittmann, lamenting the restrictions that the American government placed on the operations of the Vatican Information Service and asking him to use all his influence in order to persuade the American authorities to broaden its concessions in various respects.[53]

When Cicognani left a letter for Sumner Welles with the assistant secretary of state, G. Howland Shaw, on July 24, 1943, about the problems created by the Allied occupation of Sicily, he also requested in the name of the cardinal secretary of state "the cooperation of the United States Government for the establishment and operation of the Vatican Information Service in Sicily." He said that "innumerable requests from Sicilians on the

Italian mainland" were reaching the Vatican, and the pope ardently desired to help these families and individuals by means of postal and radio communications concerning their loved ones, in the same manner as was being done for the inhabitants of Tripolitania. He added that the Holy See was fully prepared to submit such welfare messages to competent Allied censorship.[54]

On July 29, 1943, Cicognani was pleased to inform Maglione that the American government was arranging for lists of prisoners to be immediately compiled in the theater of war operations and communicated to the papal representative two or three days after being sent to Geneva. In regard to the transmission of messages and the availability of radio, the government had replied with a negative decision to the Holy See's new request, and had asked him not to insist; no reason was given, he said, because they wanted to avoid discussions. The delegate added that he had discussed with Taylor the question of telegraphic transmissions and the ambassador had dissuaded him from insisting. The government of the United States maintained that it was bound to defend and safeguard the entire Western hemisphere with the duty of closing the way to any risk. Cicognani promised to present the cardinal's reiterated request if he wished, but the delegate held out no hope of success.[55] A fortnight later, nevertheless, Cicognani presented a note to the undersecretary of state, Sumner Welles, in which, after reviewing the preceding assurances, he indicated that Monsignor Walter Carroll had been sent to Algeria in order to supervise the inauguration and organization of the Information Service. He learned there that several lists of prisoners were already prepared and ready for transmission but that the American authorities in North Africa had not yet received instructions allowing them to permit Carroll to forward these lists to Vatican City. Carroll had informed Maglione that the local authorities were favorable to the transmission of those lists but were unwilling to take upon themselves the responsibility of approving such action without explicit directions from Washington. Hence, the delegate requested that whatever action might be possible "be taken to facilitate this humanitarian and charitable activity of the Holy See. It is a fact of experience," he added, "that the families of soldiers are oftentimes made to suffer more by uncertainty as to the fate of their loved ones than by the actual news that they have been wounded or even killed. The Holy See," he pointedly reminded Welles, "had this in mind when it undertook to transmit to the United States through its own radio facilities several hundreds of lists of American soldiers who were prisoners of war in Italy." He reminded the official that "the geographical location of the Vatican, particularly with regard to Italian prisoners of war, and the means of communication at its immediate disposal as well as its direct contacts with local bishops would appear to place it in a very advantageous position for the performance of this eminently humane and charitable work." He also argued that experience had shown in countless cases that there was really no duplication of effort involved.[56]

Cicognani pursued the matter in a visit he paid to Welles on August 21, 1943. Welles replied that he "would do what might be possible to expedite a reply to these requests."[57] Two days later, nevertheless, the delegate had to disappoint the cardinal secretary with the news that the American government had officially decided not to concede more than it had accorded in June. It added that competent authorities would now arrange to have lists of prisoners of war prepared and transmitted with dispatch; for that purpose, however, the government wished to use only the means envisioned by the International Convention of Geneva.[58]

When Monsignor Carroll arrived in Washington in September, the delegate employed him to press the Holy See's request at the War Department, which replied that it would take up the question of the information service again and would send lists of prisoners from Algiers. Unless complications arose, a decision was expected in the coming week, and the delegate was hopeful, as he cabled to Maglione on September 19.[59] His persistence and patience were at last rewarded on September 29, when the assistant secretary of state, Breckinridge Long, wrote him that the Department of State had now received the decision of the U.S. Joint Chiefs of Staff with respect to the functioning of the Vatican Information Service in North Africa and Sicily and the opening of channels of correspondence between bishops of Sicily and the Holy See. The Joint Chiefs had reconsidered their decision of May 30, 1943, and had revised to a certain extent the conditions affecting the functioning of the Vatican Information Service. The Service was now allowed to extend its activities to Italian prisoners of war in the hands of American authorities. General Eisenhower was authorized to furnish the service with rosters of prisoners on a delayed basis and to permit the transmission of welfare messages for Italian prisoners of war and persons of equivalent status in American custody. Moreover, family news service and messages from prisoners under the auspices of the Vatican Information Service were now being addressed by the archbishop of Palermo to the Holy See via Algiers.[60] Naturally, Cicognani at once apprised Maglione of the changed policy.[61]

In December, Cicognani reported to Maglione that the new undersecretary of state, Edward R. Stettinius, had informed him that Robert A. Murphy, the political counselor to the Supreme Command of the Allied Forces in North Africa and personal representative of President Roosevelt, had communicated from Algiers that the cardinal archbishop of Palermo had been notified that a special mail (courier or diplomatic messenger, *corriere*) was functioning between Palermo and Algiers. Carroll, now in Algiers, requested that the Holy See furnish to the Allied authorities information of a technical nature about the Vatican Radio, and the managers of the radio station were asked to indicate a convenient timetable for communications with Radio Algiers, that is, three times a week. As soon as such information was provided, Murphy saw no reason why the two radio stations should not begin to function regularly.[62]

The service still depended, of course, on human cooperation. In the following February Cicognani informed Maglione that Carroll had been able to send the usual messages from Algiers, but the English authorities, after many delays and favorable promises, refused to hand over lists of prisoners. Carroll had prepared a message with 60 conventional or standard sentences for civilians and prisoners to be transmitted to the Vatican by radio. The Americans gave their approval, but not the English. Five White Fathers were visiting the camps, distributing forms, and collecting names.[63]

As far as prisoners of war in the United States were concerned, Cicognani repeated to the cardinal secretary in June 1944 that from correspondence and conversations with government officials and with Taylor, he had ascertained the previous summer that the American government had decided not to permit the sending of lists of prisoners or of messages by radio, and did not even want to discuss or consider the question. The reasons adduced for the refusal were the great difficulties of telegraphic transmission in wartime and still more "the security of the whole North American continent," which the government maintained would be threatened or at least endangered by such a radio–telegraphic service. Further negotiations were not possible.[64]

In the case of one prisoner of war, the delegate had a personal interest. His nephew Gaetano Cicognani (presumably named after his brother Gaetano, the apostolic nuncio in Madrid), a soldier in the Italian army, had been captured in North Africa. It is not known how the delegate first learned that his nephew was a prisoner of war; but he assumed that Gaetano was being held by the British forces. He wrote to George W. Renchard of the American Mission, requesting that his nephew be located, that some of the priests of the Archbishopric of Algiers provide him with whatever he might need, and that he be transferred to the United States as an American prisoner in order that he might receive adequate medical attention. The American ambassador, Robert D. Murphy, supported his petition on May 24, 1944, noting: "It would be greatly appreciated if these requests could be met by the appropriate military authorities, as the Apostolic Delegate has been of great assistance to the Department of State during the present war in matters concerning relations between the Vatican and the Department of State."[65] The American vice-consul for the U.S. Political Adviser, Thomas S. Estes, on the same date wrote to the Commanding General SOS, requesting that his office be informed of the time and place of the turnover of this Italian prisoner to U.S. custody, as well as the time of his departure from

North Africa, and the time and place of his arrival in the United States so that the apostolic delegate might be advised by telegram through the Department of State. Within three days the Prisoner of War Information Bureau advised "informally" that Gaetano was currently assigned to the French Depot de Prisonniers de Guerre, Depot No. V, Department of Constantine, Algiers. He was picked up by the American authorities and transferred to the Mediterranean Base Section in the second half of July or first part of August.[66] He was apparently transported by airplane to the United States on August 26. By August 28 he was located at Fort Meade, Maryland,[67] where on Sunday afternoons his uncle often visited him.[68] The archbishop must have considered this success a compensation for all his efforts on behalf of prisoners of war.

## VATICAN–JAPANESE DIPLOMATIC RELATIONS

After the press in the United States reported that Japan was about to send a diplomatic mission to the Holy See, the Apostolic Delegation, according to its own memorandum dated March 3, 1942, requested information on the matter from the Secretariat of State. Cardinal Maglione replied and directed that the contents of his response be communicated confidentially to the government of the United States. The explanation was an account of the background of the agreement, stressing "the vast missionary interests of the Catholic Church in the Japanese Empire." In the absence of Archbishop Cicognani, the auditor of the Apostolic Delegation, Egidio Vagnozzi, requested an interview with Welles on the same day and then handed him the memorandum. After reading it, the undersecretary replied very emphatically and "with the utmost sincerity" that he "felt that this decision on the part of the Holy See was deplorable in as much as ... it would create a profound reaction on the part of the people of the United States and a similar reaction on the part of the people in many other countries including all of the United Nations." Welles recorded, "I said that at the very moment when the Japanese were committing unspeakable atrocities on the civilian populations throughout the regions they were now ravaging, when in the Philippines they had desecrated and violated churches and Catholic communities, and when the announced purpose of Japan's military leaders was to drive the influence of the white race from the Far East, including, obviously and principally, the influence of Christianity among the populations of Asia, for the Holy See for the first time in its history to receive a diplomatic mission from Japan seemed to me an incredible step." Welles believed that Vagnozzi agreed with him completely. He too "feared a disastrous effect on public opinion" in the United States. After Welles expressed the hope that the Holy Father and the cardinal secretary of state would reconsider this matter if it was not already too late, he noted, "Monsignor Vonuzzi [sic] went on to say that the step had been taken by the Vatican upon the urgent recommendations of the Apostolic Delegate in Tokyo and members of the hierarchy in occupied China who insisted that if the agreement of the Vatican was not given, Catholic Japanese and particularly Catholic Chinese would be massacred by the thousands and missions and churches would be destroyed." Welles retorted that he had no evidence, judging from the history of the past few years, that measures of appeasement of this character would have the slightest effect.[69]

Welles told Vagnozzi that he would like to have an opportunity of talking with the apostolic delegate after the latter's return to Washington, and he offered to call on Cicognani as soon as the delegate would be well enough. Instead the delegate requested an appointment with Welles and went to see him on March 6. Welles later recorded, "The Delegate stated that he had immediately sent a very full report by telegram to the Holy See and added that he had expressed in the strongest and most vigorous terms his complete agreement with the opinions and statements which I had expressed." The undersecretary told him that he had discussed this whole question with the president that very day, and he added: "The President had asked me to let the Delegate know that when he had read this report he had found it completely impossible to credit it." Cicognani told Welles that he was very happy to have this message from the president and promised to transmit it by urgent cable to the Holy See. Then he suggested that Tittmann be instructed (without any mention of the delegate's name) "to make as forceful and emphatic representations as possible to the cardinal secretary of state. He stressed particularly the importance of Tittmann's speaking with Monsignor [Domenico] Tardini in this light." The archbishop said "he was profoundly disturbed and utterly unable to comprehend any justifiable reason for the step which apparently had been agreed upon by the Vatican." It was certainly remarkable that the delegate was so critical of his superiors' decision; perhaps he recognized that it would be useless to try to defend it. Cicognani also told Welles that "in his recent trip to the west he had personally conferred with Archbishop [Francis J.] Beckman of Dubuque, Iowa, the Bishop of Fort Wayne [John Francis Noll], and Archbishop [Michael] Curley of Baltimore, for the purpose of making it clear to them that in the opinion of the Holy See they should immediately refrain from making any further public utterances which tended to create disunity in the United States and to lessen in any way popular support of the policies of the Administration."[70] In this conversation, the apostolic delegate must have cemented his good relations with the Department of State.

The delegate subsequently invited eight archbishops to a meeting at his residence on March 16 to discuss the American government's protest against the Holy See's negotiations with the Japanese government. Afterwards he informed one of the archbishops, Francis J. Spellman, that the pope wished him to go to the president and explain the Holy See's attitude and position. In carrying out this mission Spellman suggested that the Holy See establish diplomatic relations with Chiang Kai-Shek. According to Spellman's memorandum, Roosevelt was "elated" and "completely tranquilized."[71] A Chinese representative, Dr. Soong, called at the Delegation on March 23 and presented a formal note, asking for the establishment of relations. After a second meeting with him, Cicognani was hopeful that everything would work out well.[72]

### THE BOMBING OF ROME

On December 4, 1942, Cicognani called on Adolph A. Berle, Jr., assistant secretary of state, and spoke of "the threats which were being made over the British wireless that Rome would presently be bombed." He said that the pope had asked him to take up the matter with the American government in the hope that quietly, and without publicity, such bombing could be prevented. Berle recorded: "He said that the Pope had likewise taken the matter up with Archbishop Spellman, asking him to speak to the President; and that Archbishop Spellman was seeing the President about this on December 8th." He also presented a memorandum to which Berle replied "that the matter, of course, had been under consideration," that the government had the greatest desire to avoid all unnecessary bloodshed and destruction, and that it realized the ecclesiastical interests in Rome. The assistant secretary, however, observed "that the Italians were in a weak position, because their planes had participated in the bombardment of London." Cicognani replied "that he feared the Pope would have to make a protest if Rome were bombed. This, he thought, would be used as propaganda by the Axis." Berle "inquired, somewhat innocently, whether the Pope had made any protest when London was bombed. Cicognani replied that only general statements had been made. He said he realized the position perfectly: Rome was the capital of a warring state, and so forth. But he hoped some consideration would be given to the fact that Rome was the bishopric of the Pope and that almost every other building in it was ecclesiastical in character. He thought that bombing would make a bad impression on public opinion everywhere." Berle replied "that the matter would be given consideration."[73]

The secretary of state, Cordell Hull, was opposed to adopting a course independent from that of Great Britain. After Cicognani's visit to Berle, Myron Taylor on December 17 sent the president a message from the

Vatican stating that the Holy See had undertaken negotiations with the Italian government to remove Axis military installations from the Eternal City, and that the Italian government had given on December 13 oral assurances that the supreme command and the general staff, together with Premier Mussolini, were about to leave Rome. Roosevelt in a note to Hull then proposed that "England and the United States could agree not to bomb Rome" on the condition that the city not be used by the Germans or the Italians for war purposes. Hull told the British Ambassador, Lord Halifax, ". . . this Government feels, and has so indicated to the Vatican and others, that we do not want to bomb Rome or see it bombed. At the same time we have inquired why Italians and those at the Vatican who do not want Rome bombed are not proceeding to cause objectionable military agencies, properties, and interests to be cleared out of Rome before making pointed and unqualified requests that Rome be not bombed." Hull preferred to keep alive all the American Government's "rights with respect to the possible bombing of Rome" and in the meantime to put the burden on those opposed to such bombing. When the president, having received a further letter from Taylor urging some action, consulted Hull, he replied that he was awaiting the reaction of the British to his negative position on a possible ultimatum. He wrote, "The memorandum from the Apostolic Delegate indicates that the military objectives, both Italian and German, are actually being transferred from Rome and that the initiative for this action has been taken by the Holy See." He regarded this as confirmation of the position taken by the American government with respect to the British proposals. On January 12, 1943, the British ambassador sent Hull a memorandum "stating that his Government had decided, somewhat reluctantly, to abandon its idea, partly as a result of" the American attitude. The British thought it would be well, however, to keep the Italian government and the Vatican guessing about the Allied policy toward the bombardment of Rome. Accordingly, Hull approved the reply that Tittmann had been giving to questioners, that is, "that he had received no instructions from his Government on the subject of the bombing of Rome" and that the Government must be reserving its right to bomb should the military situation require it. That continued to be the American policy until the taking of Rome.[74]

After the Allies began the assault on Sicily in the third week of May 1943, the apostolic delegate requested an appointment with the undersecretary, Welles, and was received by him on May 24. Cicognani handed Welles a memorandum regarding the possible bombing of Rome. Welles recorded, "The Delegate added that the views of the Holy See with regard to this question were already so thoroughly known that he did not feel it necessary to say anything further with reference to this communication."[75]

On June 15, 1943, the delegate in a letter brought two points to Myron Taylor's attention in order that Taylor might communicate them directly to the president. First, the Holy Father recommended anew to the president the fate of the Italian people, and second, he was "saddened by the news that the possibility of the bombardment of Rome" had not been excluded. In such a hypothesis the pope would be constrained to protest. Cicognani concluded with the warning, "Those effecting such a bombardment will be held responsible by Catholics the world over and by the judgment of history."[76]

On August 2, 1943, the delegate informed Welles that the Holy See had made "representations to the present military government of Italy in order to have Rome recognized as an open city" and that consequently the new Italian government notified the cardinal secretary of state in writing on July 31 that it had decided to declare Rome an open city; it also requested the cardinal to ascertain the essential conditions that would be imposed by the Allies before the declaration would be accepted. Welles immediately sent a copy of Cicognani's letter to General George C. Marshall, chief of staff at the War Department, and asked him to have the reply sent to Welles personally so that he might communicate it at once to the apostolic delegate for transmission to Rome.[77] After waiting six days, Maglione sent Cicognani a radiogram "urgently requesting a definitive reply." When the delegate forwarded the inquiry, Welles could only assure him that the matter was receiving the "fullest consideration" of "the highest authorities of the Government of the United States." He added, "In the meantime, I am instructed by the President to state that, in accordance with the accepted principles of international law and of pertinent international agreements, there is nothing to prevent the Italian Government from undertaking unilaterally to declare Rome an open city."[78]

Twelve more days passed without any word from Washington. Hence, the cardinal secretary of state instructed the delegate to inquire further whether an official reply would be forthcoming. In carrying out this directive, Cicognani added, "His Eminence advises me explicitly that the present government of Italy is animated with serious intentions in effecting the changes required for the recognition of Rome as an open city, conformably to the provisions of international law." In a separate letter on the same day Cicognani forwarded to Welles two memoranda dictated by the Holy See's direct contact with recent events in Sicily and in Italy at large. "These reflections," he explained, "aim to evaluate recent and present happenings in the light of the future which they are molding and of the effects which they will have on the formulation of the peace towards which the Holy See continues to bend its every effort."[79] On the very next day the apostolic delegate requested an interview with Welles in order to discuss the two memoranda with him. Afterwards Welles recorded, "I told the Delegate that the memorandum from the Holy See which contained the expression of the Vatican's opinion with regard to the undesirability of continued bombing by the United Nations of Italian territory had been immediately communicated by myself to the President for his information." In regard to the other communication, however, the undersecretary could not say when a reply would be ready concerning the conditions for declaring Rome an open city. In their further discussion, Cicognani "spoke at considerable length about the present state of mind of the Italian people and of his fear that their traditional friendship and sympathy for the American people might be prejudiced if attacks from the air upon Italian cities were continued." Welles replied rather coldly that the solution would be the unconditional surrender of the Italian government. Cicognani remarked "that he had interpreted the radio address of the King of Italy" of the preceding day "as implying that the Italian Government was now ready to accept the terms offered." Welles at once forwarded the memoranda to Roosevelt.[80]

In the evening the delegate called on Welles for the second time in the same day. He read to him the telegram that he had sent to Maglione two days before, saying that "in his opinion public opinion in the United States was exceedingly uncertain as to whether the policy of the present Italian Government [Marshal Badoglio's government] of apparently continuing the war on the side of Germany was a spontaneous decision . . . or a decision which was forced upon it by German power." He had also said that American public opinion was equally uncertain as to whether the Italian government sincerely desired to find the ways and means of bringing to an end Italian participation in the war against the United Nations. In reply Cardinal Maglione sent Cicognani a telegram that the delegate also read to Welles. In it the cardinal "stated that the Italian Government desired to find as promptly as possible the means of ending its war against the United Nations, and second, that its continued collaboration with Germany was not spontaneous but was forced upon it by the German Government." As soon as the delegate departed, Welles drew up a memorandum of their conversation and sent it to Roosevelt.[81]

On the same day Cicognani wrote to the archbishops of New York, Chicago, and Detroit about the recent bombing of Rome and the possible effects on the Holy See of the "prosecution of the 'total war' campaign on the Italian mainland." Cardinal Maglione wished the hierarchy and laity of the United States to be informed that in the bombardment of Rome on August 13, two churches were hit and one of them, a new church, was completely destroyed; a great number of civilian homes in the populated areas were likewise demolished. Second, the Holy See was preoccupied, he wrote, by the prospect of extensive military operations on the peninsula. Hence, the pope had requested "that the Bishops and clergy of the United States take appropriate steps to draw attention to these facts, in order to impress the competent authorities with the gravity of the situation." The delegate asked the archbishops to discuss among themselves, as promptly as possible, what means might be best suited to carrying out these desires of His Holiness.[82]

Spellman replied that the bishops and laity of the United States had been informed of the bombardment of Rome, since these facts had been in all of the newspapers, which also carried pictures of the bombardment and its effects, including the damaged church of San Lorenzo. The bishops, through the chairman of the Administrative Board, their representative, had already manifested sorrow over the bombardment of Rome. He professed not to understand from Cicognani's letter just what additional steps, if any, should be taken at that time. Mooney and Stritch felt as he did that everything possible to do in this sad situation had been done and would be done.[83]

Mooney replied that in his opinion wide publicity given in the Catholic press to the unfortunate damage to churches resulting from the second bombing of Rome would give the bishops "another occasion to make appropriate manifestation of their consternation and regret which would find a responsible echo in the deep devotion" of the Catholic people to the person and the office of the pope. He feared, however, "that any attempt to stir up a public nationwide agitation among Catholics on the subject would have seriously unfavorable consequences for the Catholic cause," and he set forth cogent reasons in support of his position. As far as the Holy See's preoccupation with the prospect of an Allied invasion of Italy was concerned, Mooney thought that the bishops and Catholic people of the United States could "make a definite contribution by vigorously pressing for the acceptance on reasonable terms of the declaration of Rome as an open city." He thought it "possible for the Holy See on one side and the American bishops on the other to influence decisions which would in this way bring about the justified recognition of the unique status of Rome as the Center of Christendom." He was convinced that no other avenue of effective intervention was open to American bishops. He observed that no minority group of American citizens could prevail in having the American government's goodwill toward a non-Fascist Italy "turned to the military advantage of an active belligerent on the side of National-socialist Germany and Japan." He concluded by warning: "Even to make an ineffectual attempt to do so would fatally prejudice the cause of the Church and the prestige of the Holy See in this country."[84] Cicognani agreed with him, and in his reply he wrote that he understood perfectly the situation that Mooney had described and the conclusions to which it led; he added that in presenting this matter for Mooney's consideration he "was but following out the instructions of... Cardinal Maglione."[85]

When Cicognani learned of Sumner Welles's resignation in August 1943, he wrote to express his "genuine regret" and his "best wishes for whatever line of endeavor" Welles might engage in for the immediate future. He added: "My official and personal contacts with you in recent years afforded me many opportunities to appreciate your talents and accomplishments." Cicognani thanked him "most cordially for the courteous, prompt, and efficient consideration accorded to the problems" that the delegate had taken up with him in Welles's official capacity. Cicognani concluded: "This cooperation has been most helpful to me and my gratitude for it is wholehearted."[86] Indeed, the Apostolic Delegation had lost its best friend in the Department of State.

## FEEDING ROME/SAVING ROME

In the late summer of 1943 Italy itself was in dire need of food. At Maglione's prompting, Cicognani notified Myron Taylor and Archbishop Spellman, wrote twice to the secretary of state, Cordell Hull, and ascertained that President Roosevelt was apprised of the situation.[87] Hull soon communicated to Cicognani the news received from General Dwight D. Eisenhower, the commander in chief of the Allied Expeditionary Force in North Africa, about the victualing of Sicily. Hull also assured him that the competent military authority was examining his note on the need for foodstuffs in the part of Italy occupied by the Allies.[88] In the following month Cicognani wrote to Edward R. Stettinius, Jr., the acting secretary of state, that the cardinal secretary of state in a new communication had stressed very forcibly "the gravity of the food situation in Rome at that time." He added, "In view of the methodical and continued requisition of foodstuffs and animals by the occupying forces, the city of Rome is exposed to dire want of even the necessaries of life, including milk for children." Hence, the cardinal suggested "that it would be an act of great humanitarianism to provide supplies of powdered milk for immediate transportation to Rome at the moment of the Allied occupation."[89] Then in a memorandum to President Roosevelt, Stettinius enclosed "a copy of a communication from the Apostolic Delegate expressing the Vatican's hope that at the moment of the Allied occupation of Rome sufficient quantities of powdered milk to meet the needs of the children of the city" would be made available by the occupying forces.[90] Stettinius promptly apprised the delegate "of the steps already taken in connection with" his letter of October 20 "expressing the grave concern of the Holy Father over the food situation in the city of Rome." When Cicognani on November 3 thanked the acting secretary of state for his "prompt attention accorded this critical matter," he also said that in the meantime Cardinal Maglione had inquired as to the results of the delegate's bringing the problem to the attention of the U.S. government. This further inquiry emphasized the gravity of the situation; hence, Cicognani pleaded for information regarding the practical measures taken to cope with the situation, which would present itself at the moment of the Allied occupation of Rome.[91] Meanwhile, on October 30, Eisenhower had replied from Algiers: "Please assure the Apostolic Delegate that we will do everything possible to relieve suffering in Rome. Medical supplies and food will be imported, but the amounts available will be limited by total available stocks, shipping and port facilities, and military requirements."[92] Then on November 8, Stettinius conveyed the substance of Eisenhower's report to Cicognani.[93]

Meanwhile, on October 28, 1943, the delegate wrote to Stettinius that in the light of the current developments in the military campaign in central Italy, Cardinal Maglione had directed him to call attention to the danger that might soon threaten the celebrated Abbey of Montecassino, which was not far removed from the actual theater of operations. After explaining its importance, the delegate concluded: "The Holy Father, consequently, is most desirous that every possible effort be exerted to protect the Abbey of Montecassino from even unintentional damage, lest the Christian world be deprived of a monument of such historical and architectural value." Maglione had already conveyed this desire to Tittmann and to the representatives of the other belligerent powers.[94] Stettinius replied that he had made a copy of Cicognani's letter available to the appropriate military authorities with the suggestion that they inform the Theater Commander of the location of the Abbey, its historical and religious importance, and the concern of the Holy Father for its safety.[95] A memorandum was indeed promptly sent to the War Department, suggesting that word be sent to General Eisenhower on the subject.[96]

It was not only Rome and the abbeys of Montecassino and Subiaco that Cicognani and his superiors in the Eternal City wished to see spared. On January 6, 1944, he wrote to Cordell Hull that the cardinal secretary of state had directed him to advise the government of the United States that the Holy See recommended to the belligerent powers "special precautions with regard to the celebrated Cistercian Abbey of Casamari, in the Province of Frosinone." He described it as "one of the most complete examples of monastic construction . . . a classic example of Gothic style of the Burgogne [Burgundian] type," and always "a center of historical and artistic studies." He asked that the U.S. government convey this recommendation to the military commanders in the zone of operations.[97] In reply on January 14 the undersecretary of state, Edward R. Stettinius, Jr., assured him that the matter had been brought to the attention of the appropriate military authorities. On January 26, he also informed the delegate that general orders already existed "for all Allied commanders in the Mediterranean theater with respect to the protection of important religious and other monuments in Italy."[98]

At the direction of Cardinal Maglione, Cicognani wrote to President Roosevelt on February 17, 1944, stating that for some days past, Allied airplanes had undertaken an almost continuous bombardment and machine-gunning of sections of Rome, especially at the outskirts but also within the city proper. He added: "Notable damage has been caused to civilian buildings and to some churches. The recently reconstructed Hospice of Santa Galla, which is the property of the Holy See, has also been seriously damaged. His Eminence notes that since Rome was declared an open city by the Badoglio Government last August, it has been left practically without air raid shelters. The population of the peripheral zones of Rome consists largely of working people among whom there already have been many victims." The delegate added an appeal in the name of the Holy Father that the bombings of Rome be discontinued. Cicognani repeated this to Mooney and further stated that Maglione also charged him with the task of bringing the matter to the attention of the hierarchy in order that they might engage themselves for the purpose of obtaining the cessation of such bombardments. He hoped that some plan for effective action might be found promptly.[99]

Complying with this request, Mooney consulted Stritch by telephone and found that they were "in entire agreement as to the opportuneness... of trying to influence the President directly and quietly rather than through an organized public movement of protest." The two archbishops believed that more effective pressure could be exerted in that way. Accordingly, Mooney wrote to the president on February 23 "from a strictly American Catholic viewpoint" and with the clear implication that to their mind the responsibility would be on the civil authorities who were accountable to those whom they represented. Mooney thought that such an approach was best calculated to make an impression at that time.[100]

Roosevelt replied to the delegate on March 1, 1944, asserting:

The Allied military authorities in Italy are committed to a policy of avoiding damage to religious shrines and historical monuments to the extent humanly possible in modern warfare. This applies to the city of Rome as to other parts of Italy where the forces of the United Nations have been or will be engaged in active fighting.

However, we are fighting a desperate battle against a hard and unscrupulous foe whose ultimate defeat will accomplish the liberation of Italy and the Italian people. When the enemy uses all the facilities which a great center, such as Rome, affords in order to further his military campaign, thus postponing the ultimate liberation of the nation, these facilities must be denied him with all our force. When the enemy assumes a position exposing innocent civilians or uses a religious or historical shrine to his own military advantage, we have no choice but to attack and dislodge him. It is in the nature of a conflict thrust upon the world by evil powers whose strength is based on utter contempt of everything that is beautiful or holy that our military commanders may be obliged to make these painful decisions.

Our only reason in attacking any part of Rome is because it is occupied and used by the Germans. If His Holiness will be successful in persuading them to respect the sacred and cultural character of Rome by withdrawing from it without a struggle he could thus assure its preservation.

Please ask His Eminence the Cardinal Secretary of State to assure His Holiness that it remains our ardent desire that religious edifices and other monuments of our common civilization be saved from damage. To the degree that the hard exigencies of the campaign, through German ruthlessness in the use of such monuments, may not require inevitable exceptions, this principle will be applied in the conduct of the war.[101]

Cicognani enclosed a copy of this reply in his letter to Mooney of the same date, remarking, ". . . the situation is not bright."[102]

In reply Mooney agreed that the president's letter was not, indeed, "as reassuring as one could wish." He expressed the hope that the desire of preserving religious edifices and other monuments of our common civilization from damage would keep them from falling into what might be an enemy trap to discredit their cause in a war in which propaganda was such a powerful weapon.[103] Roosevelt replied to Mooney that instructions had been issued to bomb only those objectives that were of value to the enemy, and to spare, as far as humanly possible, all historic buildings and shrines. He added that this was "also the considered plan of the ground force commanders." Roosevelt assured Mooney: "we shall attempt to drive the enemy northward without a battle within the environs of Rome. The safety of military personnel must be the paramount consideration, and some monuments sacred to the Christian world may be scarred, some may be damaged, and may perforce be destroyed."[104]

After Rome was attacked from the air on March 14, Maglione wrote to Cicognani, who then transmitted the report along with certain comments of the cardinal secretary of state to the secretary of state of the United States on March 18, 1944. Maglione pleaded that such bombardment be confined exclusively to military objectives. He recalled the public declarations of Allied authorities in which it was asserted that every effort would be made to spare historical, artistic, and religious monuments. He added: "Now unfortunately the wholesale destruction and loss of life, especially among the civilian population, are the source of great concern for the fate of Rome, the center of Catholicism."[105]

On March 13, Cicognani replied to the president's letter of March 1 on the subject of the bombing of Rome. In a memorandum of the same date, he wrote: "Up to the present the destruction to sacred buildings and monuments is already enormous and involves losses that rise to many millions of dollars." The complaint was expressed "that in many cases adequate means have not been employed to carry out the repeatedly expressed desire of the President that such monuments and sacred edifices be spared from the devastation of war." He further asserted:

> These conditions have been verified also in the most recent lamentable bombardments of Rome in which the large Ostiense station was the military target. Despite the fact that the target area was very extensive and attacked under conditions of clear visibility, two churches and many homes of working people were destroyed. All these latter structures easily could have been distinguished from the objective itself. These raids resulted in the killing of hundreds of innocent persons—a fact which is the more painful since they belong to a nation already vanquished and which surrendered unconditionally.
>
> The Holy See on its part assures the Allied governments that every precaution is being used and the greatest vigilance exercised lest any of the religious monuments of the Eternal city be used for military purposes.
>
> His Eminence, the Cardinal Secretary of State, further declares that in the judgment of competent military observers a direct attack on Rome is neither necessary nor desirable...It would appear therefore that to save Rome from destruction would be in the interest not only of religion and civilization but also would offer direct military advantage.[106]

On March 22 Cicognani, after receiving a further communication from Maglione, addressed a letter to Cordell Hull on the subject of Rome. He said that the Holy Father was unwilling to assume the responsibility of not having made known the truth or of having neglected to exhort all belligerents to sentiments of humane consideration for the dangers and difficulties of defenseless civilians in all war areas. Maglione pointed out that it was the prevailing conviction there that, with adequate precautionary measures, it would be possible to limit aerial attacks strictly to objectives of military importance. He also emphasized that the continued bombings of Rome were lowering the prestige of the Allies, embittering a populace otherwise well disposed, and producing the further effect of inciting Communism, which was already rife in the great mass of the people. Maglione added that in the bombardment of Rome on March 18 the Policlinico and other smaller hospitals were badly damaged, in addition to the destruction of homes of civilians, and this made it particularly difficult to provide the necessary medical assistance for the wounded and the dying.[107] Spellman replied that he had talked the matter over with Archbishop Mooney, whom he had met at a bishop's funeral, and he felt that "both directly and indirectly" they were doing everything possible to carry out the wishes of the Holy Father.[108]

Rome was also in danger of hunger. In April 1944, Maglione cabled Cicognani that since the food shortage in the city was aggravated and provisioning overland was difficult, risky, and insufficient, the State of Vatican City was planning a transporting of foodstuffs by sea from Italian ports to Fiumicino and Civitavecchia by acquiring small ships that would sail under the Italian flag. Maglione did not expect the German government to raise obstacles, and he asked the delegate to seek a favorable response from the American government.[109] Cicognani wrote to Hull on April 19, conveying the cardinal secretary's request and adding that the English minister to the Holy See and the U.S. charge d'affaires had given assurances that word of the contemplated project had been duly transmitted to their respective governments. He enumerated the assurances that Maglione deemed necessary to receive from all the belligerent parties.[110] Cicognani would have to wait until June for a final answer.

Meanwhile, on May 2, the delegate sent Hull "for the information and consideration of the United States Government two copies of the English translation of a report prepared under the direction of the Holy See on the nature and gravity of the problem of aid to the inhabitants of Italian territory freed of the German troops."[111] On May 21, "with the further approach of actual combat to Rome," Cicognani reminded Hull that the shortage of food and medicines was becoming increasingly critical. He wrote: "The population of the city has greatly augmented in recent months and it will be extremely urgent to provide the inhabitants with alimentary and medicinal relief." Accordingly, the pope, through his cardinal secretary of state, was fervently pleading "with the Allied military authorities and civilian governments to be prepared adequately to offer relief to the suffering population."[112] In reply to the pope's appeal for "immediate and effective relief to the people of his diocese of Rome," Stettinius, now undersecretary of state, assured the delegate that his letter of May 21 had been read "with sympathy and understanding." He reminded him, nevertheless, that as long as Rome was held by the enemy the responsibility for the feeding and the general welfare of its population rested "with the so-called Fascist Republican authorities, or their German masters," who were failing to carry out their obligations in this respect. Stettinius added, however, that when Rome would be liberated from Nazi and fascist domination, the American government, in concert with its Allies, would do everything that the circumstances might warrant and which might be feasible "with a view to affording succor and comfort to the people of Rome."[113]

At last, on June 2, Secretary Hull gave the delegate a definitive reply regarding the request for navicerts and safe conducts for the fleet of vessels that the Holy See proposed to use for conveying supplies intended for the provisioning of Rome. He asserted that the matter was given the most careful consideration by the American and British governments in consultation with the Combined Chiefs of Staff and a joint reply to the Holy See was agreed upon, namely, that "to ensure the safety of these food ships whilst on outward and return passages between North Italian or other ports and Rome and to respect free zones at the terminal ports would... place severe restrictions on the Allied operations in an area of military importance"; moreover, the British and U.S. governments considered that the responsibility for supplying the population of Rome with food rested, as Stettinius had asserted, "with the so-called Fascist Republican authorities or their German masters," who were "clearly failing to carry out their obligations in this respect and thereby relieving themselves of an inconvenient strain on their communications and the consequent hampering of their own operations." Hence, the two governments did not accept the proposal "in view of the restrictions which it would place on their operations and of the relief to German obligations and responsibility which it would entail."[114] Cicognani then discharged the unpleasant duty of reporting the decision to Maglione (who had also been apprised of it by Tittmann).[115]

On May 22, 1944, Cicognani had written to Archbishop Spellman about "the desperate situation in Rome with regard to food and medical supplies," of which he had been apprised by the cardinal secretary, who had also directed him "to urge the United States authorities to provide adequate and immediate relief in the event of the taking of Rome." Cicognani accordingly wrote to the American secretary of state on that day. Now he reminded Spellman of the wish expressed by the bishops at their meeting of the previous November "to provide relief for the population of Rome." He told Spellman, however, that in his opinion it would be premature for him, together with Archbishop Edward Mooney and Archbishop Samuel Stritch, "to consider a practical plan for the sending of relief in foodstuffs to the Eternal city, for distribution by His Holiness." He feared that the relief to be given by the occupying armies would be limited, "due to their own great needs, and it would seem all-important that His Holiness dispose personally of the means afforded to succor the population. This would entail not only the offering of funds but also," he believed, "the actual shipment of food and other supplies to Vatican City," since it would most probably be impossible for the Vatican to make purchases in Europe. Hence, following Maglione's instructions, he was writing to Spellman, Mooney, and Stritch to ask their assistance "in deciding on some coordinated plan of action," which would bring these considerations to the attention of the proper government authorities as insistently as possible. He also asked them to give attention to Maglione's desire to secure the collaboration of prominent members of the laity.[116] On June 1, he also wrote to the general secretary of the NCWC, Monsignor Michael J. Ready, noting that the hospitals of Rome were almost without medicines. He relayed Maglione's assurance of the Holy See's readiness "to lend every possible collaboration for the assistance of the people," and added that various Catholic agencies had already been organized and were "ready to lend effective cooperation in this humanitarian work." He suggested that Ready pass this information on "to those engaged in the work of preparing to assist the population of Rome." On the same day, Ready sent a copy of this letter to the government official in charge of such matters, Leo T. Crowley.[117]

As the Allied offensive advanced in Italy in May of 1944, "the question of the preservation of the city of Rome from the horrors and destruction of war" assumed a new urgency. Cardinal Maglione, therefore, wrote to Cicognani again, pointing out "the opportuneness of concerted action . . . on the part of the Catholic Hierarchy and laity of the United States in an attempt to influence whatever decisions" might have been taken in this regard. The cardinal secretary felt "that efforts made by the Bishops and faithful of America could not but be fruitful of practical and lasting effects." Cicognani conveyed this exhortation to Spellman, Mooney, and Stritch and asked them to formulate some plan to be effected immediately, as soon as conditions would permit.[118]

Mooney replied in the name of Spellman, Stritch, and himself, saying that they had taken action in regard to both of Cicognani's requests contained in his letters of May 22, and they hoped it would have the desired effect.[119]

On May 29, Cicognani transmitted to Cordell Hull the complaint of Cardinal Maglione that on May 23 a "large formation of Allied planes flew undisturbed for two hours over the Monastery of Saint Scholastica at Subiaco. The famous cloister," he wrote, "was destroyed and the interior of the edifice as well as nearby buildings were severely damaged by the bombs (about fifteen) that were dropped." The community was saved, but one student and one workman were killed. Following the cardinal's statement, the delegate explained why the bombing served no military purpose. He added, "If the system that brought about this unnecessary destruction continues to be followed, it is feared that the result will be the destruction of many more renowned monuments, heritages of art, of civilization, and of religion." Cicognani asked that this communication be given highest consideration and that appropriate action be taken.[120]

On the next day Cicognani wrote to Mooney that in regard to the question of Rome being declared an open city, "although the matter was presented on various occasions, the Government of the United States avoided giving a definite answer for one reason or another. . . . The decision that will hold for the present has apparently been made."[121]

Rome was captured by the Allies on June 4, 1944. On June 17, 1944, Cicognani wrote to Mooney, Spellman, and Stritch that he had received from Cardinal Maglione two communications "regarding the use of the city of Rome by the Allies for military purposes, such as the quartering of large numbers of troops, and the transport of men and materiel." The Holy See feared that the continued use of Rome in this manner might provoke air attacks, and directed him to insist with the government that Rome be given the status of an open city. Maglione had already "consigned notes on the subject to the British and American representatives at the Vatican." Cicognani "addressed two communications to the Secretary of State," and on June 16 he "stressed the point in conversation with him." Since up to that time "no mention had been made of making Rome an open city," Maglione instructed Cicognani to inform the three archbishops in order that the American hierarchy might seek to obtain the desired result. He asked that they confer on the subject and apprise him of any conclusion that might be reached.[122]

Mooney then composed a letter to President Roosevelt, stating that the bishops of the Administrative Board of the NCWC asked him to bring to bear the full force of his influence in Allied councils to the end that Rome be made an open city under the provisions of international law.[123] When Spellman received the letter, he signed it and forwarded it to the apostolic delegate "with some observations...about the advisability of sending the letter at this time." He added: "The Delegate agreed with the logic of my observations and returned the letter to me. I have already had occasion to bring this matter orally to the attention of the President and discussed it with him and I felt that the letter might, therefore, seem to him superfluous."[124]

Meanwhile, Cicognani had received a reply from the secretary of state, Cordell Hull, and forwarded it to Maglione. Hull had assured him that the defense of Rome would be conducted with full appreciation of the special position that it occupied. He added, "In view of the present over-all military situation, especially as to the Allied air supremacy over Italy, it has been suggested that there would seem to be undue apprehension of danger to Rome. The military authorities consider that there is little likelihood of serious German air or other attacks upon the city of Rome now or in the foreseeable future." Cicognani had written Maglione that a similar answer would probably be given to the joint letter of the Administrative Board if it were sent to the president.[125] As time passed, the likelihood of German air attacks on Rome became ever more remote.

## INTERVENTION FOR THE THREATENED JEWS

Beginning in 1942, Archbishop Cicognani was actively involved in efforts to save the European Jews threatened by the Nazis. In many cases he was a willing intermediary between American Jewish organizations and the Holy See. His relations with the American government in this regard were less frequent. In May 1943, Myron Taylor at the request of the president of the American

Jewish Congress, Stephen S. Wise, submitted through Cicognani a petition to the Holy See, which was asked to intervene to free Dr. William Fildermann, a lawyer of Bucharest and president of the Union of Jewish Communities in Romania, who had been arrested by order of the prime minister and condemned to forced labor in a concentration camp, or at least to alleviate his sufferings. Cicognani asked Montini to do what he could.[126] The next month, the apostolic delegate transmitted another urgent plea from Taylor, who had been implored by Wise, to ask the Holy See to intervene in order to prevent the deportation of foreigners by the Italian government. In the Secretariat of State, Tardini noted that it could be said that nothing was known of this measure, and Maglione agreed. He added that the imminent change of government, which occurred on July 25, when Mussolini was dismissed as prime minister, led one to think that nothing of the kind would be done, but this was not to be said. Hence, Cicognani was directed to inform Taylor that the Holy See, whenever it would be necessary, would do everything possible to prevent the feared measure.[127]

Ever ready to make a humanitarian effort, Cicognani on October 15 acted on behalf of Polish rabbis who had taken refuge in Shanghai. American Jews had returned to him several times to ask that the Holy See interest the British and Polish governments. He said that the case presented difficulties for the American and British governments because many thousands of their citizens were detained by the Japanese, and the governments had to do what they could for them first. Since the Jews were few in number, 460, and peaceful people, he suggested that through the apostolic delegate in Tokyo, Paolo Marella, the Holy See make of them a special humanitarian case and intercede for their liberation.[128] It was then proposed that the rabbis be exchanged for Japanese prisoners of the United States, but the American government, through Taylor, informed Cicognani that it could not consider members of the college of rabbis for exchange and transfer to the United States since they were not American citizens. Furthermore, Japan did not permit such an exchange. The government added that there were many Americans in the Far East to be repatriated, but it thought that the questions could perhaps be studied in London by the English and Polish governments.[129] Since the American and British governments refused to intervene because negotiations were pending with Japan for the liberation of their own nationals, the American rabbis begged the Holy See to interest the Japanese ambassador to the Vatican, Ken Harada, in the case, suggesting that the Japanese government release the group in Shanghai, which consisted mainly of rabbis and teachers, without a diplomatic exchange. The American rabbis assured the delegate that once the release was obtained, the American and British governments would provide for the transportation of the detainees to some destination. The Secretariat replied that even though the Holy See was aware of the difficulty of the matter, it had not failed to interest the Japanese government on behalf of the rabbis.[130] Apparently its efforts were futile.

In February 1944, Cicognani cabled Maglione that the American secretary of state in a note dated February 21 asked the Holy See to intervene with the government of Monsignor Josef Tiso, the president of Slovakia, in order to prevent the imminent deportation and persecution of about 15,000 Jews living in that country. The American government stated that in the future it would pay close heed to the good or bad treatment that those Jews would receive from Tiso and from other responsible persons. The Secretariat of State transmitted this admonition verbatim to its envoy in Bratislava, Monsignor Giuseppe Burzio.[131] Afterward Cicognani conveyed to the cardinal secretary, Cordell Hull's thanks for the Holy See's intervention on behalf of the Jews of Slovakia.[132] In the middle of May 1944, the apostolic delegate was notified by the War Refugee Board[133] that the deportation of Jews from Hungary and Subcarpathian Russia had begun, as well as general deportations of Polish refugees known to the Hungarian police. The Board appreciated the Holy See's past action and noted that the recognition of the passports on the part of the Latin American republics did not necessarily imply immigration to those countries. Once they left the territory under German control, the American government would find a place to send them. Finally, the committee for Jewish refugees begged the Holy See to intervene with the Spanish government to the end that 238 Jews who had passports for South America and had been transferred from the camp at Vittel to an unknown destination might return to that concentration camp, because it seemed that only from there would they be allowed to leave the territory occupied by the Germans.[134]

On June 24, 1944, Stettinius wrote to the apostolic delegate that the food situation of the Jews and other persons detained because of their race, religion, and political opinions was desperate; they were in immediate danger of dying of hunger. Stettinius asked that the Holy See intervene to obtain for these prisoners the same treatment as was prescribed by the Geneva Convention for civil internees in regard to the distribution of packages under the control of the International Red Cross.[135] Cicognani reported this request to the cardinal secretary, noting that the American government had exhausted all the means at its own disposal to relieve the Jews and others detained in the camps in Germany and the satellite nations. Since it was well aware of the Holy See's humanitarian work through its correspondence with the Apostolic Delegation and valued it highly, it had asked the delegate with an official document to communicate to the cardinal secretary its desire that the Holy See strive to induce the governments of Germany and its satellites (1) to accord to such persons the same treatment as was granted to American and English civil internees, to whom it was the custom to apply the Geneva Convention, and, if that was not possible (2) to extend such treatment at least in regard to the sending and distribution, under the surveillance of the Red Cross, of packages allowed to internees. The American government preferred the first alternative; the second was to be proposed only if the Holy See judged it impossible to obtain the first. In conclusion Cicognani reiterated the government's assessment of the desperate need of these persecuted people for food.[136]

News of the relentless campaign against the Jews never ceased to flow to the apostolic delegate. The director of the War Refugee Board, John W. Pehle, asked the Holy See through him for information about approximately 4,000 Jews who had Latin American citizenship or passports for El Salvador and Paraguay, but were arrested in Bratislava and interned at Mariathal and then transferred to another place, perhaps Germany, around October 8. As news reports of massacres of non-Aryans in Hungary were received in an unending stream, the Jewish committees begged the Holy See to declare the churches of Hungary places of refuge with the right of asylum and to have the bishops and priests shelter Jews to save them from death.[137] Tardini informed Cicognani on November 29 that the Slovak government claimed that it did not know the destination of the Jews deported to Germany.[138] As far as Hungary was concerned, Tardini informed Cicognani that in pursuance of instructions from the Holy See, the Apostolic Nunciature had repeatedly intervened with the Hungarian authorities urging them not to adopt odious measures, and the episcopate also engaged in more intense activity. Then the Holy Father, on the occasion of the day of prayers and offerings called for by Cardinal Jusztinian Seredi on October 29 in favor of refugees, personally sent an open telegram to the cardinal in which once again he manifested his interest on behalf of "persons exposed to persecution and violence because of their religious confession or race or for political motives."[139] Cicognani, for his part, continued his labors on behalf of the Jews up to the end of the war.

## CONCLUSION

Amleto Cicognani's dealings with the American government during World War II were characterized by intelligence, dignity, persistence, and unflagging energy. When we consider that at the same time the internal affairs of the church in the United States demanded his close attention, we must recognize his dedication to the diplomatic relations and humanitarian causes that demanded so much time. Although in many respects he was an intermediary between the Holy See or the papal Secretariat of State on the one hand and the government officials on the other, he also seems in many cases to have stimulated to action his superiors in the Vatican and to have contributed to the shaping of their policy, just as he won the respect of the Americans. Whether Cicognani would have been more effective had he been an accredited apostolic nuncio may be discussed, but certainly he was a creditable, esteemed, trusted, and tireless representative of the Holy See in Washington during these tragic years.

On the other side, the American government was content with its means of contact with the Holy See, that is, partly the president's personal representative to the pope and his charge d'affaires and partly the Apostolic Delegation in Washington. The arrangement spared the Government the difficulty or embarrassment of establishing normal diplomatic relations but at the same time fostered Roosevelt's and Pius XII's parallel endeavors for peace.

### NOTES

In the following notes the short title *Actes* (with the volume number in Roman numerals and the item number in Arabic numerals) refers to:

*Actes et documents du Saint Sieqe relatifs a la Seconde Guerre Mondiale,* ed. Pierre Blet, Robert A. Graham, Angelo Martini, and Burkhart Schneider (Vatican city: Libreria Editrice Vaticana):

> Volume 1: *Le Saint Siege et la guerre en Europe. Mars 1939–aout 1940* (1965); English edition by Gerard Noel, *The Holy See and the War in Europe. March 1939–August 1940* ("Records and Documents of the Holy See Relating to the Second World War," Vol. 1 [Washington, D.C., and Cleveland: Corpus Books, 1968])
> Volume 4: *Le saint Siege et la guerre en Europe, juin 1940–juin 1941* (1967)
> Volume 5: *Le Saint Sieqe et la guerre mondiale, juillet 1941–octobre 1942* (1969)
> Volume 6: *Le Saint Siege et les victimes de la guerre, mars 1939–decembre 1940* (1972)
> Volume 8: *Le saint Sieqe et les victimes de la guerre, janvier 1941–decembre 1942* (1974)
> Volume 9: *Le Saint Sieqe et les victimes de la guerre, janvier–decembre 1943* (1975)
> Volume 10: *Le Saint Siege et les victimes de la guerre, janvier 1944–juillet 1945* (1980)

1. See George Q. Flynn, "Franklin Roosevelt and the Vatican: The Myron Taylor Appointment," *Catholic Historical Review,* 58 (July, 1972): 171–194; idem, *Roosevelt and Romanism: Catholics and American Diplomacy, 1937–1945* ("Contributions in American History," No. 47 [Westport, CT: Greenwood Press, 1976]), pp. 106–136; Gerald P. Fogarty, *The Vatican and the American Hierarchy from 1870 to 1965* ("Papste und Papsttum," Band 21 [Stuttgart: Anton Hiersemann, 1982]), pp. 262–291, where emphasis is placed on the role played by Francis J. Spellman, archbishop of New York; and George J. Gill, "The Myron C. Taylor Mission, the Holy See and 'Parallel Endeavor for

Peace,' 1939–1945," *Records of the American Catholic Historical Society of Philadelphia* 98 (1987): 29–49.

2. Ready's memorandum to Cicognani, April 15, 1939, *Actes*, I, #9; English edition, p. 103.

3. April 15, 1939, *Actes*, I, #10; English edition, p. 104.

4. April 18, 1939, *Actes*, I, #13; English edition, p. 106.

5. *Actes*, I, #38; English edition, pp. 129–130.

6. Cicognani to Carroll, and Carroll to Cicognani, *Actes*, I, ##44 and 45; English edition, pp. 135–137.

7. May 19, 1939, *Actes*, I, #49; English edition, p. 144.

8. June 27, 1939, *Actes*, I, #75; English edition, pp. 179–180. In this report Cicognani reviewed the exchange of views on the peace endeavors of President Roosevelt and the Holy See through the Apostolic Delegation since April 14.

9. Copy in the Office of the General Secretary, NCWC, Welles had written the final draft of Roosevelt's appeal to Hitler and Mussolini. See Frank Warren Graff, *Strategy of Involvement: A Diplomatic Biography of Sumner Welles* (New York: Garland Publishing, Inc., 1988).

10. Cicognani to Maglione, Rome, July 11, 1939, *Actes*, I, #89, with Ready's memorandum of June 29 attached; English edition, pp. 194–197.

11. Cicognani to Maglione, October 25, 1939, *Actes*, I, #212; English edition, p. 304.

12. Cicognani to Maglione, October 27, 1939, *Actes*, I, #215; English edition, p. 306.

13. Cicognani to Maglione, December 23, 1939, *Actes*, I, #232; English edition, p. 324.

14. Cicognani to Maglione, December 23, 1939, *Actes*, I, #234; English edition, pp. 327–329.

15. Maglione to Cicognani, December 24, 1939, *Actes*, I, #236; English edition, pp. 336–337. Pius XII also thanked Roosevelt personally in a letter dated January 7, 1940, *Actes*, I, #240; English edition, pp. 339–341.

16. For example, Cicognani to Maglione, June 4, 1940, *Actes*, I, #340; English edition, pp. 449–450.

17. Maglione to Cicognani, September 3, 1940, *Actes*, IV, #68.

18. Cicognani to Maglione, September 5, 1940, *Actes*, IV, #70.

19. Maglione to Cicognani, September 8, 1940, *Actes*, IV, #74.

20. Cicognani to Maglione, September 17, 1940, *Actes*, IV, #88.

21. Maglione to Cicognani, September 26, 1940, *Actes*, IV, #98.

22. Maglione to Cicognani, January 15, 1941, *Actes*, IV, #231.

23. Cicognani to Maglione, January 16, 1941, *Actes*, IV, #235; see Pius XII to Roosevelt, December 20, 1941, ibid., #203.

24. Cicognani to Maglione, February 17, 1941, *Actes*, IV, #264.

25. Cicognani to Maglione, March 7, 1941, *Actes*, IV, #282; Roosevelt's reply to Cicognani, ibid., fn. 3.

26. Cicognani to Maglione, May 17, 1941, *Actes*, IV, #353.

27. Cicognani to Maglione, May 29, 1941, *Actes*, IV, #379, with his letter to Taylor of the same date appended.
28. Cicognani to Maglione, June 17, 1941, *Actes*, IV, #410.
29. December 12, 1941, Franklin D. Roosevelt Library, Hyde Park, New York, Sumner Welles Papers; hereafter cited as "Welles Papers."
30. *Actes*, VIII, #159.
31. September 27, 1941, copy, Office of the General Secretary, NCWC. On the same day Maglione also sent the delegate a copy of the note that he had transmitted to Taylor through Tittmann regarding the Poles and Lithuanians interned in Siberia; the purpose was to obtain, through the good offices of the American government, permission to send them American relief and permission for the Holy See to demonstrate its interest in them. Cicognani was also directed to get in touch with the committee established by Poles in America to aid their fellow Poles in Siberia and to gather its advice regarding the ways that the Holy See ought to follow in order to achieve its goals: ibid. Copies of the notes: ibid.
32. *Actes*, VIII, #242.
33. *Actes*, VIII, #265. See also the note of the Secretariat of State to Tittmann, January 30, 1942: "The Holy See is desirous, now, of obtaining and transmitting some news of prisoners captured on the Russian front, just as it has been doing on behalf of those taken on other fronts. To this end, the American Authorities are approached in the confident hope that they may be able to facilitate the obtaining of information regarding prisoners in the hands of the Russians." Ibid., #272.
34. *Actes*, VIII, #288. Responding to another aspect of the general question, Cicognani reported to Maglione on February 11, 1942, that till then it had been impossible to find a radio station willing to undertake an exchange of information: hence, it was not yet advisable to begin sending information by the Vatican radio station. He asked that further attempts be limited to general news without addressing the Apostolic Delegation, which could not procure a radio set capable of receiving the Vatican station. Ibid., #282.
35. March 28, 1942, Office of the General Secretary, NCWC. Ready replied on April 14: "The Soviet authorities will not give information concerning prisoners of war nor casualties in Russian territory": copy, ibid.
36. *Actes*, VIII, #349.
37. *Actes*, VIII, #355.
38. *Actes*, VIII, #420. A summary of the efforts made by the Holy See to obtain information on the prisoners of war in Russia and to assist them from August 2, 1941, to the date of the notes, September 19, 1942, includes all the fore-mentioned correspondence: ibid., #480. Cicognani's letter of June 27, 1942, thanking Welles for his "gracious note of June 24th, concerning the exchange of information about prisoners of war and internees in Russia" and acknowledging the fact that "serious efforts" had been made "to accomplish something in this direction": Welles Papers.
39. *Actes*, VIII, #518.

40. *Actes*, IX, #119.
41. *Actes*, IX, #34. See also Welles's letter of January 10, 1943 (copy), acknowledging receipt of Cicognani's letter of January 7 and promising to make inquiry with regard to the questions contained in it and to reply as soon as he would receive an answer from the War Department; also Cicognani's letter of January 24, 1943, to Welles, thanking him for his note of January 19 in regard to inquiries concerning persons in North Africa: both in the Welles Papers.
42. *Actes*, IX, #42.
43. *Actes*, IX, #54. See also ibid., #61, fn. 2.
44. *Actes*, IX, #68, esp. Pt. X, pp. 158–159.
45. May 5, 1943, *Actes*, IX, #175.
46. *Actes*, IX, #221, fn. 1.
47. Two memoranda of conversations dated May 24, 1943, Welles Papers. Welles felt that there was "a great deal of justice" in Cicognani's second request and that "some measure of reciprocity" was desirable, provided the War Department did not feel that military danger was involved and provided that would not conflict in any basic manner with the functioning of the Red Cross. Hence, in a note written on the same day he asked Breckinridge Long, assistant secretary of state, to let him know what could be done: ibid.
48. *Actes*, IX, #221 and fn. 5.
49. *Actes*, IX, #229. See also the attached notes of the secretariat of state reviewing the steps taken since February: ibid.
50. June 28, 1943, *Actes*, IX, #245.
51. June 30, 1943, *Actes*, IX, #248. Another summary of the Holy See's efforts to obtain information on the prisoners of war in North Africa, dated June 1943, prepared in the Secretariat of State, ibid., pp. 379–381, and instructions for Carroll, same date, ibid., pp. 281–282.
52. July 1, 1943, *Foreign Relations of the United States (FRUS) Diplomatic Papers. 1943*, Vol. II: *Europe* (Washington, D.C.: United States Printing Office, 1964), pp. 958–959.
53. July 12, 1943, *Actes*, IX, #260.
54. National Archives, RG 59, 865.404/49. Shaw replied to Cicognani on August 2 that the question he had raised about the extension of the Vatican Information Service to Sicily had been referred to the appropriate military authorities for consideration, and he promised to communicate with the delegate again at a later date
55. *Actes*, IX, #277.
56. August 13, 1943, *Actes*, IX, #292.
57. Welles's Memorandum of Conversation on "Italian prisoners of war; Vatican Information Service," August 21, 1943, Welles Papers.
58. August 23, 1943, *Actes*, IX, #306. See also Carroll's report to Maglione of the same date on his efforts to set up an information service for the prisoners of war and civilians in North Africa: ibid., #308.
59. *Actes*, IX, #341. On September 17, 1943, Cicognani had written to Archbishop Spellman about (*inter alia*) his negotiations with the Department

of State over the functioning of the Vatican Information Service in Sicily: Archives of the Archdiocese of New York, S/C-20, 8.

60. *FRUS 1943*, Vol. II: *Europe*, pp. 960–961. See also the letter of the joint chiefs of staff to the secretary of state, September 21, 1943: ibid., pp. 959–960.

61. September 30, 1943, *Actes*, IX, #354. Cicognani added that Carroll was awaiting instructions from the cardinal secretary. In reply the delegate was ordered to tell Carroll to proceed promptly to Algiers and to begin sending the lists of prisoners: ibid., fn. 5.

62. December 10, 1943, *Actes*, IX, #461.

63. February 19, 1944, *Actes*, X, #64.

64. June 14, 1944, *Actes*, X, #231.

65. National Archives, RG 59, 711.65114/8-2844.

66. Memorandum (translated) from the Commissariat for War, General Directorate and Inspection of Axis Prisoners of War in North Africa, Algiers, June 28, 1944, by order of General of Division Boissau, signed by Col. Adromix, ibid. Major J. V. Sheldon, A.G.D., Assistant Adjutant General, Headquarters Services of Supply, North African Theater of Operations, United States Army, to Commanding General, Eastern Base Section APO 763, U.S. Army, and Commanding General, Mediterranean Base Section, APO 600, U.S. Army, July 15, 1944, to which was attached authorization for the release of the prisoner to U.S. custody: ibid.

67. Memorandum for the Liaison Officer, Department of State, from Military Intelligence service, War Department, signed by Major Edward H. Miller, August 28, 1944, ibid. He was called "Italian Enlisted Man," a private in rank.

68. Interview with Reverend Monsignor Donald M. Carroll, who was a secretary in the Apostolic Delegation beginning late in 1942, Chicago, Illinois, December 24, 1997.

69. Welles's Memorandum of Conversation on "Japanese Representation at Vatican City," March 3, 1942, and copy of the Apostolic Delegation's Memorandum, same date, Welles Papers. Welles had a telegram sent to Tittmann conveying the gist of this conversation. Welles to Atherton, same date, ibid.

70. Welles's Memorandum of Conversation on "Japanese Representation at Vatican City, March 6, 1942, Welles Papers.

71. Spellman's memorandum, undated, Archives of the Archdiocese of New York (hereafter cited as "AANY"), S/C-52, 14.

72. Cicognani to Spellman, March 27 and April 3, 1942, AANY, S/C-52, 14.

73. Berle's Memorandum of Conversation with the Apostolic Delegate, December 4, 1942, National Archives, RG 59, 740.0011 European War 1939/26629. The unsigned memorandum of the apostolic delegate, same date, ibid. Therein Cicognani explained that the pope was referring not only to the Vatican City State but to the entire city of Rome, since it was "his episcopal see and the revered center of the Catholic world." He added that throughout the city there were basilicas, administrative offices of the Holy See, and many international colleges and churches, and that many of these edifices were not only the property of the Holy See but extraterritorial and

enjoyed the same immunity as the Vatican City State, of which they were an integral part. Hence, the government of the United States was "most respectfully requested to use its good offices" that the Holy Father might be assured, at least informally and confidentially, that the Vatican City State and the city of Rome would be spared the destructive terrors of aerial bombardment.

74. *The Memoirs of Cordell Hull* (2 vols.; New York: Macmillan Company, 1948), II, pp. 1560–1563.

75. Welles's Memorandum of Conversation, May 24, 1943, Welles Papers.

76. Copy, Welles Papers.

77. Copies of Cicognani's letter to Welles and Welles's letter to Marshall, both dated August 2, 1943, Welles Papers. Welles's reply to Cicognani, August 4, 1943, ibid.

78. Welles to Cicognani, copy, August 8, 1943, Welles Papers.

79. Cicognani to Welles, two letters, August 20, 1943, Welles Papers.

80. Welles's Memorandum of Conversation and note to the president, both dated August 21, 1943, Welles Papers.

81. Welles's Memorandum of Conversation and note to the president, both dated August 21, 1943, Welles Papers.

82. Cicognani to Spellman, August 21, 1943, AANY, S/C-65; Cicognani to Mooney, same date, Archives of the Archdiocese of Detroit (hereafter referred to as "AAD").

83. Spellman to Cicognani, copy, August 27, 1943, AAD.

84. Mooney to Cicognani, August 27, 1943, AAD.

85. Cicognani to Mooney, August 31, 1943, AAD.

86. Cicognani to Welles, August 27, 1943, Welles Papers.

87. September 18, 1943, *Actes*, IX, #339. See Cicognani's letter, dated September 17, 1943, to Spellman, who had recently been appointed apostolic visitator in Sicily: AANY, S/C-20, 8.

88. *Actes*, IX, #347.

89. October 20, 1943, National Archives, RG 59, 865.48/107. Cicognani attached a copy of the memorandum dated October 12, 1943.

90. Memorandum for the President, October 30, 1943, National Archives, RG 59, 865.48/99-1/3; Stettinius to Cicognani, same date, ibid., also 865.48/107.

91. National Archives, RG 59, 865.48/99-2/3.

92. War Department Message, Number W 3939, National Archives, RG 59, 865.48/99-1/3; also 865.48/114.

93. Copy, National Archives, RG 59, 865.48/107. Cicognani warmly thanked Stettinius on the following day: ibid., 865.48/109.

94. Cicognani to Stettinius, October 28, 1943, National Archives, RG 59, 865.413/6.

95. ibid., RG 59, 865.413/6

96. Memorandum for Colonel Light, OPD, War Department, October 30, 1943, copy, National Archives, RG 59, 865.413/8, and a note of H. Freeman Matthews of the Division of European Affairs, Department of State, to Stettinius, same date, ibid. The papal Secretariat of State asked Tittmann

again on December 7 to remind the competent authorities once more of the great importance that the Holy See attached to the preservation of this historic monument—this after serious damage had been inflicted by artillery fire directed against the German positions on the so-called Rocca Janula mountain. National Archives, RG 59, 865.413/10.

97. National Archives, RG 59, 865.413/12.

98. Cicognani to Stettinius, January 19 and February 3, National Archives, RG 59, 865.413/18 and 21.

99. Cicognani to Mooney, February 18, 1944, AAD.

100. Mooney to Cicognani, February 25, 1944, AAD. Cicognani replied on March 1, congratulating Mooney on his "splendid letter addressed to the President" and agreeing "that the approach to the problem was well chosen" and that the presentation of it was "most forceful and at the same time dignified": ibid.

101. Roosevelt to Cicognani, copy, March 1, 1944.

102. Cicognani to Mooney, March 1, 1944, AAD.

103. Mooney to Cicognani, March 6, 1944, AAD.

104. Roosevelt to Mooney, March 9, 1944, AAD.

105. Memorandum, March 18 or 19, 1944, AAD.

106. March 13, 1944, AAD. Another copy with a covering letter from Cicognani to John T. McNicholas, archbishop of Cincinnati, March 13, 1944, Archives of the Archdiocese of Cincinnati, General.

107. Cicognani to Spellman, March 22, 1944, AANY, S/C-65, 4. Cicognani to Mooney, same date, AAD. He wrote a similar letter to Stritch on the same day.

108. Spellman to Cicognani, March 25, 1944, AANY, S/C-65, 4. See also Mooney to Cicognani, March 25, 1944, AAD, expressing hope that there was some foundation for the reports recently carried in the newspapers to the effect that the German Military Authorities would drastically reduce the use of Rome as a center of war transport and supplies. That step, he said, "would effectively minimize the danger."

109. *Actes*, X, #150.

110. National Archives, RG 59, 865.48/183. See also Hull to Cicognani, April 28, 1944, acknowledging receipt of the delegate's letter and promising to communicate with him again after "consultation with the appropriate military authorities": ibid.

111. National Archives, RG 59, 865.48/133. On May 11, Hull acknowledged receipt of the letter and the copies, thanked the delegate, and assured him that the report would receive "our careful consideration": ibid. As a supplement to that report Cicognani forwarded to Hull on August 15, 1944, two copies of an English translation of a memorandum that he had just received from the cardinal secretary of state; it was "a detailed exposition of the pharmaceutical requirements of Allied occupied Italy," pointing out that central, southern, and insular Italy were "almost entirely without laboratories for the manufacture of medicinal products": ibid., 865.48/8-1544; a ten-page report follows. In reply (August 23) Hull promised

Cicognani: "The supplemental report will be circulated to the interested agencies of the United States Government": ibid.

112. National Archives, RG 59, 865.48/154.

113. Copy, May 26, 1944, National Archives, RG 59, 865.48/154. Cicognani thanked Hull on June 1: ibid., 865.48/6-144.

114. Copy, National Archives, RG 59, 865.48/166. See also Cicognani's polite acknowledgment of receipt of Hull's letter, June 3, 1944: ibid.

115. *Actes*, X, #220.

116. AANY, S/C-65, 4.

117. Copies in AAD.

118. Cicognani to Spellman, May 22, 1944, AANY, S/C-65, 4.

119. Spellman to Cicognani, May 29, 1944, AANY, S/C-65, 4. Mooney's letter to Cicognani has not been found.

120. Cicognani to Hull, copy, May 29, 1944, AAD.

121. Cicognani to Mooney, May 30, 1944, AAD.

122. Cicognani to Spellman, June 17, 1944, AANY, S/C-65, 4. Cicognani to Mooney, same date, AAD.

123. Draft dated June 29, 1944, AAD.

124. Spellman to Mooney and Stritch, July 11, 1944, AAD.

125. Cicognani to Spellman, copy, July 7, 1944, AAD. See further correspondence on the unsent letter to Roosevelt, Mooney to Cicognani, July 19, 1944, and Cicognani to Mooney, July 26, 1944, AAD. In the latter the disturbed delegate wrote: "I was not informed of the details of the conversation which the Archbishop [Spellman] had with the President, nor do I know at what time he made this visit. During the last visit of the Archbishop to Washington I requested him to explain to the Holy See why the letter had not been sent, and I trust that he has not attributed to me the stopping of the letter."

126. June 9, 1943, *Actes*, IX, #224.

127. July 23, 1943, *Actes*, IX, #276, and the reply, July 26, ibid., fn. 2.

128. October 15, 1943, *Actes*, IX, #366.

129. Cicognani to Maglione, November 15, 1943, *Actes*, IX, #427.

130. December 21, 1943, *Actes*, IX, #478. When the American rabbis in March 1944, again approached Cicognani in this regard, he assured them that the Holy See had done its best: March 31, 1944, *Actes*, X, #127.

131. February 22, 1944, *Actes*, X, #77, and February 25, ibid., fn. 3.

132. March 31, 1944, *Actes*, X, #127.

133. President Roosevelt had created the War Refugee Board in January for the purpose of aiding the Jews and other persecuted persons obliged to leave the countries under the control of the Axis. The Board had direct communications with the apostolic delegate. The German troops had occupied Hungary on March 23.

134. May 16, 1944, *Actes*, X, #196. On May 27, Tardini outlined for Tittmann the Holy See's activity on behalf of the "non-Aryans" interned at Vittel. He cited the dates on which the Apostolic Delegation in Washington had been kept *au courant* of the developments and also had been informed of the

repeated steps taken by the Holy See in favor of the "non-Aryans" residing in Hungary, Romania, and Slovakia: ibid., p. 294 (Annexe to #212).

135. *Actes*, X, #245, fn. 1; Cicognani replied on June 26, "The Holy See will do everything in its power to obtain for these unfortunates a treatment similar to that accorded to civilian internees": ibid.

136. June 26, 1944, *Actes*, X, #245.

137. October 25, 1944, *Actes*, X, #375. On November 16 Cicognani had asked the Holy See to intervene so that the Red Cross might send packages to 250 non-Aryans holding South American passports and staying at Belsen Bergen. Tardini asked Orsenigo to pursue the matter on November 11, and the nuncio replied on December 5 that the German government had observed that the Jews holding passports from South American republics were citizens of those countries and as such had their own protectors: ibid., fn. 2.

138. *Actes*, X, #375, fn. 3. Burzio reported on December 5 that only 13 of the deportees had been recognized as citizens of the United States: ibid. Later (December 16) he forwarded to the Vatican a list of the persons deported in spite of their American nationality or their passports from American states and added that in most cases these documents had not been taken into consideration; the 13 American citizens were then in the concentration camp of Bergen Belsen (near Celle in Hannover).

139. November 3, 1944, *Actes*, X, #385.

# CHAPTER 14

# A FEW BITS OF INFORMATION

## AMERICAN INTELLIGENCE AND THE VATICAN, 1939–45

### DAVID ALVAREZ

THE VATICAN CAME TO THE ATTENTION OF AMERICAN intelligence services rather late during World War II. This is not to say that policy-makers cared little for news from Vatican City. With most other world capitals, Washington shared a belief that the thick walls of the Palazzo Apostolico protected a trove of secrets assiduously collected and transmitted to Rome by Catholics around the globe. This conviction was especially prevalent in the State Department where the desire to access those secrets was the primary justification for establishing, in the form of the Taylor mission, an American diplomatic presence at the Vatican. Despite this interest, American intelligence was slow to focus on the papacy. In the early months of the war this hesitancy was a function of the particular characteristics of the intelligence bureaucracy in Washington. The two agencies principally concerned with collecting foreign intelligence were the intelligence staffs of the Army and the Navy. These staffs served the needs of their respective services and, consequently, emphasized the collection of military and naval information. Their information came primarily from open sources (newspapers, military journals) and the observations of army and naval attachés at American embassies. Given their organizational posture, these staffs had little reason to pay attention to the militarily insignificant Vatican. It is unlikely that questions about the armament of the Swiss Guards or the force levels of the pontifical police would have interested even the most conscientious officer in the Military Intelligence Division. The occasional item of news on the pope might find a place in the files of the War and Navy Departments, but there was no systematic effort to collect intelligence on the Vatican.

The creation of a civilian intelligence organization, first in the form of the Coordinator of Information (COI) in July 1941 and then as the Office of Strategic Services (OSS) in June 1942, had little immediate effect on the coverage (or noncoverage) of the papacy. During its brief life, COI was preoccupied with establishing its bureaucratic credibility and fending off hostile takeover bids by the Army and Navy, neither of which fancied a competitor in the field of intelligence. It had little opportunity to organize intelligence operations against anyone, although at the time of its demise it had begun to send representatives overseas to collect information.[1] OSS proved a more substantial and long-lived institution and its director, William Donovan, favored an aggressive approach to intelligence collection, but initially its attitude toward the Vatican was rather passive. For several months after its foundation, the successor to COI was preoccupied with bureaucratic battles with the armed services over its proper mission and during this time foreign operations were largely put on hold. When OSS finally took the field, military issues predominated over diplomatic in the competition for policy-makers' attention. On the list of intelligence priorities, the Vatican was nudged lower by other targets arguably more relevant to immediate military needs, such as the preparation for the invasion of North Africa (Operation Torch), or by special operations that caught the fancy of the notoriously mercurial Donovan. Political geography was also a problem. Vatican City remained a small neutral island in a sea of Fascism. Any Allied intelligence service faced imposing problems in gaining access to papal territory and personnel. In the first year of its existence, OSS simply did not have the capability to run operations directly against the Vatican (it wasn't even running operations into Italy) and Donovan's organization had no personnel assigned to the Vatican intelligence problem. Some information was acquired ("collected" would suggest more purpose than was present) through indirect means: press and radio reports, interviews with political exiles and refugees, and gossip from diplomatic cocktail parties. There was, however, little system and less direction. As might have been expected the results were at best mixed. Most of the "intelligence" was uncorroborated and, consequently, of uncertain credibility. Many of the reports, like a report that Monsignor Mario Zanin was the apostolic delegate to China, were merely trivial; others were almost comic in their absurdity. The same report that breathlessly announced that Monsignor Zanin was delegate to China, also revealed that there were 10,000 native seminarians preparing for the priesthood in China, a figure that exaggerated the number of seminarians by a factor of more than ten.[2] A source who had not been in Italy since April 1941 reported in

January 1943 that when the source left Italy the chief of the cipher office at the papal Secretariat of State was an Irish priest (unidentified) who was a member of the Irish Republican Army and exhibited his violent Anglophobia by publicly proclaiming that he praised God for every German bomb that fell on London. As an extra touch the source revealed that this priest was a "crack golfer." As a matter of fact, no Irish priest worked in the secretariat of state in 1941. The cipher officer was an Italian monsignor, Amadeo Finnochi, who did not play golf and almost certainly was not a member of the IRA.[3]

Before the fall of Rome, Washington's most reliable source of information on the Vatican was neither the Office of Strategic Services nor the military intelligence services but President Roosevelt's special mission to the pope, Myron Taylor, and his assistant, Harold Tittman. Tittman, who remained in Rome while Taylor made flying visits from the United States, was a particularly conscientious and levelheaded diplomat. After Pearl Harbor and Italy's subsequent declaration of war against the United States, he was compelled to move into Vatican City, which was already a claustrophobic home to the diplomatic missions of several other governments at war with Italy. During his enforced residence in the Vatican, Tittman worked diligently to inform Washington of the attitudes and intentions of his hosts, but his efforts were constrained by several factors. Papal protocol and diplomatic custom limited his access to the cardinal secretary of state, Luigi Maglione, the two undersecretaries, Monsignors Domenico Tardini and Giovanni Montini, and (infrequently) the pope himself. These were, of course, excellent sources, but their conversations with Tittman were inhibited by their concern for Vatican neutrality and by a desire to address certain topics (the bombing of Rome) while avoiding others (the political situation inside Italy). Tittman was also constrained by the insecurity of his communication lines to Washington. He entered Vatican City with neither a cipher nor a radio. Under the terms of the wartime censorship arrangements imposed on the Vatican by Italy, Tittman (and other Allied diplomats inside the papal city) could communicate with their governments by means of the papal diplomatic pouch, but only on subjects directly related to their representational mission. Since the security of the Vatican's diplomatic pouch could not be assured, Allied diplomats had to be careful in their reports. Finally, Tittman knew he was under surveillance by the Fascist secret police who used their contacts in the Vatican police force to monitor the activities and contacts of Allied diplomats inside papal territory.[4]

The intelligence situation only began to improve after the Allies occupied Rome in June 1944. With Allied authorities in control of the city administration, the police, and the phone and cable lines, the problem of access to the Vatican and its personnel lessened and OSS quickly established a station in the Eternal City. American intelligence now took more interest in the papacy. With the occupation, Axis diplomatic missions to the pope sought refuge inside Vatican City, occupying the same apartments now vacated by their Allied opposite numbers. Just as the Germans and Italians had suspected American and British diplomats inside the papal enclave of espionage and subversion, Allied intelligence decided that the Axis diplomats required close surveillance. Many Fascist officials from Mussolini's now-discredited regime had taken refuge in monasteries and religious houses in Rome and these fugitives required apprehension or at least surveillance. Finally, Washington was increasingly concerned about the Vatican's attitude toward the role that communist parties and the Soviet Union would assume in postwar Italy and Europe as a whole. These concerns made the Vatican an increasingly attractive target for American intelligence. Initially, the newly established OSS station in Rome limited its work on the Vatican to establishing informal contacts with papal officials who helped American intelligence and counterintelligence monitor the movements and activities of former Fascist officials who had sought sanctuary in ecclesiastical buildings in Rome.[5] In the closing months of 1944, however, OSS embarked on three offensive operations that specifically targeted the Vatican.

The story of the VESSEL Project, the most notorious of the operations, is well known to intelligence historians. In the fall of 1944, OSS Rome began to receive documents from a source inside the Vatican. These documents, copies of telegrams exchanged between the Secretariat of State and its nuncios, minutes of the pope's meetings with cardinals and bishops, memoranda from various dicasteries, exposed the most secret proceedings of papal diplomacy and administration. One day there would be a report that the pope had instructed the nuncio in Belgium to monitor collaboration between Catholic associations and left-wing political organizations; the next day an item revealing that the pope had recalled the apostolic delegate from Iran to prepare a plan for opening relations with the Soviet Union; the following day a copy of a cable from the papal representative in Tokyo summarizing the political situation in Japan.[6] American intelligence now had a source at the very heart of the papacy and the intelligence product from this source circulated at the highest levels of American government including the White House. Concerned about domestic Catholic opinion toward cooperation with the Soviet Union, the White House must have been especially pleased with VESSEL reports indicating that the Vatican was interested in establishing relations with Moscow. Policy-makers were also excited by the copies of telegrams from Monsignor Paolo Marella, the apostolic delegate in Tokyo. These telegrams included factual descriptions of military and naval operations, informed speculation concerning Russian policy toward Japan, appraisals of political developments in Japan, China, and Manchuria, and discussions of possible papal mediation in the Pacific War.[7] It all seemed too good to be true. It was too good to be true.

The VESSEL material was the product of the fertile imagination and skillful pen of Virgilio Scattolini, journalist, pornographer, film critic for the Vatican daily newspaper, *Osservatore Romano*, and the most brazen intelligence fabricator of World War II. As early as 1939, Scattolini decided that he could make more money selling to interested parties accounts of personalities and political events in the Vatican. In his apartment near the Spanish Steps, he concocted stories based on a careful scrutiny of the pope's audience schedule and a large dose of fanciful detail concerning the alleged content and results of such audiences. Gradually, even the audiences became imaginary as he sought to "improve" his reporting. The closed, secretive, and (to outsiders) mysterious world of the Vatican inadvertently abetted this confidence game by creating an audience of journalists, diplomats, and intelligence operatives desperate for any information about papal affairs and by inhibiting any effort to confirm the veracity of the often dramatic revelations. Scattolini's lucrative practice was interrupted by the Italian police in 1942, but after the liberation of Rome he returned to his old stand and his unsuspecting clients soon included newspapers, banks, embassies, and several intelligence services.[8] His edifice of lies began to collapse in early 1945 when the State Department was astonished to read in a VESSEL report that Myron Taylor had met secretly with Ken Harada, the Japanese ambassador to the Holy See. Asked to account for this unauthorized and unreported meeting, Taylor vehemently denied any contact with the Japanese representative. As intelligent consumers began to scrutinize more carefully the VESSEL product, doubts multiplied. In mid-February, OSS headquarters warned its Italian outpost that the VESSEL material "has earmarks of being concocted by a not too clever manufacturer of sales information. As a result, for the time being we are withholding the dissemination of most of this material." Two weeks later Washington reiterated its suspicions: "Whereas some unimportant items of Vessel material may be based on factual knowledge of the source, the more important items are believed to be manufactured by the source out of whole cloth or are plants."[9] Surprisingly, OSS chose to believe that the VESSEL items concerning Japanese and Far Eastern affairs were more credible (they were not) than items dealing with other subjects. With one voice OSS warned policy-makers that VESSEL reports on European events could not be trusted, while with another voice it assured the same policy-makers that the source's information on Japan was accurate.

At least one student of wartime intelligence has concluded that Scattolini could bamboozle OSS only because American intelligence had few other sources on the Vatican.[10] Whatever the VESSEL Affair says about OSS sources, it clearly reveals American intelligence's almost perfect ignorance of the

Catholic Church in general and the Vatican in particular. There is no other way to explain the ready acceptance of descriptions of administrative practices and relationships that often verged on the ludicrous. On one occasion OSS Rome confidently passed to Washington a VESSEL report that ecclesiastical authorities were proceeding with plans to construct an airport in the Vatican gardens. One can only stand in awe of Scattolini's effrontery in passing this report off on the Americans. By accepting this fantasy as legitimate, the gullible OSS representatives would have had to know absolutely nothing about the physical, economic, and cultural geography of Vatican City.[11]

At the same time that its Rome station was falling victim to a confidence trickster, OSS headquarters launched another operation against the Vatican. This operation centered on a Belgian Dominican, Felix Morlion, and his Catholic news service, the Center for Information Pro Deo (CIP). The affair remains shrouded in mystery, but it seems that OSS expected that the Dominican (working under the cover name "Bernard Black") would use his clerical and journalistic credentials to insinuate himself into high ecclesiastical circles in Rome and report the results of his conversations. Morlion passed his reports to a woman identified in the surviving documentation as "A. Smith." This cutout was a protégé of Morlion and moved easily in American ecclesiastical circles. OSS subsidized Morlion's travel and residence in Europe and arranged for him to receive, through covert OSS channels, press clippings, pamphlets, and books in the hope that such items would assist him in "explaining the American reaction to world events in order to receive the ideas of the people with whom he deals."[12] It is unclear how much Morlion was a witting agent of American intelligence. He may have convinced himself that he was merely dealing with Americans who wished to assist the work of his press agency much as they may have helped other journalists. OSS representatives seem to have presented themselves as "friendly good-natured people who assist him in a task which [they] think is a worthy one." In her communications with him (which passed along secure OSS lines), Smith referred only to "the men who have taken an interest in our work." Witting or not, Morlion was a difficult agent to run. On the one hand his access to Vatican authorities seemed impressive. He met with Cardinal Jean Tisserant and discussed the prelate's appraisal of the political strength of various groups in liberated France. He was also in a position to describe the attitudes toward Russia and postwar Europe of various cardinals and monsignors including Monsignors Tardini and Montini, the undersecretaries in the Secretariat of State.[13] On the other hand, his reports tended to be pedantic, theoretical expositions of Catholic social thought and history. Smith (who almost certainly was a conscious instrument of the OSS) chided Morlion for submitting reports on issues of only historical interest and pressed him for factual and timely information about current developments at the Vatican. She and her OSS controllers were much more interested in the Vatican's reaction to the Yalta Conference than a review of the nineteenth-century origins of the Catholic labor union movement.[14]

At the same time that OSS was running (if only from a distance) Felix Morlion against the Vatican, it introduced into Roman ecclesiastical circles one of its own officers working under commercial cover. Martin Quigley, who had worked for OSS in Ireland, appeared in the Eternal City under the guise of a marketing representative of the American film industry seeking postwar outlets for Hollywood movies. Quigley had been sent to Rome "to produce information through Catholic church organizations and individuals in Rome and through whatever contacts could be developed at the Vatican." He had also been personally charged by William Donovan to "be alert at the right time to attempt to open up communications to Tokyo looking to the surrender of Japan."[15] To preserve his cover, Quigley lodged quietly with an Italian family near the Piazza Argentina, arranged business meetings with leaders of the Italian film industry, carefully avoided any contact with the OSS station housed in a large villa on Monte Mario, and passed his reports only through dead-drops. For all this discretion, the Vatican was soon aware of his true work in Rome. In a directive strangely at odds with his assignment to work under cover, he had been authorized by Washington to reveal the nature of his mission to selected individuals if by so doing, he could advance that mission. Shortly after arriving in Rome, Quigley had revealed his OSS identity to Father Vincent McCormick, an American Jesuit attached to the Rome headquarters of his order, and Enrico Galeazzi, a high lay functionary of the Vatican who had the confidence of Pope Pius.[16] Galeazzi revealed to his superiors that the young man working as a representative of American film interests was also an intelligence officer.

Quigley moved unobtrusively through Roman ecclesiastical, social, and business circles, and cultivated various sources who are identified in his reports by code names (BOOM, ANCHOR) or by vague references such as "a lay Vatican official" or "an Italian lawyer with close Vatican connections." He passed to Washington reports on such subjects as "*The Pope's Health,*" "*The Vatican View on Trieste,*" "*Cardinal Tisserant on Russia,*" and "*The Vatican and Relations with Russia.*"[17] His access to ecclesiastical circles was good, in large part because of his friendship with Father McCormick, who had lived in Rome since before the war, and this friendship opened many doors. McCormick, for example, connected Quigley with Father Robert Leiber, the Jesuit who served as the pope's confidential assistant.[18] Since influential Vatican officials, such as Leiber and Galeazzi, were aware of Quigley's espionage mission, it is likely that they revealed to the intelligence officer only what the Vatican wanted Washington to know. On one occasion Galeazzi actually passed to his American friend a Vatican document detailing anti-Catholic activities (including the execution of priests) on the part of the Communist partisans in Yugoslavia.[19]

The work of Felix Morlion, Martin Quigley, and (in his perverted way) Virgilio Scattolini were examples of what intelligence historians call "human intelligence" (Humint). During World War II, however, human intelligence was displaced in importance by another method of intelligence collection, signals intelligence (Sigint). Signals intelligence is concerned with the extraction of information from intercepted communications, especially the diplomatic and military communications of foreign governments. Since such communications are likely to be encrypted to protect their contents, signals intelligence includes the arcane practice of cryptanalysis or code breaking. It is now clear that in terms of quality and quantity Sigint was, for both the Allies and Axis, the most important source of information throughout the war. Terms such as "Ultra," "Magic," "Enigma," and "Purple" are now central to the vocabulary of historians who explain the political and military history of the war. For all its successes, however, Sigint was little help to governments seeking information about the Vatican.

During the war, the United States, through the agency of the U.S. Army's Signal Intelligence Service (SIS), established a comprehensive program to intercept and decrypt the diplomatic communications of other countries. At its headquarters at Arlington Hall, a former finishing school outside of Washington, SIS read all or part of the secret communications of more than 35 governments, hostile, neutral, and allied. SIS had begun to intercept Vatican communications (mainly messages between the Secretariat of State and its nunciatures and delegations) before the war, but for lack of staff had been unable to study the encryption that protected the messages. For some time after the U.S. entry into the war in December 1941, the Federal Bureau of Investigation ran the only active American operation against papal communications. In a clandestine operation whose details remain classified to this day, the FBI, suspecting (incorrectly) that Axis intelligence agents in North America used the papal diplomatic pouch to communicate with their controllers in Europe, placed the mail of the Apostolic Delegation in Washington under surveillance.[20] The situation changed in September 1943 when, with the Italian armistice, Italian diplomatic traffic virtually disappeared from international communications circuits. SIS shifted several cryptanalysts from its Italian section to a newly created Vatican section.[21]

The new section began work by reviewing the several thousand Vatican diplomatic messages that had accumulated in Arlington Hall's intercept folders. Like most foreign ministries, the papal Secretariat of State used several different cryptosystems, each designated by a color, to protect its confidential communications. Most nunciatures and delegations held two or three of these ciphers, although the more important missions might possess the entire repertoire. In 1944, for example, the Apostolic Delegation in Washington was using six different ciphers to communicate with Rome. The Vatican section first attacked a system known as the *Cifrario Rosso* (Red Cipher). This was a relatively unsophisticated papal cipher that had been in service since the early 1930s, a dangerously long time for a diplomatic cipher. The Vatican rightly considered this system insecure and used it only for routine administrative messages and relatively unimportant matters. With the assistance of their counterparts in the British code-breaking establishment, the Government Code and Cypher School, who had begun to attack Vatican ciphers the previous year, the Americans progressed rapidly against Red and by the spring of 1944 most messages in this system were readable. Unfortunately, it was the only success. Neither the Americans nor the British were able to crack the high-grade ciphers used by the Secretariat of State for its more sensitive communications. Arlington Hall assigned to the problem some of its best code breakers, including two who had been on the team that had cracked Japan's high-grade cipher machine, the famous "Purple" machine, but the pope's ciphers resisted every attack. In the summer of 1944, Arlington Hall simply gave up on Vatican cryptosystems and turned their attention and resources to more promising targets. Some intelligence on the Vatican was obtained indirectly by intercepting and decrypting the messages of the Japanese, Portuguese, Spanish, and Latin American ambassadors to the Holy See.

American cryptanalysts were surprised at the sophistication of Vatican cryptosystems. Reviewing their experience, they noted that "The difficulties encountered showed that considerable intelligence was matched against the analysts," and they concluded that they were dealing with "a cryptographer of no mean ability."[22] Their effort was also hampered by the complete absence of compromised (stolen) cryptographic materials and the communication discipline of papal diplomats. The nuncios and delegates kept their telegraphic traffic to a minimum; consequently, relatively few messages in the high-grade systems were available for study. The attack against a special cipher introduced in September 1943 by the Secretariat of State for communication with the delegate in Washington was constrained by the fact that after a year of surveillance only 46 messages thought to be in this system had been intercepted, too few to support serious cryptanalysis.

Washington closely guarded the secret of its code-breaking program because its success depended in part on foreign governments remaining unaware that their ciphers had been solved. In the case of the Vatican this concern was aggravated by fear of a domestic political reaction should Catholics or Congressional representatives from heavily Catholic constituencies learn that the U.S. government was eavesdropping on the confidential communications of the Holy Father. As a result, the American effort against papal ciphers was cloaked in particular secrecy. At Arlington Hall the code-breaking teams were organized according to the language or country of the systems they were attacking. The systems themselves were identified by a trigraph in which the first two letters were an abbreviation of the country and the last letter indicated the particular cryptosystem in the sequence in which it had been taken up by the analysts. The Swiss desk, for example, would be working on SZA, SZB, and SZC, while the Turkish team might be studying TUA and TUB. Under this administrative arrangement the team assigned to papal ciphers would have been organized as the Vatican desk in the Italian section (Italian being the working language of the Vatican) and its targets would have been identified as VAA, VAB, VAC, and so on. This was not the case. The Vatican operation was included among a handful of super-secret projects that for security purposes were identified only by color. In this scheme the Vatican team was known as "Gold" section.[23] The ciphers they studied were assigned the digraph KI (Red Cipher = KIA), a label that gave no hint of the target government's identity. Although internal memoranda at Arlington Hall routinely identified the countries whose systems were under study, no reference to the Vatican ever appeared in status reports from Gold section.

The special security surrounding the attack against papal communications had a negative (though unintended) impact on American intelligence opera-tions against the Vatican. As we have seen, the only papal cipher solved by American code-breakers was the so-called Red Cipher. This was, however, the only cipher available to the Apostolic Delegation in Tokyo. Apparently, the pope's Secretariat of State was never able, during the war, to arrange a method for safely sending new, improved ciphers to Monsignor Marella. This proved a serious constraint on the delegate's ability to communicate securely with Rome, because the Secretariat of State believed (correctly) that the Red Cipher had been cracked by the signals intelligence services of several governments. All of Marella's messages to Rome were decrypted and read by Arlington Hall at the same time that OSS was purchasing VESSEL reports that purported to be verbatim copies of the same messages. A comparison of the decrypted messages with the purchased versions would have immediately exposed the VESSEL documents as fabrications.[24] Unfortunately, OSS knew nothing of Arlington Hall's modest success against papal communications. Relations between the SIS and the OSS were distinctly cool, especially after an OSS operation against the Japanese embassy in Lisbon caused the Japanese to consider changing their ciphers. Any such change would have been a calamity for American intelligence because the decryption of Tokyo's messages had long been the principal source of intelligence on Japan. The work on Vatican communications was also too sensitive to be shared with other agencies, especially one as notorious for leaks and misadventures as OSS. As a result, one American intelligence service continued to swoon over elaborately detailed reports from the pope's representative in Tokyo while another service held proof that those reports were forgeries.

While it is often difficult to evaluate the effectiveness of intelligence operations, it is clear that American operations against the Vatican (at least until the Japanese surrender) were less than resounding successes. The VESSEL project was a debacle that did nothing but misinform and confuse policy-makers. The few reports from operation BLACK that survive in the archives suggest that Washington received from Felix Morlion more socio-logical and philosophic speculation than hard political information. Martin Quigley, a level-headed and conscientious reporter, probably produced more real intelligence than all other sources combined, but he worked alone and without funds and his most important sources knew he was an American agent. Signals intelligence, normally the most reliable source of information, faltered in the face of the pope's impenetrable ciphers. Several factors contributed to this lackluster record. Technical problems (e.g. the complex-ity of papal ciphers, the difficulty of communicating securely from Fascist Italy) often complicated the efforts of American intelligence. These efforts were also undercut by the resistance of the target. In intelligence parlance, the Vatican was a hard target. The ecclesiastical character of the papal admin-istration created a wall higher and more impenetrable than the stone walls surrounding Vatican City. Aside from laborers, gardeners, guards, and a few technicians in the library and museums, all posts in the administration were filled by priests or members of religious orders. The ecclesiastical flavor of Vatican City was so intense that even the small pharmacy, the telephone switchboard, and the papal kitchen were staffed entirely by nuns or lay brothers. This ecclesiastical community, distinguished by dress, education, lifestyle, and discipline from the secular world, represented a closed society that consciously recognized boundaries between itself and secular society. The citizens of this ecclesiastical community were also products of an admin-istrative tradition and culture that emphasized prudence, secrecy, and, above all, allegiance to the Church and its pontiff. More than one intelligence service found this ecclesiastical society a formidable obstacle.[25]

Intelligence efforts were also hindered by long-standing administrative practices in the Roman Curia, which tended to reserve important matters to only a handful of officials. If it is true that the security of a secret is in inverse proportion to the number of people who know that secret, then secrets in the Vatican were very secure. Throughout the war, Pope Pius reserved all major and many minor diplomatic and political questions for himself, and he frequently kept his own counsel. When requiring advice or information, he turned to a handful of collaborators: his confidential aide, Father Robert Leiber, the cardinal secretary of state, Luigi Maglione, or the latter's two deputies, Monsignors Domenico Tardini and Giovanni Montini. Even members of this inner circle were often ignorant of important policy initiatives.[26] The small size of the Secretariat of State further limited the number of people who were privy to diplomatic secrets.[27] There were few knowledgeable sources for intelligence sources to cultivate or suborn.

American intelligence efforts were further undermined by an organizational mindset that projected a distorted image of the target. American policymakers shared the popular assumption that the pope sat at the center of an organizational web along whose strands ran currents of information from all parts of the globe. In 1941 a senior American diplomat asserted, "It needs no flight of imagination to recognize the accumulation of information that is gathered into the hands of the high dignitaries of the Church. Through its representatives the Church has access to the thoughts of men in every chancery in Europe and in remote villages in every country."[28] Such comments reflected the widespread belief that the world's Catholics, in all their millions, but especially the tens of thousands of priests, nuns, and monks, were loyal and compliant agents of the pope, passing to Rome the secrets of individuals and governments.

There was, in fact, little substance to support this belief. There was no Vatican intelligence service. The Vatican never sought systematically to mobilize the faithful for intelligence purposes. It never occurred to most Catholics that they should report particular events to Rome. It has become increasingly clear that during World War II, the Vatican was actually rather poorly informed about events. Both the British and French ambassadors to the Holy See reported to their foreign ministries their surprise at discovering how weak the Vatican was in this regard. The British envoy noted that for news of the war the pope relied primarily upon the BBC.[29] Still, the myth of the Vatican's intelligence capabilities persisted and it had an insidious effect on American intelligence. Believing that the pope had agents everywhere and that these faithful minions had access to secrets beyond the reach of secular governments, American intelligence was a gullible consumer of every street rumor and an easy mark for the most outlandish fabrications of a Virgilio Scattolini. The inability to confirm information independently merely demonstrated that the Vatican's sources were far superior to Washington's.

During the war, American intelligence services contributed little but misdirection, confusion, and uncertainty to American policy toward the Vatican. At the end of 1943, the German embassy to the Holy See warned Berlin about the assertions and rumors concerning the Vatican that, at times, overwhelmed the diplomats and intelligence agents in Rome. "There is no shortage in this respect," the embassy reported, "But what is needed instead of this deluge of unreliable reports, is to get the few bits of information that are really important."[30] Those few bits constantly eluded American intelligence.

## NOTES

1. Bradley F. Smith, *The Shadow Warriors: OSS and the Origins of the CIA* (New York: Basic Books, 1983), pp. 93–94, 104.
2. "Zanin, Msgr. Mario," June 23, 1943, Rome-X2-OP-2, Box 1, Reel 6, Records of the Office of Strategic Services, Record Group 226, National Archives and Records Administration, College Park, MD (hereafter cited as OSS).
3. "Vatican Priest," January 1943, ibid.
4. Owen Chadwick, *Britain and the Vatican during the Second World War* (Cambridge: Cambridge University Press, 1986), pp. 168–170; David Alvarez and Robert Graham, S.J., *Nothing Sacred: Nazi Espionage Against the Vatican, 1939–1945* (London: Frank Cass, 1997), pp. 145–148, 155–156.
5. Max Corvo, *The OSS in Italy, 1942–1945: A Personal Memoir* (New York: Praeger, 1990), p. 220.
6. Report #104311, November 14, 1944, Box 1178; Report #L51213, December 11, 1944, Box 421; Report #L49138, November 25, 1944; all in Research and Analysis Branch, Intelligence Reports, OSS. These reports were distributed to the State, War, and Navy departments.
7. "Vessel Reports," June 6, 1945, COI/OSS Central Files, Entry 92, Box 595, folder 6, OSS.
8. Alvarez and Robert Graham, *Nothing Sacred*, pp. 16–17.
9. Magruder to Caserta, February 17, 1945 and March 3, 1945, Records of the Radio and Cables Branch, Entry 90, Box 6, folder 73, OSS.
10. Timothy Naftali, "ARTIFICE: James Angleton and X-2 Operations in Italy," in George C. Chalou, ed., *The Secrets War: The Office of Strategic Services in World War II* (Washington, DC: National Archives and Records Administration, 1992), p. 232.
11. Casserta to OSS (Magruder), January 22, 1945, Records of the Radio and Cable Branch, Entry 90, Box 6, folder 63, OSS. In order to accept this report OSS had to believe that a plane would land on a runway less than 100 yards long, laid out on the side of a hill, and surrounded by multistory buildings, including the highest structure in Rome (St. Peter's Basilica).
12. Dolbeare to Van der Hoef, n.d., Field Station Files, Box 121, folder 483, OSS; ABBOTT to DIANE, April 5, 1945, Field Station Files, Box 121, folder 481, OSS.
13. BERNARD [Black] to A. Smith, February 18, 1945, Field Station Files, Box 121, folder 481, OSS. There is some evidence that Morlion or someone connected with the BLACK Project paid informants and sought to establish a regular agent network. An unsigned, undated memo in the BLACK files notes, "F reports Grey gave out of local funds 30,000 for trial of various lay sources... These [sic] expended end of Sept. to end of Dec. to pay Andreotti, Giano, and others."
14. A.S. to BLACK, February 15 and March 9, 1945, ibid.
15. Martin S. Quigley, *Peace Without Hiroshima: Secret Action at the Vatican in the Spring of 1945* (Lanham, MD: Madison Books, 1991), pp. 26, 80.

266

16. Ibid., pp. 27–28. In May 1945, in the course of a futile attempt to open a negotiating channel with Tokyo through the Japanese embassy to the Holy See, Quigley would also reveal his OSS identity to Monsignor Egidio Vagnozzi, a diplomat in the papal Secretariat of State.

17. Many of Quigley's reports can be found in Box 2, folders 72–75, Martin Quigley Papers, Georgetown University Library, Washington, DC.

18. McCormick's diary entry for February 19, 1945 notes, "P. Leiber in A.M.—talk on Russia, etc. for Martin Q." Extracts from the diary of Father McCormick, Box 2, folder 32, Quigley Papers.

19. Quigley, *Peace Without Hiroshima*, p. 28.

20. Memorandum for the Director from Edward Tamm, September 28, 1942, and "Allegations of the Misuse of the Washington Papal Embassy Diplomatic Pouch" (date and author deleted by censor). Documents released to the author by the FBI under the provisions of the Freedom of Information Act.

21. For a survey of the "Vatican problem" at Arlington Hall, see David Alvarez, "No Immunity: Signals Intelligence and the European Neutrals, 1939–1945," *Intelligence and National Security* 12 (April 1997): 30–31. For a technical history of the effort to crack papal ciphers, see "Vatican Code Systems in the SSA, 1943–44," Box 1284, Historic Cryptographic Collection, National Security Agency Records, Record Group 457, NARA.

22. "Vatican Code Systems in the SSA, 1943–44," pp. 57, 59.

23. The group working on Russian ciphers during the war was known as "Blue" section.

24. In contrast with the dramatic military and political content of Marella's messages as reported by VESSEL, the contents of the actual messages as intercepted and decrypted by American code-breakers were so trivial that Arlington Hall declined to include them in the intelligence summaries circulated to policy-makers.

25. In postwar appraisals of intelligence opportunities at the Vatican, American and British diplomats admitted that it was almost impossible to extract, even from their own nationals in papal service, any information about papal affairs. Memorandum by McFadden, December 5, 1947, Political-General, Box 17, Records of the Personal Representative of the President to Pope Pius XII, Record Group 59, NARA; Memorandum by Parson, May 22, 1948, Memoranda-Confidential, Box 19, ibid.

26. In the autumn of 1939 when Pius decided to act as a link between London and the anti-Nazis resistance in Germany, neither Maglione nor his two deputies were aware of the pope's activities.

27. Even in comparison to the foreign ministries of minor powers the Secretariat of State was an exceptionally small organization. In the first year of the war the Secretariat employed 31 individuals, including archivists and typists. That year the foreign ministries of Norway and the Netherlands had staff of 119 and 80 respectively.

28. Hugh Wilson, *Diplomat Between Wars* (New York: Longmans, 1941), p. 28.
29. Chadwick, *Britain and the Vatican*, pp. 201–202; David Alvarez, "Vatican Intelligence Capabilities in the Second World War," *Intelligence and National Security* 6 (July 1991): 593–607.
30. Quoted in Alvarez and Graham, *Nothing Sacred*, p. 130.

# CHAPTER 15

# A PECULIAR BRAND OF PATRIOTISM

## THE HOLY SEE, FDR, AND THE CASE OF REVEREND CHARLES E. COUGHLIN

### CHARLES R. GALLAGHER

FATHER CHARLES E. COUGHLIN OF ROYAL OAK, MICHIGAN, was the single most controversial Catholic priest in America during the Depression era. Through the medium of radio, he led a crusade against Communism which linked bitter anti-Semitism with Catholic ideals. During the height of his popularity he commanded a weekly radio audience of 30 million listeners. Indeed, historian Alan Brinkley of Columbia University has labeled Coughlin one of the significant "voices of protest" of the era.[1] One Coughlin scholar has even argued that by the mid-1930s, many Americans considered Father Coughlin to be the second most important political figure in the country, surpassed only by President Roosevelt.[2]

In 1936, FDR wrote to Breckinridge Long that the country was suffering from a hard bout of "Father Coughlin...influenza."[3] Of course, Roosevelt was complaining of the political aspects of Coughlin's rabid anti-Rooseveltianism and his incessant harping on the economic failures of the New Deal. But by 1938, things were getting a bit worse. Historian Mary Christine Athans has noted that in the late 1930s, "a build-up of anti-Jewish material" became more prevalent in his speeches and publications.[4] In fact, it was probably Coughlin's anti-Semitic vitriol that ultimately reserved him a special niche in the pantheon of American history. Other demagogues, such as Francis Townsend, Huey Long, and even Gerald L. K. Smith, all employed various forms of specious rhetoric, but none of them employed overt anti-Semitism to the extent of Father Coughlin. The Radio Priest was both political *and* anti-Semitic. Consequently, he was both a political *and* a religious problem for President Franklin D. Roosevelt.

In a strange drama that could only be written for Father Coughlin, the Roman Catholic Church decided to adopt the policy of vigorously reprimanding Coughlin for his *ad hominem* attacks on President Roosevelt, while remaining silent on his virulent anti-Semitism.[5] Over the years, this question of Catholic silence amid the rage of Coughlinite anti-Semitism has been a vexing one for American Catholics.[6] The Church's utter silence on this issue has cast a cloud of skepticism over modern Jewish–Catholic dialogue. In the academic world, Professor Jay P. Dolan of the University of Notre Dame writing in *The New York Times Book Review* in August 1996, indicated that the primary unresolved question for the Roosevelt administration—and even for Catholics today—was why the Catholic Church refused to silence the Radio Priest for his anti-Semitic diatribes.[7]

In this chapter, I would like to offer one possible answer to this complex question. Simply put, I contend that the Vatican administrator in charge of handling the case, Monsignor Joseph Patrick Hurley, was an intense anti-Semite who consciously expurgated any mention of Coughlin's anti-Semitic rhetoric from the official reports that he was preparing for his superiors at the Vatican. Second, I will show that Hurley's anti-Semitism played a large role in shortcircuiting President Roosevelt's vigorous initiatives to get the Holy See to crack down on Coughlin for his anti-Semitism.

An examination of the process of anti-Semitic sanitization cannot be addressed without an analysis of the person responsible for the actions. Joseph Patrick Hurley was born in an Irish enclave of Newburgh, Ohio, in 1894. His discomfort with Jews was evident at an early age. Between 1904 and 1914, a *shtetl* of Orthodox Jewish Ashkenazim began to encroach upon Hurley's Irish-Catholic neighborhood and ethnic tensions increased.[8] But it was after his secondary schooling—as he studied for the priesthood for the diocese of Cleveland—when his animosity toward Jews broke the surface.

As a 21-year-old seminarian, he consistently began to refer to the Jews as "Kikes." An examination of Hurley's Biblical Theology notebooks from St. Bernard's Seminary in Rochester, New York, reveals, for example, that "Moses led the kikes through the Red Sea."[9] Moreover, later in his life Hurley would speak of an "international Jewish conspiracy," a "conspiracy" with its "tentacles" spread throughout the world.[10] In addition, Hurley subscribed, under an alias listed to a post office box, to the virulently anti-Semitic Catholic underground magazine *Alerte!*, with its complete references to the Jewish "Brotherhood" and its plot to control world finances.[11] In fact, it could be argued that much of Hurley's own anti-Semitism mirrored, and in some cases was more insidious, than Father Coughlin's.

But after seminary, Hurley's career took a remarkable turn toward international diplomacy. In 1926, Hurley's former seminary professor, Edward A. Mooney, tapped him to be his secretary when Mooney was appointed apostolic delegate to India. Over the next eight years, Hurley's star rose through the ranks of Vatican diplomacy so that by 1934, he was named the first American to be officially attached to the Secretariat of State of the Holy See.[12]

Part of Hurley's new job at the Vatican included attending to American dignitaries visiting the Holy See on official business. But even in his new position, at least a mild form of his anti-Semitism shone through. In 1935, when C. Everett Clinchy of the National Conference of Christians and Jews wrote to the secretary of state to arrange a meeting and an audience with the Holy Father, Hurley told him, "in effect, that the Holy See would not touch him, or receive him officially." In this case, Hurley acted as the bureaucratic roadblock that inhibited Clinchy from explaining the aims of the NCCJ to the Vatican. "Of course, he saw neither the Holy Father nor the Secretary of State," Hurley later wrote, indicating that he had politely dismissed Clinchy and "sent him on a tour of the Vatican City and the Galleries." In Hurley's mind, the Conference was nothing more than a "Jewish move to head off persecution in the United States"—a key statement since it points up that Hurley was cognizant as early as 1935 that American Jews could be open to persecution.

Be that as it may, by 1936, Hurley had been assigned to administer the Coughlin situation in the United States. In May of 1936, as Coughlin was vigorously attacking Roosevelt and his policies, Hurley was commissioned by Pope Pius XI to secretly visit the Radio Priest at Royal Oak. He "tried to send a message to Charlie telling him that the Pope desired that he keep in mind always that he was a priest and that prudence and charity should guide his utterances."[13] While this secret interview failed to address Coughlin's more subdued anti-Semitism during the period, it does point out that Hurley was actively briefing the pope on the Coughlin affair and that he had advised the Holy Father to personally intercede to quiet Coughlin.

One year later, Hurley's role in the Coughlin situation took on greater importance when Pope Pius XI appointed Edward A. Mooney, Hurley's former boss and confidante, to the archbishopric of Detroit. Now, with Mooney in place as Coughlin's bishop, an informal hot line was opened between Mooney in Detroit and Hurley at the Vatican. In late 1937, Hurley wrote to Mooney indicating that he had been placed in charge of "handling the case" for the Vatican.[14] One year later, when Coughlin announced over CBS radio that German Jews were indirectly responsible for their fate on

*Krsytalnacht*, the storm cloud burst and Coughlin's rank anti-Semitism became the number one concern of the American media, the Roosevelt administration, and the American Catholic Church. In St. Peter's Square, however, Coughlin's new turn toward anti-Semitism raised neither questions nor concerns.

After Coughlin's November 20 speech endorsing Hitler's *Krystallnacht* policy, Archbishop Mooney wrote a somewhat frenzied letter to Hurley, asking him to lobby the Holy Father for a public statement to silence Coughlin.[15] But as the secular media and American Jewish organizations hounded Mooney for a statement, Hurley casually dismissed the Coughlin incident in Rome. In a December letter to Mooney, Hurley wrote, "Nobody seems bothered about it here." The only groups to protest Coughlin at Rome were "some irate Jews of the gonnif Variety."[16] Personally, Hurley felt that international Jewish organizations had "made too much of an outcry about the speech."[17]

It was only after a second letter from Mooney that Hurley explained more closely the Vatican's attitude. He wrote to Mooney that he had "kept the bosses informed of the developments"; that his superiors were interested, "but that [was] all." In a significant statement, Hurley wrote: "Nor has the Pope brought up the question on the several occasions on which I have been with him lately."[18] This statement is crucial because it shows a deliberate breakdown in bureaucratic communication. By the very nature of his position in the Secretariat of State, it was Hurley's job to bring the Coughlin crisis to the attention of the pope, not vice-versa. Clearly, Pius XI was uninformed on Coughlin because Hurley shirked his professional responsibility to bring it up. But someone who was willing to bring up the Coughlin problem was Franklin Delano Roosevelt.

After the death of Pope Pius XI and the election of Pope Pius XII in March of 1939, Roosevelt made a concerted effort to place a representative at the Holy See. In December he appointed Myron C. Taylor the "Personal Representative of the President to His Holiness Pope Pius XII." Within the year, Taylor called a meeting with Vatican authorities for the sole purpose of rectifying Coughlin's anti-Semitism. By 1940, Coughlin and his "Christian Front" organization were stirring up social unrest and threatening to subvert the government. On March 8, 1940, Taylor arranged a meeting with Luigi Cardinal Maglione, Pius XII's new secretary of state, to discuss the Coughlin situation in detail. What he wanted was a Vatican censure of Coughlin's anti-Semitism. The secretary for the meeting between Taylor and Maglione was Monsignor Joseph P. Hurley of the Secretariat of State.[19]

From the Vatican documents selectively released in 1965 as the *Acts and Documents of the Holy See Relative to the Second World War*, we learn that Taylor's conversation "revolved around the racial movement in the

United States"—a euphemism for Catholic anti-Semitism. In his conversation, published under the subheading "Notes of Monsignor Hurley of the Secretary of State," Taylor cut directly to the chase with the two prelates, indicating that before he left from his last visit to the United States, "President Roosevelt gave him a memorandum concerning an anti-Jewish movement in the towns of Brooklyn, Baltimore, and Detroit"—all Coughlinite strongholds. Taylor continued, "The President was informed that the movement [was] supported by Catholics in those cities..." Then, in order to impress the Vatican with the importance of dealing with the issue, FDR pulled one of his own diplomatic backflips. In order to get the Vatican moving, Roosevelt pointed out that he was "afraid that, as a result, anti-Catholic feelings may be reawakened in the nation."[20] The fact that Roosevelt was trying to persuade a surefooted American Catholic Church that the persecution of a historically despised minority religion would rekindle a bout of Know-Nothingism, underscores the lengths that FDR was willing to go to in order to quash Coughlinism.

In terms of diplomacy, the only commitment drawn from the Holy See was a promise by Cardinal Maglione that he "was ready to study the question and to examine a note on the matter." But three months later, Taylor was back at it again. Nothing had been done, and so a second discussion was arranged with Maglione and Hurley. This time, Taylor pointed out that he was:

> Still concerned with the Coughlin question and connected matters in the American Church, especially the attitude of certain papers such as *Social Justice*, *The Brooklyn Tablet*, *America*, and several other diocesan journals—all of which have quarreled violently with the President's conduct of American Foreign policy.

Finally, Taylor let it be known that he wished the Vatican to take action against Father Coughlin and his "anti-Jewish movement." But before we analyze the Holy See's response to Taylor's concerns, it is important to point out that the "Notes of Monsignor Hurley of the Secretariat of State" as published in *Actes et documents* are the only documents that the Vatican has seen fit to release concerning the entire Coughlin affair. Moreover, these documents are some of the only documents that make any reference to the Jews or anti-Semitism in the entire six-volume series. Regardless of this, it must be pointed out that in no instance was the Vatican concerned with Coughlin's anti-Semitism. According to the published text, it was only *Myron Taylor* who was concerned with extinguishing Coughlin's anti-Semitism. Therefore, it must be held in mind that publication of the "Notes" in 1965 suggests a concern only on the part of Taylor and not on the part of the Vatican. By selectively releasing the "Notes" in 1965, the Vatican created only an *illusion* of concern for the Jews. This illusion is substantiated further by examining the internal documents that were generated through Taylor's diplomatic efforts.

The original responses to the Taylor *demarches* of March and July 1940 have never been released by the Holy See. But unbeknownst to the Holy See, Hurley was keeping copies of his notes on the Coughlin affair and retaining them in his personal archive. These documents are reviewed here for the first time. The most important Coughlin-related document in Hurley's archive is a position paper written on July 2, 1940, and submitted to the substitute secretary of state for Extraordinary Ecclesiastical Affairs, Monsignor Domenico Tardini. This paper, entitled "Opinion Written for His Excellency Mons. Sostituo," was Hurley's summation of the Coughlin problem and his suggestions to his principals for handling the situation.[21] The document mirrors exactly the information relayed by Taylor to Hurley and Maglione at their second meeting—except for the crucial fact that nowhere in the two and one-half page document is there any mention of anti-Semitism.

The opening paragraph mentions that "such Catholic papers as SOCIAL JUSTICE, THE BROOKLYN TABLET, AMERICA and several of the Diocesan journals have consistently taken an attitude in support of Father Coughlin and in bitter criticism of American internal and external policy." But in the whole two and one-half pages, there is not one mention of Coughlin's anti-Semitism. The summary only highlights the *political* aspects of Coughlin's campaign. There is one remark about the "intemperate activities of Father Coughlin," and yet another about Coughlin engaging in "partisan politics and other kinds of intemperate activities," but no mention of Roosevelt's and Taylor's main concern—the rise of Catholic anti-Semitism. So, as Hurley placed his memo in the Vatican pipeline, the concerns of Franklin Roosevelt were left to be washed under with the tide.

In addition, on July 25, Hurley sent a confidential letter to Edward Mooney in Detroit outlining the gist of his July 2 position paper on Coughlin. He told Mooney: "I recently wrote a memorandum for the Boss here in connection with another complaint which had been presented [Taylor's second meeting]. My recommendation was that the matter be left in your hands; you had done much to temper Coughlin' s speeches and had obtained his promise to discontinue broadcasting during the summer; that for obvious reasons, it would be better for the H [oly] S [ee] not to intervene at this (late) date." Signing off, he wrote to his mentor, "So far, I do not know the result of my demarche; but I sincerely hope that Domenico did not again succeed in torpedoing it."[22]

But there was no reason for Tardini not to "torpedo" it. There was nothing new in the report. Coughlin had been ranting against Roosevelt's policies for six years. The reports moving up the ladder indicated that nothing had changed. Coughlin was still considered a political problem, not a religious one. But Hurley would not allow Coughlin to become a religious problem at the Vatican because he himself endorsed anti-Semitism. On two separate occasions, President Roosevelt and Myron Taylor tried to hammer home that something had to be done about Coughlin's anti-Semitism. In fact, they must have been bewildered to think that such a dire religious situation failed to get even a practical response from the Vatican.

In the final analysis, it becomes clear that Monsignor Hurley had deliberately filtered out any references to anti-Semitism as he prepared his reports for his superiors. On "several occasions," he failed to alert the pope to Coughlin's new turn toward intolerance. When he received two official diplomatic notes from President Roosevelt, he sanitized the subsequent policy memoranda of all references to the Jews. The only reason for such behavior can be the personal anti-Semitism of Hurley himself.

While he disdained Coughlin for his politics, Hurley secretly sympathized with his anti-Semitism. He expressed no moral outrage and failed to offer any consideration of Catholic intolerance. In fact, in a 1937 conversation with William Phillips, then the U.S. ambassador to Italy, Hurley expressed the opinion that "a little anti-Judaism may not be such a bad thing."[23] Thirty-five years later, he became the only bishop of the entire Second Vatican Council to officially and publicly protest the signing of *Nostra Aetate*, the landmark document which condemned anti-Semitism as incompatible with Catholic thought.[24]

In retrospect, it is clear that Hurley was a tragically sad choice to have anything to do with the Coughlin situation. While Hurley castigated Coughlin for his anti-Roosevelt tactics from 1934 to 1938, he deliberately misrepresented the Coughlin threat after the "anti-Semitic crisis" of 1938. But Vatican complacency can be contrasted with Franklin Roosevelt's activism. It was Roosevelt who recognized the Coughlin threat for what it was; and it was Roosevelt who ordered his representative to see that Coughlin was silenced by the Holy See. Incredibly, it was the politician who was thinking like a priest. It was Roosevelt who was staking out the high moral ground. And, ultimately, it was Roosevelt who would silence Coughlin in 1942.

### NOTES

1. Alan Brinkley, *Voices of Protest: Huey Long, Father Coughlin and the Great Depression* (New York: Knopf, 1982).
2. Susan Zickmund, "The Shepherd of the Discontented: A Rhetorical Analysis of the Discourse of Father Charles E. Coughlin" (Ph.D. diss., University of Wisconsin, 1993), 1.

3. Brinkley, *Voices of Protest*. On Roosevelt's early concern about Coughlin's anti–New Deal program see: Ronald H. Carpenter, *Father Charles E. Coughlin: Surrogate Spokesman for the Disaffected* (Westport, CT: Greenwood Press, 1998), p. 105.

4. Mary Christine Athans, *The Coughlin–Fahey Connection: Father Charles E. Coughlin, Father Denis Fahey, C.S.Sp., and Religious Anti-Semitism in the United States, 1938–1954* (New York: Peter Lang, 1991), pp. 164–165.

5. The best summaries of the Catholic Church's handling of Coughlin are found in Donald Warren's *Radio Priest: Charles Coughlin, the Father of Hate Radio* (New York: The Free Press, 1996) and Leslie Woodcock-Tentler, *Seasons of Grace: A History of the Catholic Archdiocese of Detroit* (Detroit: Wayne State University Press, 1990); Alan Brinkley, *Voices of Protest: Huey Long, Father Coughlin, and the Great Depression* (New York: Knopf, 1982); also see Sheldon Marcus, *Father Coughlin: The Tumultuous Life of the Priest of the Little Flower* (Boston: Little, Brown, 1973); and Charles J. Tull, *Father Coughlin and the New Deal* (Syracuse: Syracuse University Press, 1965).

6. Ronald Modras has set forth that "it was a pre-Vatican II Catholicism in which anti-Semitism did not arouse moral outrage and where institutional consideration outweighed virtually all else," which permitted Coughlin's toleration. See: Ronald Modras, "Father Coughlin and Anti-Semitism: Fifty Years Later," *Journal of Church and State* 31 (1989): 246. Contemporaneously, a Father Feige of Fordham University stated that the Catholic Church did not muzzle Coughlin because to do so would violate his rights as an American citizen. See: letter to the *New York Times*, August 30, 1939. Father Francis Talbot, editor of the powerful Jesuit periodical *America* simply endured Coughlin as "a thorn in the side of Catholics." See: *America* (August 23, 1939).

7. Jay P. Dolan review of *Radio Priest: Charles Coughlin, the Father of Hate Radio*, by Donald Warren, *New York Times Book Review* (August 25, 1996): 20.

8. *Plat-Book of the City of Cleveland, Ohio and Suburbs* (Philadelphia: G.M. Hopkins, 1912), plate 29. Corroborate this with the *Encyclopedia of Cleveland*, ed. James Van Tassel and Edward Grabowski, *sub vero*, "Jews and Judaism."

9. Hurley personal notebook, St. Bernard's Seminary, 1916; St. Bernard's Seminary file, Archives of the Diocese of Saint Augustine (hereafter ADSA).

10. Personal interview, Catholic source contemporary with events, May 16, 1996. The subject of the interview recalled that the remarks were made during a dinner conversation in Rome at the second Vatican council.

11. *Alerte!* was arguably the most malicious anti-Semitic Catholic periodical of its day. Published by the "Advocates of Our Lady," and mailed from a post office box in South Bend, Indiana, it was in print from 1954 to 1960.

12. Hurley to [Doc] Mooney, November 15, 1934, Mooney administration uncatalogued collection, Box 9, Archives of the Archdiocese of Detroit. Others have argued that Francis Cardinal Spellman was the first American attached to the Secretariat of State. Spellman officially served as the

playground director of the Knights of Columbus in Rome and was never officially listed as an *addetto* in the Secretariat of State. Spellman was unofficially attached to the First Section of the Secretariat. See: Robert I. Gannon, *The Cardinal Spellman Story* (New York: Doubleday, 1962), p. 47.

13. Earl Boyea, "The Reverend Charles Coughlin and the Church: The Gallagher Years, 1930–1937," *Catholic Historical Review* 81 (1995): 213.

14. Hurley to Mooney, November 21, 1937, Mooney administration, uncatalogued collection, Box 9, Archives of the Archdiocese of Detroit.

15. Mooney to Hurley, December 22, 1938, Mooney administration, uncatalogued collection, Box 9, AAD.

16. Hurley to Mooney, December 26, 1938, Mooney administration, uncatalogued collection, Box 9, AAD.

17. Ibid., Box 9, AAD.

18. [Joe] Hurley to [Doc] Mooney, January 16, 1939, Mooney administration uncatalogued collection, Box 9, AAD ("gonnif"; Yiddish, variation of "ganef"; thief, scoundrel).

19. "Notes of Msgr. Hurley of the Secretariat of State," in *The Holy See and the War in Europe: March 1939–August 1940*, ed. Pierre Blet, Angelo Martini, and Burkhart Schneider (Washington, DC: Corpus, 1965), p. 352.

20. Ibid., p. 352.

21. Hurley to Domenico Tardini, "Opinion Written for His Excellency Mons. Sostituo," July 2, 1940, Hurley administration microfilm collection, reel 30, doc. # 141C, Archives of the Diocese of St. Augustine. The letter box containing the original copy of this memo was destroyed sometime after Hurley's death in 1967. The author is indebted to Michael V. Gannon, former archivist of the Diocese of St. Augustine, for microfilming the documents.

22. [Joe] Hurley to [Doc] Mooney, July 25, 1940, Hurley administration microfilm collection, reel 30, ADSA.

23. William Phillips Papers, 55M-69, vol. 17, p. 2705, Houghton Library, Harvard University, Cambridge. In reference to the rise of Italian anti-Semitism, Phillips indicated: "Hurley feels as I do the danger that the anti-Jewish campaign will get into the hands of extremists and away from control of the Duce." There was no criticism of the anti-Semitic campaign itself, just a fear that it would get out of the hands of Mussolini.

24. *Acta Synodalia Sacrosancti Concilii Oecumenici Vaticani II*, vol. 4, pt. 2 (Vatican City: Vatican Polyglot Press, 1977), p. 190.

# PART 4

# REFLECTIONS ON THE *SHOAH*

# CHAPTER 16

# THE PURPOSE OF THE DOCUMENT, *WE REMEMBER: A REFLECTION ON THE SHOAH*

## REMI HOECKMAN, O.P.

THE HOLY SEE'S COMMISSION FOR RELIGIOUS REFLECTION with the Jews, published on March 16, 1998, a document entitled *We Remember: A Reflection on the Shoah*. As you undoubtedly know, this document attracted a great deal of attention on the part of those to whom it was addressed—that is, the Catholic faithful *throughout the world* (not only in Europe where the *Shoah* took place), with the hope that all Christian believers would join them in accepting the challenge, and indeed inviting all men and women of goodwill to reflect on the matter—as well as on the part of those to whom, primarily, the document was not addressed, although we did most sincerely ask our Jewish friends "(to hear us with open heart)."

In the years following the decision by our Commission to begin a study process that could result in such a document—we did this at the express request of His Holiness Pope John Paul II and on the basis of his teaching— our Commission engaged in a process of consciousness-raising and reflection on the *Shoah* at every level in the Catholic Church and, in a special way, in different local churches in Europe. In fact we set out with the idea that one single document would cover all that the Catholic Church, throughout the world, might wish to state on this terrible tragedy of our century. However, in the process, we soon became aware of the great differences of experience, and thus also differences in perception, which existed in the different local churches. For instance, what the Church in Germany or Poland wanted to say in this regard was not at all identical, and their statements were not altogether appropriate for the experience of the churches in other continents, for example, in the Middle East and Israel, or, for that matter, in Lesotho, Swaziland, or Papua New Guinea.

The Bishops' Conferences in Germany, Poland, the Netherlands, Switzerland, France, and Hungary went ahead. Each published a courageous statement that, while dealing with the same issue, related in a special way to the particular experience of the people in their countries—something that proved to be absolutely necessary. The Catholic Church in the United States did something similar in a statement made by the chairman of the U.S. Bishops' Committee for Ecumenical and Interreligious Affairs. The Italian bishops followed by presenting a formal letter to the Italian Jewish community. And the Slovakian bishops published a statement as well. The way was thus open to the Holy See to speak to, and on behalf of the universal Church. In fact, we wished to reach the minds and the hearts of Catholics in all those countries that were not only far removed, by geography and history, from the injustices that in the past have been inflicted by Christians on the Jewish people, but that are also far removed from the scene where the *Shoah* actually took place.

Unfortunately, this fact has been overlooked by many, or, by those who are solely interested in Vatican confessions of guilt and mea culpas, it has simply been ignored. The latter have put even more obstacles in our path. As the issue seems to contain great potential for the promotion of particular agendas, the temptation to make use of it in the face of the Church can be difficult to resist. Some Jewish leaders did not resist, as became clear at the 1994 Jerusalem meeting of the International Catholic–Jewish Liaison Committee, when a confidential progress report on our work was leaked to the media. The incident that then occurred was very serious indeed, because it not only meant a breach of trust on the part of some of our Jewish dialogue partners (although most of the Jews present were as much disgusted as we were), but because it undoubtedly harmed our work as well, and delayed the publication of the document considerably. Instead of assisting us in preparing the minds and the hearts of those to whom the document was going to be addressed, they "pressurized" them into a defensive attitude from the very beginning!

On the other hand it ought to be said that the reflections and insights of many of our Jewish friends have inspired, guided, and supported us in the process of preparation of the document. I just would like to mention a couple of examples. The Dutch Rabbi Awraham Soetendorp, for instance, who is himself a survivor of the *Shoah*, told the participants at the Eisenach Conference of the International Council of Christians and Jews, in 1995, that the real meaning of repentance (*teshuva*) is not to be burdened with guilt but to learn from experiences and to turn the mistakes and the transgressions into a passion for a new future. And in the United States, Rabbis Jack Bemporad and Michael Shevack are telling us the same thing in their great little book *Our Age*. "No one should be so obsessed with the past that they prevent themselves from moving into the future. No one should *live* in the past," they affirm. Yet they also point out that "the past is not something you should ever toss away and forget... quite to the contrary, it must be remembered, heeded, learned from, so that it will never repeat itself" again.

That is exactly what we had in mind when we prepared our reflection statement on the *Shoah* and named it the way we did: *We Remember*. On several occasions the Holy Father had been extremely strong and clear on this, but especially so on the occasion of a Concert in commemoration of the *Shoah*, which took place in the Vatican on April 7, 1994. "We remember," he affirmed, "but it is not enough that we remember... we have a commitment... This is our commitment. We would risk causing the victims of the most atrocious deaths to die again if we do not have an ardent desire for justice, if we do not commit ourselves, each according to his own capacities, to ensure that evil does not prevail over good as it did for millions of the children of the Jewish nation."

In order to understand the purpose of our document, one has to understand that first. The pope wanted a document that would help Catholic believers all over the world "to renew the awareness of the Hebrew roots of their faith"; to learn from history about "the ways in which the image of the Creator in man has been offended and disfigured," also by Christians; to learn about the *Shoah*, "the inhumanity with which the Jews were persecuted and massacred during this century... for the sole reason that they were Jews"; to become aware of the "heavy burden of conscience of their brothers and sisters [in Europe] during the Second World War," but also before, something that calls for a sense of solidarity and penitence also on their part today. As the document says: "At the end of this Millennium the Catholic Church desires to express her deep sorrow for the failures of her sons and daughters in every age. This is an act of repentance (*teshuva*), since, as members of the Church, we are linked to the sins as well as the merits of all her children... [This] is not a matter of mere words, but indeed of binding commitment." It is indeed the Holy Father's fervent hope, and it is our hope as well, that by remembering the past the document will also "help to heal the wounds of past misunderstanding and injustices," thus "enabling memory to play its necessary part in the process of shaping a future in which the unspeakable iniquity of the *Shoah* will never again be possible" (Pope John Paul II to the President of the Commission for Religious Relations with the Jews, March 12, 1998). In other words, we do want to remember, but with a purpose.

Moreover, we did and do share with many of our Jewish friends the conviction that a document such as ours will contribute significantly to combating attempts to deny the reality of the *Shoah* or to trivialize its significance for Jews, Christians, and indeed all of humanity. We want all Catholics, all Christians, in fact all people everywhere, to know about it. We want everyone to know that, putting it in the words of the Pope, "guilt must always be the point of departure for conversion." In other words, the document *We Remember* has clearly an educational purpose, and this is something that many Catholics (and Jews) have warmly welcomed. For instance, Cardinal William Keeler and Dr. Eugene Fisher, speaking on behalf of the U.S. National Conference of Catholic Bishops' Secretariat for Ecumenical and Interreligious Affairs: "We must look at the implications of this document for our educational programs, its opportunities for rethinking old categories as well as probing the most difficult areas of moral thought. To take the Holocaust seriously is to look back at centuries of Christian misunderstanding both of Judaism and of the New Testament itself, as the text emphasizes, and seek to replace them with more accurate appreciations of both. How shall we embody what this statement calls us to do in our classrooms and from our pulpits?"

Today we are pleased to hear of concrete applications and implementations in teaching and preaching of our document, as it was intended. In my opinion this is the answer to the document. It is also the answer to reactions such as "too little, too late" and other similar utterances. In fact, some of our Jewish partners shared with us their answer to these kind of reactions. I quote only one: "Let us resolve to pursue [our efforts] toward the goal of understanding and combatting the pathology of group hatred and persecution, in an atmosphere free of polemics. We are not responsible for the prejudices of the world into which we were born, but we are responsible for fighting them. We are not accountable for past events over which we had no control, but we are accountable for the future. We are jointly responsible for facing history and for forging new traditions of human and spiritual solidarity—for the sake of our children, our world, and the sanctification of the One who is Holy to all of us" (Judith Banki, program director of the Marc Tanenbaum Center for Interreligous Understanding).

As far as I am concerned the keyword (and the key reality in this matter) is reception: reception of what and why we remember by Catholics in the first place, but also by other Christians, and indeed by every man and woman of goodwill everywhere. Anything that hinders that process does not deserve our consideration. One should take seriously comments such as that made by Gustav Niebuhr in *The New York Times* of March 29, 1998: "Response to what is often a cautiously worded document must be measured against extraordinary changes in Catholic–Jewish relations since the early 1960s, a progress from distance and frigidity, to high-level engagement and warmth." Otherwise, one must be prepared to risk losing much of what was gained in Jewish–Catholic relations up to now. Obviously Orthodox Rabbi David Rosen of the Anti-Defamation League, the president of the International Council of Christians and Jews, is not prepared to take that risk. Interviewed in his office in Jerusalem by Ross Dunn for the Ecumenical News International News Service (September 17, 1998), he is reported to have said: "For those involved in the dialogue, there is an increasing sense that we have a responsibility to move towards the future more and more, while at the same time saying that one has never exhaustively dealt with the issues of the past... The church is not part of the problem for the Jews anymore, it is part of the solution." Other informed Jewish friends have been emphasizing the same. To them as to ourselves I would say: keep that in mind. Let us continue to become ever more part of the solution instead of wasting our energy in "nursing" the problems. The generations that will come after us will tell the difference.

**David Alvarez**   A former Scholar-in-Residence at the National Security Agency, Dr. Alvarez is Professor of Politics at Saint Mary's College of California. He is the author of *Secret Messages: Code Breaking and American Diplomacy* (2000) and *Spies in the Vatican: Espionage and Intrigue from Napoleon to the Holocaust.*

**Steven M. Avella**   An Associate Professor of History at Marquette University, Dr. Avella has written and edited numerous books on the American Catholic experience, including *This Confident Church: Chicago Catholicism: 1940–1965* (1992) and *In the Richness of the Earth: A History of the Diocese of Milwaukee* (2002).

**Michael Barone**   Formerly the Senior Staff Editor at *Reader's Digest*, Mr. Barone is currently Senior Writer for *U.S. News & World Report.* He is the author of *The New Americans: How the Melting Pot Can Work Again* (2001) and *Our Country: The Shaping of America from Roosevelt to Reagan* (1990). As well, he is the coauthor of the biannual *The Almanac Of American Politics*, which published the sixteenth edition (2002) in August 2001.

**Michael H. Carter**   Mr. Carter is a graduate student in the Department of Political Science at the University of California, Berkeley, and Graduate Theological Union.

**Philip Chen**   Mr. Chen is a Fellow at Nuffield College, Oxford, England.

**John S. Conway**   Dr. Conway is Professor Emeritus, University of British Columbia, and the author of *The Nazi Persecution of the Churches* (1996).

**Gerald P. Fogarty**   Reverend Gerald R. Fogarty, S.J. is the William R. Kenan, Jr., Professor of Religious Studies and History at the University of Virginia and the author of *The Vatican and the American Hierarchy, 1870–1965* (1982).

**Charles R. Gallagher**   Mr. Gallagher was the Archivist for the Archdiocese of St. Augustine in Jacksonville, Florida. He is now a member of the Jesuit Order living in Boston.

**Remi Hoeckman**    The Reverend Dr. Remi Hoeckman, O.P. was Secretary to the Holy See's Commission for Religious Relations with the Jews.

**Peter C. Kent**    A former Dean of Arts at the University of New Brunswick, Dr. Kent is the editor of *Papal Diplomacy in the Modern Age* (1994). His book *The First Cold Warriors: Pope Pius XII, the Roman Catholic Church and the Origins of the Cold War* is forthcoming. He is currently a Professor in the Department of History at UNB.

**Richard G. Kurial**    Dr. Kurial is Associate Professor of History and the Dean of Arts at the University of Prince Edward Island, Charlottetown, Canada.

**Ajay K. Mehrotra**    Dr. Mehrotra received his Ph.D. from the University of Chicago in 2000. He is currently a Fellow at the Miller Center of Public Affairs at the University of Virginia.

**Michael Phayer**    Dr. Phayer is Professor Emeritus of History at Marquette University in Milwaukee, Wisconsin and author of *The Catholic Church and the Holocaust* (2001).

**Francis Sicius**    Dr. Sicius is Professor of History at St. Thomas University in Miami, Florida and the author of *Word Made Flesh: The Chicago Catholic Worker and the Emergence of Lay Activism in the Church*.

**Robert A. Slayton**    Dr. Slayton is Chair of the Department of History at Chapman University in Orange, California.

**Anthony Burke Smith**    Dr. Smith was Program Associate at the Greenberg Center for the Study of Religion in Public Life at Trinity College in Hartford, Connecticut. He is currently Assistant Professor in Religion at the University of Dayton in Ohio.

**Robert Trisco**    Monsignor Robert Trisco is Professor of History at the Catholic University of America and Editor of the *Catholic Historical Review*. He is the author of *Bishops and Their Priests in the United States* (1988).

**David B. Woolner**    Dr. Woolner is the Executive Director of the Franklin and Eleanor Roosevelt Institute in Hyde Park, N.Y., and Assistant Professor of History and Political Science at Marist College in Poughkeepsie, N.Y.

# INDEX

and Germany, 173–4
and the Jewish question, 155–60
and Poland, 154–5, 167–70
as secretary of state, 11
and the Taylor mission, 25, 28, 143,
    145, 147, 150, 179, 184, 192,
    213, 217
and unconditional surrender, 31
elected pope, 22–3
POAU (Protestant and Other
    Americans United), 180, 190,
    192, 194, 195, 200, 202
Polish Corridor, 154
Polish Home Army, 170
Potsdam, 154, 175
pragmatic pantheism, 112
prisoners of war, 214–24
Prohibition, 7, 16, 27, 28, 81

*Quadragesima Anno*, 49
Queretaro constitution (1917), 126
Quigley, Martin, 259, 260, 263

Ready, Michael, 26
Red Army, 166, 170, 172
Red Cross, 215, 217, 219, 220, 241, 242
Red Mass Sermon, 105, 107
Reform Liberalism, 107
Regime Fascista, 212
religious liberty, 121–33, 135, 136,
    169, 170, 191
Renchard, George W., 223
*Rerum Novarum*, 49
Roman Catholics, 59, 74, 75, 106, 121,
    122, 180, 182, 184
    *see* Catholics
Roman Jews, 153, 156–8
Roosevelt, Eleanor, 4, 63, 179, 180
Roosevelt, Franklin Delano,
    and Al Smith, 55–6, 59, 61–4
    and the American Catholic
        Hierarchy, 11–13, 17, 19, 22,
        29–36, 37, 39, 171, 239
    on the bombing of Rome, 226, 233–5
    comparison with Peter Moran, 93–4,
        97–9, 101

and the Democratic Party, 4–5, 7
and Father Coughlin, 79, 269–75
and James Farley, 8
on the Good Neighbor Doctrine,
    126–8
and John Ryan, 48–9
and Joseph Kennedy, 8
and neo-scholastic thought, 106,
    108–9, 114–15
and the New Deal, 7, 15–18, 182
Protestant patrician, 3, 4
on Soviet recognition, 122, 124–5
and the Spanish Civil War, 9,
    129–31
and Tammany Hall, 6
Roosevelt, James, 4, 19, 21
Roosevelt, Theodore, 5
Roy, Ralph Lord, 202
Rural Farm Homestead Movement, 97
Rural Farm Program, 101, 102

*Sacramento Bee*, 70
Sacred College of Cardinals, 167
Sangnier, Marc, 95
Saskatchewan, 95
Scattolini, Virgilio, 257, 260, 264
Schrembs, Bishop Joseph, 19
Schuler, Robert, 58, 59
Seabury, Samuel, 6
Senate Foreign Relations Committee,
    127, 180, 193, 194
Seredi, Cardinal Jusztinian, 242
Shaw, G. Howland, 220
Sheen, Fulton, 134
*Shoah*, 281–4
Signal Intelligence Service (SIS), 260
signals intelligence (Sigint), 260
Sinclair, Upton, 67–70, 74, 75, 77, 81,
    82, 84, 85
Smith, Alfred E., 6, 11, 15, 56, 58,
    60, 62
Smith, Gerald L. K., 270
Social Justice, 16, 21, 29, 30, 48, 49,
    51, 79, 94, 97, 107–9, 114,
    273, 274
Social Security Act, 18, 49